Prescott

The Biography

Colin Brown

First published as *Fighting Talk* in Great Britain 1997 by
Simon & Schuster
Africa House
64–78 Kingsway
London WC2B 6AH

This revised edition published 2005 by
Politico's Publishing, an imprint of
Methuen Publishing Limited
11-12 Buckingham Gate
London SW1E 6LB

10 9 8 7 6 5 4 3 2 1

A CIP catalogue record for this book is available from the British Library.

ISBN 1 84275 108 5

Printed and bound in Great Britain by Bookmarque Ltd, Croydon, Surrey

CONTENTS

FOREWORD

When I decided to write a biography of John Prescott, presciently titled *Fighting Talk* by the publishers, I did so because he seemed a complex character, and far more interesting than the Old Labour 'bruiser' portrayed in the press. I had spotted at an early stage that he was prepared to challenge the left-wing orthodoxy of the time about renationalisation with his ideas about private enterprise investment in public services. I was also intrigued by the fact that the Prescotts owned their own semi-detached house – a rare thing in the 1950s – and his father had been a Justice of the Peace and a controller on British Railways. These facts jarred with the public image of Prescott as the working-class warrior and suggested a more middle-class upbringing for someone who, as he joked later, had learned to keep the 'coal in the bidet'.

As I delved into the biography, with many riotous conversations with his friends, and a magical exploration of the Prescott attic in Hull, I began to find a much more complex character than I had imagined, who, in spite of the tough exterior, was privately warm, sincere and beset with self-doubts. I was privileged to be allowed into the close-knit circle of family and friends who protect him, and it was his late mother who told me that John was a sensitive child. His favourite film is *Billy Elliot*, but I doubt that it is solely because of the romantic portrayal of the miners' strike. Billy, the aspirant ballet dancer, was also a sensitive child who triumphed against those who doubted that a boy from a humble background could make it to Covent Garden. The young John Prescott learned to box to survive in the harsh seas of militant trade unionism on Merseyside. He has been routinely sneered at by Westminster sketch-writers for strangling the English language, but I suspect none of those with an Oxbridge education could have persuaded a pier head mass meeting of angry members of the National Union of Seamen to go back to work, as he did when barely out of his teens.

By far the biggest misjudgement by Prescott's critics in the media was that he would 'blow up' and 'storm out' like George Brown, an earlier Labour deputy leader, before the end of the first term. They underestimated Prescott and continue to do so. Many who have known him in government say that his relationship with Blair has been the rock on which Labour has won three successive elections.

Fighting Talk finished at the point when Labour was elected in 1997. I have written the updated chapters to complete the part of the story I know. This was never an authorised biography, and its subject has not cooperated with the updated chapters. It may be a friendly account, but I make no apologies for that. It merely balances the scales slightly for a politician who, having been vilified for most of his career at Westminster, is in danger of becoming a national institution.

Colin Brown, 7 August 2005

INTRODUCTION

Third Term

As he prepared to fly to Moscow to represent the Prime Minister at the VE Day marchpast in Red Square on 8 May 2005, John Prescott's patience with Downing Street was near breaking point.

Three days earlier, Blair had been elected for an unprecedented third term, but there had been none of the triumphalism of Blair's 'new dawn' when he arrived in Downing Street fresh-faced and confident in 1997.

Labour's majority had been slashed to 65, excluding the Speaker, and the party's share of the vote had fallen to 35.26 per cent – a fall of over 5 per cent and the smallest share of the vote for any winning party in postwar history. On the streets, Prescott had been confronted with the hostility of the voters to Blair. Largely as a result of the war on Iraq and the failure to find the weapons of mass destruction that were supposed to justify it, trust in Blair across the country had crashed.

The result was widely seen as a 'bloody nose' for Blair, in spite of winning an historic third term, and it would have been even worse had not Gordon Brown helped to shore up Blair's collapsing personal support in a series of carefully stage-managed events during the election campaign. These started with a soft-focus party election broadcast in which they were seen discussing the good times they had shared together, in an echo of the 'docu-drama' a year earlier called *The Deal.* The lasting image of the campaign was Blair buying an ice cream for Brown. Prescott privately called it the 'love-in'.

It was in sharp contrast to the unceremonious way Brown had been removed from the campaign strategy team before the election by Blair, who had put Alan Milburn in his place. The calculated insult to Brown had inspired a series of reports that Brown would also be removed from the Treasury after the election, when Blair would reassert his authority and put a fresh New Labour stamp on his government.

It had not been easy to persuade Brown to bury his own resentment with Blair over the way he had been treated and return to the front line of the campaign. Alastair Campbell, Blair's former communications director, brought back for the election, had gone up to Scotland to persuade Gordon to return to the campaign strategy team. Prescott also had used all his influence on Brown and Blair to broker their rapprochement for the good of the party. One of Prescott's allies said that Prescott had spoken to Blair in the bluntest terms before the election about bringing Brown into the campaign. 'He really laid it on the line to Tony,' said the source. 'He told him, "If you don't sort it out we will all suffer." It was a fairly tough meeting.' Now all that hard work was being put at risk and Prescott was worried that it would sour their relations once more.

Although he remained loyal to Blair as his deputy, Prescott had spent the previous four years ensuring that when the time came, there would be a smooth transition of power between the two men. Blair's last word on the subject, in October 2004, had been that he would stand at the next election, but stand down after serving a 'full term'. Brown's discomfort over what Blair meant by a 'full term' was brutally exposed in the run-up to the election, when he was questioned about the meaning of 'a full term' on the BBC *PM* programme by Eddie Mair:

MAIR: What does 'full term' mean?

BROWN: It means what Tony Blair says.

MAIR: What do you think it means?

BROWN: Well, that's for Tony Blair to say. It's not for me, eh, to, eh, say what Tony Blair should do. It's up to Tony Blair.

MAIR: You are saying you don't know?

BROWN: A full term is exactly what Tony Blair said today: full term.

MAIR: Isn't it insulting the electorate?

BROWN: I don't quite know what point you are getting to. Tony Blair says he's serving a full term. If Tony Blair says he is serving a full term, you had better ask him whether full term means something to what you are suggesting.

MAIR: I don't know what it means.

BROWN: He says he is serving the full term. Full term means full term.

MAIR: You keep repeating that. Isn't that insulting to the electorate, who don't know who is going to be Prime Minister and for how long?

BROWN: Tony Blair said in answer to a question how long

would he serve and he said he would serve a full term.

MAIR: How long does that mean?

BROWN: It means full term.

MAIR: Five years, four years?

BROWN: A full term is normally how long a Parliament runs; of course it is for the Prime Minister to decide how long a Parliament runs.

MAIR: You understand a full term to mean he will be the Prime Minister until the next election is called?

BROWN: That is what he's said, and that is what he said again today.

Left-wing MPs who had opposed the war on Iraq, top-up fees and foundation hospitals found trust in Blair had collapsed and were not prepared for him to serve a 'full term' after winning their seats. Within 24 hours of his victory, some MPs were lining up to say: 'Blair must go.' There were reports that there would be a showdown with the 'awkward squad' at the first meeting of the parliamentary Labour Party.

As Prescott prepared to fly to Moscow, Downing Street launched a counter-attack, briefing the media that having just won an historic third term, Blair had no intention of leaving office until he was ready. That Sunday the *Observer* headline said: I WON'T QUIT VOWS BLAIR AS CABINET RIFT OPENS – BLAIR REVEALS 2008 DATE FOR DEPARTURE. Blair now seemed to be retreating from the understanding he had reached with Brown, and Prescott, who was party to the deal, was angry.

'He can't just tough it out,' Prescott told his allies. Prescott had remained totally loyal to Blair, as he had promised when they were elected together as leader and deputy leader in 1994, but this was now testing his loyalty to the limit. He had no intention of helping Brown force Blair out, but he feared that the Number Ten briefers were now threatening to provoke another outburst from Brown, who, according to Prescott's friends, had warned Prescott in the run up to the election: 'He's ratted on me, and he will rat on you.' That was a reference to the long-disputed dinner at Granita restaurant, in which Blair is said to have promised to hand over to Brown in the second term.

Prescott was still sore over a report in the *Sun* in the run-up to the election that Blair intended to recall David Blunkett, the former Home Secretary, to the Cabinet as a new 'minister for respect', taking over the local government functions of Prescott's department while Prescott took on an 'enforcer' role on government delivery. Prescott had not read the *Sun* news story, telling friends, 'I don't read the poxy paper.' But he was well aware of its contents, and when Blunkett was promoted by Blair to another department, Work and Pensions, Prescott was further annoyed to see himself being portrayed as the 'Cabinet wrecker' for allegedly blocking the move.

In fact, Blair at no time mentioned Blunkett by name when he discussed the reshuffle with his deputy on the eve of the election. Blair was well aware of Prescott's views about the former Sheffield City Council leader. The Deputy Prime Minister had dismissed Blunkett as 'arrogant' on the BBC radio *Today* programme after a withering assessment of the Cabinet had been published in Blunkett's biography by Stephen Pollard. Blunkett had suggested that Prescott did not like him, because they were too alike, saying: 'He doesn't like that I do what he is good at himself – saying it as it is.'

Blair was emollient, asking Prescott for his help over the reshaping of the government for the third term. He wanted Prescott to take on a wider diplomatic role, deputising for Blair on more trips abroad, such as the Moscow event, while the Prime Minister presided over the G8 and the EU summits that coincided in the UK in 2005. According to Prescott's allies, he told Blair he was quite prepared to help but if he thought he was going to give up his department and do the 'enforcer nonsense', he had another think coming. Prescott was well aware how that would be reported in the press – PRESCOTT DEMOTED. He reminded Blair that he would be playing some sort of role in the transfer of power to Brown, when the time came, and he was therefore not going to be railroaded. He asked Blair to promote his Local Government Minister Nick Raynsford to the Cabinet to take charge of the new post as a reward for Raynsford's handling of the difficult brief in Prescott's office. 'He's worked like a Trojan,' said Prescott, pointing out that Raynsford's expertise would be needed in dealing with three forthcoming major problems: the revaluation of council tax, the reform of the council tax system, and finding a way of affording public sector pensions for the future, on which the unions had threatened to strike. Blair had his own protégés to promote, including his education adviser, Andrew Adonis, and refused. Within hours, Raynsford resigned from the government. Prescott asked instead for David Miliband, a trusted friend of Blair's, who was young, bright and likeable, and whose brother, Ed, worked for Gordon Brown, to act as his deputy., to which Blair was happy to agree.

Now, three days after polling, the Blair camp was fending off the calls for Blair to go by insisting that the Prime Minister would continue to serve a full term. To Brown and Prescott, the presumption inside Downing Street that it was 'business as usual' was untenable, given the rescue operation they had mounted to help ensure that Blair was elected for a third term. Prescott feared there would be great bitterness in the party at the way the Blair camp was continuing to insist that Blair would serve a full term. The party would want to know the date for Blair's departure and, in his opinion, it had a right to know. The resignation speech by Michael Howard, the defeated Conservative Party leader, had brought the issue to a head, in Prescott's view. Howard had surprised many in his own party who had been urging him not to repeat the mistake of William Hague by resigning in haste after the election while the party was still in shock at the Tories' unprecedented third successive defeat. There was speculation that Howard might stay on to fight the European referendum and then go. That timetable seemed to Prescott and Brown a good framework for Blair's departure. It would give Blair eighteen months, not the three and a half years the Blair camp had suggested, to complete his term of office, and prepare for an orderly succession. As a passionate party man, Prescott always thought in terms of party timetables, and it seemed right to him that Blair's departure or

Brown's coronation should fit in with the annual party conference in 2006, which could provide Blair with a platform for his swansong, leaving Brown to take over as leader in the spring or summer of 2007. However, if Blair prevaricated until the autumn of 2008, as his aides had clearly implied in their brief to the Sunday newspapers, Brown could be left with little more than six months as Prime Minister to prepare for the next general election in the spring of 2009.

Prescott forcefully relayed the message to Blair that he did not think the party would allow him to carry on, regardless of the election result, for another three or more years. The Tory Party had always prided itself on its ability to use the 'men in grey suits' to tell a leader when he or she had stayed on too long. The unspoken threat hanging in the air was that if Blair persisted in frustrating Brown's ambitions for the leadership, Brown would confront the Prime Minister and tell him his time was up. Blair got the message. By the time the 'showdown' meeting with the parliamentary Labour Party took place on Wednesday 11 May, the mood in the Blair camp had changed. There was no more grandstanding. However, Blair was not ready to be marched over by his own troops. As the Labour MPs filed into committee room 14, the Blair camp had made sure that the 'awkward squad' in the left-wing Campaign Group would not have it all their own way. They would be challenged by loyalists who were primed to point out that they had just won an historic election thanks to Blair's appeal. Blair sat at the front of the room, at a desk on a raised platform, normally occupied by a committee chairman and clerks. The meeting was packed, with 300 MPs jammed into the room; some, who failed to find a space to squeeze into when they opened the door, trudged back to the bars to hear about Blair's speech from those who managed to get in. Blair was flanked by Brown and Prescott, who had returned from Moscow.

Blair looked and sounded confident. Some said it was the best speech they had heard him deliver. It was cleverly judged, and strongly delivered. There would be no retreat on the modernising agenda and no return to a more left-wing version of New Labour. If they remained united behind the agenda for modernising public services, he said, 'a fourth term is there for us'; but if Labour moved to the left it would 'cede the centre ground to the Tories and that's where elections are won in this country'. However, the key sentence that quelled the unrest was Blair's appeal for time to ensure 'a stable and orderly transition', which everyone present understood to mean a transfer of power to Gordon Brown. He had not gone so far as to provide a timetable, but he had done enough. There was to be no more talk of a 'full term'.

The next day, when Blair held his first Downing Street press conference after the election, he was asked whether he would serve a full term, but he carefully sidestepped the issue, saying: 'I have got nothing to add to what I said in the election campaign; that remains the position. I actually wasn't invited to make any specific comments on it at all yesterday. And I suppose what I think the party, and in a sense the country, just wants to see is for us to get on with the business now. That is really what it was.'

Tory campaign chiefs privately said they could track Labour's improvement in their own opinion polling from the moment that Brown was brought back into the front line of Labour's campaign team. Turning a Tory jibe on its head, 'Vote for Blair and get Brown' had a winning appeal with the voters.

The election had diminished Blair's waning power, but in doing so it had changed the relationship with his deputy. Prescott had been loyal to Blair for more than ten years, in spite of all the clashes, irritations, speculation, backhand briefings and occasional bust-ups with Downing Street, but now Prescott was preparing for a different role, as the kingmaker for Brown. He was also preparing for his own departure, for he had privately made it clear to Blair when there was speculation that Prescott was about to retire that he would not step down before Blair. Prescott took the view they were yoked together by the party when they were elected together in 1994. In recent months, there have been signals from Brown's allies that Brown may ask Prescott to stay on. It is not clear at the moment what the future holds for Prescott, but it is difficult to see him opting for complete retirement. When eventually he does step out of frontline politics, he will be able to reflect on a long and remarkable political career. The boy from Prestatyn who failed the eleven-plus has come a long way.

PART ONE

CHAPTER ONE

The Dawn of Prescott

Never turn back.
Prescott's dad, Bert.

John Prescott is Welsh.

This comes as a surprise to many who assume that his roots are in the working-class industrial towns of the north of England. That came later.

John Leslie Prescott was born in Prestatyn on 31 May 1938 to John Herbert (Bert) Prescott, a railwayman, and his wife Phyllis. His mother was attended by a visiting midwife. She remembers it was a painful birth, but then it was typical of John to be difficult. Bert Prescott, a Liverpudlian, was the signalman at Prestatyn station when John Leslie arrived, weighing in at over nine pounds, and showing the midwife he had a lusty pair of lungs.

Some claim that his Welsh antecedents were kept secret on the orders of Labour Party 'spin doctors', to avoid Prescott's being called 'a Welsh windbag', as Neil Kinnock was. Those who believe that do not know Prescott. It would not be easy, even for Labour spin doctors, to repackage Prescott, Man of Harlech.

It is hardly surprising there is no trace of the lilting voice of Wales in his accent. Prestatyn, a resort on the coast of north Wales, is on the English-speaking fringe of Wales, and the future deputy leader of the Labour Party left the region before his fifth birthday, when his family moved to the south of Yorkshire. They lived until he was ten years old in Brinsworth, a small town crushed between the two steel-making giants of Sheffield and Rotherham.

It is from his childhood in South Yorkshire that Prescott gets his northern vowels, flat as a cap. There is also a lashing of Scouse, thrown in like spice, which he picked up in his formative teens on Merseyside. This has made him sound like a working-class warrior should – northern, blunt as a fist, stripped of artifice.

His parents were impeccably, solidly working class, with strong trade union connections. But, like much of Prescott's life, it is not the whole story. His family spent five years among the Lowryesque streets of Rotherham, and his mother found it a trial. The remainder of his early years were spent in the leafy suburbs of Chester, in a comfortable postwar three-bedroom semi, with a stable family background, the eldest of three sons and two daughters. His mother doted on John and she was unashamedly 'well-to-do working-class'. His father became a Justice of the Peace in Chester, and ruled the family with magisterial discipline. As in most families, there were tensions, but when Prescott went away to sea it was to find his fortune, not to escape trouble at home.

Prescott was born in the front bedroom of a comfortable seaside bungalow called Wendover. The Prescotts had rented the newly built three-bedroomed bungalow at 10 Norton Avenue from Charles Birch, a local auctioneer and valuer, after they were married.

Birch had built the row of semi-detached and detached bungalows on a flat field he bought in 1936 from a seed merchant, facing the Irish Sea, and separated from the beach by a couple of other rows of seaside bungalows in roads with grand-sounding names, such as The Mall. Wendover, Norton Avenue, was within a minute's pram ride to the sand dunes and the beach by the Pavilion Lido, Ballroom and Café, where the Nova leisure complex now stands. It was a perfect spot to bring up a young boy, until Hitler invaded Poland.

Prescott's parents had met at a 'sixpenny hop' in Hoylake, on the northern tip of the Wirral peninsula by the Mersey, where Bert's family had settled. Bert got his first job as a porter at Meols, the next stop along the line from Hoylake. He was a porter with big ambitions, and first spotted Phyllis as she stood on the platform one day. She was a maid at a large private house in the area. He chatted her up at a local dance.

The Prescotts had been as much a fixture in Liverpool as the Liver birds: Bert's grandfather had been a printer in the city, producing handbills and labels with gold leaf dabbed on with a rabbit's foot; Bert's father, Tom Prescott, was employed by Pickford's, the shipping firm. The family lived at Anfield, so close to the football field that when Tom was a boy and the team was also in its infancy he helped to deliver the oranges at half-time to the players on the pitch. Bert was a sickly child, stricken by rickets, the disease associated with poverty, and after an operation on his legs, to reset the bones, his family moved to Hoylake to enable young Bert to bathe them regularly, under doctor's orders, in sea water.

As a result of his illness, Bert was no great dancer, but it was the period of the great British dance bands, playing hits from the American musicals, which were packing people into the pictures and local dances. Carroll Gibbons and the Savoy Hotel Orpheans had just recorded 'Shall We Dance?' from the Fred Astaire–Ginger Rogers film, which was on general release; and Roy Fox and His Orchestra had a hit with 'Things are Looking Up'. The war was just two years away.

Phyllis was 'in service', and had come from a proud line of miners in north Wales. Phyllis Parrish was a vivacious girl who had come from the Welsh borders town of Chirk, an English-speaking mining community where the Parrishes went back several generations. Her father, William, was a miner at the Black Park colliery, treasurer of the miners' union, and a committed member of the fledgling Labour Party. He was a union official for 50 years. 'He was a very strong character,' said Phyllis. 'And that's where John gets his socialism from. I remember my father crying, and he was a stern man – men didn't show tears in those days – when Ramsay MacDonald turned out to be a turncoat.'

The first Labour Prime Minister, whose second administration was riven by ideological splits with its idealistic left wing, presided over cuts in unemployment benefit in 1931, in spite of a rise in unemployment to nearly three million, as part of a desperate effort to prop up the pound on the gold standard. He surrendered Labour's hold on office to a coalition National Government with the Tories and the Liberals, and imposed cuts that would have made Denis Healey blanch. Such lessons in working-class betrayal were driven in hard in the Welsh mining communities. The treachery of right-wing Labour leaders to the aspirations of the working classes was a lasting theme in the coalfields, and left a powerful impression on William Parrish to be passed on to his grandson.

There were ten children in the Parrish family, and Phyllis was the third daughter, born in 1918. Her father doted on Phyllis. 'You've got more about thee than any of 'em,' he used to tell her.

She was eight years old when she went knocking on doors to get people in Chirk to take copies of the socialist *Daily Herald*. At 78, 'Battling Phyllis', as she has been called, was still knocking on doors for the Labour Party, as an active member of the Upton Labour Party on the outskirts of Chester, and has been a delegate of the European 'pensioners' Parliament' with Jack Jones.

Prescott's grandfather was once pictured on the front cover of the *Daily Herald*, when the mines were nationalised. The caption, in his grandfather's words, was 'We fought for this!'

William Parrish used to keep the miners' union ledger, carefully noting down the items bought by the union for its members. The small bound ledgers are among the political books that line three walls of Prescott's study at home in Hull. They speak directly of another age, in pencil. 'Relief committee held in the union office on December 15 1936 … Herbert Roberts £2. George Davies (lodge) 10s. Paid Moody for tools

£2.12.0.' There is also William's certificate exempting him as a collier from service in World War I, dated July 1916 when he was aged 33. One of William Parrish's lifetime battles was to get the mining industry nationalised and to take the pits out of the hands of the private owners, an objective achieved by the Labour government after World War II.

'John was steeped in it,' his mother recalled.

William Parrish was in his 84th year, living at 3 Woodside Cottages, Black Park, Chirk, when John was adopted as the prospective candidate for Southport in the 'swinging sixties'. William's local newspaper in Chirk commented that he must be proud that his grandson had followed 'his predilection', a hint, perhaps, that William might have shared his ambition to become an MP, had he been born in a later generation.

Phyllis had many suitors, and she broke up with Bert for a time, but Bert was something of a charmer with women, and courted Phyllis when she had returned to her family in Chirk, love being made easier because he was able to get free travel as an employee of British Rail.

Bert and Phyllis were married on 25 November 1937 at the Presbyterian Church, Hoylake, on the northern tip of the Wirral peninsula near Liverpool, the Reverend Howell Williams officiating. She was 19 and Bert was 26. He had just been transferred to Prestatyn when they were married.

Phyllis gave her address to the registrar as the Sandringham Café, Victoria Road, Prestatyn, where she got a summer job. After they were married, they rented their first house at 7s 6d (37½p) a week in Prestatyn. It was on the site where the

Prestatyn holiday camp now stands, and right by the beach. Because it was a fully furnished holiday home, the rent shot up to £5 a week when the summer came, and they had to leave. With Phyllis pregnant, they had to find cheaper accommodation for the summer and rented an unfurnished bungalow at 10 Norton Avenue for 19s (95p) a week, where, in May, John was born. He was given his father's first name, and the second name of Leslie was chosen because it was fashionable at the time. Prescott shares a name with matinée idol Leslie Howard.

Norton Avenue was less than a mile from Prestatyn station, and some of his first steps were taken on the short walk with his mother to the station's signal box, to take his father his sandwiches.

Being in the signal box, on a busy seaside line, was trying for young Bert, who had ambitions for better things. On one occasion, Phyllis visited him in the signal box, which was against company rules. To his consternation, she was spotted by his boss from a train as it was stopping in the station. The railway official quickly made for the signal box. 'You've had a woman in here, Prescott,' said the official. 'Can you see a woman, sir?' said Bert.

Phyllis remembers dangling outside the signal box window above a ten-foot drop, until the official had left. 'I loved that man, but some of the tricks we got up to …'

Bert had a reputation for larks. A lifelong racing fan, Bert in later life got into Goodwood racecourse on the cheap by tagging behind a coachload of blind punters from St Dunstan's.

'Who are you?' asked the gateman, noticing that Bert was sighted.

'I take down their bets,' said Bert, with a nod at the blind men.

Prestatyn station was a bustling holiday stop on the breezy coastal line from Chester to Holyhead. Bert was pulling levers in the signal box as part of his training to become a weighing inspector. It involved a few months in each branch of railway station work, including working as a clerk in the booking office. There were four platforms at the station, which replaced an earlier one in 1897, and it was a busy scene in the holiday period that summer in 1938. There were branch lines operating to the farms in the Welsh hills that stood guard over the town, and steam trains depositing holidaymakers from the Lancashire conurbations of Liverpool and Manchester. There were few large hotels in Prestatyn, and fewer entertainments. Horse-drawn traps transported day-trippers from the impressive Victoria Hotel at the station along Bastion Road to the beach for a fare of 1d (½p) until 1939, when the war broke out.

At the height of the summer, for the whole hot month of August 1939, Bert and Phyllis let number ten to holidaymakers from Liverpool. One of the hits of the time was 'Love Is Here To Stay', recorded by Jack Harris and His Orchestra. Phyllis, with a one-year-old son, and pregnant with their second son, Raymond, went to stay with her family in Chirk for a break, while Bert went to summer camp with the Royal Welch Fusiliers.

It was a fateful choice for a holiday. At eleven o'clock on the morning of 3 September 1939, with Bert still away at the camp, war was declared on Germany.

Territorial Army members like Bert were immediately mobilised, and Phyllis did not see him again for nearly a year. When he returned, he had had his left leg amputated below the knee.

Bert had joined the TA because he was a drinking pal of the brother of a jockey. Bert shares a love of horse racing with John's wife, Pauline, and telephone calls from the Prescott home in Hull to her father-in-law are often about hot tips for the track. Before the war, Bert followed the career of a prominent jockey, R.A. Jones, whose brother was a TA recruiting sergeant. Sergeant Jones conned Bert into joining in peacetime, to go to the summer camp with his pals.

Bert's first duty after war broke out was in the orderly room, where he had to send out the police to round up other TA volunteers for the call-up. This cushy number was short-lived, as Bert and his friends were redesignated as the 60th Anti-Tank Regiment by the Ministry of War under Leslie Hore-Belisha, a competent minister, now remembered principally – in a lesson to all politicians – for the beacons at pedestrian crossings. After training at Aldershot, Bert and his regiment were sent to France via Calais in the British Expeditionary Force with orders to join French forces to halt Hitler's Blitzkrieg in its tracks.

In his first speech as Prime Minister, Churchill, who had been appointed on 10 May 1940, had offered Britain 'nothing but blood, toil, tears and sweat' to win the war. For those like Bert in France, with resistance collapsing all around, it looked like being their blood, their toil, their tears and their sweat. Modern history records how the Panzer tank divisions swept across trench defences where World War I became bogged down, but Bert remembers his part in the defeat of Hitler quite differently: the German army cut through the British ranks on motorcycles with sidecars, which outmanoeuvred their Anti-Tank Regiment.

As a quartermaster sergeant, Bert Prescott had been in charge of five vehicles with orders to find food, ammunition, gas capes and other essentials wherever he could and to deliver them to sergeant-major battalion troop commanders. They were heading for the town of Rouen on the Seine with orders to protect Paris, as part of a plan produced by a 73-year-old French general, Maxime Weygand, to defend France. Weygand's plan was for all available French and British forces to take offensive action to halt the onward thrust of the German advance. Bert's footnote in history came when Churchill, at a crucial planning meeting in Paris on 22 May 1940, noted that the British forces had no more than four days' food left. All the supplies and war stores of the British Expeditionary Force, including those in Bert's possession, were concentrated along the coast from Calais southwards towards St Nazaire; 'and that General Gort's paramount concern was to preserve this line of communication, which was absolutely vital to him'.

Within three days, the impossible Weygand plan had collapsed, and the BEF was in retreat to Dunkirk. Bert and his troops never got to Paris. The 51st Highland Division, which had the task of defending the capital, was cut to pieces, and Bert's mob fell back on Rouen. It was eight days after the BEF had been evacuated by the heroic flotilla of small boats from Dunkirk.

'We were continually bombed,' recalls Bert. He was ordered to deploy into a wood. 'It was early in the morning on the fourth of June. I was shot in the knee. Nobody knew where it came from. There was a panic.'

Badly injured, Bert was taken into Rouen, but with the order for general evacuation of the BEF, he was moved in the retreat to the port of Le Havre to be shipped home. 'The capture of Rouen in the west and the crossing of the Marne in the east,' says the writer Alistair Home, 'now meant that Paris, the sacred capital, was inevitably compromised ... On 3 June Paris was bombed for the first time.' Rommel sealed off Rouen. 'We never imagined war in the west would be like this.'

Bert was waiting to be evacuated on a ship in the harbour, when his ship was sunk as it came into the port. Bert thought his chances of getting out had gone down with it. In the chaos, with the Germans closing in, he was evacuated on a long and agonising journey west by train to La Baule, a resort town near the port of St Nazaire on the Atlantic estuary of the Loire river.

The casino on the seafront at La Baule had been turned into a temporary hospital, with a crude operating theatre. The bullet had smashed through his tibia and fibula, and ploughed down the shattered bone to lodge in his ankle. The surgeons amputated his leg below the knee. As he recuperated from the shock of the operation, the casino came under attack from the howling fighter-bombers of the Luftwaffe. The patients who could run fled into the grounds of the casino and were cut down. 'Dozens were killed in the gardens,' said Bert. Unable to move because of his injuries, he survived the attack. After a day or two, he was moved the few kilometres south to the port for evacuation.

Entering the docks at St Nazaire, later to be the scene of a daring commando raid on the German submarine pens in 1942, the fleeing British forces came under savage attack by the German bombers. Bert's evacuation ship, a cargo vessel called the *Worcestershire*, was one of the last to reach Britain. The next ship to leave the port blew up, with a bomb down the funnel, and Bert knew of no others that made it home.

The German XV Panzer Corps smashed west, crossing the Seine at Rouen, and pursuing the retreating British army across Normandy and Brittany. They entered Rennes on 18 June. By the time they reached Nantes on the Loire, Bert was sailing home.

For six weeks, Phyllis, living with her two children at a cottage in the Welsh hills at Froncysyllte near Llangollen, had no knowledge of his fate. His regiment was not among those evacuated from Dunkirk. She traced him through the Red Cross to a hospital at Warwick.

Bert, in his eighties, is regarded as a 'character' – he is a familiar figure at Labour Party annual conferences, gatecrashing cocktail parties by announcing himself, with absolute honesty, as 'John Prescott'. Having an unquenchable spirit for life, he gets abroad to time-share apartments he has in Spain and Malta.

But, as with most of those who lived through it, the war changed his life, and, for both Bert and Phyllis, life would never be quite the same again. Not that Bert – who lives in a pensioner's sheltered flat in Chester and drives a car – would complain. Dennis Skinner, the Labour MP – who became a good friend of Bert's in his later years through John – tells the story of how Bert's false leg once got caught in a turnstile going into the Westminster Underground station, on one of his frequent trips to London to see his son in the Commons. 'Come back,' said Skinner, seeing Bert was stuck.

'Never turn back,' said Bert. It was a motto for life.

Invalided out of the army, Bert rejoined Phyllis at his mother's house at Upton, a comfortable suburb of Chester, and signed on at the Labour Exchange on crutches. He was initially given a job checking on the benefit claims by the wives of servicemen. However, under the wartime industrial rules, British Railways (as it was called then) had been forced to keep his job open. Just before he had gone to the war, Bert had qualified for promotion to become a railway controller, and now he was told that his job was open for him, in Rotherham, in the old West Riding of Yorkshire.

It was an opening Bert and Phyllis would have preferred had been closed.

In 1987, John Prescott was taken back to Norton Avenue by David Hanson, the Labour candidate for the Conservative seat of Delyn, which covered Prestatyn. Hanson, a student at Hull University, had first met Prescott when he was the MP for Hull, and Hanson (no relation of the international magnate) was a campaigner against apartheid in South Africa. He had asked Prescott to address a meeting at the university to attack investments in South Africa by the university, where Prescott gained a BSc in economics. Prescott was at that time leader of the Labour delegation to the forerunner of the European Parliament and was busy in Strasbourg on Euro business, but Hanson's meeting appealed to him. Prescott flew to the meeting in Hull, attacked the university, and caught the next flight back to Strasbourg. After that they became firm friends.

The visit to Norton Avenue some years later was recorded for posterity with a photograph, and Hanson recalls that Prescott was understandably fascinated to be taken back to see his Welsh roots, although he found he could remember little of the house.

Ten Norton Avenue – it has lost its name over the years – has no outward sign of having been Prescott's birthplace. It is a comfortable, whitewashed three-bedroom semi, with newly double-glazed windows in a well-to-do working-class part of the town. Few in Prestatyn seem to be aware of the fact that he was born here. An estate agent selling property in the area was unaware, and not quite sure whether it would help or hinder his sales.

The visit to Norton Avenue failed to do the trick in the 1987 general election: a Tory, Keith Raffan, won the seat. It was not until 1992 that Hanson snatched it from the Conservatives. Prescott's birthplace, and the rest of Prestatyn, was moved, through boundary changes, into the Vale of Clwyd, won by Labour in the landslide on 1 May. There are no plans to erect a blue plaque to Prescott there for the foreseeable future, although his family felt sure that the fact he was born at number ten was a good omen.

CHAPTER TWO

The Most Typical Family in Britain

I'm not thick-skinned. If anything, I'm too sensitive.
John Prescott.

Wartime Rotherham came as a terrible shock to the young family from north Wales.

The girl from the Welsh hills was used to coal dust from the pits, but it was nothing compared with the soot in Brinsworth. Like Mrs Ogmore Pritchard in Dylan Thomas's *Under Milk Wood* ('And before you let the sun in, mind he wipes his shoes'), Phyllis was house-proud. She was called 'the Duchess' by her neighbours because she bothered to clean the windows. There were standards to be kept, and she was determined to instil them into her two boys. Her insistence on being properly turned out was something she passed on to John, who is still criticised by the left for his penchant for smart clothes.

There was filth and grime everywhere – even one of the local towns is called Grimethorpe – and the row of railway cottages in Ellis Street, Brinsworth, where the Prescotts arrived in 1941, was covered in soot from the local railway yards. Dwarfed by Rotherham and Sheffield, which together made up a steel centre to rival the Ruhr in Germany, Brinsworth was like hell on earth to Phyllis. 'It broke my heart when I went there,' she said.

Prescott keeps a painting of a back-to-back terrace in the kitchen of his eight-bedroom house in Hull to remind him of his Rotherham childhood. In fact, the house they stayed in at Brinsworth was built of red brick; the terraced row of cottages in the painting is of Yorkshire stone, but the impression is right: it looks rather gloomy, with dark shadows, as though it has just been raining. His mother does not like it, because it also reminds her of Rotherham, but Prescott insists it is part of his childhood. He could, just as easily, have put up a painting of a semi-detached house to remind him of Upton, a suburb of Chester; he was to spend more time there. But these were his formative years, the years that made him think of his background as working class, and Yorkshire.

It was a few fields, a few houses, on the edge of a truly Satanic landscape. Writing in 1937, George Orwell described Sheffield, into which Rotherham merged, as 'the ugliest town in the Old World'.

The Tinsley steel mills, a long dark canyon of high-sided factories and fiery furnaces, were swept away in the Thatcherite 1980s, to be replaced by vast American-style shopping malls, with green, glass roofs. It is hard to imagine now, standing in the atrium with shoppers all around, what it was like when the Prescotts arrived.

The city seemed to be on fire, producing steel round the clock for the war effort. Furnaces shone red in the pitch-black night, and could be seen from the cold moors overlooking the city, turning metal into molten lava, which erupted in sparks like volcanoes. Workers were so hot, the local pubs had especially cold pints of beer for the breaktimes, and the pubs had appropriate names, such as the North Pole.

'Wigan is beautiful compared with Sheffield,' Orwell wrote in *The Road to Wigan Pier*.

> *And the stench! If at rare moments you stop smelling sulphur, it is because you have begun smelling gas. Even the shallow river that runs through the town is usually bright yellow with some chemical or other. Once I halted in the street and counted the factory chimneys I could see; there were 33 of them, but there would have been more if the air had not been obscured by smoke.*

Added to the assault on the eyes and the nose, the industrial hell of the steel city also attacked the ears. Everywhere, recalled Orwell, was the 'whizz and thump of steam hammers and the scream of iron under the blow'.

Bert's job with British Railways was to direct the trains around the steel-making plants. It was a hazardous business. The cargoes included white-hot metal, which had to be moved across the rails at Steel, Peach and Tozer, which ultimately became part of British Steel, having been nationalised in the sixties.

In Rotherham, Bert Prescott could have been forgiven for thinking that Hitler was out to get him. Having survived the retreat from France, Bert arrived in Rotherham after Hitler's Luftwaffe had launched the Blitz on the area.

German bombers almost wiped Sheffield city centre off the map in 1940, the Luftwaffe bomb-aimers mistaking the long straight outline of the High Street for the Tinsley steel plants in the blackout. Some Sheffielders say the damage was no worse than the planners visited on their city in the 1960s.

Bert had initially gone to southern Yorkshire on his own, to find lodgings, and it was nearly a year before Phyllis insisted on moving to Rotherham with their young family to be with him. Phyllis, now with three children – John, Ray, and a newborn baby, Dawn, who was just three weeks old – had been living near Bert's mother in the leafy suburbs of Chester. It seemed far removed from the stress of war, until one night in April 1941, when the German bombers attacked a local airbase.

'The Germans got through to bomb the airfield, outside Chester,' says Phyllis. 'It was a terrible night. Bert was in Rotherham. The air-raid warden came round telling us what to do. I had all three children under the kitchen table. We put the mattress under the table to protect us from any bombs that were dropped. This night it was ghastly. Bang, bang, bang. An aeroplane was shot down above our house; next door got it, and part of a German plane came down in our garden. I was shook up. I just couldn't take it.'

Bert pulled strings: there were no houses to be had in Rotherham, but there was a street there for footplatemen by the big railway depot at nearby Canklow. 'It was a filthy place. You couldn't take them for a walk without getting soot on them. They used to clean the chimneys of the trains. The kids loved the engines,' says Phyllis.

John's earliest childhood memory is of the strips of silver paper that the German bombers dropped over Rotherham to confuse the radar during the war. 'We'd find them in the garden.'

Bert had found the family a house at 10 Ellis Street, in a row of railway cottages near the marshalling yards at Brinsworth. Although it was grimy, there were large rooms, where Phyllis and the children could spread out, and there were fields full of bluebells, buttercups and dandelions behind St George's Church. There were three streets in that part of Brinsworth – Ellis Street, Duncan Street and Atlas Street – and in the evening, parents went strolling with their children. They could survey the whole of Brinsworth, at the top end of the playing fields opposite the school, near a pigeon loft. Soot settled on everything, including the washing on Mondays. But Brinsworth also had a smell to it: of smoke and grime and grease which emanated from the old railway sheds at the top of Ellis Street, where many fathers worked.

Forty years later, Prescott returned to see his old house at 10 Ellis Street. It was early one morning, at the height of the miners' strike; he had been on the picket line to meet the morning shift at Corton Wood colliery, and he was with Kevin Barron, the local MP; and Dick Caborn, a long-time friend and Labour MP with a Sheffield seat, who played a key part in Prescott's career. It was around 6 a.m., in a sleeping street of deathly quiet, and Caborn remembers urging Prescott to 'hush up' or they would get arrested. Prescott was thrilled to see the old place again. 'He was saying in a big loud voice, "It's just the same. There – that was my room."'

In spite of the war, and the surroundings, it was a relief for the Prescotts to be a family again. The Prescotts were to stay in Rotherham until John was ten. Brinsworth junior school was just across the road, and that was where he first went to lessons. It was a small village school, with three or four classrooms, dull and dingy when the weather was overcast, with draughty outside toilets. Bigger children used to torment the juniors when they went across the playground to use them. It was a basic education, but with caring teachers. The headteacher was Miss Hill, who was barrel-round and topped with grey fuzzy hair, but possessed of bright eyes. She lived in Bonet Lane, near the farm, where the village dairy was. There were cut-out letters in the classrooms from which Prescott and the children learned the alphabet, with the teacher, Mrs Bagshaw, hammering on them, and her class parroting the letters in unison.

Phyllis, who later became a fully qualified needlework teacher, passed on her skills as a part-time teacher in night classes at the school. She also used to make most of the clothes that John wore. 'I met the teachers and they were good. It was a good school.'

As he grew up in Brinsworth, John Prescott cut his teeth on organising for the Labour Party. Bert had been a member of the party before arriving at Brinsworth, having joined as a railwayman on Merseyside, but he became actively engaged in local politics in the town. Bert found that operations were being run by a group of councillors, who were mostly fellow workers on the railway. They were all elected as independent councillors, and Bert decided to throw a spanner in their works. 'I picked nine stooges as Labour Party candidates, and opposed the ruling group with the backing of the party. I got my nine stooges in, and the consequence of that was, much to my chagrin, I was chosen as chairman of the council. I was also having to give these engine men their jobs, because I was the controller. They were furious about the whole thing.'

The Brinsworth council was eventually swept away in local government reorganisation, but there are plans to honour Bert's wartime chairmanship with a plaque.

John was recruited as a party helper by his father, stuffing leaflets through doors, and joining in the fun when Bert ran the local carnival committee. John was seven when, in 1945, Churchill was thanked for his wartime leadership by being turfed out of office by the returning soldiers who had had enough of the officer classes and voted Labour.

The landslide Labour victory produced the great reforming Labour government of 1945, which ushered in the NHS, with Nye Bevan acting as the midwife.

It would be easy to assume that Bevan would be one of Prescott's political heroes rather than the Labour leadership of the time. But he regards Ernie Bevin and Clement Attlee as guiding lights.

'Both of them were practical politicians, both were interested in ideas and how you could convert these into reality,' he says of Bevin and Attlee. But Attlee was from a middle-class background, and for Prescott his rise was less impressive. Bevin, on the other hand, was someone Prescott could feel affinity with. He was from a humble working-class background and rose by sheer application to become Foreign Secretary.

Bevan was a left-winger, a rousing orator, with his socialist roots driven deep into the Labour Party in the Welsh valleys, and a man of vision. But Prescott's politics are imbued with a streak of pragmatism that shuns ideology, and the 'gift of the gab', for the need to be practical. He is a believer in politics as the 'art of the possible'; it is a streak in his character, regarded as the flaw of a compromiser by some prominent members of the Campaign Group of Labour MPs, which has led the alienation of the 'hard' left. He fundamentally rejects that view.

'There are those priests of the Left who want to keep their conscience and there are those who will get their hands dirty. I belong to the dirty hands brigade. I risk getting it wrong.'

Phyllis found some of the people in Rotherham as difficult to live with as the environment. 'Salt of the earth they called themselves. Some were as rough as they come. It was a tough place.'

She was always keen to lift the family up by its bootstraps. She saw nothing wrong in the working classes enjoying the fruits of their labours. This, though, was a view of socialism out of favour with the socialist elite in the days of Militant, when to drive a Jag, as John Prescott did, was tantamount to being a class traitor. Phyllis went one step further: she even wore a fox stole to a Labour Party reception, much to John's embarrassment.

John shared her view of socialism. There was no intellectual analysis of socialism requiring hair-shirt self-denial for the Prescotts.

'There's nowt too good for the working class' summed up Phyllis's view of socialism. That anticipated by nearly three generations the Blairite desire to reconnect the Labour Party of the 1990s with the aspirations of ordinary people.

While at Brinsworth junior school, young John had his first taste of showbiz, which he still enjoys. He was Grumpy in the school play *The Seven Dwarfs*. His mother was also theatrical in her own way. The British Red Cross raised money for the soldiers with amateur nights at the local British Legion club in Rotherham. 'There was an ankle competition going on, so I entered,' she said. 'I took the three kids along to it. They put a sheet across and all you saw were the ankles. I won the competition,' she remembered with pride.

John recalls that most of their holidays were at union conferences, in Scarborough or Bridlington. But that is the shortened memory of childhood. Bert was keen on using his free travel on British and Continental railways to broaden their horizons, including taking a trip to Evian, on Lake Geneva, where he gambled in the casino with the holiday money. Fortunately, he won.

In 1951, they also went to Brighton for the final of the competition for the 'Most Typical Family in Britain'. The competition finals were at Brighton Pavilion, near the site where the conference centre was built. This was the scene of Prescott's triumph in 1993, when he swung the vote behind John Smith in the debate on one-member-one-vote democracy in the Labour Party.

At that time, Bert and Phyllis had four children: John, thirteen; Ray, twelve; Dawn, ten; Vivian, seven. They had a fifth child, Adrian, who was born in 1958, when Phyllis was 43. In the 1960s, Bert and Phyllis divorced after 25 years of marriage, when John was in his twenties. They both married again, Phyllis to a civil servant called Ron Swales, who has since died. But the break-up of their marriage was another severe test for their eldest son. John remembers going to the local police station when he was about thirteen to report his father. 'My dad's a magistrate,' he said. 'I've seen him kissing another woman.' The police escorted him home – and told him not to tell his mum.

Putting aside the tensions that were to lead to the break-up ten years later, the Prescott family went to Brighton to win, and Phyllis used up her clothing coupons – rationing was still in operation – to make the children presentable on stage.

'The first prize was a thousand pounds – think of that in those days,' said Phyllis. They had a 'question time', and the judges were British stage and radio stars, including Tony Hancock – before his *Blood Donor* days with Galton and Simpson on television – when he was famous as the stooge in the radio programme *Educating Archie*. The Prescotts were invited to Brighton Pavilion with five other families to be quizzed on such questions as 'Who looks after the money in the family?' and 'Who does the housework?'

On the stage, they asked John, then aged thirteen, how he got on with his brother, Ray. John had his arm in a sling, having sustained an injury when he was pushed over by Ray in a dispute about his bike. John's answer was characteristically frank.

'Oh, all right, but he will steal me bike.'

Photographers and reporters followed the Prescotts around Brighton all week, and they were the favourites to win. The result came as a shock to Phyllis, and even some of the audience.

Even over 40 years later, his mother still nursed a sense of having been cheated out of the first prize. It was won by a couple with only one child; the husband had never been in the war, making them untypical in 1951, and the answer that still rankled four decades later came when the mother was asked who looked after the family money. She said they did not have that problem: they had a bank account and a chequebook. To the Prescotts, in postwar Britain, that was unheard of.

Later, the Prescotts heard there was an inquiry and it was discovered that the winners were distantly related to one of the council leaders who was running the competition.

The Prescotts had to settle for the runners-up prize of £50 and a silver rose bowl, with the inscription 'Brighton – Typical Family Competition Finalist, 1951'. It still rests on Phyllis's sideboard. 'I was all for the family,' said his mother.

In spite of his taste of the spotlight, John 'was so shy in those days. He really was. He would withdraw into himself,' said Phyllis. 'But he was very protective towards his brother and sisters.'

In postwar Rotherham, when his father was away – he had been transferred back to Cheshire with British Railways – John acted as the head of the family. He was not yet ten years old. 'We were very, very close,' said his mother.

The sensitive side of John Prescott is one of the many paradoxes in his life. He gained a reputation for being the Mr Angry of the Labour Party, with bust-ups in the tearoom of the Commons, and aggressive Tory-baiting performances on television. The private John Prescott bears little resemblance to the public figure, known as 'Thumper'.

'I'm not thick-skinned. If anything, I'm too sensitive. I do some pretty straight talking. The assumption is that if I am rough in presentation, if I have no smooth edges, then I'm less intelligent.'

During the 1992 leadership election, Prescott was asked to name his greatest strength. 'I hope it is the quality which I believe to be essential to every human person – sensitivity. If you lose sensitivity, you've lost everything.'

CHAPTER THREE

Eleven-Plus Failure

> *Though I have a lot of time to catch up on, I will make the grade in the future.*
> John Prescott, aged twenty, in a letter to his mother.

Failing the eleven-plus was a defining moment for John Prescott, who left school at fifteen without any qualifications.

It went far deeper than a choice over whether he played rugger at grammar school or soccer at the secondary modern school. Rejection, and an inescapable feeling of inferiority, became a recurring theme which has persisted through to his middle age. He is still fighting it.

'When I hear people who've been well educated talk in the House of Commons … it's an arrogance. They've been blessed, if you like. They can't tackle you on the ideas, the substance, so they go for the form. Those of us who've come through a bad education system are resentful about that. I have to live with my lack of education daily in the way I string words together in the House of Commons,' he said.

The eleven-plus examination, the most important in his life, came on John Prescott, as it did on thousands of other children, rather suddenly, without sufficient preparation. Other children shrugged off the setback, and made the best of a bad break in life. The shy boy from Upton took it like a personal affront, and now to some members of the family seemed 'sullen' with the pain of failure.

The Prescotts had moved into a new semi-detached house in a cul-de-sac at 29 Pine Gardens, Upton, on the outskirts of Chester. Les George, Prescott's form master, remembers that, like the other 'Uptonites', John was 'always immaculately turned out'.

The Prescotts were early converts to the 'property-owning democracy', as Baroness Thatcher later described home-owning. Bert Prescott had moved back to Chester with British Railways and, unusually for the time, got his name down for the private three-bedroom semi-detached house on a site by the local railway station after Phyllis had returned from Rotherham with the children in 1948. It cost £1,200 and Bert had some help from the British Legion to buy it. Bert was given priority because he had four children. The house was ideal: there was a big garden for the children to play in, and it was near the BR station where the Safeway supermarket has since been built.

John had acted as 'the little man of the family' in Brinsworth, after his father had been moved back to Chester by British Railways. Before leaving his Yorkshire childhood behind him, John sat the eleven-plus examination at the Brinsworth junior school. (He got his results while attending a small church school in Upton in Cheshire.)

Like countless classes of other eleven-year-olds, Prescott puzzled over sums that did not add up, and IQ tests that were like a strange foreign language of symbols. Ticking the boxes was a hit-and-miss affair, which would affect the rest of his life. R. A. (Rab) Butler's 1944 Education Act had ensured education in state schools for all children up to the age of fifteen; but at eleven, the brightest were given an IQ test and streamed off to grammar schools, while the rest were sent to secondary modern schools. There was little preparation for the one-day tests in many schools. Some sat them without quite knowing what it was all about. Prescott, like most children, was pitched in and required to sink or swim. Tick off the right answers, and grammar school beckoned. Tick off the wrong ones too many times, and the secondary school was the only option. Young John ticked too many wrong boxes.

His former teachers say the odds were stacked against children like Prescott, who got their results in Cheshire in 1948–9. According to Les George, the county had so few grammar schools that it was harder to pass; but Prescott ignored the entreaties of his family to shrug it off.

'I was shattered. My brother and sister passed and went on to grammar school, so I was the only one who didn't. It gave me a great sense of failure.'

There was a palpable feeling of failure in the choice of schools and type of education which was now presented to Prescott, J. L. Even the name 'secondary modern school' seemed to suggest something second-class. If he had passed, he would have gone to Helsby Grammar School in the self-satisfied semi-rural suburbs of Chester near to his home.

He felt the system had let him down. That conviction

produced in Prescott a detestation of selection in education that lay behind his outburst 48 years later, at the decision by Harriet Harman, a fellow member of the shadow Cabinet, to send her son, Joe, to a grammar school, in spite of party policy.

Failing the eleven-plus, Prescott was put down by the education authority for the Grange Secondary Modern School, at Ellesmere Port, a windswept town, dominated by the oil refineries and chemical plants on the mudflats by the mouth of the Mersey.

There were four ability streams for the school of about 500 boys, from A for the most able down to D for those who required remedial teaching. John stayed in the top A stream throughout his five years at the school. He was regarded as bright by his teachers, of exam ability. He left without any qualifications because, in those days, there were no GCEs for secondary school pupils to sit at the end of their five years (and GCSEs did not make their appearance – as a replacement for the CSE and the GCE O level – until 1988). Only the gifted sat external exams for further education. It was ten years before he had the chance to find himself through education. 'One of the most attractive things about him is that he does this work out of the zest of a man who has discovered himself; he found out by gradual degrees that he was bright, that he understood intellectual concepts, that he was more than a shrewd heavy with good union contacts, that problems engaged his mind,' Edward Pearce wrote later in the *Illustrated London News*.

John had been promised a new bike by his father, if he passed the eleven-plus. As he failed, he never got the bike. Ray got a new bike, when he passed, but only the first payment was paid by his dad. The Prescott boys were taught the economic facts of life at an early age.

There was a more traumatic insult to add to the injury over the bike for the eleven-year-old John. Before leaving the village school in Upton, he wrote a love letter to a girl from his class he was sweet on.

'Our lives split. I can remember sending her a letter expressing my desire – love, if you like, a young kid's feelings – and she sent it back with the spelling mistakes corrected. That summed up the division. The message was that suddenly you are less than they are. It tends to leave you with a bit of an inferiority complex. And aggression comes partly from reacting against that …'

His family think he is being oversensitive, but Prescott says it 'knocks you back' when your words are thrown back in your face. The problems of spelling – and syntax, too – are a recurring problem for Prescott. His friends say his mangling of grammar – combining consonants so that words are merged, dropping sentences, shortening words by abandoning their endings – is because he is in too much of a rush to get out what he wants to say. He was told it might be caused by a form of verbal dyslexia, but if so, it was a disability he could use as a weapon. He cannot resist making jokes, and he likes wordplay, so would frequently refer to Peter Mandelson, Prescott's bête noire, as 'Mendelson', which made the 'Prince of Darkness' sound sinister.

The late Jean Rook wrote: 'Mr Prescott's articulation can be as graceless as a jack-knifed lorry, a fact of which he's quite touchingly aware.'

The snooty girl he left behind passed the eleven-plus and it remained a sore point for the rest of his life. He has often told the story of how he lost his *first* girlfriend to the cruelty of the eleven-plus system, but a couple of years ago the *Daily Mail* devoted a full page to its report of how it had tracked her down and discovered that, like him, in spite of her dismissal of his letter, she had failed the eleven-plus too. Pamela Reaney lived in a comfortable semi-detached house in Brinsworth Hall Avenue. In fact, she was the 'wrong' girl. Pamela Sen, as she is now called, does not remember the letter incident, and Prescott says the girl who wrote [corrected] the letter was not Pamela at all: she lived in Upton and he is not revealing her name.

Pamela was a carpenter's daughter, and more well-to-do than the kids in the terraces like Prescott. Now married with two grown-up sons, Pamela still lives in Rotherham, but has a hazy recollection of young Prescott. 'He was just somebody at school. You are a bit giddy at that age.'

He did go back to Brinsworth to meet her again when he was about thirteen and took her a box of Newberry Fruits. 'He must have liked them because they weren't my favourites. Perhaps he wanted to say something to me about how he felt, but he just asked if I would write to him and for a while we exchanged letters.'

He is remembered by his former school friends, as 'well-dressed and clean', and likeable. Prescott and another boy, Jack Wilson, were the class favourites. Norma Broadhurst from 14 Ellis Street fancied John but she was heartbroken when he returned to Brinsworth a year after moving back to Chester and did not visit her.

But the struggle with syntax and spelling came to symbolise the lack of a good education, which Prescott felt was a right he had been denied by a class-based system that benefited the rich. In spite of his Rambo image, Prescott was emotionally thin-skinned and sensitive.

He was acutely conscious of the class divisions around him, even as a child. He remembers at Scout camp the 'middle-class kids took beautiful things with them, like wrapped-up chocolates. All I had was scones.'

It developed into an inferiority complex which in later life, he realised, led to a defensive reaction, causing the aggressiveness that he is only now learning to control. If there is any mellowing in the Mr Angry of the Labour Party, it is because he understands better how his own personality was shaped by the sense of failure at the age of eleven.

In 1989, when he was running against Roy Hattersley – a grammar school boy – for the deputy leadership the first time, he said, 'I do believe I'm a socially inferior person. There are some places I'd never go alone, like the theatre or a posh restaurant. I'll only go in a group I can hide in. It's Me and Them with the Tories, and I'm not happy socialising with 'em.'

His son, David, said Prescott will not book a table at a restaurant, but has no nerves about addressing a mass rally of Labour supporters. He can lose himself in a big crowd. On his own, his shyness overcomes him.

Dennis Skinner, the MP for Bolsover, with whom he shared a flat in London after becoming an MP, has few foibles about 'inferiority', but then *he* passed the eleven-plus. Skinner, the grammar school boy, in spite of his image as an archetypal mining MP, tried to convince Prescott that the eleven-plus was only a test of memory; some had it, others did not. He also tried to persuade Prescott not to overburden himself with the mastery of facts, and, when, speaking, to stick to a single theme. 'I used to tell him that a speech was like a trunk of a tree. Get the theme, then put the detail out on the branches.'

Prescott was inclined to put in the detail first, producing a bush of facts, and would not be dissuaded from doing it his way. 'I love the detail. I immerse myself in detail, whether it's in organisation or policy. The vision is the house. I like the bricks,' he said.

Colleagues testify to Prescott's love of detail, sometimes finding him sitting up late surrounded by papers, writing a speech packed with facts. Friends say he does not lack intelligence. 'He absorbs facts like blotting paper. He is really very good with detail. He is certainly intelligent,' said Mike Craven, who was Prescott's personal assistant and researcher in the mid-1980s.

Raphael Samuel, Prescott's tutor in history at Ruskin College, Oxford, taught Prescott economic, social and labour history. 'It was a disturbing experience. My student seemed a very incarnation of Jude the Obscure, with a tremendous appetite for learning, fiercely independent opinions, and a determination like the tragic hero of Hardy's novel, to crack the secret of knowledge – in his case, economics rather than classics. He loved argument, and tutorials were apt to erupt in fierce disagreement ...'

Prescott's GBH upon the English language has provided easy copy for the sketch-writers. Matthew Parris, a former Tory MP turned sketch-writer for *The Times*, has parodied Prescott's syntax so sharply it has almost drawn blood.

Parris's account of Prescott's speech on the Budget in 1995 is a typical example:

> *Have you ever watched a disaster movie? Have you seen the look on the pilot's face as the plane spirals, engines aflame, towards the sea? Gripping the levers he fights the urge to panic. Every facial muscle is tight, hysteria close to the surface.*
>
> *This was the look on the faces of the Hansard reporters as John Prescott's Budget speech gathered speed yesterday afternoon. Wrestling with the controls of their stenograph machines, two ladies from the Official Report stared forward, white-faced, as their mission to turn chaos into prose disintegrated. Who says it's not glam to be a Gallery reporter? Mission impossible! Join Hansard and tame Prescott's grammar!*
>
> *Down at the dispatch box, the deputy leader of the Labour Party was knocking seven bells out of the English language. The ladies tugged at their headsets, but it was no good: there was nothing wrong with the technology. The output was true to the input. The input was Prescott. It was without form, and void.*
>
> *Their task to make this intelligible was hopeless. Even Pauline Prescott in the Special Gallery looked stunned. He cannot, surely, talk like this at breakfast?*

Faster and faster Prescott went, misplaced participles flying like stones from the wheels of his wagon. At breakneck speed he took a tight corner from a 10p tax band into the Private Finance Initiative, scattering nouns and adjectives as he went. When he ran out of verbs, he ploughed forward on nouns alone, whole strings of them: 'Holland, France, Belgium, Scandinavia …': laundry lists of facts, but with no grammatical line on which to peg them. In moments of passion, he started throwing in the definite article randomly: 'from the fourteenth to the eighteenth in the world competitiveness league'.

From time to time an intervening Tory back-bencher would try to block his path like a cow in the road. Carnage! Losing a fender here, a spoke, a headlamp there, losing coherence all down the line, Mr Prescott gabbled on.

Sometimes, as if to tease, he would return momentarily to his written text.

From his oratory a flash of lucidity would shimmer for an instant, mocking reason as mirage mocks the eye, then dissolve as Prescott re-entered the stream of his own consciousness.

Once he hit a tree. The tree came in the form of Michael Heseltine, who repeated a question from Alex Salmond, the Scottish National Party leader, about VAT on fuel, to which Mr Prescott had no idea of the answer. Wallop! The great man came to a shuddering halt.

For a second, silence, a scratching of the head and the hiss of escaping steam. Gordon Brown whispered something. Prescott threw the wagon into reverse, disengaged from the tree, then, with a crash of gears, 'I keep getting explanations as to why it should be. I think I stick to my argument …', plunged senselessly on.

Prescott says he had not heard of the VAT proposal. Parris, who looks down on the chamber from a seat in the press gallery that was above and behind the Labour front bench in opposition, went on:

The notes on the Despatch Box in front of him appeared to include a selection of figures. Mr Prescott threw these into his discourse with wild abandon, muddling his billions with his millions. A passage followed concerning the Tories' wasted opportunity in Europe. He listed the advantages we had thrown away. First among these, he said, was the predominance of English as an international medium of communication. What he had to share, he said, was a 'common language'.

The Hansard reporters tugged again at their headsets. But they heard right.

Prescott knows his grammar is bad, and there is little he can do about it. For him, it is sometimes exasperating, and sparks his famously short fuse. Given the press he gets, it is hardly surprising he does not like debating in the chamber of the House of Commons, which he once said was like 'having a pack of wild dogs set loose on you'.

He was not brought up in Oxbridge debating societies, and

has no time for clever debating points. He is uncomfortable with the elaborate nineteenth-century rules of behaviour in the Commons, and prefers to bludgeon his Tory opponents. Often the direct assault can hearten the Labour back bench, and the audience outside the Commons, far more than a clever speech that draws no blood. The Commons has the atmosphere of a gentlemen's club – its architect, Charles Barry, was also responsible for the Reform Club in Pall Mall – and Prescott is undoubtedly seen by the Tories as one of the rougher, 'country' members, easily provoked into throwing rolls across the dining room. Many Tory MPs in the Thatcher and Major governments have known each other since their prep school, or university, and some have been debating against each other since their Oxbridge Conservative Association days – the pro-European Kenneth Clarke first crossed swords with the Euro-sceptic Nicholas Budgen at Cambridge; Cabinet colleagues John Gummer, Michael Howard and the former Chancellor Norman Lamont were all in the so-called 'Cambridge mafia', and were all pictured with Clarke at his wedding. On the New Labour benches, the former trade union officials, like Prescott, have been replaced by confident, well-educated, white-collar professionals. Lawyers such as Tony Blair are fully equipped for public speaking – they were trained to marshal an argument with telling effect. Prescott's public speaking was learned at the pier head in mass meetings of striking seamen and dockers, where the crowbar was a useful debating tool. He does not lounge confidently with his feet on the Despatch Box table from the front bench, with the insouciance of the aristocrats of politics, like Tony Benn – Bert Prescott's hero. John Prescott was taught to sit up straight. There is an easy confidence which comes to the public-school-educated, born-to-be-in-power politicians which Prescott has never possessed.

'I recognise that my style of speaking tends to intimidate Tories – it's almost daring them to get up and say something. They've also learned over the years that I've mastered details – it isn't huff and puff. My problem is I've so much to say, I try and say it too fast and fall over myself. When I listen to bits of me on tape, it's gobbledygook. That's to do with class and confidence. A barrister pauses to show reflection. I come from the background of strike meetings where, if you paused, some bugger got in.'

During his successful challenge for the deputy leadership, Prescott got his own back on Parris in a BBC *Breakfast News* programme, when Parris was on the panel. Parris tried to goad him about his problems with grammar. 'You bridle about it. You bridle, don't you?' said Parris.

'I didn't have your education. What was yours? Yale and Cambridge and Swaziland. I'd love to have had that, but I didn't. I'm a secondary-modern-school lad. But I'll tell you this: nobody ever misunderstands what I mean even if they don't understand the grammar.'

It is a point Parris concedes. Writing about Prescott's regular clashes as shadow Transport Secretary with John MacGregor, the former Transport Secretary, Parris noted that MacGregor could be clearly understood, but had nothing to say; Prescott's syntax may have been challenged, but at least we knew what he meant. 'You can always tell what Mr Prescott is trying to say. It's just that it never comes out like that,' observed Parris. Prescott admits Parris has a point. 'I didn't like that but I couldn't deny it.'

Prescott has a sharp sense of humour, which has sometimes got him into trouble, and he is big enough to laugh at himself. He has entertained the Labour supporters by performing a sketch in the Labour Red Revue – an end-of-the-pier show – at the annual party conference, in which he parodied himself, like Parris's rendering of the Lord's Prayer in Prescott-speak: 'Our Heaven which Thou art hallowed in Be Thy name Father to give us ongoing daily delivery …'

In 1995, after a minor accident, he had a routine brain scan. Phyllis Clarke, secretary of the Hull constituency Labour Party for the past 30 years, teased him. 'Did they find any syntax?'

'Not a trace,' he laughed.

Deep down, however, he resents the impression given by the press that bad grammar or poor syntax may be taken to mean that he lacks intelligence; that he is 'a bit of a thicko'. It may have been partly to prove the world wrong that he persevered, after he was married, with a degree course at Hull University. When he arrived at the shadow Cabinet table, he realised that they were no brighter than he was. 'It seemed like a world far away inhabited by giants, but when I got there I found they were only on the same level as me.'

The Grange Secondary School was regarded as a good school with high standards – some of his contemporaries went into the professions, including one who became a doctor and another who became an executive with Shell. However, the Grange – now an evening centre for further education – was noted more for its football record than its academic achievements with the 'rejects' from the grammar school system. The school's ethos was that 'everybody should be happy, hard-working and courteous'. It tried to turn out decent citizens rather than university material. The headmaster of the Grange, Bill Roberts, was passionately keen on football, and he trained the England schoolboys international soccer team for eighteen years. Ex-pupils who were there with Prescott remember the excitement when the FA Cup was brought to the school by a former local boy, Joe Mercer – later to succeed Alf Ramsay as England manager – after his team, Arsenal, beat Liverpool in the final.

You had to be good to get into the school football team at the Grange; two boys went on to play for England, and a number were of county standard. Prescott preferred swimming. The boys from the Grange had to shiver in the open air from early April at the Rivacre Baths in Ellesmere Port, an experience that hardened him for scuba diving, which he later enjoyed in his spare time, until he burst an eardrum with pressure underwater. Prescott, showing typical thoroughness, qualified as a diver to investigate the exploitation of workers by US companies who were pioneering the exploration of oil in the North Sea. More used to rigs around the shallower American waters, they did not have submersibles when Prescott took up the campaign for North Sea rig safety. Training off France and Italy, he met Jacques

Cousteau, the French underwater explorer, and put his skills to good use by swimming underwater along the Thames for the two miles from Chelsea Bridge to Downing Street to deliver a petition to Number Ten in his diver's wetsuit, to protest about dumping of nuclear waste in the sea. He became one of the first people in 400 years to see the *Mary Rose*, Henry VIII's warship, when as the parliamentary Private Secretary to Peter Shore – the Secretary of State for Trade, whose responsibilities included wrecks – he was allowed to dive on the wreck on 13 July 1974, a few months before Prince Charles. She was located in the mud and silt in the Solent, where she had keeled over and sunk in 1545 as she went to meet the French. Prescott has a framed limited-edition print of the ship proudly displayed in his lounge at home in Hull, recording the event. In the silt, he found the timbers 'amazingly well preserved'.

Georgie Crump, one of his long-term friends from his seafaring days, recalls that, when they had a reunion party at his home in Cheshire, one of the former Cunard stewards – an expert diver who used to dive from the bridge of the ship when it was anchored in Dubrovnik – jumped into the Crump family swimming pool, and swam over three lengths underwater. The former steward is now making a living diving for golf balls in the alligator-infested waters surrounding the golf courses in Miami. But Prescott said he could beat him. Prescott did four lengths underwater. It was a rare example of Prescott winning an argument by holding his breath.

There is also a certificate from the Association for Spina

Bifida and Hydrocephalus to prove that John Prescott MP completed 9.7 miles (600 lengths) at the RAC club over a duration of nine and a half hours for the charity in November 1979. And there are memorable photographs of a tired-looking Prescott being helped out of the water by two *Penthouse* pets.

George Wall, who was in the same class as Prescott, remembers that John was a 'very quiet, studious type ... He was not very jolly.'

His mother was concerned by his shyness. 'He was so shy he would not let himself go. These days, they would have something done about it,' says Phyllis.

The 'Uptonites' used to arrive at school by bus, keep themselves to themselves, and return by bus after school. Girls went to a separate school building on a neighbouring site, but the few miles between Upton and Ellesmere Port separated the Upton boys, including John, from the social life of the school in the evenings. He did, however, like the stage, a passion that enhanced his performances in later life. He regularly appeared in the school plays put on by Mr George, and there is a school photograph of Prescott dressed as a toff in top hat, silk scarf, and bow tie with a lowly road-mender from a play about a hole in the road.

It is another of the paradoxes about Prescott that he has grown up with a reputation as a rebel with a temper in the Commons, but as a teenager he was never a juvenile delinquent; his father saw to that. In an era when rock 'n' roll was taking off, and teenagers were ripping up cinema seats at showings of *Rock Around the Clock* with Bill Haley and the

Comets, John preferred swing bands, and still has a love of jazz, as an habitué of Ronnie Scott's. He was never a teddy boy. He never had a motorcycle, and he never wore a leather motorcycle jacket. Compared with Prescott, Tony Blair the long-haired pop singer was a teenage tearaway.

Through his active membership of the Labour Party in Upton, Bert Prescott was appointed a local magistrate, and he was an authoritarian father at times. When John was about eight, he, his brother and some friends in Rotherham set a field on fire after Sunday school, and his father 'shopped' his sons to the police.

'I was playing with matches in a field with my brother and a couple of others. We set light to the grass and tried to put it out with our jackets – and ruined the jackets, of course. All the fire engines came. We stank of smoke and had to explain it to our parents,' says Prescott.

However, he was more shocked by the fact that it was his father who turned them in.

'My father reported me to the police. I felt terrible. It was very authoritarian. I was small; [the policeman] was a damn big bobby. And there was the shock that my father was reporting me.'

The policeman gave him a dressing down, and a severe warning 'with lots of nods and winks between him and my father'.

By the time the family had moved to Pine Gardens, Bert Prescott was a rising figure in the local Labour Party and on the local bench of magistrates. He made sure none of his own children appeared before him, however minor the misdemeanour. But there was total embarrassment when Bert Prescott JP, John and Ray were caught 'scrumping' apples from an orchard; Bert defended his sons, and talked his way out of the situation – insisting it was an abandoned orchard – but he was not afraid to use his stick to impose some discipline.

These juvenile indiscretions appear to be the only 'crimes' on young Prescott's charge sheet. His headmaster, Bill Roberts, told his mother when he was due to leave, unqualified, at the age of fifteen, 'He has never given us one ounce of trouble.'

So why did he fail at school? He was not disruptive, girlfriends were not a distraction, he was not preoccupied with sport, according to those who were at school at the time, and he was pushed by his mother and father to work hard and succeed. The most compelling reason appears to be that he was a late starter – he let the lessons pass him by, ignoring the appeals of his parents to buckle down and pass exams. There was no spark to light his imagination after the crushing disappointment of his eleven-plus failure, apart from the occasional school play.

The famous Prescott syntax problem was hardly noticed at the school. 'He was a good, average pupil,' said his form master, Les George. 'He lost enthusiasm for education after the eleven-plus. It was when he started studying with the WEA [Workers' Educational Association] at Ruskin that it changed. I told him, "You have got a good brain. Use it,"' said Mr George.

And Prescott senior says of the young John, 'He wasn't interested in school at all. He didn't show any interest in homework. He wasn't a lad that would push himself. Whether he didn't hear, or didn't understand what they were talking about, I don't know, but he wouldn't raise the question. He was submissive in a way. He would take what was coming. I was the same as John, in a way. I didn't go to school until I was seven, and I left at fifteen. All I ever learned, I did through reading.'

His mother agrees: 'John didn't seem to have any interest in anything until he went to sea. That's when he started. He was always conscious that he never did anything with his education.'

She says she treasures a letter he wrote at sea when he was 20:

> *Though I have a lot of time to catch up on, I will make the grade in the future. One day, be assured, you will have something to be proud of me, mum.*

CHAPTER FOUR

Hollywood Waiters

> *A whisky and soda for me, Giovanni, and a gin and tonic for my friend.*
> Nicholas Soames, Tory MP for Crawley, barracking Prescott in the Commons.

The stewards on the luxury Cunard liners were so smartly dressed that they were nicknamed 'the Hollywood Waiters'. They wore white shirts with swallowtail collars, bow ties, white waistcoats and black trousers which were always immaculately pressed. Like John Travolta with plates, they added a dash of showbiz to the serving of breakfast, lunch, tea and dinner in the grand saloon rooms. And they knew how to charm the customers for tips.

'It was a good life. We were very wealthy. Americans were very generous and with two tables of fifteen each tipping $10 – about £8 – you made $300/$400 every seven days which was a fortune then. We looked good. They used to call us the Hollywood waiters. We used to dress in these jazzy evening suits – wing collars, bows, white waistcoats – as a young kid, I loved the dressing up. And, if I was honest, there was also the fact that women found us attractive.'

Being caught in a woman's cabin was a punishable offence at sea. It was treated in marine law like tampering with the goods in the hold, and the young stewards could be charged with 'broaching ship's cargo' if they were not careful. For a first offence, the penalty was a 10s (50p) fine and a day's pay; for a second offence, it was a £1 fine, two days' pay and a big smile.

'The captain would sit there, in full uniform with a peaked cap, and a Union Jack on the table, and ask if you were guilty,' Prescott later recalled.

Was he ever caught? Prescott was asked this by the *Evening Standard* in 1992, when he was running for the leadership of the Labour Party. 'There is a long pause as honesty wars with discretion, then he roars with laughter and answers, "Let's say I never faced those charges".'

In fact, his former colleagues all say there was not much time for shipboard romance on the seven-day trips to New York, but the cruises to the Caribbean, around the Mediterranean or, on one occasion, a millionaires' world cruise, were more relaxed. Some accounts sound like *Carry On Cruising*: on one occasion, two beautiful and very tipsy Chester women were found wandering in the passage to the stewards' rooms, with no clothes on.

There were also endless numbers of famous people to meet. 'I was a waiter to Anthony Eden when he went to sea after he'd resigned. I was always interested in politics and I used to argue with people on my tables – judges and senators and politicians. Then there were more rows because all my rubbish was piled on the table while I was arguing. It was a good period.

'I did manage to get one bit of British merchant navy legislation changed. Now if you're caught with a woman passenger, you are no longer charged with broaching ship's cargo,' he said.

Shipmates remember that Prescott had a photograph of Pauline Tilston, a Liz Taylor lookalike, pinned up by his bunk. Pauline and John were not yet married, but his friends recalled he was already 'smitten' with his girl back home.

Life in the 'glory hole', where ten or twelve stewards had their bunks in the bows of the ship, was as fuggy as a changing room, congested, and, above all, noisy. Prescott's bunk was next to a big pipe that carried the anchor chain down through the bows to the sea. It could be run out at any time in port, usually when they were catching a few hours' sleep after a long voyage, and it made a thunderous clanging din, according to Georgie Crump. It was hot, and stuffy, and no place for a young man to study, but Prescott was taking a correspondence course at Ruskin College, Oxford, through the WEA, and in impossible circumstances. That led to tiffs with his workmates, who were full of the boisterous joys of life at sea, and barely out of their teens.

An old photograph of his group in the 'glory hole' shows Prescott in shirtsleeves, laughing. After photographic enlargement, the reading material which one of his mates was studying can clearly be seen to be a girlie mag called *Nugget*.

'It was like a ten-berth ranch house, right in the forward end of the ship,' says Crump.

Crump, who lived near Chester, used to pick Prescott up on his motorcycle, and take him to the Liverpool docks, where they boarded the Cunarders for America. 'He was the worst pillion passenger I ever knew. He would always try to steer the bike from the back seat.'

On their few hours off each day, they could retire to the Pig and Whistle, the crew bar, where Wrexham lager cost 2s (10p) a pint.

The shifts were punishing. The stewards had to be up at 6.30 a.m. on the Atlantic run to carry out the 'menial' duties that John complained of in his letter to his mother. One task was to carry the beer from the stores to the bars. If anyone died on the voyage, they were kept in the cold store with the beer. Waiters were sometimes greeted by the sight of a coffin when they went down for the beer barrels in the morning.

Each waiter was given a cleaning chore to perform, washing the floor in the main corridors, or the saloons, before their real work started. The main routine was to lay out the places for the two servings of breakfast in the main saloon; wait on at breakfast; clear the things away; at noon lay out the places for lunch; serve the lunch between 1 p.m. and 2 p.m.; from 3.45 p.m. to 4.40 p.m. serve afternoon tea on the promenade deck or the lounges and the library; and catch an hour's cat nap before dinner was served from 6 p.m. until 8.20 p.m.

Prescott's 'saloon boss', Owen Thompson, struck a deal with one of the officers to give Prescott more time, in more peaceful surroundings, to do his studying. He was put on the afternoon watch to stop the passengers stealing the silver from the restaurant.

'We were having a lot of silver stolen out of the restaurant,' says Thompson. 'Between lunch and dinner there was never anyone around, and we were losing salt and pepper pots, and silver mustard bowls and teaspoons as souvenirs. The catering officer decided we would have to have somebody on watch in the afternoon. John was studying then, and it was very hard for him, so we came to an agreement. He kept an eye on the restaurant in the afternoon, and he did his studying at the same time.'

Thompson, whose son, Phil, became an England international football star with Liverpool, retired to Kirkby after a lifetime on board ship. He had no trouble remembering Prescott's time at sea when I spoke to him: the former shipmates still met each Wednesday in a Liverpool café for a cup of tea and a chat about the old days on board the Cunarders.

The *Britannic*, on which they served together, was 'a very good sailing ship – she was low in the water, broad, and very good in heavy weather,' said Georgie Crump. She also had a reputation for 'wonderful food and some sumptuous meals created by her chefs', according to Derek Whale, an historian of the Liverpool liners. 'Her artistic cold-buffet displays resplendent with decorated whole salmon, meats of all kinds, with elegant figures sculptured from solid blocks of ice, were so picturesque and appetising that it seemed sinful to mutilate them.'

She was the last of a distinguished line of ships of the same name, the last of the White Star liners. She was also one of the last great liners to leave Liverpool, when the fleets of transatlantic passenger ships were replaced by Boeing 747s. The first *Britannic* was scrapped in 1903 after serving as a troop ship in the Boer War; the second, a giant vessel with four funnels, was a hospital ship in World War I until she was torpedoed by a German submarine on 21 November 1916 – an outrage not confirmed until 1977 with an underwater investigation by Jacques Cousteau, the underwater explorer. The *Britannic* on which Prescott served was built by Harland and Wolff in Belfast and launched in the mahogany and brass heyday of the luxury liners on 6 August 1929. Her maiden voyage was from Liverpool to New York, on 28 June 1930. She had two squat funnels in the distinctive buff and black colours of the White Star line, weighed 26,943 tons, survived the war as a troop ship, and she was an old favourite in Liverpool by the time Prescott joined her as a boy in his late teens. She sailed for the last time to the breaker's yard at Inverkeithing in January 1961, after completing two million miles, and carrying over 1,200,000 passengers on Atlantic crossings and cruises. Among the passengers were Stanley Baldwin, Rita Hayworth and Aly Khan.

The *Britannic*, which stayed under her White Star colours even when she was owned by Cunard, also went on summer cruises in the Mediterranean. Her journey took her first to Madeira, then on to places that sounded like something from Hollywood movies to the young waiters – Casablanca, Alexandria and Venice. Georgie Crump remembers there were always fights when they docked in Venice, because the Italians did not like the Liverpool boys going ashore, stealing their girls.

There was also more time on the cruises to enjoy the facilities on board. They included a fully equipped gymnasium run by a boxing celebrity from Liverpool, Dom Volante, who had been a featherweight in the 1930s and still cut a dash 20 years later in his white peaked cap and blazer. Nominally a steward, Dom would try to keep the passengers entertained on the voyages; he accompanied the film star Cesar Romero on early-morning runs twelve times around the deck; he caught the Archbishop of Canterbury when he fell from an exercise horse a month before he performed the coronation of the young Queen Elizabeth II; and Dom taught Prescott to box.

Prescott had taken up boxing at the Butlin's holiday camp in Pwllheli on holiday with a bunch of pals. Dressed in shorts and pumps, Prescott took on a youth who could box and also had a beautiful girlfriend in the front row. Prescott had his eye on the girl, and found himself kissing the canvas before he had time to throw a punch. After that, he decided to learn the *right* way to box.

Volante organised boxing bouts among the ship's company as part of the entertainment for the cruise. On one voyage around the Mediterranean, Prescott fought his way to the final. The bouts were held on the deck, in a makeshift ring, in the full heat of the day, with the 'scallywags', the rough lads from Liverpool who made up part of the ship's company, cheering on from any vantage point they could find.

Prescott was a regular in the makeshift boxing ring, and on one cruise in 1957 was presented with the top prize – two bottles of beer plus two hours' overtime bonus – by Sir Anthony Eden, the former Prime Minister. They were on the cruise liner *Rangitata*, bound for New Zealand through the Panama Canal; Eden had resigned over the Suez debacle, and had taken the cruise to get over the trauma of his personal disaster.

Owen Thompson remembered that, for one final bout on the *Britannic*, the crew were hanging out of the lifeboats to get a better view of the contest.

There had been horse play in the crew's quarters with wet towels, and Prescott had found that life was hard on board ship. His father had heard stories of bullying at sea, but his son was taught how to handle himself. Knowing how to box was a useful skill for a young man, who was having the manners of childhood knocked off at sea. 'It was every man for himself,' one of his shipmates recalled.

Prescott was up against one of the ship's toughs, who had plenty of support. With hundreds watching, including the passengers and men, Prescott slugged it out. The blow with which he caught his opponent may have been a lucky one, but Prescott laid him out, and won the contest, for which he was given a silver trophy. Prescott was nineteen.

He later presented the cup to his former teacher, Les George, who had moved on to become headmaster of Christleton High School, a comprehensive with 1,300 pupils, near Chester. It is now the inter-house swimming trophy, and each year, pupils from Christleton High School compete for the Prescott Cup, which the Deputy Prime Minister won with his fists.

It was not always under the Queensberry rules. 'I have been in my share of fights when I was at sea. When a ship gets in the lads will go ashore and get bevvied. I've been in some problems, yeah. A Belfast lad pulled a razor on me in New York once. He was drunk. I just moved away. Got him the next day.'

His ability to use his fists once came in useful as shadow

Transport Secretary, when he was making a video for London Television, in the rush hour on the platform at King's Cross station.

Filming had been fraught. For one thing, Prescott had not learned his lines. For another, he was in the middle of a take when he was forced to stop because the direction board right above his head bore the single word 'cancelled'.

And he was in no mood for humouring drunks. A tramp with a bottle of Strongbow cider staggered into the shot and said, 'That's a nice silk tie you have on, comrade.'

In a stage whisper, Prescott told the drunk, 'If you don't get out of this shot, I'll stick one on your chin.'

The drunk reeled backwards and, in front of a crowd, shouted at Prescott, 'Come on – stick one on me then.'

For once, the shadow Transport Secretary decided to duck a challenge.

Prescott had gone to sea after a stint as a porter, and a commis (or apprentice) chef, because the Cunarders offered him the prospect of more money, with the bonus of seeing the world and being paid for it.

When John left the Grange Secondary School, Bill Roberts told the boy's mother he was a 'wonderful lad' but would not go far academically. 'He is honest. He has never given us one ounce of trouble. He is going to make a wonderful citizen, but you must accept he won't be academic.'

The headmaster said one thing John excelled at was catering. 'He is very good at going for the fish and chips,' he said. It was half in jest, but it gave his mother an idea. She recalled, 'He was talking down to me a bit, but I thought: Well, he's still got to make a living.'

At fifteen, John got his first job as a junior porter at the White Hart Hotel on Lake Bala, north Wales, at the rate of £2 0s 7d (£2.03) a week. His wage was regulated by the Wages Councils Act.

'I can recall refusing my first tip by saying, "Oh, it's all in the service of the hotel."'

He quickly learned the importance of minimum-pay scales. The manageress ordered him to take the tip next time. 'If you don't want the tip, I'll have it,' she warned him.

'I thought I was just doing my job – helping with the cases, cleaning shoes. I soon got over that, and made a lot of money from tips.'

There were high hopes that one day Bert might have a hotel, with John in charge of the catering side. After working at the White Hart for six months, Bert got John a job as a commis chef under a French chef at the Patten Arms, a hotel in Warrington. John moved out of the kitchens, because it meant he would earn more money.

'I thought, I'm working twice as hard as a waiter but he's getting twice the money and this seemed daft,' he said.

After becoming an MP and a front-bench spokesman, Prescott fought against the Tory abolition of the wages councils, and he never forgot his own experience of low pay. 'The government are threatening to remove protection for young people under 21. That will affect half a million of our youngsters who are on low wages, such as my son, who was an apprentice hairdresser. He was receiving only £23 a week. It would have affected me in the days when I was a commis chef and worked under wages council regulations. I know the conditions of wages councils because I had to live under them. Not many Conservative MPs could tell us about that.'

John stayed there for a couple of years, training as a chef, and studying for his City and Guilds exams.

He also learned about hangovers when he was sixteen.

'There was a Christmas dinner for the staff and guests of the Patten Arms and an American guest bought everybody a Drambuie liqueur. I wouldn't go into the restaurant because I was too shy, so I stayed in the kitchen and did the meal. Then I drank this one Drambuie and it went to my head. I went to the dining room and drank everybody else's. There were 50 people in there but some were supped up, so I must have drunk 30 glasses. It made me violently ill. I couldn't go into a bar without feeling violently sick if I smelt Drambuie.'

The experience put him off drinking. 'I'm still not a great drinker. I drink to get drunk, not particularly for pleasure, and that's not very often.'

Close colleagues knew when he was going on a bender because he was inclined to announce it.

The attractions of hotel life began to pall, however, as locals came in from the cruise ships in Liverpool, with money to burn. His natural rebelliousness made him unsuitable for the army, and the merchant navy was an alternative to National Service.

When he was seventeen, he went to sea to seek his fortune.

There is no evidence that, like other boys, he was running away to sea to escape trouble at home.

'The idea of going to sea was very attractive. You could say to people, I'm off to America. You can imagine the feelings of a young lad sailing out of Liverpool on the great Cunard liners. The first ship I joined was the old *Franconia*, Churchill's ship at Yalta, going to New York, then on to Quebec. I was a commis waiter and liftboy.'

Prescott and Georgie Crump make unlikely doubles for Frank Sinatra and Gene Kelly in *On the Town*, but it must have felt as if the movies had come alive when the Hollywood Waiters arrived in New York, New York!

On one occasion, Prescott and three shipmates pushed a washing machine along Broadway and down 52nd Street to their ship. It was for Prescott's mum, and it was a monstrosity on great iron legs. The souvenirs were not usually so large, but his mother proudly told me, 'I had my first washing machine from New York.'

It was tough on board ship, and Prescott the boy quickly became Prescott the man. His mother remembered receiving a photograph from New York which signalled the end of childhood: 'It was his eighteenth birthday. He sent me a photograph. He had never smoked; he didn't drink; he had never caused me any problems with girls. He had a pint of beer in one hand, and was smoking with the other. That was symbolic. He was a boy no more. It was as if he wanted to make a statement.'

Prescott travelled all over the world, waiting on the tables of the rich and famous, including Archbishop Makarios, when he went to Cyprus. But some of the reports of his exploits are tinged with the romance of the sea. He denies spilling soup in the laps of passengers who upset him, but he says that, if they clicked their fingers, he did look under the table for the dog.

One profile of Prescott, written in 1988 when he was threatening to run for the deputy leadership for the first time, said: 'On Caribbean cruises from New York, he used to argue with blue-rinse Americans on the virtues of the National Health Service as he fed them.' In fact, it was an American millionaire, a man, whose son had a hare lip and a cleft palate. Prescott's youngest brother was born with the same disorder, but had it corrected on the NHS. 'I said to this American, "Why didn't you have your son's condition corrected?" He said, "To be frank, I don't have the money ..."'

For Prescott that summed up the importance of having the NHS available to all regardless of the ability to pay, and it is an anecdote he has often quoted.

Those who lived and worked with him on board the *Britannic* in the 1950s do not remember his being a shipboard firebrand. He was one of the lads, learning the ropes, having the time of his life. But he was also showing signs of being a leader of men. They would come to him with niggling grievances, and he would try to put them right. Belonging to a 'bosses' union' like the National Union of Seamen in those days offered no protection to a member of the crew who was acting as shop steward. He was sacked from ship after ship, returning home to tell Pauline that he was laid off again, and flat broke.

When Prescott was a transport spokesman for the Labour

Party, Nicholas Soames, Winston Churchill's grandson and a wickedly funny Tory MP, guffawed, and shouted a now famous order at Prescott.

Soames recalls he had been at the Cavalry Club with his good friend Ian Gow, Margaret Thatcher's former parliamentary aide, who was later murdered by the IRA in a car bomb. They had had a very good lunch, and Gow said when they sat down in the chamber, 'I say, Captain, that chap Prescott – wasn't he a steward in the merchant navy?'

'I said, "A whisky and soda for me, Giovanni, and a gin and tonic for my friend." I never meant it to be offensive. I like Prescott. It was just meant as a joke.'

Many versions have appeared, but the true version is the one quoted here.

Years later, Prescott was asked whether it had hurt him. 'What's wrong if somebody has a job selling you a gin and tonic? Why is there contempt for people doing that job?'

In another interview, Prescott said, 'I don't mind that. Lord Caradon once said: "Haven't we met somewhere before?"

'I told him: "Yes, on the *Britannic* in the Mediterranean when you were having lunch at the captain's table. I was the waiter."' It was in 1959 when Caradon, then Governor General, was having secret talks with Makarios off Cyprus. It did not stop Prescott voting for Caradon's brother, Michael Foot, for the leadership in 1980.

There was another 'historic' meeting in 1959 when Prescott's ship put in at Larnaca in Cyprus for a day for the talks with Makarios. John's brother Ray, then twenty, was in the RAF and stationed nearby at RAF Akrotiri. Prescott's local paper described how the 'two Chester brothers' had met in Cyprus.

John (21) had taken a four-pound cake to present to his brother and they made a joint call home to their parents. They had arranged a football match between an RAF eleven and a side from the ship, but it had to be called off because the ship's team was kept on duty for the talks.

A few months before the *Britannic* was scrapped, Prescott played a decisive role in an unofficial seamen's strike at Liverpool, which even some of his closest colleagues at Westminster know little about.

The strike, in 1960, brought the liners to a halt; they were tied up for weeks, and it was to be a turning point in Prescott's life. If there was a moment when he showed true leadership, it was now.

CHAPTER FIVE

'Paul'

That is part of politics. You have to bite your bottom lip.
Pauline Prescott.

The first time that Pauline Prescott met Cherie Booth, Tony Blair's wife, was at the Institute of Education lecture theatre in Bloomsbury when their two husbands were elected to the leadership of the party.

'She gave my hand a squeeze. Cherie was just as nervous as me,' Pauline told me. Too much can be made of the fact that they had never met before; they found a rapport, but it underlined the point that the Blairs and the Prescotts are from different backgrounds. Cherie Booth and Pauline Prescott both come from Merseyside, but they move in different circles of friends, a point Pauline recognised, saying, 'There is a fifteen-year difference between us, and Cherie was a barrister …' Pauline, a former hairdresser, spends a great deal of time in Hull, in John's constituency, in a supporting role, away from the metropolitan dinner parties in Islington. She has her own northern network of friends, including the wives of John's closest allies in the party: Ann McCartney, Janet Snape, Di Meale and Margaret Caborn.

Pauline is not overtly 'political', unlike Cherie, who once stood for Parliament, or Glenys Kinnock, now a Member of the European Parliament. But she can look after herself, and she is highly protective towards John.

She met John when she was a hairdresser at Quaintways, a department store in Chester. John was suffering one of his many enforced periods of shore leave, when he was laid off by the shipping companies for union activity, and took a part-time job as a chef in the kitchens at the store.

Bert Prescott, John's father, was a friend of the general manager. John's mother would often make the short journey into town to get her hair done at the store, sometimes by Pauline. 'If I was going to have my hair done, the boss would make sure I had a cup of tea,' says Phyllis. 'Pauline was only a junior then. She used to say, "I was frightened to death I was going to do your hair."'

Quaintways had a jazz club, where the resident band was the Wall City Jazzmen – a six-piece outfit of piano, clarinet, trumpet, double bass, trombone and drums – who were still together in 1997 and playing in Chester.

One day John's mother and father went in to watch them jiving. 'There was John throwing Pauline over his shoulder,' said his mother. John's face fell into its now famous grimace at the appearance of his parents. 'You know how John's face can go … We call it his Family Face.'

They met around 1957, when John was nineteen and had been at sea for two years. Pauline Tilston was a local Chester girl, from a working-class family, with dazzling good looks. Her father was a bricklayer, and her mother was a housewife.

Pauline said: 'John was dating a friend of mine. He went to New Zealand, and my friend married somebody else. When John came back, I'd finished with my boyfriend and we just got together. I'd always liked him, and we started going out together. I was glad my friend had dropped him.'

Pauline's uncle was a boxer called Fred, who was known in the ring as 'Tilly' Tilston. He was a celebrity in Chester before the war, and the nickname stuck. Pauline is still known as 'Tilly' by her friends in Chester, with whom she had a reunion in 1996, but to John, she is always known by the shortened name 'Paul'.

'Pauline was always the girl for John,' said his mother.

John went out with other girls, and in New Zealand he met someone else, but that came to nothing. He gave Pauline a tiki love charm, which he had picked up in New Zealand, and which she wore on the day of the deputy leadership elections. 'I had other boyfriends. He had other girlfriends. I was glad he had.'

As a former hairdresser, Pauline has always taken great care over how she looks, and, if there is more than a passing resemblance to Elizabeth Taylor, it is from Taylor's *Cat on a Hot Tin Roof* period.

Pauline has preserved her figure without dieting or working out in the gym, and she can be feisty. Shortly after they had set up home together, Pauline was cooking John's supper, when he complained she could not boil an egg like his mother. 'I got two eggs thrown at my head,' he recalled with a smile.

Pauline said, 'He was always going on about trade unions. I didn't understand all this sort of stuff. I remember once, he was due to pick me up at home. He didn't arrive.'

John took up the story. 'I was out on strike for six or seven weeks. I had been out on a big march through Liverpool. When I got home, there was a note from Pauline ...'

He still has the note she wrote when, for a few hours, she had walked out on him. Written in ballpoint ink on blue notepaper, it begins 'Darling, dear ...'. Both words are crossed out, and the note continues:

> *John,*
>
> *So glad your* [sic] *back from your march and that you could make it. Well I've just gone on a march so you can bloody wait for me.*

It was signed 'Love Pauline' but she crossed the 'Love' out.

'But you came back,' he said.

'Paul' and Prescott's romance survived a lengthy engagement, with John away at sea regularly, sometimes for long periods of up to six months.

When he was in America, Prescott cut records to send messages back to Pauline. As her birthday falls in early February, he coupled birthday greetings with a Valentine's message. She still has the 45-rpm-sized discs with the effusive love messages – 'Darling, Darling – I Love You' – from the homesick sailor, who was to become Deputy Prime Minister. They were unlikely ever to make the hit parade, but they did the trick. John and Pauline were married on 11 November 1961 at Upton Parish Church. Two years later, on 5 April 1963, they had their first son, Jonathon. Their second son, David, was born on 22 June 1970, three days after John was elected as an MP. They were not baptised at birth: Prescott gave them what David calls the 'socialist alternative', to make up their minds about religion when they were old enough to choose for themselves. Neither has so far felt the need to do so. Bringing up two sons in a constituency so far from London had its own strains. Their father was away at the Commons for most of the week, and at weekends, when it was not the constituency to attend to, he was busy with trade union and Labour business. Prescott was a devoted father nonetheless, but the distances between father and sons were difficult to overcome.

David's first memory of his father was at the age of four when he saw his dad on the television. 'He liked celery and I went to the fridge, got a stick of celery out, and tried to feed it to him through the screen.' David brushed off suggestions that he should have been home more. 'John missed us growing up, and I didn't always understand why at the time. There's a phase all politicians' children go through. I wanted to rebel and be who I was for myself, but that was just puberty … On the other hand, I've had Michael Foot and Tony Benn stay at our house. And it could have been worse. I could have been David Mellor's son.'

In spite of the distances, they have remained a close family (Jonathon lived at home until recently) and they are fiercely protective of each other. Working in London, David shared the flat John rented at Maritime House, the old NUS building in Clapham. There is a photograph of John and Pauline when they were in their twenties, and David is the spitting image of his father at that age.

Being an MP's son was not easy. 'My friends took the mickey when the election posters came through the post and there was a picture of me smiling with my dad.' Jonathon and David used to get called names at school – in the schoolyard, 'MP' was perversely interpreted as 'Mucky Pig'. Both David and Jonathon attended the local secondary school, Bramsholme, and there were no favours in selection for the local MP's boys. David put down another secondary school, Andrew Marvell, as his first and second choice. He was given a place at Bramsholme, his third choice, where – unlike his father – he shone at athletics, representing Hull as a sprinter at the 100 metres. David also formed a lifelong passion for rugby league.

The sons, unlike the father, are 'Tykes' (Hull folk do not seriously regard themselves as Humbersiders), but John is an adoptive Yorkshireman. 'He's a Taff but they all think of him as a Yorkshire lad. He loves that. It makes him feel he belongs.'

The first house the Prescotts bought was a three-bedroom semi-detached, a few doors along from John's mother, in the cul-de-sac at 22 Pine Gardens, Upton, where he had been brought up. His mother lived at 29, which was often turned over to the local party to use as committee rooms, and the local Labour Party secretary lived next door. Prescott joined the Labour Party when he was eighteen in 1956, but it was 1964 before he had his first taste of running a campaign as the Labour agent in true-blue Chester in the general election. The Labour candidate was the colourful publisher Anthony Blond. Phyllis Prescott remembers they were stunned when he arrived from London: the candidate stayed at the Grosvenor, the most expensive hotel in Chester, and turned up for the campaign trail in a pink Lincoln Continental, which they plastered with Labour stickers. 'John was knocking on doors at that time.' No amount of help could win him the seat. 'He never got anywhere,' said Phyllis. The Tory MP for Chester was Jack Temple, and, in 1965, Prescott went to see him at his constituency surgery.

The Labour agent went to see the Tory MP to press upon him the case for legalising vasectomy. Prescott did not want a vasectomy himself. 'I just thought it wrong that it was a criminal offence for a doctor to perform the operation, but it was legal to carry out an abortion.'

He got a polite letter from Temple. 'I was glad to see you at Unionist Buildings on Saturday last and will certainly be most happy to look into the question of the special "by-pass" operation to which you referred. Frankly, this was something I had never heard of myself, but it clearly needs careful consideration.'

In due course, Prescott's public-spirited action bore fruit. Vasectomy was legalised.

John and Pauline lived at number 22 until 1966, when they moved to Hull to allow John to take up a full-time course at the university. In spite of having a child, Pauline went along with his plans, although it meant she had to keep them both on her earnings as a hairdresser, when she found work in Hull. Setting up home was hard with a husband who was continually being laid off work owing to his union activities. When he was working, there were the long absences at sea.

When the Prescotts first moved to Hull, they lived in a more modest, modern house in the Cottingham area of the town, but in 1968, when he was selected for the Hull East seat, they moved to a chalet bungalow in Sutton Park, to fulfil his promise to live in his constituency. It was adapted to serve its purpose as an MP's home, with one bedroom used as a 30-foot meeting room with a small platform put in for social events. They would have stayed in that house, but were forced to move when boundary changes left it outside his constituency.

John's mother joined them in their house-hunting, a pastime John took little interest in. Phyllis spotted a large house for sale at a reasonable price, and pushed John to take a closer look at it. At first, he would have nothing to do with it, saying it was too big, but his mother persisted.

Addison House in Saltshouse Road, Sutton-on-Hull, was in the perfect spot for his constituency: on a long road which forms the backbone of East Hull, handy for his agent, Harry Woodford – who lived on a council estate within walking distance – and within easy reach of his voters, spread out on council estates all around the surrounding area. It had plenty of room for entertaining, and a large garden for the children to run around in. But the eight-bedroom detached house with turrets front and back, tucked discreetly behind a high hedge, was every inch a house for the upper middle classes. Buying it showed he had arrived, but it was not without a conflict of conscience.

Prescott has learned to live with the sniping about his house and his cars. A fellow Labour MP, Austin Mitchell, once said to him, 'For God's sake, I don't know how you can drive a Jaguar?'

Prescott said, 'I told him, "I stick the key in the ignition and turn it. How the bloody hell do you drive yours?" My house and my Jaguar are symbols to me of where I've got to.'

Pauline does not drive, and that can lead to the impression that she is cut off in the big house. But she says she likes to live quietly while he is away.

The house has been used as a local party headquarters, and a dining room has been equipped with a boardroom table, lent by a friend, with ten chairs from the old NUS executive office at Clapham, which he rescued when they were about to be thrown out in the union's move to merge into the Rail, Maritime and Transport union (RMT). In doing so, Prescott scavenged an important piece of trade union and Labour history.

The grey-green leather chairs are the ones in which Harold Wilson's 'tightly knit group of politically motivated men' sat in the 1966 national seamen's strike, when they met as a national executive to plot their next moves.

He is keen to preserve bits of Labour history that come his way. On the walls of the dining room are framed copies of 1922 trade union certificates, from the Millers' Society to the Association of Tramway Owners. He took them when they were being discarded by the local trades council. One for the Dock Workers and General Labourers Union, the forerunner of the TGWU, was signed in 1922 by Ben Tillet.

Pauline freely admits she did not want to live in the house when they bought it, but she has grown to love it. When she first saw it, Christopher Lee and Count Dracula came to mind. It is a large Gothic edifice with eight bedrooms, a dining room, lounge, farmhouse kitchen and large garden, set back from the road, behind twin gates and a short driveway, with gargoyles on the downspouts and twin turrets on the rooftop. There is a steep staircase to Prescott's study at the back of the house, where the servants' quarters used to be. There are no servants now. The wood floor in the airy mock-Tudor hallway takes a day to polish. Pauline does all the housework herself, although a gardener helps to keep the garden neatly trimmed. It is a fine example of the arts and crafts movement, inspired by William Morris; but in Hull, surrounded by plain postwar council housing estates, it became known to their friends as 'Prescott's Castle'.

Pauline likes to pull up the 'drawbridge' to give John time to relax at home, and play CDs of Ella Fitzgerald, Sinatra and Sade when she is in the kitchen. She is also an avid fan of horse racing, and sometimes goes to the races at Doncaster with John's father, Bert; they often exchange tips over the telephone. It was Pauline's love of horse racing, which she also shared with Robin Cook – who had a tipster column in a Scottish newspaper – that led to the Labour shadow Cabinet turning out for a 'rolling rose race day' at Brighton races before the 1995 annual party conference. The National Union of Journalists had planned a demo at the races by running a pantomime horse in the 3.30, but it had to be scratched when the horse costume was inadvertently delivered to grateful Labour Party officials.

'Politics is never discussed at home,' says Pauline. 'John can switch off.' Addison House was being used as a Salvation Army hostel and John bought it for £28,000 – a fraction of its worth today. Pauline asked the owners for assurances that it was not inhabited by resident ghosts. She was told that, on the contrary, it had been filled with prayers; a stone pulpit is one of the more unusual features of the neatly planted garden, from which leading Labour figures have 'preached' at their parties in the garden. If the Prescotts kept a guest book, it would read like a *Who's Who* of the Labour movement. All the party leaders from Callaghan have stayed there: Foot, Kinnock and Blair, and trade union leaders such as Sam McCluskie, the NUS general secretary to whom Prescott was very close. Ray Buckton and Jim Slater 'preached' socialism from the garden pulpit with their wives shouting, 'What about the workers?'

Addison House had been used by doctors before the Salvation Army took it over, and was a seed merchant's house when it was built at the end of the Victorian era in 1906. Britain was then a world power, and Hull a booming port.

The next-door neighbours were the Duffills, a middle-class family, whose son, Graham, grew up with Prescott's sons, and was a news editor at *The Times*. David, too, became a journalist. It is perhaps strange, then, that the house has proved a bastion against the press at times. Appearing on the BBC's *Question Time*, John described how the press were trying to smear him with false rumours about an affair. Within the hour, the house was besieged by journalists seeking interviews with Pauline. David was on his first day at a press agency in Hull, and had the task of interviewing his own mother over the telephone from his office for his first 'scoop'. He also advised her not to go too close to the window because she would be in range of the photographers.

David was involved in another 'scoop' after Norman Lamont's mother, who lived in the region, disclosed that her son was going to resign as Chancellor. As the national press beat a path to her door, David telephoned Mrs Lamont. The Chancellor's mother announced she wanted £10 for every question she answered but, by the time he got to her door, she had changed her mind. David pushed tenners through Mrs Lamont's letterbox, but they were pushed back out again without a word. Stumped for an angle on the non-story, an inspired colleague at the freelance agency came up with the solution: LAMONT'S MOTHER IN U-TURN. David moved down to London, reporting for some years for the *People*, before joining *GMTV* as a freelancer. Doorstepping President Clinton and John Major for a story, David became the first of the Prescotts to get to Chequers.

Prescott senior has few outside interests beyond politics, and is not a regular at Hull City football matches, even when close friends such as Peter Snape, the MP and his former campaign manager, come up to watch Hull play Snape's team, Stockport County. His reading is mainly non-fiction: history, biography, and normally related to the Labour movement. The few works of fiction he has read are usually related to politics, such as Orwell's *Animal Farm*.

'It's part of his feeling that he lacked a proper education. He constantly wants to better himself, and feels that fiction is a waste of time,' said one close friend.

Having sailed into New York, into bebop, goatee beards, jive talk, big cars, smart suits, and clubs, Prescott was hooked on jazz. Breaking his socialist principles, he admits to owning one share in a private company – Jazz FM. In London, he was a regular at Ronnie Scott's club, and Marion Montgomery is a personal friend of the Prescotts. 'It's anti-establishment, it's free-ranging, not allowing anything to be of a convention. It's a disorder of things that has its own structures and conventions. It's a great leveller. You can be in all classes and enjoy jazz,' said Prescott.

Another regular at Ronnie Scott's, Conservative politician Kenneth Clarke, Health Secretary, Home Secretary and Chancellor under John Major, shares Prescott's love of jazz, and his robust 'two fingers to the world' approach to life. They sometimes turned up at the club at the same time, although never shared a table. When a TV programme was being filmed for the club's thirtieth anniversary, Prescott realised that being seen in Ronnie's with the Chancellor might send the wrong signal to the voters in Hull East, but he could not ignore Clarke. He found a simple solution. 'Hiya Ken. How many hospitals have you closed today?'

There is a showbiz side to Prescott, which he may have inherited from his mother: he loves acting, and did a double act in Labour Party revues as the cockney Tory bigot Alf Garnett with the professional actor Anthony Booth, Cherie Blair's father, who played the 'Scouse git' in the television sitcom *Till Death Us Do Part*. Prescott can fairly claim to have been the first to inject some showbiz into Labour's presentation, long before the spin doctors thought of it. He organised the first Labour showbiz rally with jazz bands for a Euro-festival in June 1979 at Leeds Town Hall; the political 'stars' included James Callaghan and François Mitterrand.

On a train to Hull in 1988, when he was running for the deputy leadership, Prescott shared a compartment with Michael Winner, the director of such hit films as *Death Wish*, and they struck up a friendship.

Winner was going to Scarborough to shoot the film *A Chorus of Disapproval*, Alan Ayckbourn's story about an amateur drama group, and invited Prescott and Pauline to watch the filming. During a break between takes in a theatre at the resort, Winner organised a bingo game, and got Prescott to call the numbers.

'He was very good. He called bingo with Anthony Hopkins and Jeremy Irons.' Winner, a lifelong Tory, adds, 'He was a very nice chap. I knew Scargill before he was Scargill, and Ken Livingstone. They could have gone either way, being successful or going a little too far … I always felt that John would not take that route, he would put himself into the mainstream.'

Equity, the actors' union, later complained about one of the amateurs sharing a scene – involving a passionate kiss – with Jenny Seagrove. The professional daily rate was £200. Seagrove's 'lover' in the scene, a local Scarborough man, said later, 'I got peanuts, only £10, but I would have done it for nothing … I enjoyed every minute.'

Prescott is notorious for sitting up late working on papers, and sometimes he 'switches off' in embarrassing places. The Bishop of Durham was speaking in Durham Cathedral on one occasion, during the Durham Miners' Gala, when the clear drone of Prescott's snoring could be heard. On another occasion, he realised he had gone to sleep during a shadow Cabinet meeting, and had been snoring. As he snapped to, Tony Blair was smiling at him, and saying, 'I'm not boring you, am I?'

Among Pauline's closest friends at Westminster was Betty Boothroyd, the former Speaker of the House of Commons, whom she first met when Betty – who could still do the high kicks she learned as a Tiller Girl – was a Member of the European Parliament, and John was the leader of the British group. 'We once went through the duty-free, and Betty said, "Just watch this, we'll sort out the men from the boys – the boys buy cologne; the men buy perfume."'

Pauline was a frequent visitor to the Commons, and the Speaker's House, where the Speaker hosted dinners for ministers and opposition MPs, business leaders, sportsmen and -women and television stars, including Ian Richardson, the ruthless Conservative Prime Minister in the Michael Dobbs series *House of Cards*.

Walking through the Ways and Means corridor near the Members' Lobby, with John, they met John Major. There was some good-natured banter between them about 10 Downing Street. Major told Prescott: 'We're just keeping it warm for you – when you get rid of Tony Blair.'

Pauline was sitting in the gallery when Michael Heseltine – who in 1970 had praised Prescott's maiden speech – poked fun at Prescott over a love poem to the deputy leader by Fleur Adcock. It was two minutes before Prescott was to deliver his major speech on the Budget as deputy leader of the Labour Party.

Hansard records that Mr Heseltine said, 'I do not want to give the impression that just because no one talks to him, they do not love him. It has become abundantly clear through the media of the *Times* that at least someone loves the deputy leader of the Labour Party …'

After reading the section of the poem – 'certain protuberances under our clothing brushing each other's front' – Heseltine read the mock 'line': '"when my mother saw us, and I woke up". I must say, it was a merciful release for somebody.'

Hansard does not record, but those who were there remember the impact of Heseltine's words being regarded as 'over the top'. There were jokes, unrecorded in Hansard, from the Tory bench about waking up next to Prescott in the morning. Pauline had to sit and take it.

'Quite a few of our MPs said that that was horrid,' she says. 'There was no need for that. I thought it was awful, but that's part of politics. You have to bite your bottom lip.'

Pauline was hurt by the press reports after the leadership contest implying she and Cherie Booth were from different planets when it came to dress sense. The words of one press report have been burned into her memory.

Under a headline, A TALE OF TWO WIVES, the *Daily Mail* compared her to Bet Lynch, the former landlady of the Rovers Return in *Coronation Street*. 'Mrs Prescott walked on stage after her husband's victory to plant a lipsticked kiss upon his cheek, each step of her high heels crushing the myth that the wives of Labour MPs have to be drab.

'Compared with Cherie Blair and Margaret Beckett, she

looked like Bet Lynch arriving by mistake at a session of the Open University.'

'I thought that was absolutely horrid,' says Pauline. After that, she decided it was pointless speaking to the press. She has an open nature, but has refused all appeals for interviews. That did not stop the newspapers fishing for items about her in the run-up to the general election. Journalists from two tabloid newspapers approached the shop in Beverley, in the East Riding of Yorkshire, where she buys dresses, for information on her dress preferences and the price tags.

She has a highly protective network of friends, and they refused to give any details, but warned Pauline that a pack of news hounds was sniffing around for information. Pauline finds it astonishing that they should be interested in such trivia. However, there was a suspicion that the subtext of such 'fashion' stories would be the allegation that Pauline and Cherie spend more on their clothes than many Labour voters have to spend on their weekly food bill.

Pauline does not shop in expensive haute-couture stores in Bond Street or Harvey Nichols for her clothes: she buys her outfits locally in Hull and neighbouring Yorkshire towns. John buys all his suits off the peg from a small tailor in Hull, and Pauline chooses his ties.

Barbara Follett, wife of the thriller-writer, once advised Harriet Harman to drop her soft, peasanty Laura Ashley look and adopt power shoulder pads. No one ever tried to advise Pauline on how to dress. They did not have to.

'Labour Party women are very smart now. There's a difference between being well dressed, and overdressed, but you should always be as smart as you can. If you don't, the press will always try to turn it against you.'

Some years later, I was on a train with Prescott and his aides when he took a call on his chunky mobile. As he spoke, he gripped the phone more violently. We were in an open carriage, but he did not hide his anger. He was furious with frustration, battling with his anger not to shout out loud, beating his fist on the table. It was times like this, he said, when he wondered whether it was worth it. He told me that a number of newspapers had been sniffing round for a story about 'Prescott's love child' and had discovered that it was not his, but Pauline's. Alastair Campbell had been keeping the papers at bay, threatening them with the Press Complaints Commission for intruding into his personal life. He was angry that the newspapers were only interested in the story because of who he was, and although, strictly speaking, it was nothing to do with him, they were claiming it was in the public interest.

There was one further twist that turned it almost into tragicomedy: Pauline's long-lost son, Paul, who was put up for adoption before she married John, was an officer in the 'Red Caps' (the Royal Military Police), a Tory supporter who had joined the Young Conservatives when he was fifteen, and he enjoyed fox-hunting. He had known he was adopted, but had never known the identity of his real mother until being confronted in 2001 by a *News of the World* reporter.

'This woman turned up from the *News of the World* and said did you know your natural mother is Pauline Prescott,' he told me later. It was a shock, but he said the fact that it was the wife of the Deputy Prime Minister 'was not a problem at all'. He found being put in touch with his natural mother deeply moving.

'I had no idea who she was or where she was. Unless you have looked at somebody and thought she is my flesh and blood, it's difficult to understand. I have never had that before. That was very moving for me.'

He was also relaxed about being an extended member of the Prescott family, in spite of being poles apart politically. Paul told me: 'I had seen him in Whitehall. I saw him on television in Rhyl when he thumped that guy and I thought, Bloody well done. I would have done exactly the same thing. I think I found an affinity with him. I thought there must be more to Prescott than the press say. I never slagged him off. And he has turned out to be a really nice guy. He is a great family man and very loving.'

I had been let in on the family secret by Prescott's mother, Phyllis, who sadly died in 2003, after the publication of *Fighting Talk*.

The story about 'Prescott's love child' was to haunt Prescott through the next two years, as one newspaper after another investigated and was repelled by Campbell. The saga had two immediate consequences – it reinforced Prescott's view that Britain has a 'lousy' press, that it is more interested in 'tittle-tattle' than policy; and it strengthened his respect for Campbell.

The tale was to have a happy ending, however. Towards the summer of 2003, Pauline and her son Paul were due to go to the Trooping of the Colour together. They had been to restaurants, and had to explain they were mother and son to avoid other wrong conclusions being drawn, but appearing in public could raise renewed questions about their relationship, and could even undo the 'truce' negotiated around their story between Campbell and the press. Pauline told John she would like to get the whole story out in the open so that she and Paul could feel comfortable together in public. John readily agreed, and set about organising a media strategy for handling the story, which they discussed in the Prescotts' flat on the top floor of Admiralty House with a few close aides and Paul, one sunny morning as the royal bands were practising. The two newspapers that already knew about the story, the *Sun* and the *News of the World*, were in the same stable, and could make their own arrangements for sharing it. As I had been sitting on the 'secret' for some years, I was allowed to report it for the *Sunday Telegraph*, for whom I was then political editor.

So it was that one morning in July, Arthur Edwards, the star photographer of the *Sun*, a reporter from the *News of the World* and myself turned up at the Prescotts' house in Hull for the interviews with Pauline and Paul. John kept in the background as we taped the interviews and they posed for photographs together. The resulting 'exclusives' dominated the newspapers the following weekend. My report said: 'A 47-year-old foxhunting, Conservative Lieutenant Colonel in the Royal Military Police spoke yesterday for the first time about how it felt to discover that his stepfather is John Prescott, the Deputy Prime Minister and champion of Labour's left wing.

'Timothy Paul Watton was still coming to terms with the fact that after nearly half a century of living with his adoptive parents in Staffordshire, and rising through the ranks as an army officer, he has a new family, with two grown-up half-brothers, Jonathon, 40, and David, 33, and a name that can still send shivers down the spines of many Tories: the Prescotts.'

I quoted Pauline saying she had always had a quiet moment by herself each year, on her son's birthday on 2 January. She told me she went through her personal agony, wondering what had happened to the son she had not seen since 1959.

'I used to keep myself to myself on January 2,' she said. 'It was agonising. There was always the guilt, but I knew deep down that I had done the best thing for Paul – and it has proved to be right.'

Paul said he had been brought up by loving adoptive parents. His adoptive father had died, but his mother expressed happiness that he had been reunited with his natural mother. Paul was also warmly embraced by the Prescotts' two sons, and life in the Prescott household went on with an extra member at family gatherings.

Before Labour came to power, Pauline told me she was proud of John's achievements, and believed he had failed to gain the recognition he deserves for the thinking he has put into the development of modern Labour policy. Among the plethora of policy papers he had produced, three stood out as milestones in Labour's road to modernisation: on the regions, job creation and trade union reform, and transport. The staff were exhausted by his boundless energy. 'He was always ringing up at 11.30 at night and saying, "I've seen Neil and I've got this idea ..." The only way we could get away at weekends was to put the answerphone on and pretend we were away,' said one of his former staff.

'He is the H.G. Wells of the Labour Party,' Pauline said. Such a remark would be quite likely to cause John to growl with embarrassment, but she made it clear from the outset that, although she is sweet-tempered, she was a match for the man later described by Cecil Parkinson as 'the Rottweiler of the Shadow Cabinet'.

Pauline had an unshakeable faith in Prescott's ability to get to the top. When his confidence might have been sagging, she provided the unquestioning support and ambition that have fuelled his drive to succeed against all the odds of education and class at the Commons. 'Without my mother, he would not have got where he has,' said their son David.

Above all, she has provided a solid home for him to return to. 'Home was always vital to John. He needs a place to relax and calm down and get away from it all,' David added.

John never goes near a gym, but he likes to relax in a tracksuit and sweatshirt. They do not smoke, and John is meticulously tidy, but Pauline does the housework and some of the gardening.

At home in Hull, Pauline would lay out generous plates of sandwiches for visitors prepared in the large farmhouse-style kitchen, which is the hub of activity in the house. The *Daily Mail* said it had been noted that 'Pauline, described as tidy and house-proud, carefully cut the crusts off the paper-thin ham sandwiches she served up along with tea in delicate china cups.' Whatever else happens to the Labour Party, there has been a reassertion of traditional Labour values over the wholemeal in the Prescott household. If Cherie were to come to tea, she would find that the sandwiches were served with the crusts on.

John is a rapid eater, like someone constantly on the move, a habit he says he picked up because he was taught not to see food wasted. 'My overeating is partly the legacy of my father, who said your plate had to be bloody empty before you left the table because of the starving in China. Recently I've started leaving little bits but I feel guilty about it.'

The temptation proved too great when Prescott led a Labour stunt at Westminster in September 1995 attacking Tory 'porky pies', or lies. To catch the attention of the Fleet Street picture editors, Labour spin doctors laid out a baker's dozen of large pork pies at a press conference in the Commons, each marked with a label saying 'Tory Porkies'. In his press release, Prescott said, 'Britain can watch John Major's lips as he eats another plate of Tory pork pies.' But after the press conference, rather than see them go to waste, a peckish Prescott tucked into one of them in a back room. Fortunately for the spin doctors, the Fleet Street snappers missed the chance to catch a photograph of the Labour deputy leader making a meal of 'Tory porkies'.

CHAPTER SIX

Shaping the Bullets

> *Thirty years later he is still very very much the same person – opinionated, articulate … you clearly knew where he was coming from.*
>
> Denis Kavanagh, former tutor at Hull University.

On 4 October 1963 at 9.55 a.m. a telegram was delivered to 29 Pine Gardens from the principal of Ruskin College, Oxford, H.D. 'Billy' Hughes: PLACE AVAILABLE 1963 OR 1964 STOP CAN YOU REPORT 8TH OCTOBER – HUGHES RUSKIN COLLEGE.

Prescott was serving on the Royal Mail vessel the RM *Amazon*. He received a Marconigram from his stepfather, Ron Swales: UNIVERSITY SEAT CONFIRMED STOP GRANT AWARDED CONGRATULATIONS RON.

It had been a hard-won battle, which Prescott had begun when he took up a correspondence course at sea with the WEA. He had overcome the hostility of his own trade union leaders, who refused his grant, and rejection by his Tory Cheshire County Council, to win the place at the college. Now, when it came, he was on a slow boat through South American waters.

Being on board ship, he was not able to go for the interview on his appointed day, but the college admitted him without the interview. Raphael Samuel, his history tutor, said he seemed to have been accepted on the strength of a glowing report from his old form master, Les George, and a 'distinctly queasy one' from the NUS. Mr George, then head of Christleton County Secondary School, wrote:

> *John Prescott was an outstanding pupil in a very good 'A' stream ... He took a full part in all school activities and it was obvious that his personality would ensure his becoming a leader in whatever sphere of work he chose. At fifteen he could have transferred to the Grammar School but chose instead to study on his own to achieve success in his profession. Since then I know he has shown a keen interest in education and has never missed an opportunity of improving his own standard. He is now an assured, widely travelled man of considerable experience.*

In fact, Prescott had left school at fifteen with no O-levels to his name, and a big chip on his shoulder about the system that rejected him with the eleven-plus.

Prescott was 25, a father, and yearning for education when he entered Ruskin College. 'My mind was opened to the pleasures of learning, of shaping the bullets with which to fight. Ruskin gave me self-confidence in mobilising my arguments. It taught me I had no need to feel inferior to anybody.'

It nearly ended in disaster. Prescott walked out in the middle of his first-year mock exams. He was tired by continuing his trade union activism, and by the struggle to keep up his education. That first exam made him feel out of his depth. Angry and frustrated, he got up, handed his empty papers to a surprised invigilator, and walked out. For him, it was over. But when he got back to his room, he found a note scribbled on the back of a brown envelope, which he has kept safe all these years. It was from Raphael Samuel and said: 'John – why not take the papers? Do it in your own time …' He was not used to the more relaxed university ways. It had never occurred to him to take papers away from an examination, even his mocks, and do them in his own time. He seized the second chance.

It was at Ruskin that Prescott, in spite of the fiery rhetoric of Nye Bevan, adopted Ernest Bevin as his hero. 'I came from the Left and had been fed the diet that Bevin was to the Right and therefore wasn't one of our heroes. When I read the history of this man, his contributions to the Labour movement, a giant in the things that he did – organising, modernising the trade union structure. He was one of the first to recognise the importance of Keynes's ideas, that the Government could have a role. That was great intellectual ability from a man who they tell me was very roughly spoken, could not sound his aitches.

'When I read history books about Bevin, I was in awe of it.' Bevin was from a working-class background, with deep roots in the trade unions, and rose to become Foreign Secretary. He was a powerful speaker, and his attack on Lansbury's pacifism before World War II at the party conference led to Lansbury's resignation as leader of the party. Attlee was also in awe of

Bevin, and bowed to his judgement in supporting America with the Marshall Plan. Prescott also noted that Bevin protected Attlee, to whom he was ferociously loyal. If there is any guide to how Prescott sees his relationship with Blair, it is Bevin's role with Attlee. 'In 1947, when his stock stood perhaps at its lowest, Dalton and Cripps made a concerted effort to displace him. Morrison refused to commit himself. When the conspirators approached Bevin – their candidate for the succession – he at once told Attlee. Sure of Bevin's support, Attlee took the conspiracy in his stride, never referring to it and keeping the plotters in office.'

One of Prescott's end-of-term reports described Prescott as an 'earnest, hard-working student'. Samuel was 'increasingly impressed with his great natural intelligence' and commended his 'fine command of detail' and taste for 'theoretical argument'.

On his first day at Ruskin, he was set a 2,000-word essay to complete by Friday: 'Power corrupts – absolute power corrupts absolutely. Discuss.' Prescott did not have a clue how to begin the project, but there was another in his class, a bus-driver, who had seemed so confident, who went to his room, packed his bags and left the college when faced with the essay question. 'It was then I realised that I wasn't the only one terrified about failing. I started talking to other people on my course and they felt the same as me. But quitting wasn't the answer.'

Samuel recalled that Prescott wrote very long essays. 'The handwriting was not easy to read and his sentences were not always grammatical – occasionally they stopped, disconcertingly in mid-passage, as though the energy of thought had outrun delivery. But he usually had something urgent to say. He was also ready to take risks, chancing his arm, for instance, by introducing a passage of poetry into an economic history essay or, in Labour history, using the source to challenge the authorities.'

Friends testify to his restless mind. Rodney Bickerstaffe, former general secretary of UNISON – the health workers' and public employees' union – who supported Prescott at key moments in his career, said: 'He does have an excellent brain; the brain works faster than his mouth sometimes; it's a form of verbal dyslexia. He has ideas tumbling out; his mind races ahead. If he is on theme "A" he jumps to theme "C" and then "G", one thought leading to another.'

It was a process that, more than any other, made Prescott free-thinking, free from the chains of party dogma, to challenge the Whitehall orthodoxy of the supposedly better-educated, better-equipped shadow ministers and advisers who prepared Labour for government. It enabled Prescott to ask seemingly simple questions: 'Why can't we have private finance for British Rail?' And, at the same time, to reject old-style nationalisation.

The daring tendency to throw poetry into economic theory identified by his tutor was not so surprising. Like many young men enthused with language and learning in the sixties, Prescott fancied himself as a bit of a poet. Adrian Henri, one of the Liverpool poets, fused jazz and beat poetry:

'if you weren't you, who would you like to be?'
Paul McCartney Gustav Mahler
Alfred Jarry John Coltrane
Charlie Mingus Claude Debussy
Wordsworth Monet Bach and Blake

Anything was possible, although Prescott might have baulked at being Paul McCartney. And he never wore a goatee beard.

At Ruskin, Prescott had used a melancholy poem in a poetry seminar:

'Preciousness'

Have I got to wait till four.
Or Have I time to ignore
the heaving belly on my bed.
Instead of lying silent, calm and
Still. I shed some tears.
Some trickling, trembling tears;
that reach my thighs and feebly
Stroll to touch my knee.
The tears have gone. Uprooted from
The soul. The preciousness has
left. And leaves in its tender
shielding place – an oppressiveness;
and like the tears is set apart
Parted from the soul. No longer
part of all the sacred fears.

The churning blackness of a
deeply hidden night
has engulfed the peeling walls
struck with the hardness of a
steady chime.
And alone in the facelessness
of times unfavoured cause
– there is no heart to open
No love is pure.
And the fickle, vanishing air
– consistent in its despair –
finds here at – least we are
as one.
It is fitting to let this fragile
budlike burden, in all its
uncurled glory – know the
world. In the helpless absence
that floods reality. And in the
greyness of an unhappy dawn
this yearning, yielding human mold
Is giving me a hold on life.

When he got to Hull University, Prescott confronted one of the most famous poets of his time, Philip Larkin, who was the university librarian. They met in the street. He asked the poet, 'Do you do seminars?' Larkin did not answer. 'He looked down his nose at me and walked on.'

Poetry's loss is politics' gain.

Prescott was not intending to go to university, but applied for a place at Hull as the only way of remaining in his union, when he was again blocked for advancement in the NUS by its general secretary, Bill Hogarth, who saw Prescott as a troublemaker. Even after being accepted in October 1965, he tried to get into Parliament, first through the Hull by-election, for which he was not selected, and then in the no-hope Tory seat of Southport.

Raphael Samuel had suggested that he go to Hull to study under John Saville, a highly respected left-wing professor of economic history.

Saville, who took him for economic history, found that it was in seminars, arguing the toss with fellow students as well as with the tutors, that Prescott excelled. Professor Denis Kavanagh, who subsequently went to Liverpool University, was in his first teaching post when he took Prescott for politics.

'He was a self-made young man who had worked in the National Union of Seamen and he was clearly such a rough diamond. What I find really quite remarkable thirty years later is that he is still very very much the same person – he was opinionated, articulate, in class sessions you clearly knew where he was coming from. He didn't apologise for himself and thirty years later, his whole persona is very similar to what it was thirty years ago, which I think is very much to his credit.'

It was hard at first, however. Prescott was studying economic statistics – which he now fires like machine-gun bullets – and did not know anything about logarithms. He spent a week in a library trying to understand the theory about how they were calculated, before someone told him they were all set out in a book of tables. 'I learnt that you should not be afraid to ask questions to the answers you seek. That's an essential requirement for the second-chance student.'

But in his first year at university, Prescott was heavily preoccupied with his union and political activities. In addition to fighting a parliamentary seat, the 28-year-old student was deeply engaged in the first national seamen's strike in half a century.

Working for the NUS and joining the seamen's picket lines in strikes around the country while he was a student took their toll on Prescott's formidable energies. When he came to sit his finals, he was exhausted. During one paper on economics, he walked out of the examination, just as he had at Ruskin, but again, he was helped through by his tutor. Saville arranged for him to take the paper later in the year, and he passed.

His mother kept the programme from Prescott's graduation day, Saturday, 6 July 1968. During the entry of procession, the city organist, P. Goodman, played Bach's Toccata in C. The civic dignitaries included the Lord Mayor and the town clerk, and the mayors of the boroughs. On page six, under conferment of degrees, John Leslie Prescott's name appeared under the heading: bachelor of science in economics with honours (class iii).

Prescott returned to Ruskin on 13 June 1996, to deliver a heartfelt speech in defence of the comprehensive-school system. 'It is based not on theory but on my practical experience, warts and all, as an eleven-plus failure, as a correspondence-course freak with the WEA, as a mature student here at Ruskin – the joy of my life – as a graduate of Hull University, as a parent of two children who attended comprehensive schools, and as an MP hearing the worries constituents feel … about the so-called "right school".'

He avoided mentioning his disagreement with Harriet Harman's choice of a grammar school for her son Joe – he did not need to: his views were clear. They had been drawn from his life, notably his failure of the eleven-plus, and the 'scarring experience' of being designated as a failure and being split from the 'girl I carried a torch for'.

It marked you for life as either a first-class or second-class citizen, he said. 'Grammar schools provided the classics like *Julius Caesar* for their pupils. At secondary modern, I had to make do with *Dick Barton*.'

That the privileged got the knowledge and knowledge was a privilege was one of his first lessons in life, he said. 'People like me were expected to be pigeonholed, branded, a ceiling put on their ambitions. Some people thought I had reached my educational peak by the time I was a waiter on the liners. "Another gin and tonic, Giovanni," as one Tory MP bawled at me while I was speaking in the House.

'But in my twenties, I arrived at Ruskin College without an O-level or an A-level to my mind. I had organised a couple of strikes – an acceptable qualification for Ruskin.

'But in spite of studying hard, getting a degree at Hull University, and 26 years' service as an MP, I'm still seen by some to be inadequate. Can you believe that 40 years on from that corrected love letter, I still get pulled up by the likes of Matthew Parris for bad grammar? As he said about my OMOV [one member, one vote] speech, "John Prescott went twelve rounds with the English language and left it slumped and bleeding over the ropes." And by some I wasn't seen as leadership material because they thought I might fluff my lines at the Despatch Box …

'The overwhelming impression I have is that even in these so-called enlightened times, society still mocks people with learning difficulties that language and knowledge can be used as obstacles to the lifelong learning process and a convenient barrier between the educated and the less educated.'

CHAPTER SEVEN

Striker

This tightly knit group of politically motivated men …
Harold Wilson.

In 1960, Prescott and his shipmates joined an unofficial strike, which was to lead the future Deputy Prime Minister into direct conflict with the Labour government under Harold Wilson.

Prescott, then 22, courting Pauline and shortly to get married, had been on the *Britannic* in the high summer of 1960 when the strike hit every port in Britain. It affected all sorts of vessels, from ocean liners to cargo ships and colliers.

Ships were tied up at the docks for weeks. Three *White Empresses* – of France, England and Britain – were tied up together at Gladstone Dock, Bootle. The *Empress of England* missed a voyage when half her deck and engineering crew walked off three hours before sailing time. Some passengers on the *Queen Mary* offered to serve their own meals to allow their ship to sail after the catering staff walked out at Southampton.

For Prescott, it was a formative experience that was to affect the rest of his life. It was also to drive him to make his first public speech – to a mass meeting of over three thousand striking seamen.

The seamen were demanding better pay and conditions, but the strike was fuelled by the belief among the rank and file that the National Union of Seamen was a 'bosses' union'. Prescott was caught in a power struggle between militants on Merseyside and the union 'old guard'.

The leader of the NUS, Sir Thomas Yates, was 64 and had been in office since 1947. He was so close to the shipowners that, when he opened a union office in Dover, he invited the owners along to celebrate as though it was the launching of a ship. By their 'closed shop' alliance, the union was able to dictate who worked in the industry, and the shipowners were able to maintain a merchant fleet with poor pay and conditions and long hours – 84-hour weeks were the norm – for the men. They worked together to crush incipient strikes. The owners also had the backing of successive governments, who saw the industry as being of national strategic importance.

Striking was not only the last resort, it was also illegal for merchant seamen under the Merchant Shipping Acts. There had been strikes in the past, roughly at five-yearly cycles, in 1946, 1951 and 1955, which were all unofficial. In the 1955 dispute, the striking seamen were issued with conscription papers threatening them with National Service, if they did not resume work.

The unofficial strike was sparked off in July 1960 when the men on the *Carinthia*, a Cunard liner, had walked off in a row over four lads – perhaps prototype Beatles – being 'logged for insolence' for playing guitars after midnight and upsetting the passengers. It ignited discontent that had been smouldering for years.

A breakaway group formed a strike committee, and called a wildcat strike of seamen in Liverpool, which quickly spread to other ports. Prescott, like thousands of other seamen, also had contempt for the union, but had been trying to organise on board ship to change it from within, arguing a union was only as good as its members made it. He did this by encouraging the men to demand postal ballots for the election of their union executive. As some of the larger ships could command up to a thousand votes – they had a vote for every five years of service – Prescott quickly came to the notice of the union 'old guard', whose power he was directly challenging. He was regarded as a marked man by his own union, and an important recruit by the breakaway group.

They wanted him to join the strike committee, but he refused, insisting that the only way to change the NUS was to do so from within. He agreed to act as an adviser and persuaded the leaders to call themselves the National Seamen's Reform Movement to make it clear they were not trying to replace the union, but to reform it.

The wildcat strike caught the union and the owners by surprise. The union leaders and employers were attending a Safety of Life at Sea (Solas) conference in Geneva, and it became clear that to continue the strike would mean the loss of pay for up to three weeks, until the two sides could get back and negotiate a settlement. Simon Mahon, the MP for Bootle, and Eric Heffer, leader of Liverpool Trades Council – he became the

MP for Walton in 1964 – intervened and sought a temporary settlement to allow a return to work, pending negotiations. They held talks with Sir Thomas Yates and his general secretary elect, Jim Scott, and the shipping owners, and reached a national deal under which the men at all the affected ports around Britain, including Southampton and London, would go back to work with the promise of negotiations on pay and conditions, without fear of victimisation.

With that guarantee, the Reform Movement leaders agreed to suspend their strike, but the terms, which were not released to the press, had to be put to mass meetings of the men in their ports the next morning. In Liverpool, the mass meeting was to be held 'on the 'Oller', a piece of waste ground or hollow bomb site, near the pier head, where the Holiday Inn now stands.

The terms were to be read out on the 'Oller by a strike committee member called Vic Lilley, but a member of the Reform Movement who was due to bring a loudspeaker van to the meeting was involved in a row with the organisers, and refused to turn up. As a result, Lilley had to shout the details to the mass meeting without a microphone. Few could hear the terms, and he was shouted down; they agreed to meet again in the afternoon, when a microphone had been rigged up. Meanwhile, meetings in other ports went smoothly, and over lunch, the strikers in Liverpool heard radio reports that all around the country there was a general return to work.

When they reassembled at 3 p.m. – as the pubs were closing their doors after lunchtime – thousands of men arrived on the 'Oller and many were in an angry mood at the acceptance of the terms for a return to work at other ports. Some had spent the intervening hours in the pubs getting 'bevvied'. There were angry shouts of 'sell-out'. Lilley read out the terms, but after suffering a heavy barracking he told the crowd, 'You're right, lads,' and tore up the paper setting out the agreement.

The Reform Movement leaders in Liverpool were now in disarray. They were looking for a way out, and, in a private meeting with Prescott, they discussed whether the terms for a return to work still applied after they had been torn up. And who was going to get up and ask the men, who were in an ugly mood, to do a U-turn? Prescott was the obvious choice: he was young, conversant with the negotiations, and burning with indignation at the way the men were being led.

Jim Scott warned Prescott that he could not take over a union with an embryo breakaway group inside it, and if the unofficial leaders called a strike again, 'I have got to destroy them.' Scott said, 'I would rather tie our ship up in the Gaellock [where they used to lie idle in Scotland]. It's a fight to the death.' Heffer confirmed to Prescott that that was his understanding of the union's attitude.

That night, Prescott asked his father what he should do. Bert, older and perhaps wiser, knew clearly the risks that John was running, and advised him not to go ahead with it. He told his son that he did not have the experience to ask Liverpool's seamen to stand on their heads within 24 hours. But Prescott said he had to do it.

There is no record of Prescott's first speech – there were no camera crews or shorthand-writers at the 'Oller – but, from accounts of those who were there, it was typical Prescott: fiery, thumping and direct. With a working-class sense of solidarity bred into his veins, he told them that they should stick together to the agreed national terms for a return to work; they should go back united, with their heads held high.

Liverpool was a violent city with strong community loyalties, and on the waterfront intimidation was a fact of life. Anyone disobeying the strike orders, even those issued by an unofficial group in defiance of the union, was likely to be 'sorted out' by some of the heavies around the docks.

When Prescott's call for a return to work was put to a show of hands, only about 250 hands were raised.

Prescott called for another show of hands. This time 500 went up.

Another show, and the number had crept up to 1,000.

Prescott called five times for the men to show their hands. By the final call, he had got a majority to end the strike.

With an uneasy truce, Prescott went to sea again on a month-long cruise on the *Britannic*, but the 'peace' lasted only about a week. The underlying cause of the strike – the power struggle between the NUS leadership and the Reform Movement – had not been settled.

On 9 August, the union reached a deal with the owners, represented by the Shipping Federation, and the Employers' Association of the Port of Liverpool. It provided for a 7.5 per cent pay increase, and a 44-hour week in port with a non-contributory pension. With double pay for Saturdays, it would mean many would get 15 per cent more and some 20 per cent.

The employers said they would have no dealings with 'any agitators who accept no responsibility themselves and seek to upset an industrial agreement which has been constitutionally arrived at by those on both sides who are responsible for carrying it out. To act otherwise would be to encourage mob rule.'

Undeterred, the next day, 10 August, the militants again called the rank and file out on unofficial wildcat strike.

Prescott was crossing the Atlantic bound for New York when he was summoned to the bridge of the *Britannic* by the skipper. The captain had been handed a telegram by the radio officer addressed to John Prescott, 'convener of the *Britannic*', from Paddy Neary, chairman of the Reform Movement. It was informing 'convener' Prescott that the terms were unacceptable and the strike was back on. The captain challenged Prescott about the meaning of the message; he was alarmed that he had a rebel on board plotting action. Prescott told the captain he was committing an offence by interfering with the Royal Mail, and intercepting his messages. But Prescott, who had never been a 'convener', was disturbed by the news.

The strike was against the leadership of the NUS under Yates as much as the men's pay and conditions at sea, and Prescott realised it would be a fight to the death. Yates claimed the ring-leaders were communist agitators intent on bringing Britain to a standstill – a charge that was to be repeated famously by Harold Wilson in 1966 when it was levelled at Prescott's associates on the executive of the NUS.

Among the leading members of the Reform Movement who

were to take over the control of the NUS executive five years later with Prescott were Jim Slater, representing seamen in the north-east; his successor at the NUS, Sam McCluskie from Scotland; and Joe Kenny from Liverpool.

A Communist Party handbill issued in support of the unofficial strike described Slater as a 'true stalwart much maligned by the NUS'. It said: 'Seamen take note! We of the Communist Party know of your trials and tribulations but take heart and act accordingly.' It named Slater, Joe Kenny, Jack Coward and Gordon Norris as 'but a few of the men sympathetic to our cause'. It was issued by the Communist Party at 16 King Street, London WC2.

But the Reform Movement leaders denied they were acting for the Communist Party. Seamen in Liverpool were handed an open letter from the Reform Movement attacking the NUS leadership:

> *Brother Yates has taken it upon himself to label this movement, its officers and its objectives communistic. He has classed the movement of ship's delegates as a communist plot. The attempt to class this rank and file movement as Communist dominated is almost too ridiculous to answer. The Reform Movement denies this accusation in the strongest possible way.*
>
> *We earnestly request that you join your shipmates in our main cause to clean up the National Union of Seamen so that it truly represents us and to improve our shipboard conditions.*

> *Aims: to bring about substantial reform inside the NUS by legal and constitutional means so that the NUS will become the true voice of British seamen which we suggest is not now the case.*

It was signed by Paddy Neary, chairman of the Reform Movement; Ken Kean, secretary; Barney Flynn; and Vic Lilley, national organiser.

With the strike entering its fifteenth day, the employers joined with the NUS to force a return to work. The Shipping Federation and the Employers' Association of the Port of Liverpool issued a press release on 25 August, repeating the warning of 9 August that they would not negotiate with any strikers, and would deal only with the NUS. British shipowners were 'not prepared to agree to any system of shop stewards on board ship which is designed to undermine the authority of the master and forment [sic] discontent among the crew'.

There was a further sting in the tail. The unofficial strikers would be blacklisted.

It said the unofficial strike had already victimised the loyal seamen, the shipping companies, the public and the national economy.

'There can be no guarantee that all strikers will get back into the Merchant Navy in the same or a similar capacity as previously,' the press release continued. 'Some by their conduct in the strike have proved themselves quite unworthy members of the Merchant Navy and it is unlikely that they could ever be re-admitted to it.'

These terms were clearly unacceptable to many who had been involved in the unofficial strike, and they may have been designed to strangle the Reform Movement at birth.

Change was already taking place in the NUS, with Jim Scott, a highly respected and tough union official, elected as the general secretary to replace Yates at the end of the year. He died within eighteen months, before the changes to the NUS were carried out, but he was determined to stop the NUS being replaced by the Reform Movement, which he was prepared to crush if necessary.

The leaders of the unofficial strike were convinced they would get official recognition from the TUC at its annual conference in the Isle of Man and they could replace the NUS as the main negotiating body for the seamen. There was some circumstantial hope for their ambitions. The NUS had been regarded as a pariah union after it was thrown out of the TUC for supporting the strike-breaking Nottingham miners' organisation in the General Strike of 1926.

Prescott consulted his father, by now an official in the Transport Salaried Staffs' Association (TSSA), led by Ray Gunter, about the chances of the Reform Movement's gaining TUC status. Bert Prescott approached Jack Braddock, husband of Bessie Braddock, the battling Liverpool MP, and was told that there was no chance, confirming Prescott's view that they would not succeed with their breakaway from the official union.

When Prescott's ship docked again in Liverpool, he was once more thrown into the dispute and it sailed without him to America. He could see that the leaders were engaged in a fight to the death, which he believed would do neither the men nor the movement any good. And in a city like Liverpool, where passions run deep, there was also the threat of violence after five weeks on strike with one leader in jail. Prescott privately called on the strike leaders to organise a secret ballot of the seamen, but they refused to put it to the test, and he gradually distanced himself from the leadership as they headed for the brink.

Again, Heffer sought to mediate a way out for the men, in talks with the union leaders and the shipowners. It was agreed that the improved terms and conditions would be available if they agreed to an immediate return to work, but the leaders of the breakaway group would have to take their own chance.

Another mass meeting was called on the 'Oller, and Prescott was this time one of the crowd at the front. After setting out the strikers' case, one of the ringleaders asked whether there were any questions. Prescott's voice rang out: 'What about a secret ballot?'

They were not having anything to do with ballots. The leaders were in to the bitter end. But one of them asked whether anyone wanted the microphone.

'I'll have it,' said Prescott.

Some in the crowd shouted, 'Give it him.'

Prescott jumped up on the makeshift platform, and addressed the mass meeting. Standing in front of the sea of faces, he told them, 'You all know me …' They did. They had gone along with his argument last time. He told them they had been out for seven long weeks, but it was breaking down. Ports in the south were again going back to work, leaving Liverpool once more out on a militant limb.

'We are now the remaining rump of the dispute; the union and the owners have now combined to smash us.'

Now he was asking them again to stick together and to go back united. Prescott was convinced their leaders were taking them up a blind alley. There would be no recognition by the TUC, no hope of replacing the NUS, only defeat – and oblivion.

So Prescott called for a ballot for the next day on the 'Oller. At that point, the leaders of the unofficial strike snatched the microphone out of his hands. He got down from the platform and cut a swathe through the body of men. They parted for him, and he walked out of the meeting.

Owen Thompson, Prescott's saloon boss, was there. 'There were thousands of men there. He got up and we all admired it. It took a lot of guts to do it.'

Others too could see the writing on the wall for the strike leaders, and decided to return to their ships. Unlike workers in factories, the seamen were a mobile workforce and many had voted with their feet by leaving Liverpool for jobs on ships out of Southampton. It was a trend that was to accelerate the decline of the merchant fleet on Merseyside.

Within a few days, Prescott and others were back at sea, but the anger and intimidation followed them. One steward on his Cunard liner, who had worked throughout the strike, was so intimidated that he took his own life, slashing his throat in the toilets on board ship. They also tried intimidation on Prescott, but he could handle himself, and it soon died out.

However, the experience never left Prescott. There were many lessons it taught him for later in his political life: that it was crucial to bring the union, or the party, with you, if you were to act as a leader. Courage was not enough. Prescott had the courage of youth, the courage of his own convictions, but he was haunted by the experience, which is told here for the first time.

And it is why, years later, he told Neil Kinnock that 'courage is not enough … You might be right, but it doesn't make you right. You have to carry people.'

It convinced Prescott of the importance of ballots in the workplace, long before the Labour 'modernisers' took up the theme. There was another long-term lesson he learned from the 1960 strike: the importance of changing structures from within. It confirmed Prescott as a reformer, but not a revolutionary. It also showed that, even as a reformer, Prescott would always play the role of outcast, both from his union and the 'boss classes', always swimming against the tide.

A few months after it was over, Prescott was in New York and met Brendan Behan, who was in the Big Apple for his play, *The Quare Fellow*, on Broadway. Behan, a hard-drinking, rumbustious Dubliner and Republican, who had been sent to borstal for trying to blow up a British warship, strongly identified with the seamen, and had sent a telegram of support to Paddy Neary, imprisoned for contempt of court after Neary had ignored a court order restraining him from agitating in Southampton for the strike. Prescott still has the telegram, which he got Behan to sign: 'To Good Old Johnny – a lightning strike is a good strike, but an unofficial lightning strike is better! Brendan Behan.'

Prescott's intervention helped to bring about a settlement, but some of the leading reformers, including Prescott, were determined to go back and change the NUS from within. At the end of the year, Yates announced his retirement. By 1966, some of the leaders of the Reform Movement, including Slater, Sam McCluskie and Joe Kenny, had taken over the executive of the NUS, and called the union out on an official strike for the first time since 1911. And again, Prescott was in the vanguard, acting as an adviser to the NUS.

Prescott continued to be regarded as a troublemaker by his employers for representing the men on board ship. On one occasion, he found himself alone when he refused to do a scrub-out in his Hollywood Waiter outfit. 'I would say, "We're all sticking together on this, Mister Officer. We think you're wrong and we're not going to do this." And then everybody else says, "Yes we will." And then you're left on your own and you say, "Sod you lot, I'm not." And you end up sacked.'

He was frequently accused under the Merchant Shipping Acts of being 'indifferent to discipline', which meant that he had been agitating on behalf of the men for better conditions on board ship. On the *Andes*, he covered it up by acting as the chairman of the 'social club'.

The passengers were bemused by 'industrial action'. On one occasion, Prescott got the stewards to down tools by leading a conga dance. They danced off the ship into the port. When they returned, they were singing the Drifters' big hit of the time, 'Will You Still Love Me Tomorrow?' – one of their favourite numbers. One passenger who met Prescott again on another cruise had no idea he had witnessed illegal industrial action on board ship. 'You were such a happy crew,' he said.

On the *Mauritania*, one-time holder of the Blue Riband for the Atlantic crossing and sister ship of the ill-starred *Lusitania*, Prescott acted as an unofficial convener. He organised union meetings at midnight in the passenger restaurant and had posters printed on the back of the Cunard menus. On one side, they carry a fine-coloured portrait of RMS *Mauritania* sailing proudly into port with sunshine sparkling on the river. On the other in large black letters was printed the message:

> *National Union of Seamen – this concerns YOU*
>
> *Are you a person who complains about your Union? Have you ever participated in your Union affairs? Here's YOUR chance to ACT NOW. Within the next three months a ballot will be held for the Executive Council. This council is answerable to you and is the ruling body of the Union for the next two years. It is YOUR RESPONSIBILITY to see the right men are elected. Register NOW for YOUR right to vote. Remember!!! A Union is only as good as its members make it.*

Further details were available from J. Prescott, tourist waiter; S. Myles, first-class waiter; B. Bennet, cabin-class waiter; Miss J. Thomson, stewardess; J. Garret, swimming-pool attendant; J. Moody, tourist bedroom steward; F. Wright, tourist chef; K. Cann, first-class bedroom steward.

His early exercises in organising ballots – which in a small, badly organised electorate could influence the election of national officers – also upset the trade union bosses, but it proved a useful preparation for the leadership elections to the Labour Party two decades later.

The owners did not recognise shop stewards and the skipper decided to get rid of Prescott when they docked in New York. The captain called Prescott and told him, 'I want you off the ship. I don't care a damn.'

Prescott's shipmates supported him, and walked off the ship too. They told the captain his ship would not be sailing out of port, wrecking the plans for a twelve-hour turnaround for the next voyage. The captain backed down, and brought Prescott back on the ship.

His discharge papers record Prescott's service at sea with a passport photograph and a description: 5ft 7in; brown eyes; dark hair; fair complexion; tattoo or other distinguishing marks – nil (unusual when many seamen were tattooed). Prescott was number R624748 in the records of the Ministry of Transport and Civil Aviation. It also bears testimony to the captain's change of course. His discharge in New York was scratched out. Instead, he was officially discharged in Southampton, when the ship returned to port. He still has his papers bearing the mark 'not for Cunard' and 'not for Union Castle'. That was how the Deputy Prime Minister was blacklisted from some of the leading shipping lines.

Prescott's record as a troublemaker followed him round the ports. In the end, he ran out of ships on which to serve. On the *Andes*, he was accused of mutiny. The air-conditioning had collapsed when they were sailing around the Greek islands in the Mediterranean in high summer, and it was left to Prescott to complain to the ship's officers about the heat in the rooms.

'All the lads had come to me and said, "Are you going to get something done about this?" We were asking to sleep on deck and we wanted an awning over the deck.'

Prescott went to the ship's butcher and borrowed a temperature gauge. Armed with his temperature reading soaring into the nineties, Prescott went to the captain to complain.

Reports of Prescott's troublemaking in New York had reached the captain and he was determined to crush it before it began again. The skipper said, 'I am told you are going to lead a mutiny. The next stop is Piraeus. You are going to lead the crew off.'

He denied the mutiny charge, and finished the trip, but his days were now numbered on board ship. The union was also hostile to his activities. Prescott was convinced that it had been infiltrated by Special Branch and knew seamen who were installed by Special Branch to spy on union activists like himself.

'As a seaman I saw Special Branch activities with my own eyes. The Special Branch was involved in the seamen's disputes.' Shortly before going to Downing Street with an NUS delegation, he was in the NUS headquarters when Special Branch arrived. He was asked to step outside, while the officers had words with one of the union officials. They were seeking help in identifying agitators, who had been secretly photographed on picket lines. Prescott had no doubt they were given all the assistance they wanted. He is convinced that some NUS officials and the police colluded as members of the Freemasons, which was one of the reasons why the union leadership did not include Catholics.

As an MP Prescott led delegations to the Home Secretary, Roy Jenkins, to protest about Special Branch engaging in anti-trade-union operations, which he believed exceeded their founding principle 'to combat a potential threat to the State'. He also took up the case of Kenneth Joseph Lennon, a possible agent provocateur for Special Branch who was mysteriously killed in April 1974. Ten years later, during the miners' strike, he protested to Leon Brittan, then Home Secretary, about treating trade unionists as 'the enemy within' by having Special Branch spying on the picket lines.

The happy days on board ship were over. But there was more trouble brewing for Prescott ashore. His single ambition was to become a full-time NUS official, but he was blocked by Bill Hogarth, the union's general secretary. Prescott had won a place at the trade-union-backed Ruskin College, Oxford, through which many trade union and Labour MPs had passed, but Hogarth vetoed the provision of an NUS scholarship for him to take up. Hated by the union leadership and the shipowners, he had no one to turn to, except the local Cheshire County Council, which was Tory-controlled. It turned him down.

'I wanted to be a trade union official. I had a row with the general secretary. He was not introducing shop stewards at sea fast enough. I said he was playing games for the employers. He took the scholarship from me … They told me to apply to Chester [where the county has its HQ] for a grant.

'I said I wanted to be a trades union official and the Tory authority refused me the grant. Then I lost the place.'

Fighting adversity again, he would not give up. He was

advised by Billy Hughes, the head of Ruskin College, to apply again and this time to say he wanted to be a teacher. Prescott got 30 people to confirm he wanted to be a teacher, including his former boss at the Patten Arms and the Workers' Educational Association.

This time, Prescott J., would-be teacher, was approved the grant. But when he emerged from Ruskin College, Oxford, with a two-year diploma in economics and politics in 1965, his union would not have him as an official.

'It was Hogarth. He said I could not have a job, nor would they allow me to stay active in the union or to be sponsored by them in education.'

Out of work, and blocked by Hogarth from becoming a full-time official, Prescott considered joining the Rossendale Union of Boot, Shoe and Slipper Operatives as general secretary, but, when he told them he expected the TUC rate for the job, the offer never materialised. Perhaps it was just as well. The RUBSSO hardly had the street cred of the NUS.

He took a temporary post as a recruitment officer with the General and Municipal Workers' Union under David Basnett. Prescott had the job of trying to recruit new members in factories where the bosses had resisted the union. They included the Liquorice Allsorts factory in Belper where he played a trick on the management by persuading them to allow a meeting inside the factory gates under an awning if it rained. His notice for the meeting said 'if raining' in small print. There was more trouble at Copious Pickles in Leeds where he put up a notice claiming the owner 'says unions do a good job'. The owner sued and the union got its first writ. Prescott felt he was not cut out for recruiting in pickle factories, and wanted to get back to the NUS.

His tutor, Raphael Samuel, suggested that he should go to Hull University and study under John Saville, a left-wing professor of economic history. He did not need to go through the usual university clearing system: the vacancy was waiting for him.

Pauline backed him in his ambition, although it meant they had to uproot from Chester, which had been her home all her life, to go to Hull, where John, at the age of 27, became a full-time university student. This was when Pauline, with Jonathon, then aged two, went out to work as a hairdresser to keep them, and worked at one of the big stores in Hull.

Having started his university course in October 1965, Prescott was led by his passion for politics to stand, in March 1966, for Labour in the unlikely setting of Southport, a gentle Victorian resort, which thought itself a cut above Blackpool, on the Lancashire coast. It was so sleepy that the days when the tide came in made news on the front page of the local paper.

It was also solidly Tory, and the ideal place for Prescott to get his first experience of a 'no-hoper' under his belt. With Tony Blair two months away from his thirteenth birthday, Prescott stood against the Conservative MP Sir Ian Percival, who later became the Solicitor General in the first Thatcher government. A personal message to the voters of Southport carried a photograph of Prescott with his blond-haired son, and Pauline looking very beautiful with a Jackie Kennedy hairstyle. It said the candidate, aged 28, was studying marine economics at Hull

University. 'His special interest is economics and he holds strong views on the existence of underprivileged sections within the Welfare State. He hopes to meet many of the electors of Southport in the course of a concentrated doorstep campaign.'

His electoral address also described Prescott as a seaman, although he had ceased his seafaring two years earlier.

In his address to Southport voters, Prescott said, 'I have the pleasant but responsible task of maintaining the high political standards set by the government of Harold Wilson …'

Three months later, Wilson denounced the seamen as 'a tightly knit group of politically motivated men' for going on strike and bringing the country to its knees. There was nothing in the family photograph of Prescott to suggest to the voters of Southport that they had a dangerous man in their midst on whom Special Branch had a record.

Wilson alleged that Communists were manipulating the executive through Slater and his clique, even though they were still outnumbered by Hogarth and his allies.

He was convinced that they were seeking to foment revolution on merchant vessels to smash the Labour government's prices and incomes policy. On 13 May, Wilson had called 48 seamen's leaders excluding Prescott to 10 Downing Street for talks in a vain attempt to persuade them to abandon the strike and accept the main findings of the Pearson inquiry into pay and conditions in the merchant navy with a brokered deal from the employers.

After they refused, the Wilson government prepared for the worst. Emergency powers were held in reserve to allow the armed services to move goods into and out of the ports and airlift mail to Northern Ireland; they were not needed, but daily the crisis mounted, and there were threats of its spreading to the dock workers led by Jack Dash in London.

On 20 June, Wilson told the Commons the NUS was being manipulated by 'this tightly knit group of politically motivated men, who, as the last general election showed, utterly failed to secure acceptance of their views by the electorate, but who are now determined to exercise backstage pressures, forcing great hardship on the members of the union, and their families, and endangering the security of the industry and the economic welfare of the nation'.

The Labour Prime Minister refused to accept that it was a genuine trade union dispute over pay and conditions, which his incomes policy had exacerbated. He was accused of dodging the issue, by blaming reds under the NUS hammocks. Wilson was challenged by the press and the unions to provide the evidence. Prescott had been told by a Labour MP, Peter Jackson, and a researcher for the BBC *Panorama* programme, which was doing a documentary on the seamen's strike, that he would be named by Wilson in the Commons. Prescott was a potential target because he had been the author of a searing attack on the government's handling of the dispute in a pamphlet called 'Not Wanted on Voyage – the Seaman's Reply'. It was written by Prescott on behalf of the Hull strike committee because the NUS would not reply to the Pearson report on the seamen's strike.

Prescott, a marked man, was in the public gallery of the House of Commons to hear Wilson open a debate on the extension of the emergency powers on 28 June in which he was to be named. He had been given a ticket for the Strangers' Gallery by Michael Foot.

Wilson took the unusual step of laying out some of the evidence supplied to him by Special Branch – the rest was covered by the Official Secrets Act and would not be released for at least 30 years, January 1997, and probably longer in the case of Prescott's own file.

Naming the ringleaders, Wilson told the Commons that Bert Ramelson, in January 1966, had succeeded Peter Kerrigan as the Communist Party's industrial organiser; the chairmanships of the two strike committees at two major ports in London and Liverpool were taken by two Communists, Jack Coward and Roger Woods; a leading member of the NUS negotiating committee, Gordon Norris, was a Communist, who sometimes operated under the name of George Goodman.

Wilson claimed one of the Communists' objectives was to use the strike to destroy the government's prices and incomes policy, and he alleged they had used NUS leaders to further their ends.

'If I refer to Mr Joseph Kenny and Mr James Slater, neither of them a member of the Communist Party ... They live in Liverpool and South Shields respectively and over the past few weeks, when attending the executive council in London, they have stayed at the same flat as Mr Jack Coward. Of course, they are free to stay where they like, but Mr Ramelson has visited the flat when they were there and Mr Norris has been in constant touch with them. They have been in continual contact with Mr Ramelson and Mr Norris.'

Wilson was acting on surveillance and intercepts. According to the journalist and writer Chapman Pincher, 'Wilson was provided with irrefutable evidence by MI5, including records of bugged conversations and photographs of intercepted documents, that the strike was being orchestrated by a few Communists imposing their will on the others and determined to bring in the dockers and other workers so that the country could be brought to a standstill.'

Prescott had been closely involved in the strike, and had been to some of the meetings with Slater. Had Prescott been named, his future political career would have been ruined. But Wilson was constrained in what he could say about Prescott because he had been the official Labour Party candidate in Southport only ten weeks earlier in the general election.

The 'evidence' produced by Wilson looked hopelessly circumstantial. It led to a backlash from the left wing of the Labour Party, and it was ridiculed in most of the press. 'If Mr Wilson really believes that the sole threat to his incomes policy comes from the Communist Party, he has hopelessly misunderstood what is happening not only in the unions but in the ranks of his own party.' That verdict, in the *New Statesman*, was shared by Tory-supporting newspapers.

Tony Benn recorded: 'It made me sick and reminded me of McCarthyism. The Left attacked him almost unanimously with powerful speeches by Michael Foot, Eric Heffer and Ian Mikardo. In a sense Harold said nothing that was new, since every trade union leader knew it and we were all afraid that by going in for these tactics, he would simply make the anti-

Communist smear a weapon that every Tory could use against us in the future.'

Wilson went round the Cabinet and forced each member to define his position. Richard Crossman, a member of Wilson's Cabinet, recorded in his diary:

> *In the evening I talked to Tam Dalyell* [Labour MP] *at length about this whole naming affair. We both feel it is an example of Wiggery-pokery. George Wigg* [Paymaster General] *has been busy on this for weeks, organizing the counter-security against the trade union communists, collecting the whole story into his hands, trying to get it into the press and, when he couldn't, selling it to the PM instead.*

To forestall any possibility of an attack from the opposition, Wilson then decided to brief Ted Heath, the Tory leader, on Privy Counsellor terms 'and for good measure to bring to our meeting [MI5's] senior people responsible for these matters, and one of the operators "in the field"'.

Crossman found it difficult to stomach Wilson's 'McCarthyite' attempts to produce evidence of the Red Plot. 'We are trying to smash the seamen although we have just given huge concessions to the doctors, the judges and the higher civil servants. It is an ironical interpretation of a socialist incomes policy,' said Crossman.

'Not Wanted on Voyage – the Seaman's Reply' was regarded as a brilliant critique of the Pearson inquiry into the causes of the dispute, particularly of the Minister of Labour, Ray Gunter.

Characteristically, Prescott did not shy from attacking the personalities. He attacked each member of the board to show theirs was a loaded report. As ever, education and class were in Prescott's charge sheet: The Rt Hon. Lord Pearson, Prescott noted, was 'educated at St Paul's School and Balliol College, Oxford. His clubs are the Garrick and Roehampton.' The implication was clear: what did Pearson know about the plight of ordinary seamen?

On A.J. Stephen Brown Esquire, BSc – president-elect of the Confederation of British Industry – 'the employers' organisation', Prescott's note said: 'The CBI launched a strong attack on the seamen at the beginning of the strike and have continued to accuse the NUS of ruining the country.'

On Hugh Armstrong Clegg – an expert on industrial relations and professor at Warwick University: 'he was a member of the Devlin Inquiry into the Docks problem, and therefore supports the strengthening of private employers' power in that industry.'

On Joe O'Hagan – chairman of the TUC finance and general purposes committee: 'it was an astute political move to include him on the Pearson Inquiry since it was obvious that if the seamen rejected the Report, they would have to appeal to the TUC for support. Since the Report failed the seamen, it was rejected, and in their approach to the TUC, met Joe O'Hagan in the chair at the meeting …'

The press barons, who had battered the NUS for its strike, were individually attacked by Prescott. He identified their own interests in the shipping industry: Sir John Ellerman – a shipowner – also had a big stake in the *Daily Mirror* group, which had been 'very tough on the seamen'; the millionaire Harold Drayton had a big stake in shipping, television and the provincial string of papers owned by the United Newspapers group.

Roy Mason, the Minister of State for Shipping, took a sideswipe by Prescott for being too close to the owners – 'This backward, selfish group of owners through their spokesman, arrogantly claim that "the national interest" so often thrown against the seamen by Press, TV, and Government, IS THE SAME THING AS THE SHIPOWNERS' INTERESTS.'

It was an aggressive victim's view of the press, which persists to this day.

'Despite the common misconception largely encouraged by the mass communications of Press, TV, and Government, the Inquiry's suggestions, which neatly juggle with percentages, offer no firm basis for positive improvements in their fight for a 40 hour £14 week. To talk of a basis for compromise shows a fundamental lack of understanding of exactly what seamen are being asked to accept.'

He set out in detail the seamen's claim, and its justification, challenging the inquiry report, point by point.

'The job of the inquiry was to discredit the seamen's case, and to deliver up the sailor for sacrifice on the altar of George Brown's Incomes Policy,' he concluded.

Prescott, clearly relishing the use of the 'bullets' given him at Ruskin, fired them bang on target at the shipping companies by challenging their claims that they had insufficient profits to pay for a better deal for the seamen. He quoted the Jenkins

Committee Report on Company Law 1962, to demand access to the companies' accounts.

Reviewing the causes of the decline of the British merchant fleet, Prescott blamed the owners for stifling competition, and therefore change, by organising cartels. 'The placing of family representatives on each other's Boards of Directors kept potential competition in check,' he said.

The anger of the seamen was caused not by Communists but by an intense feeling of injustice after 'huge increases for members of parliament, judges, top civil servants, Ministers of the Crown, and the doctors.

'It becomes hard to accept that all these professions can get increases well above the norm, on already comfortable salaries, while the lower earning groups as in the cases of railwaymen, busmen, and now seamen, are forced to run the gauntlet of "threats to the State" and massive press campaigns for the merest fraction above the norm on a basically low wage.'

The incomes policy had lost all pretence of being concerned with social justice. It was one law for the rich, another for the poor. The incomes policy had become wage restraint, Prescott protested, although the 1966 strike did not shake Prescott's faith in some form of incomes policy, provided it was just.

'It is time for seamen, and the rest of the labour movement to rethink its attitude to present policy, and to sign perhaps a Declaration of Dissent rather than of Intent. Thereby, we would register our demand that the policy be withdrawn and we start again with a socialist incomes policy, which controls and plans all forms of incomes.'

That required a radical reform of company law to force companies to reveal what their profits really were, at the same time as 'radically altering our system of taxation to achieve a great redistribution of wealth in a socialist direction'.

And he thundered, 'We say that the shipping industry's crisis should be finally resolved by NATIONALISATION.'

The emphasis in capital letters was Prescott's. The conclusion of his pamphlet, published for 1s 9d (or 9p – the same price as the Pearson report) still has echoes over three decades later, long after the findings of the Pearson report have been forgotten.

He was allowed to join the union as a full-time official, but Hogarth made it clear to Prescott that he would never allow him into the union leadership. He was offered the 'consolation' prize of sponsorship by the union to become an MP. They needed someone like Prescott, who was a fighter, committed to the union, and equipped with his education at Ruskin and Hull, well versed in mercantile marine law, to act as their spokesman in the Commons. Four months later, he was adopted for Hull East, but he had to wait two years for the general election to gain a seat in the Commons. In the meantime, the union put him to work, advising the Labour government on changes to the Shipping Acts. In the months before the 1970 election, Prescott went to Downing Street for the first time with an NUS delegation, including Slater, to press for the abolition of outdated penal clauses, covering such offences as 'breaching ship's cargo', for which the Hollywood Waiters had been docked pay. The legislation had been drafted with Hogarth's agreement, but Prescott persuaded the general secretary that he could not have given his consent.

They were met at Number Ten by Wilson, wearing a Trinity tie. He had just come from the Scilly Isles, where he went on holiday. Prescott does a painfully accurate imitation of Wilson patronising the seafarers with ill-informed chat about the wind direction, which he got wrong. 'It was blowing an easterly …'

Then Wilson took them to the Cabinet Room, where they sat down at the table. Again more Wilson banter. 'You're sitting where the Lord Chancellor sits,' he told Prescott. Prescott was unimpressed. He wanted to get on with the negotiations. Prescott led for the union. Wilson said the problem was that the legislation was already in the House of Lords, but he offered a pledge that it would be reviewed. Prescott pointed out that, after he had described the executive as a 'tightly knit group of politically motivated men', the union might not take his word at face value. Wilson conceded that Prescott might have a point, and told them that the government would make an announcement in the House of Lords, saying the legislation would be reviewed. It was one of the few Bills to go through with a promise to change it once it was on the Statute Book.

Prescott then said, 'There is another problem. What if you aren't here?'

'I don't envisage my plans being upset,' said Wilson.

CHAPTER EIGHT

JLP MP

A lot of people seem to get political promotion by doing the crawly things. Conscience is an important part of my make-up.

John Prescott, one year after becoming an MP.

At general elections, a sign is erected by the Labour Party local workers near to the Humber Bridge telling motorists: YOU ARE NOW ENTERING JOHN PRESCOTT COUNTRY.

Hull East has been in Labour hands since 1945, and for half that time, it has been Prescott's domain.

Until Prescott was adopted for Hull East in 1968, the Hull constituency had been held since the war by Commander Harry Pursey. The commander, who claimed to have had distinguished service in the Royal Navy during the war, lived for most of the time in Putney, London.

When Commander Pursey announced retirement before the general election of 1970, the constituency party was flooded with applications. They included a number of prominent Labour candidates who were on the lookout for a safe seat, including Tom Ponsonby, later the Labour Chief Whip in the

Lords after he inherited the title of third baron from his father in 1976. Although it was a port, there were only four or five delegates from the National Union of Seamen in the CLP, but they included Sam McCluskie, the union organiser, later to become general secretary of the union, and Ken Turner, who followed in his footsteps. They wanted an NUS spokesman in the Commons.

'John was the obvious choice,' recalls one old hand in the constituency. 'We later learned that John – he obviously wanted to keep this quiet – got the support of the Transport and General Workers' Union because the T&G wanted to take over the NUS. Jim Slater was resisting it, and a number of delegates from the T&G immediately appeared at the selection conference.'

These days his supporters might be accused of packing the meeting, but it is claimed that up to 50 T&G delegates appeared to swing the vote in Prescott's favour. If there was any deal done about the future of the NUS, it was never fulfilled. In 1990, the NUS was merged with the NUR, the railway union, to form the RMT (the Rail, Maritime and Transport union). The *Yorkshire Post* reported on 11 November 1968: 'Seamen's official to be candidate. A graduate of Hull University who is Hull district secretary of the National Union of Seamen, Mr John Prescott, 30, of Cornwall Street, New Village Road, Cottingham, was chosen yesterday as prospective Parliamentary Labour candidate for East Hull. Commander Harry Pursey (Lab) who was first elected for the constituency in 1945 had a majority at the last election of 23,072.'

Prescott was already well connected in Hull but had faced stiff competition. Charlie Brady, an USDAW (shopworkers' union) organiser, wanted Ponsonby to get it, but his 'ferocious' organising skills were hampered before the selection campaign got under way when his union sent Brady to the Far East. He came back before the selection, but by then it was too late. There was a strong NUR contingent, and Harry Woodford was on the shortlist. He was a pint-sized worker from the railway sheds, who, despite being small, could wield a big hammer. Harry became Prescott's agent.

Another on the shortlist was Alex Clarke, husband of Phyllis Clarke, the secretary of the Hull East CLP. The Clarkes were pacifists from London.

Prescott has never been a member of CND. His friends cannot remember his going on peace marches, and he has taken little interest in defence in the Commons, except to cross swords with James Callaghan, the last Labour Prime Minister, when Callaghan supported the retention by Labour of the Trident missile system. Prescott's anger was not raised by the substance of the issue, but by its timing – shortly before the 1987 general election – which might have undermined Labour's electoral chances. When challenged by his regional daily paper about Denis Healey's remark in Moscow that the Russians 'were praying for a Labour victory', he snapped, 'When was the fucking *Yorkshire Post* interested in the Labour Party? I am not saying anything about Denis Healey, thank you, comrade.'

Phyllis Clarke was still as committed as ever when I spoke to her in 1996, and remained the secretary of Prescott's CLP.

At the selection meeting, Prescott challenged the impartiality of the chairman, who was – like Harry Woodford – a member of the NUR. 'John was literally on edge – pacing up and down because it meant so much to him,' recalled another who was there. Looking back on his first year as an MP, Prescott said, 'For me selection, not the election, was the climax.'

The organisers had little doubt that the Prescott camp would have lodged a formal complaint if he had lost, and would have demanded an inquiry into the selection. As deputy leader, he now sits in judgement on such disputes. In early 1996, Prescott had great sympathy with local Labour activists in Swindon who complained that a Blairite was being foisted on them. When the complaint was heard at the NEC, Prescott voted with the left-wingers, like Skinner. It was the first time that Prescott had voted against the leadership on the NEC since the leadership elections.

Having won the selection, he set about healing the wounds, telling Harry Woodford he wanted him to continue as his agent. It has been a long and solid relationship. Harry, who lived in a 1960s council house on the estate a short walk from 'Prescott's Castle', made his mark in local government in Hull, becoming Lord Mayor and secretary of the Labour Group. Regarded as 'a character' by his friends, he was the only one in Hull to be honoured by having a landmark named after him, while still alive. The Woodford Leisure Centre is a bustling sports complex, which was paid for partly from an idea that Harry borrowed, after spotting some boys on a beach in Brighton when he was on holiday, selling raffle tickets to raise money for a sports field.

Harry was the organiser, while Prescott was in London.

The timing of the June 1970 general election was a traumatic experience for the Prescotts. Pauline was pregnant with David, their second son. Prescott even included the news in his election address to his voters. 'Your Parliamentary Labour candidate is 32 years of age, married with a seven-year-old son. Pauline, his wife, is expecting a baby on June the eighteenth – election date.'

Pauline later recalled, 'David was not born until the twenty-second. John was telling everybody that Pauline is due to give birth on the eighteenth. I said, "John, you cannot say that."'

Prescott was determined his son would be born in time for the election, and brought into the world with his dad as an MP, which produced some odd ideas for inducing the birth. 'He used to sit me in the car, and race me around in it. It didn't work,' said Pauline.

His Tory opponent was a young Cambridge graduate being tested out in a no-hope seat: Norman Lamont. The result was announced at 1.20 a.m. on 19 June. At the count, Lamont said to Pauline, 'I didn't expect to see you here ...' For Pauline, that was an understatement.

The local newspaper said, 'Perhaps the most excited supporter of Mr Prescott was his raven-haired wife, Pauline. Smart and erect in a striking red frock, nobody would have guessed that she was within a few hours of giving birth to her second child.

'All yesterday, this birth had been expected hourly. But the baby did not arrive and Mrs Prescott was able to realise her dearest wish, to watch her husband declared the East Hull victor.'

Prescott had a majority of 22,123. That night, James Johnson and Kevin McNamara were also returned as Labour MPs for Hull constituencies. A photograph appeared with the report, showing Prescott's mother, Phyllis, at the count, wiping away 'tears of joy' at her son's being elected.

The local paper said Prescott had won a 'sporting battle of bright young men' over Lamont, whom it described accurately as 'a 28-year-old Shetland Islander and banker'.

Lamont, it said, 'pale but smiling bravely', was greeted by boos, and crackers went off below the balcony of the town hall, where the count was made, but Labour supporters shouted, 'Give him a chance.'

The Tories had increased their vote on the night from 11,385 to 14,736, which Lamont said was 'a very good result indeed'. Despite the 'acute political differences, Mr Lamont and Mr Prescott were on good terms last night and there was general admiration for the sporting fashion in which Mr Lamont accepted his defeat. He went off smiling, with officials of his party to East Hull.'

In 1984, when they faced each other again across the Despatch Box, Prescott railed against the government for creating mass unemployment deliberately to reduce wage levels as the government had in the 1920s.

Lamont recalled election night in 1970. 'He made a powerful and outrageous speech after the count. He made the same speech tonight.'

Lamont had a hard time during the campaign. It was one of the rare occasions when the Tories held control of the Hull council, and council house rents had been doubled with the help of a young bright councillor, a chartered accountant called John Townend, now the MP for Bridlington and chairman of the hard-right 92 Group of Thatcherite MPs.

Prescott speaks fondly of the memory of Lamont's campaign. 'They used to spit at him.'

Lamont, who had been a researcher at Conservative Central Office, said it was partly because his father, a surgeon, lived in Grimsby, that he fought the Hull seat. He was to get a second chance in a by-election, two years later, when he secured the Kingston-upon-Thames seat that lasted him until it was abolished in boundary changes in 1996. After a lot of searching, he was finally selected for the Tory seat of Harrogate, where his Yorkshire family connections again came in useful.

When, in October 1965, he was accepted by the university, Prescott was still drawn by a political career and narrowly failed to get adopted as the official Labour candidate for a parliamentary by-election in Hull in January 1966. It proved to be a contest of national importance. Labour was challenged by Richard Gott, a *Guardian* journalist standing as an independent against the Vietnam war. It was an early test of Prescott's loyalty to the party; he sympathised with the anti-Vietnam campaigners but stuck loyally with Labour. During the campaign, Barbara Castle, the Transport Minister, promised to build the Humber Bridge. Crossman recorded going up for the campaign in his diaries; Crossman issued a statement showing he had raised the idea of a Humber Bridge in September the previous year, so that 'Barbara's speech wasn't a last-minute bribe'. Nevertheless, the by-election has become synonymous with the offer of the bridge to buy by-election votes. It was important for another reason. The by-election on 27 January 1966 was won by Kevin McNamara with a 4.5 per cent swing, the biggest swing to Labour in ten years. That convinced Wilson of the wisdom of an early election, which he called two months later. This was when Prescott, using his contacts on Merseyside, where he had been an agent in 1964, was adopted to fight his first parliamentary contest as a candidate in the no-hope Tory seat of Southport, while he was in his first year at university. He remembers being supported by Lord Longford. They rowed in the car about abortion on the way back from a public meeting. Prescott strongly supported the women's right to choose in the Abortion Reform Bill introduced a month later, April 1966, by the Liberal MP David Steel. Pauline and John stayed in a pleasant Southport hotel for a month, and enjoyed the campaign, which, nationally, saw Labour increase its majority to 97 in the Commons. Wilson recorded that seats never held by Labour since 1945 fell to the party that night, including Exeter, Oxford and Hampstead. They did not include Southport. Prescott returned to Hull to make up for lost time.

Nineteen sixty-six was also the year when England won the World Cup at Wembley, Simon and Garfunkel sang 'Scarborough Fair', the Rolling Stones followed 'Satisfaction' with 'Get Off My Cloud', and Bob Dylan had the 'Subterranean Homesick Blues'. The campuses in California were soon to be filled with LSD-powered flower followers, but Prescott, as a mature student of 28, was beating to a different rhythm in Hull. The summer of '66 meant only one thing: the seamen's strike. Wearing a black leather jacket, he was heavily engaged in the action with Jim Slater. It was four years before he became an MP.

Standing on the balcony at Hull town hall in 1970, Prescott said, 'We have won a great victory in East Hull. We will no longer tolerate Conservative rule, either nationally or locally ...' But he was wrong. Labour's national majority was wiped out, and Prescott was destined for opposition. The national result was the greatest upset in a general election since Attlee's victory over Churchill in 1945.

Wilson had gone to the country in warm sunny weather, with the balance of payments in healthy surplus – the reduction in imports caused by the seamen's strike may have played a small part – and Labour was 'apparently coasting to victory on a warm tide of national well-being'. By the end of the campaign, the trade figures had slipped into the red, and West Germany had come back from 2–0 down with twenty minutes to play to beat England 3–2 in the World Cup quarter-final.

Heath's Tory government came from behind like West Germany to win 330 seats to Labour's 287, with a Conservative majority of 37.

It was a bitter blow for the newly elected backbench MP for Hull East. Although Wilson was returned to office in 1974, the highest post in government Prescott had over the following 26 years was as parliamentary Private Secretary to Peter Shore.

Thursday, 2 July 1970 was a day for celebration, however. His mother carefully preserved the menu for the Members' Dining

Room for her son's arrival at the House of Commons. The choice (with English translations) for luncheon 'on the occasion of the State Opening of Parliament by Her Majesty Queen Elizabeth II' was:

Consommé Royal (clear soup garnished with baked savoury egg), Vichyssoise, Coupe Florida (grapefruit and orange)

Fried fillet of sole, Tartare Sauce
Mushroom Omelette, Noisette of Lamb Nicoise (garnished with tomato and french beans), Fried Breast of Chicken Princesse (garnished with asparagus tips), Roast Ribs of Scotch Beef and Horse-radish Sauce

Potatoes: Roast, Boiled, Creamed, French Fried, Garden Peas, French Beans, Cabbage

Fresh Fruit Salad and Cream, Cassata Veronique (Tutti Fruiti ice cream, butterscotch flavour) Apple Crumble and Fresh Cream

Coffee

Mrs Prescott wrote across the cover photograph of the Houses of Parliament: 'The Proudest Day of My Life (Mum). Lunch with John in the House of Commons, John Taking his seat as MP.'

The MP for Hull East learned the hard way about the importance of the trappings and ceremony of Parliament. He made his maiden speech during the second reading of the Harbours (Amendment) Bill on 14 July, three months after being elected. 'Some older members advised, "Take your time, son, and get the feel of the place first". But this view did not attract me. Once over, it is a great feeling and you walk around with more confidence.'

Prescott had tried to make his maiden speech twice before but had 'failed to catch the Speaker's eye'. He stayed up all night on three occasions writing different speeches. The first two went into the litter bin, possibly because he refused to bow to the Speaker, until he realised that MPs depended on 'the goodwill of the chair'.

'So I compromised and now bow. There are aspects of ceremony which are designed to cool tempers and it can play an effective role even if you hate a fellow you have to be polite. Ceremony depersonalises the proceedings.

'But there are many other things which I consider crazy and a load of rubbish.'

Putting on a top hat to make a point of order during a division was among them. Dennis Skinner, another young rebel – from the mining constituency of Bolsover – was inclined to sing 'Give me the moonlight ...' whenever that happened. Skinner was also known to offer snooker chalk to the whips when they arrived in the chamber carrying a long white 'wand of office'.

In spite of the irritations, Prescott approved of Parliament on the whole. 'People in the constituency think of you as an extension of themselves – proud that you are active. You are their Robin Hood – they have voted you in and have a stake in your progress.'

Prescott's election address had said, 'We are convinced that in electing John Prescott, East Hull will have acquired a Member of Parliament whose youth, energy and understanding of Hull's problems will be of direct and everlasting benefit to the people of Hull and East Hull particularly.'

His maiden speech was true to that promise. All maiden speeches traditionally are meant to focus on the constituency of the new member, and a convention has been observed that they should be non-controversial. Prescott followed the rules, but stretched them to the limit in setting out his stall on dock law and the welfare of those at sea.

He went through the routine of describing his constituency and its connections with seafaring – as long ago as 1890, it returned Samuel Plimsoll – and graciously paid his respects to Commander Pursey (the former MP had been responsible for raising the banks of the River Hull, to stop flooding, but there had also been a great deal of gossip surrounding his private life – Pursey had had several affairs). 'He was both colourful and controversial, and his presence will be sorely missed in the House,' said Prescott with considerable diplomacy.

Prescott also displayed his own self-deprecating sense of humour. The people of Hull, he said, were renowned for their 'warm Yorkshire hospitality and generosity and shrewd judgement of character – never was this so amply demonstrated than in the recent general election when the Labour candidate was elected with no evidence of the national swing against the Labour Party'. He liked to think that it was due to the personal qualities of the Labour candidate, but accepted that the Tory council's decision to raise council rents in Hull from £3 to £9 a week 'played no small part'.

The main themes of his speech would become well-trodden ground for Prescott over the next 26 years: the need for an integrated transport system, public ownership, industrial democracy, and private money financed by loans to pay for public investment.

As the first MP sponsored by the National Union of Seamen in the Commons, Prescott warned the Heath government that seamen were expecting the Tories to fulfil the pledge made by the outgoing Wilson government to review the penal clauses in the Merchant Shipping Acts.

'The seamen will not tolerate those penal clauses remaining in the Acts. I hope that the Government will take due note of this, particularly as this was the running sore which led to the problem of the 1966 strike,' he said. They included the punishment for 'broaching ship's cargo', which caused Cunard stewards occasionally to appear before the ship's captain on a charge.

The Bill was a technical measure, and the second reading ended without a vote, but Prescott used it to pin his colours firmly to the mast of nationalisation.

There was continued industrial unrest on the docks, and the seamen's dispute was fresh in the memory.

He told the Commons, 'It should be noted by the government

that almost the same problems are peculiar to both docks and shipping, and, I suggest, for exactly the same reason. Both have a history of casual labour, controlled in the supply by the employer, disciplined by means of fines and penalties, plagued by a higher record of occupational accidents and deaths, and further soured by the lack of welfare facilities and amenities …

'The only solution is to take both industries into public ownership in the interests of the nation.'

He quickly displayed the uncompromising side of his nature, which has characterised his political career. 'A lot of people seem to get political promotion by doing the crawly things.

'I like to think I do things because they are right – controversial or not. Conscience is an important part of my make-up.'

Prescott's maiden speech lasted fifteen minutes, the maximum allowed, and was praised by the parliamentary Secretary to the Minister of Transport – a sparkling rising star in the Tory ranks called Michael Heseltine.

Heseltine said it was 'one of the most remarkable maiden speeches I have heard in the House … I am pleased to have the opportunity of congratulating him from this bench, and I am sure that we shall hear from him on many occasions with equal enjoyment in the near future.'

Prescott did not hear that kind of praise from Heseltine when 'Prezza' faced 'Hezza' across the Despatch Box as Deputy Leader of Her Majesty's Opposition.

Prescott's part in the seamen's strike was quickly put to one side. His expertise was an asset to the opposition under Wilson, as a string of shipping controversies arose, and, within his first year in the House, Prescott was made a front-bench Labour spokesman on shipping by one of those he had criticised in 'Not Wanted on Voyage': Roy Mason, now a Labour life peer. Asked why he appointed Prescott, Lord Mason said with Yorkshire bluntness, 'Because he was good. He came in with all his experience in shipping, the merchant navy, and safety at sea. He knew his subject.'

His first experience of standing at the Despatch Box was on a quiet Friday, when he spoke for Labour on shipping safety. His dad was in the public gallery to witness the event. The *Hull Daily Mail*, 6 May 1971, recorded:

> *With Mr Mason absent, the Opposition asked Mr Prescott to sum up for them in a Front Bench capacity during the debate. After his 30-minute speech he was congratulated on the 'maiden' attempt by the Government spokesman who told the House: 'I thought he made a very good job of it.' Later, Mr Prescott told me: 'I was not affected by nerves. But I did learn one thing. Summing up can leave you in an unhappy position. Everyone else has said just about everything there is to say by the time your turn comes.'*

The Hull prison riots in 1976 led to Prescott's first serious report since 'Not Wanted on Voyage'; it was to be a model for a steady stream of Prescott policy papers over the next decade. Employing exhaustive research, Prescott delved into the reasons why the prisoners had systematically destroyed the prison and gone on a rooftop protest. He did not spare the Labour government in his report to the Home Office inquiry. A tougher regime was made worse by Chancellor Denis Healey's spending cuts, which meant the guards were forced to lock up the prisoners for longer, with less exercise time and less education. A former governor had allowed prison representatives – shop stewards – to be appointed by the prisoners, and Prescott was reported to support allowing prisoners to join a trade union.

Prescott noted that the prisoners vented their anger not on the 'screws' but in graffiti on the walls of the prison, complaining about the lack of conjugal rights. 'Sexual deprivation must surely constitute one of the worst and potentially most harmful aspects of loss of liberty. These are powers which produce frustrations and tensions.'

He did not blame the prison officers, but was seen by them as the prisoners' friend. When he later visited the jail, they tipped off the police that the shadow Minister for Transport's Jaguar was displaying an out-of-date tax disc. Prisoners may have got more conjugal visits thanks to Prescott, but he paid for it by being pilloried in the press for failing to pay for his road fund licence on time.

CHAPTER NINE

Into Europe

Probably my most momentous decision.
John Prescott, *Hull Daily Mail.*

The splash headline in the *Hull Daily Mail* on Friday, 8 August 1980 was almost too amazing to be true: MP'S 'NO' TO £400,000 EURO JOB.

The leader of the opposition, James Callaghan, had approached Prescott, one of the first 'Euro-sceptics', with the offer to become one of Britain's European Commissioners to replace Roy Jenkins at a salary of about £400,000 over five years.

'While being flattered, I had no hesitation in saying I could not accept the offer,' said Prescott. That was not quite true. He telephoned Pauline first to get her approval to turn it down.

'I rang the wife and told her the money. She said, "My God, can I go and buy that Brueghel print at W.H. Smith's? Seven pounds?" I said, "You can go and buy the original on the money that comes out of Europe."'

It took ten minutes to turn it down. 'I don't believe in the constitution of the Common Market or its economic philosophy, basically a capitalist philosophy.'

Pauline went out and bought the Brueghel print anyway, and it is on the wall in the kitchen. Prescott said he thought the amount of money he could have earned, with pensions and expenses, was 'obscene', but his main reason for turning it down was that it would have meant giving up his parliamentary career. 'I told him I'd be cutting my throat by taking it.' Callaghan had expected him to say no and Prescott had no regrets. 'I feel my decision was the right one. The next two or three years will be the most momentous in British postwar politics. I would like to play my full part in returning Labour to power and improving the prospects of my constituents, particularly the unemployed, who are suffering from the effects of present Tory policies.'

Prescott, then 42, had been leader of the Labour Group in Europe since 1976 and had demonstrated that, for all his Euroscepticism, he was assiduous in arguing Britain's case in the forums of Europe. He voted against Britain's entry in 1971 and 1972 and shared a platform with Peter Shore in the 'no' campaign on the referendum, but he accepted the result. In 1973 he became a delegate to the Council of Europe and served on the European Assembly from 1975 to 1979. 'My first speech in the European Assembly was concerned with defending the concept of national interests.' (Hansard, col. 1754, 23 February 1978.)

Callaghan felt that Britain needed a powerful advocate, such as Prescott. Jenkins stayed on as President of the European Commission until 1981, when he returned to form the SDP with the other members of Labour's 'gang of four'.

Shore, then a Cabinet minister, had made Prescott his PPS on the strength of his Euro-scepticism and his effectiveness in arguing his case in Europe, where he was far better known than in Westminster. But no area of policy better illustrated Prescott's willingness to accept democratic decisions, and compromise when necessary, than Europe. 'The political reality in my view is that the electorate will not be given the chance to vote in another referendum on the issue, nor if they were, would they vote to come out.'

It has set him apart from some of his more uncompromising left-wing friends, such as Dennis Skinner. The rejection of Skinner's brand of protest socialism began over Europe. They had rows over the subject, when Prescott decided, following a vote by the parliamentary Labour Party, to join a delegation of Labour MPs to the Council of Europe. In the year he campaigned with Peter Shore to pull Britain out of the Common Market, Prescott joined the delegation of twelve MPs and six peers to the European Parliament in Strasbourg. There were others in the delegation who had voted against British membership of the EEC, including Gwyneth Dunwoody and John Evans. The group included Betty Boothroyd and Lord Castle, husband of Barbara Castle, then Secretary of State for Social Services. Lord George-Brown, the former Foreign Secretary, wanted to be in the group in 1975, but was vetoed by Wilson. The following year, Prescott became its leader, when he succeeded Michael Stewart, another former Foreign Secretary.

Some fell to the gourmand's temptations of Strasbourg and Luxembourg. Willie Hamilton, another member of the group, said, 'By our standards, the expenses and allowances in Europe were in the nature of a very full pig trough. The food and drink were excellent, and the Parliamentary proceedings at Strasbourg and Luxembourg were terminated every evening at an early hour to ensure that the "good life" could be enjoyed to the full. In addition, there were trips to all parts of the globe, and expenses were so generous that members could afford, and were allowed, to take their spouses with them.'

It went against the grain for Prescott to be sharing in such undoubted luxuries. At Westminster, he had been one of the early advocates of the register of members' interests and had argued in favour of MPs being barred from making earnings outside Parliament. In December 1974, he took up the issue of a ban on outside earnings in a letter to Harold Wilson, then Prime Minister, following the John Stonehouse affair. Wilson gave him the brush-off, arguing it would be best to accept the conclusions of a select committee which had just proposed the register, 'before considering whether or not there is a need for any further move'. Wilson said the register would give MPs in future the 'opportunity to forestall unjustified criticism'. That was not Prescott's view. He put forward his own motion on the declaration of members' interests to the parliamentary Labour Party, calling for all forms of outside interest and income to be registered, and fully disclosed, in addition to unearned income and all gifts over £10. He had campaigned on the slogan 'One man, one job', a view he holds today. In July 1996, he was not present for the controversial vote to increase members' salaries by 26 per cent – he had broken a bone in his ankle, and a plaster cast on his right leg was being removed on the day of the vote – but like many

MPs he was torn between demanding the right rate for the job and avoiding being branded a 'fat cat' MP. Although Blair supported Major's call for pay restraint, by voting for 3 per cent, Prescott privately took the view that MPs should be paid more, provided they moved to end their outside earnings.

While others may have enjoyed the Euro gravy train, ministers and observers noted that Prescott was in the engine, hard at work. Guy de Jonquieres, the Common Market correspondent of the *Financial Times*, reported: 'Far from working to undermine the European Parliament, Mr Prescott is often to be heard haranguing his colleagues for failing to take their responsibilities seriously enough. His brusque and impatient manner has set some people's teeth on edge, but he has won respect as an aggressive debater and a shrewd tactician who clearly delights in taxing EEC Commissioners and ministers with awkward questions.'

David Owen, the Labour Foreign Secretary, was also impressed with the diligence of the anti-EEC MP in his European duties. 'Some on the Left, like John Prescott, were developing as European socialists and becoming adept at handling the politics of the European Parliament.' Roy Jenkins, who resigned the deputy leadership of the Labour Party and later became the President of the European Commission, was on the receiving end. He ruefully recorded Prescott's name in his diary like a bout of bad indigestion:

> *Commission, followed by a Socialist lunch at the Parc-Savoy, which is almost my least favourite of the grand Brussels*

> *restaurants and an extraordinary lavish place to be chosen by the Federation of European Socialist Parties. They had disinterred old Sicco Mansholt* [Dutch commissioner] *to preside and had about five or six others, Fellermaier, Prescott etc. The object was to launch a considerable attack on the Socialist Commissioners, but particularly upon me, for not being more political in the worst sense of the word, i.e. that we didn't run the Commission on a more party-political basis, that we didn't have more purely party votes, that we didn't devote ourselves enough to doing down the dirty Christian Democrats, Liberals etc.*

David Marquand noted: 'Two former anti-marketeers – Lord Bruce of Donington and John Prescott, the leader of the Labour Group – played leading parts in the work of the Parliament, of a remarkably constructive kind.' Marquand argued strongly for a directly elected Parliament; Prescott saw it was inevitable, and, after opposing it, was won round to supporting direct elections, provided the powers of the European Parliament were circumscribed.

One of the attractions for Prescott – apart from those listed above – was the recognition that issues affecting his union, such as safety at sea, and his constituency were often supra-national, and open to European law. It is a strategy he has followed in Europe ever since. The dichotomy is that while Prescott remains deeply sceptical of European federalism and monetary union, he has fostered links with the European socialist group and European unions to advance Europe-wide protection for workers, including the Social Chapter, on which Britain had an opt-out.

One such issue was the Cod War. Prescott infuriated Roy Hattersley, the Foreign Minister in charge of the negotiations, when he intervened. 'While Foreign Minister Roy Hattersley was talking tough, he flew to Iceland to seek a compromise.'

In February 1976, Prescott flew to Iceland to negotiate a way out of the gunboat 'war' which was threatening to lead to bloodshed over the unilateral declaration by the Icelandic government of a 200-mile exclusion zone from its fishing grounds. To an MP representing a fishing port, which stood to lose jobs as a result of the Icelandic action, talk of a compromise was dangerous stuff. 'I'm afraid that if this goes on much longer, some of my constituents may get killed in this dance of death.'

He was going with a great deal of goodwill on the Icelandic side. They had invited him on several occasions before, but he had never accepted. 'I feel the time has come to really find out what the strength of their case is. These are circumstances in which all politicians should at least try to make the effort of talking directly to people who are involved in both sides of this dispute.'

The British government's stance was uncompromising. The Icelanders had no legal basis for their unilateral action, and would be stopped by force if necessary from attacking British trawlers. The stand-off was so serious that Dr Joseph Luns, the NATO Secretary General, was invited into talks with James Callaghan, then Foreign Secretary; Fred Peart, Minister for Agriculture, Fisheries and Food; and Hattersley, to find a settlement to the diplomatic crisis.

Meanwhile, Prescott was conducting his own diplomatic mission. After more talks, Prescott returned to London with what he believed was a deal, which would enable his trawlermen in Hull to carry on fishing in the disputed zone, albeit for a reduced catch. In Prescott's view, something was better than nothing. He was called to a meeting with Hattersley. Instead of the pat on the back, he was handed a copy of a signal which had been wired to key diplomatic posts around the world from the Foreign Office 'immediate Oslo, Reykjavik, Washington, saving to all other Nato posts, Stockholm'.

It was signed by Callaghan and was marked confidential. It was sent cipher category A and by diplomatic bag.

> *Icelandic Fisheries: rumoured intervention by Mr John Prescott MP*
>
> *1. The US Ambassador to Iceland told Young (Reykjavik) on 16 March that Agustsson had been informed that John Prescott MP was empowered by me to reach an agreement with Iceland if he found himself able to do so. (Agustsson told the US Ambassador that Prescott had recently spoken in this sense to a member of the Icelandic MFA in London.) Agustsson had passed on to the US Ambassador a formula providing for a measure of continued British fishing off Iceland that Prescott had allegedly given to his Icelandic contact.*
>
> *2. According to the Norwegian Ambassador to Iceland (speaking subsequently to the US Ambassador) Hallgrimsson told him the Icelandic Cabinet had been discussing the Frydenlund*

initiative when news of Prescott's approach arrived. The Icelandic Cabinet had therefore deferred further discussion of the Frydenlund initiative in the belief that HMG were about to make a more precise offer through Prescott.

3. *There is no truth in the story that Prescott has authority to act on my behalf. We still await an Icelandic response to the Frydenlund Initiative (My Tel 53). Please make this clear to Frydenlund with the request that the Norwegian Ambassador in Reykjavik should pass this on to Hallgrimsson. But please do not tell Frydenlund of the US Ambassador's initiative.*
4. *Reykjavik please tell Martin (American Embassy) that there is no truth in the Prescott story.*

Details of this had never been published before.

It was an odd reversal of roles: Prescott, the pugilist and a Euro-sceptic, negotiating for peace; while the pro-European Hattersley, urbane and reasonable, lampooned as 'hot lunch' – after advocating hot lunches for schoolchildren – was ready to fight for British jobs. In the many testy exchanges that followed in the Commons over the exclusion zone and the Common Fisheries Policy, it became clear why this had happened. Hattersley believed he was upholding the rule of law. The Euro-sceptic leader of the Labour Group in Europe was up to something quite different. He once said, in a different context (trade union law), that he believed there were some circumstances in which you could break the law. This was one. Prescott believed the Icelanders were right to insist on an exclusion zone and he believed the answer was for Britain to declare its own 200-mile exclusion zone to keep out European fishery fleets.

'The insane policy on which we seem to be embarking is putting at risk the lives of men on our trawlers and that we are bound to reverse that policy when we renegotiate the fishing policy of the EEC. To that extent would it not be better to concede Iceland's case, seek an opportunity to ask for exclusive fishing rights with the EEC, and "do an Iceland" on the EEC? Would not the situation be better served by our calling together all the EEC ministers together with those of Norway and Iceland to discuss conservation and exploitation within the 200-mile limit that we shall adopt next year?'

As a pro-European, Hattersley found Prescott's proposals unacceptable. The Cod War was settled when Tony Crosland took over from Callaghan as Foreign Secretary and adopted an inferior version of Prescott's plan. But Britain never 'did an Iceland' on Europe. In retrospect, Prescott had a good Cod War. The British government did not. There could have been no more powerful reason for Callaghan's wanting to appoint the 'Mouth of the Humber' to speak up for Britain than that. Prescott, after turning down Callaghan's offer, and abandoning his role in Europe for the hard slog in opposition under Thatcher, never dropped his Euro-scepticism, but adapted – his critics say compromised – to change. This led to his apparently having faced both ways at times: he had opposed the Channel Tunnel and on 8 November 1973 had warned in the Commons that it would not be economically viable. Yet once it was built he campaigned for the fast rail link to the tunnel. He had been against a directly elected

Parliament in principle, but was the first to advocate it to act as a counterweight to the Brussels bureaucracy. When the idea was taken up by Owen, Prescott had voted against the legislation to put it into effect (he was in good company – also voting against direct elections were Margaret Beckett, Michael Meacher, Ann Taylor and Robin Cook along with six Labour Cabinet ministers). In 1983, he joined Bryan Gould and Stuart Holland in urging the party to fight wholeheartedly for the direct European elections in spite of continuing party opposition on a socialist agenda, including opposition to the European Monetary System, reform of the Common Agricultural Policy to allow in New Zealand lamb and butter (New Zealander Gould's reason for resigning as Peter Shore's PPS after Prescott), and Keynesian reflation through monetary cooperation.

There was another irony in Prescott's clashes with Hattersley, which would end in the deputy leadership contest in 1988. Hattersley, the grammar school boy, was just as committed to his region as Prescott, if not more so, having been born there, as he often reminded his readers. Hattersley's *Goodbye to Yorkshire* was a beautifully crafted elegy, as romantic as a Hovis ad, to a disappearing Yorkshire of his youth, including the fishing industry at Hull. Hattersley was only six years Prescott's senior, but had studied at Hull University fifteen years before him – like Prescott he gained a BSc economics degree; he knew the town well. It was a fighter's town; it was a Roundhead capital in the Civil War; the town where Wilberforce, the anti-slavery campaigner, had been the MP. But above all it was a seafarer's town. Brought up in the hills around Sheffield, the blue-scarved student Hattersley was shocked by the flatness of Hull. It was the 'place where England ended ... after this, there could only be sea.' Hull was the docks, and it lived on fishing. 'When the wind blew north, the smell of the Fish Dock would swirl through the backyard and into the kitchen. Suddenly I understood that Hull was about the sea not the land. It was there because, in an earlier age, the ocean had been its benefactor. By 1955 the tide had gone out.'

Those words were written about the same time as Hattersley was fighting the Cod War for Britain. Prescott had hoped to be in ministerial office if Callaghan had won in 1979. In opposition, he was made second in command to Albert Booth, the shadow Transport Secretary, who later became the head of the South Yorkshire bus fleet. They had a young researcher called Peter Mandelson, who soon left to sharpen his career in television. After the election of Michael Foot as leader, Prescott was given a new role, as spokesman for the regions, and threw his heart and soul into producing the first comprehensive policy for regional government, which was to be the bedrock of his strategy for the next fifteen years.

'Alternative Regional Strategy – A Framework for Discussion' was a brilliantly lucid exposition. The drive was Prescott's; the clarity was supplied by his assistant, Dave Taylor. It criticised the failures of the party to give regional planning higher priority in the past; called for decentralised economic planning; and targeted the crisis of unemployment which Labour insisted – and the government denied – had been deepened by Tory policies. Prescott and his deputy, Tom Pendry, had gone on an exhaustive rural ride of Britain, drawing on local government expertise, and unplugging a well of academic interest.

Pendry was so worried about the non-stop regime that he warned Pauline that Prescott would kill himself with work, if he did not slow down. He did what he could to reduce the pressure on Prescott by acting as his unofficial driver. But the format was set for his later policy papers, and the team included David Blunkett, then leader of Sheffield City Council. At the heart of the matter was the clash of ideology between the Thatcherite economics and Prescott's style of planned intervention.

There was a wider acceptance that 'something must be done' after inner-city rioting in 1981, which shocked the Cabinet. Michael Heseltine, then Environment Secretary, after an emotional trip to Toxteth, Liverpool, became personally committed to bringing enterprise to the cities. But Prescott had a different agenda. In place of quangos, Prescott believed in handing down power to the people through regional assemblies; his paper admitted they could help to balance the power for the regions of England in a Labour Cabinet against the domination of Scotland and Wales – and London. 'British life is dominated by London and the South East region. London is the centre of industry, commerce, culture and government. Inextricably related to this is its less readily admitted position as the centre of the country's status system.'

As the party of the underdog, he said, Labour had become the party of the underprivileged regions. Without the vote of the north of England, Scotland and Wales, it would never regain power. But the system of government – Whitehall and

Westminster – was 'pervaded with metropolitan values'. The perception that the 1981 recession hit particularly hard in traditional smokestack industries was not borne out by the figures in the appendix to the report – they showed that while unemployment in Yorkshire and Humberside had risen by 117 per cent in two years since the Tories had come to power, it had risen by 136 per cent in London and 131 per cent in the south-east generally; in fact, the worst hit was the West Midlands with a rise of 173 per cent.

'Planning means you look at industries and ask yourself what assistance you can give to them,' he said in 1986. One searing experience had been the closure of Imperial Typewriters in his constituency by an American multinational in the early 1970s. Prescott felt impotent as the women workers took over the factory for three months and produced an alternative plan.

'The multinational just laughed,' said Prescott. 'We said to them: we have the plans, we have the skills, what the hell do we want you for? They said: we have the market. A Labour government must say to these multinationals: no, you don't have the market because we have a countervailing power. How we use public expenditure, how we effect price controls, how we effect planned market systems, even import and quantity controls; all have an influence.'

Experience in Europe had also shown him the value of regions, such as the German *Länder*, in winning Euro-cash. 'We are the only major country in Europe without a proper regional government structure. This puts our regions at a disadvantage in making effective use of European money. Too much is spent on Whitehall's priorities; too little on those of the regions.'

He proposed regional assemblies 'with real power and resources' and a 'senior minister' for the regions. Prescott appointed an independent commission under Bruce Millan to report on devolution. As it reported in May 1996, and Jack Straw polished Labour's own policy, Prescott was put in the frame to become 'governor of the regions', equivalent to Secretary of State for Scotland and Wales. It was seen as one way of enabling Prescott to push his goal for full employment, which was to be the theme of his next great paper, and his third and successful campaign for the deputy leadership. But that would also require agreement on the economic strategy with the then shadow Chancellor, Gordon Brown, and that was far from clear.

CHAPTER TEN

The Odd Couple

Pauline called us the Odd Couple.
Dennis Skinner.

When Prescott arrived at the Commons in the aftermath of Labour's general election defeat on 18 June 1970, he met another 'new boy' with a reputation for causing trouble – Dennis Skinner, the mining MP for Bolsover. It was not surprising that the two firebrands from the NUS and the NUM became close friends.

The Skinners were in the front line of the class war in Derbyshire. Dennis had been a local councillor, leader of the Derbyshire miners' union, and his brother was a ringleader in the rebel Labour council at Clay Cross, also in Derbyshire.

Dennis Skinner had been a miner from 1949 to 1970, when he became an MP. Built like a miner's whippet, he was an accomplished cricketer and footballer, and might have made the grade in soccer if politics had not intervened. His natural position was as a striker.

Dennis Skinner was also very bright. He was six years older than Prescott and, after Tupton Hall Grammar School, had –

like Prescott – studied at Ruskin College, Oxford, where, he jokingly says, he 'read tennis'. Skinner became a strong tennis player on the courts at Oxford, and passed on his passion for the sport to his son, a county class player.

Skinner had been an MP for some time, living in digs at King's Cross, when a demolition order on the house made him look for alternative rooms. Prescott suggested they could share a flat at the NUS headquarters in Old Clapham.

It had three main rooms and was situated over the garages at the back of the Georgian town house which the NUS had turned into offices. It had been a grace and favour flat for an ambassador to Chile, but under the new regime at the NUS, under Jim Slater, the union gave first refusal to its first sponsored MP at a market rent.

Prescott and Skinner had separate bedrooms, and shared a living room with a television, a bathroom and a kitchen; they shared the rent, and returned to the flat after the Commons at night for nearly 20 years. But, from the beginning, Prescott took a different path from Skinner. Within twelve months of entering the Commons, he became a junior trade spokesman on marine affairs under Roy Mason, the shadow Trade and Industry Secretary.

They were also quite different characters, socially. 'Pauline called us the Odd Couple,' recalls Skinner.

Skinner liked to watch sport on television. Prescott would want the television switched off, unless there was boxing or a current-affairs programme to watch. 'He would come in and I would be watching Jimmy White [the snooker player].

Sometimes he would watch, but he always wanted to switch over to *Newsnight*.'

Prescott would be up at the crack of dawn the next morning, and off to his office.

Sometimes Skinner would hitch a lift in Prescott's Jaguar, but at night they would go their separate ways, Prescott sometimes winding down after the Commons at Ronnie Scott's with other friends, including Tom Pendry.

Skinner refused to engage in the convention of 'pairing' with a Tory MP to enable him or her to miss votes if other engagements intervened, and stayed until the House rose each evening. In the early 1980s it was regularly long after midnight before the police would shout, 'Who goes home' at the closing of the day's business.

Prescott by the mid-1970s had paired with the Tory MP for Harrow East, Hugh Dykes, an ardent pro-European, who remained his parliamentary 'pair' until 1997 when Dykes left Parliament after crossing the floor to join the Liberal Democrats. He is now a Lib Dem peer. Dykes and Prescott got to know each other as members of the opposing delegations to Europe. They exchanged insults across the chamber.

'He used to call me the Bookies' Runner from Harrow. I used to call him the Fisherman's Friend from Hull,' recalls Dykes.

Some parliamentary pairs become close friends, in spite of their politics, but Prescott has never befriended any Tories, including Dykes. 'He still thinks I'm a wicked Tory. But he sends me a Christmas card.'

Dykes, a Heathite, was so passionate in his support for

Europe that he was regarded as a 'Federast' by the Tory Euro-sceptics and he was far more enthusiastic than Prescott. Prescott opposed Britain's entry to the Common Market in 1971, but his early hostility to Europe mellowed into constructive use of its institutions, particularly its help for the regions, something which he had worked hard for within the Labour Party.

Europe became the biggest political dividing line between the Odd Couple. Skinner argued that it was wrong for Prescott to compromise his views by accepting a post on the Labour delegation from the Commons to the (then putative) European Parliament.

It was a post approved by the PLP and Prescott went as a Labour Euro-sceptic, but it was against Skinner's puritan principles to compromise. He would have nothing to do with Europe, and they had rows about Prescott's constructive engagement in European politics.

That marked the sharpest difference between the two men. But they were close friends, and Skinner gently tried to advise Prescott on how to improve his speeches in the Commons. 'I often used to say speeches have got to be totally political in that place,' said Skinner. 'It's not a court of law. You do as you like. In that zoo-like atmosphere, you have to be political …

'He hated the Chamber.'

Skinner was portrayed at Westminster as the 'wild man' of the working class, and the 'Beast of Bolsover'; he could have become a major player like Prescott in the development of Labour's thinking, but Skinner was a recidivist rebel, and refused to accept the discipline of any front-bench responsibility. After building up support in the unions and the constituency parties, he got elected to the Labour Party's ruling National Executive Committee, and acted as a thorn in the side of Neil Kinnock – a role he later played with Tony Blair – but he remained wedded to the Labour backbench.

Skinner has made his position his own, in the first seat below the gangway. From that seat, he has raised heckling from a sedentary exercise to an art form. His interventions have gone into the history books, and radio broadcasting of Parliament has earned him fan mail from across the world, including the United States. He gives the impression of being the court jester, but his act is carefully thought out, and his interventions have at times brilliantly captured the moment. The flash of Skinner's wit has also, at times, brought out flashes of brilliance in his victims: during Margaret Thatcher's valedictory speech in the Commons, after she had been knifed by her Cabinet, Skinner suggested that she might like to be president of the European bank; she liked that. There was a grudging respect between the two.

Skinner would not compromise even in his style of dress. Prescott had picked up the habit of dressing smartly in his Hollywood Waiter days, and adopted a suit when he first came to the Commons. Photographs of his first day at the House show him smartly dressed, with neatly pressed trousers. The suit looked new. Skinner still wears a tweedy sports jacket, and is never seen in a suit. 'There's always been a struggle with Dennis between the priest and the politician,' said one of Prescott's friends.

From Prescott's view, purity without power was pointless. It relegated the backbench role to little more than showmanship.

One analysis of the voting record of MPs in the 1970s, which Skinner can still quote from memory, showed that he had voted against the Labour government on 156 occasions, more than any other MP. Kinnock, the rising star of the left, had voted against the government a mere 72 times. Prescott was not in that league as a dissenter. One of the reasons was that, from 1974 to 1976, he was a parliamentary Private Secretary to Peter Shore, the Trade Secretary, in the Wilson government. For two years, he had the of job acting as 'eyes and ears' to Shore, and gave it up when he became leader of the Labour Group in Europe; Shore then added to Prescott as his PPS with another left-wing anti-Market Labour MP, Bryan Gould. Shore was one of the leading intellectuals of the left, and an ardent anti-European, who picked Prescott because of his performance in Europe. It was unpaid but his job as a PPS put Prescott officially on the payroll vote of the Wilson government.

It could be said that, while Skinner and Kinnock were rebelling, Prescott was in effect carrying Shore's 'bags' – one of the routine tasks of being a PPS is to carry the red boxes for secretaries of state – but it gave Prescott a first-hand insight into the workings of the Cabinet and the government, sitting in on meetings of departmental ministers with Shore, and it tested his loyalty to the leadership.

Gould confirmed to me that voting against the government was a sacking offence – he was forced to resign as Shore's PPS by James Callaghan after voting against the Labour government over 20 per cent tax on imported food, including New Zealand lamb. Shore, then Environment Secretary, registered his protest at the sacking by never appointing another PPS until the Callaghan government fell in 1979.

It caused tensions in the flat, and within Prescott himself, as Prescott the Class Warrior fought with Prescott the Party Loyalist. 'Like a lot of people,' says Skinner, 'he decided to climb the ladder. Every so often this tormented soul would say, "I am going to pack it all in." He was always threatening that. It happened about once every six months.'

Skinner saw the struggle continuing inside Prescott as he rose from the backbenches.

'It was as if there was a schism within him. He wanted to be the class warrior, and then he was meeting these people he felt were intellectually superior: Kinnock, Smith, Blair ...'

Prescott found it hard to relax, and seemed to his flatmate to be constantly on the telephone to trade union contacts or journalists.

They also argued about Prescott's lifestyle. Asked about being middle-class on *Breakfast with Frost*, Prescott said, 'It was an argument I had with Dennis Skinner some years ago.'

Kinnock felt he could have had more support from Prescott when the Labour leader was engaged in trench warfare against the left-wing Militant Tendency. Prescott's friends say that Prescott was never sectarian about the party; he would not easily exchange pleasantries with Tories, but for his own party he was never keen on expulsions (until the Militant Coventry MP Dave Nellist admitted to Labour's National Executive Committee that Militant was a party within a party, and that was in 1992). In 1989, Prescott told the *Independent*: 'We seem to have given the impression that the activists are somehow anti-

Labour. But our future lies in building on the activist base.'

Kinnock could have used Prescott's weight with the left in his battles with Militant. At the 1985 Labour conference in Bournemouth, Kinnock delivered his famous, coruscating attack on the Militant leaders of Liverpool City Council for the 'the grotesque chaos of a Labour council – a Labour council – hiring taxis to travel around a city handing out redundancy notices to its own workers'. Kinnock spat the words at Derek Hatton, sitting fuming in the audience, while Eric Heffer, a blustering, soft-hearted left-winger with a Liverpool seat, stormed off the platform in protest. Kinnock knew he was trampling on big egos.

Heffer's antics were lampooned in the *Guardian* 'Pocket Cartoon' the next day. It depicted a man in a bookshop selecting 'Short walks by E. Heffer'. The same day, the cartoonist, Bryan McAlister, had a telephone call from someone wanting to buy the original. It was Heffer.

There were few bigger egos to deal with than that of Arthur Scargill, the NUM president, whom Kinnock had likened to a World War I general – a donkey leading lions to their fate on the barbed wire of their picket lines.

Kinnock wanted to support the miners and their families, but equivocated his support for fear that it would be seen to be endorsing the tactics of Scargill, which included bloody confrontation with the police and 'scab' workers on the picket lines. Kinnock's own Welsh miners were the first to go back, proudly with brass bands playing at the head of a march. But Prescott in Hull was close to the seat of Scargill's kingdom, South Yorkshire.

At the height of the miners' strike, Prescott went to an NUM rally in Sheffield city hall. It was like the old days on the pier head with the NUS. He threw his prepared text away and delivered a thumping message of solidarity from the heart, which had the miners cheering for more; it went far beyond the authorised Kinnock line on the strike, but for Prescott that did not matter. The event was recorded by the NUM on video, and copies still exist. It clearly captures the emotion of the moment.

The rally was held on 8 November 1984, when the miners had been out on strike for eight months, and Tony Blair had been an MP for just ten more.

There were about two thousand miners and their wives packed into the main hall, shouting and chanting 'here we go, here we go' like the kop at Hillsborough, and a further three thousand spread across two overspill halls. Miners filled seats, aisles and every available piece of floor space in every corner of the city hall, including two balconies. On the platform were local Labour MPs, including Flannery, Maynard, Cryer, Caborn and Skinner. Seated at a long trestle table on the platform were the NUM executive, led by Scargill, who was to be the star turn, and for the Labour Party, Stan Orme, the energy spokesman; Jim Mortimer, party General Secretary; and Prescott, the employment spokesman. The speeches were interspersed with more chanting: 'Arthur Scargill – we'll support you ever more' and 'The miners, united, will never be defeated'.

The defiant mood was infectious, but it is heartrending to see it now. They were the cannon fodder for the two generals – Scargill and Nigel Lawson. Their pits have been closed, and their communities devastated. With the benefit of hindsight, they had little chance of winning, without the all-out mass strike that Scargill wanted.

Lawson describes how, as Energy Secretary, he called in Scargill for talks. When Scargill left his office, Lawson told officials there was no way he could do business with the president-elect of the NUM. He prepared for confrontation.

The so-called Ridley plan for resisting a miners' strike had been drawn up by Nicholas Ridley for Margaret Thatcher in 1978 while she was still leader of the opposition. Thatcher ordered a climbdown when David Howell, then Energy Secretary, was confronted with a strike in 1981, and it finished his ministerial career with Thatcher. Lawson knew there would be another challenge, and had been secretly planning for a strike since 1982, according to Lawson's memoirs. Thatcher and Lawson were determined to avoid the humiliation suffered by Heath at the hands of the miners in 1974, when he lost the election on the issue 'Who governs Britain?' There would be no three-day week under Thatcher.

Lawson spent two years preparing for a strike, and he did so with the meticulous eye for detail of a general planning for war. The imperative was to get stocks of coal into the electricity stations to survive a strike; he set about secretly arranging for that to be done. There were also secret plans to airlift by helicopter the chemicals needed for electricity generation. Jim Prior, Employment Secretary, and last of the wets, warned it would look provocative; Lawson said it would show the miners they could not win.

As part of the preparations, Lawson sacked a Labour-appointed chairman of the CEGB and appointed Walter Marshall in his place, because he knew the scientist would be committed to keeping the power stations open. He considered appointing Roy Mason, the former Labour Cabinet minister, as chairman of the National Coal Board but opted for Ian MacGregor, the chairman of nationalised British Steel, to fight Scargill in a strike. Scargill called a strike ballot in 1982. 'At that time we were still not adequately prepared for a strike,' Lawson recalls. On the eve of the ballot, Joe Gormley, the outgoing NUM president, was 'prevailed upon' to urge the miners to reject the strike in an article for the *Daily Express*. 'I later persuaded Margaret to offer Gormley a peerage ...'

Then Lawson waited. Thatcher persuaded Peter Walker to take over as Energy Secretary when she made Lawson her Chancellor. Walker claims credit for the victory over the miners in his own memoirs, but the plans for trench warfare had been laid before he arrived. His role was in winning the propaganda war.

The strike started in March 1984 and lasted almost exactly a year. Lawson was surprised – not that a strike occurred, but that Scargill was so inept to start it in the spring, when the warm weather would make it easier to keep sufficient coal stocks at the power stations. Scargill kept reporting there were only weeks of coal supplies left, and the government would not last out the winter. In fact, there was a year's supply and in the end enough to run for two years.

The ostensible reason for the strike was the need to close loss-making pits which were costing the taxpayer £1 billion a year.

In his profit and loss account of the strike after it was over, Lawson calculated it had cost around £2 billion in higher public spending and nearly £3 billion in higher borrowing; GDP growth had dropped; industrial production had been brought to a standstill; the balance of payments had worsened; unemployment was exacerbated; it had caused a sharp increase in interest rates; the pound had fallen sharply; and it had damaged Britain's image abroad. On the plus side, the government had won.

'These one-off costs did not in any way colour my attitude towards the strike. It was essential that the Government spent whatever was necessary to defeat Arthur Scargill.'

Opening the Sheffield rally – one of a series across Britain – Mick McGahey, the president of the Scottish NUM and a former chairman of the Communist Party of Great Britain, was given a rapturous reception. 'This series of rallies is not some pep pill for miners. It is a reaffirmation of our position – we are out, we are staying out. We have come too far. We are not turning back …'

They cheered ecstatically.

And he told Kinnock, 'Get your eyes off the opinion polls in the *Mirror* and the *Sun* – come and meet your opinion-moulders.'

In the demonology of the miners, scabs were at the top of the list, but Kinnock could not have been far behind. They hated his equivocation. He equivocated because he could not support Scargill, who had failed to get a ballot for the strike. Every mention of Kinnock's name was booed.

Prescott, who followed McGahey to the rostrum, carefully distanced himself from the Labour leadership. Instead, the shadow Employment Secretary offered the solidarity of the National Union of Seamen, to which he passionately belonged. He was introduced as 'a friend of workers'.

Prescott said, 'The thing you didn't say is that my most famous claim is that I share a flat with Dennis Skinner, and we're known as the Odd Couple …' As the cheering died down, he added, 'Trust a politician who knows how to get a cheer.

'I am here to make it absolutely clear I give my fullest support to the miners' struggle in this particular strike.

'I give it – how could I [do anything] else? – from a mining family in Wales. But I also give it as a seaman for ten years.'

He spoke of the seamen's struggle, 'which was unofficial and illegal. It was illegal because it was illegal for seamen to strike. We broke the law to strike to change the laws.

'As a seaman, I want to say to this multitude today … we were grateful for the support you gave us in 1966 when we were attacked as the "politically motivated men", when Harold Wilson and the Labour government savaged us for going on strike to improve our conditions.'

He made it clear he believed it was right – in spite of the Tory trade union laws banning sympathy action – that trade unions needed to back up the miners.

But underneath the rally-rousing rhetoric, Prescott expressed a real anxiety in the Labour Party that the strike could split the Labour movement. Above all, he wanted loyalty to the party.

'Let's be clear. I am in Parliament because the seamen found the laws worked against them. We knew the Labour Party could change those laws ... Whatever the stresses and strains in this movement, don't let's forget, you need a political arm, as well as an industrial arm.'

Prescott came to share Kinnock's contempt for Scargill's tactics, believing that the strike could have been settled without inflicting more pain on the miners and their families. But he failed to conceal his feeling that Labour should have done more to support the miners in their struggle. In December 1984, the shadow Employment Secretary walked out of a press gallery luncheon – in full view of lobby journalists – in protest at a speech by Leon Brittan, the Home Secretary. 'I was not prepared to sit there and listen to a declaration of war on what these people call the "enemy within".'

Prescott, who had always supported ballots in the NUS, believed Scargill should have had a ballot of his men much earlier, and accepted the outcome. But he felt that by distancing Labour from the strike, as it dragged on in the coalfields, Kinnock was cutting off the party from its own people, as he was in danger of doing over Militant.

'It was the same with the activists on the picket lines in the trade unions. We appeared to look as if we'd distanced ourselves from them. Sometimes they're right, sometimes they're wrong. But we do have a connection between us. They are part of our movement.'

The parting of the ways for the Odd Couple came in May 1988 when Mr Justice Michael Davies in the High Court ordered the sequestration of the £2.8 million assets of the National Union of Seamen and imposed a fine of £150,000 over a strike at Dover.

After the judgement on 3 May, *The Times* reported: 'Last night one of the team of four sequestrators from the firm of chartered accountants Spicer and Oppenheim, Mr Roger Powderill, arrived at the union's main asset, its Maritime House headquarters in south London.

'Tenants, including Labour MPs John Prescott and Mr Dennis Skinner, who rent £18 a week flats in the building, overlooking Clapham Common, could be evicted.'

Little knowing what her action would portend for the Odd Couple, Margaret Thatcher, in the Commons, said she would uphold the right of strike-breaking seamen to go to work. 'Everyone has a right to go to their place of work without hindrance.'

In spite of attempts by Sam McCluskie, the NUS general secretary, to purge the union's contempt for allegedly allowing the Dover strike to continue, the fines went up to £300,000 and the dispute escalated. There were old memories of the 1966 seamen's strike, of ports standing idle, of the miners' strike, and a direct challenge to Thatcher's authority.

Prescott went on union protest rallies, including NUS picket lines at Dover. He was good at the impromptu speeches to mass meetings, but was clearly choosy about the company he kept and the issues on which he protested – Skinner does not recall seeing him on any of their CND marches, for example.

At a May Day rally, the day before the court action, Arthur Scargill, defeated but unbowed, said the seamen and the trade union movement should tell the courts and Thatcher to 'get stuffed'.

From the same platform, Prescott attacked Thatcher for claiming the unions were the enemy within, and in doing so touched on the old sore nagging away at him – his secondary school education. 'It was not trade unionists educated in secondary modern schools but people from the Establishment educated in public schools that were the traitors in our midst.'

But, as the strike dragged on for six months, Mr Justice Michael Davies increased the fines, the union leaders dissociated themselves from the strike, and it became clear this was not going to be a rerun of the miners' strike or 1966. The power of the courts, and Mr Justice Michael Davies, began to look excessive.

The judge even managed to upset the police, after rebuking a local Kent police chief for appearing to sanction the mass picketing in a BBC interview. The Police Federation came to the support of the superintendent against the judge. By mid-July, Prescott was in the midst of his own campaign for the deputy leadership of the Labour Party. He went with Skinner to Dover docks where they joined the pickets to denounce the judge for ruling that the mass picket was unlawful.

'The judge is wrong and we want to make that clear to him today,' said Prescott. The government had turned 'our courts into employer courts which offer no support to the individual employee and every support to the employer'. He told cheering demonstrators that it was time to take a stand.

The strike marked the high-water mark of the courts' use of the Thatcherite legislation against the unions. By the time it had ended, sympathy had shifted away from courts, sequestration orders and judges to settle disputes.

But life for the Odd Couple would never be the same again. Skinner had moved out of the NUS flat, insisting that he would not pay rent to 'Thatcher's sequestrator', and refused to return.

They remained firm friends, however. Skinner backed Prescott to the hilt when Prescott clashed with Kinnock over the style of the deputy leadership role that year, but voted for Heffer, a fellow member of the Campaign Group, in 1988, when Prescott made his first challenge for the job no one really wanted.

Prescott, as deputy leader, still believed Skinner was a vital voice in the Labour Party, reminding the Labour leadership of its responsibilities to its rank-and-file members. He may seem at times like grit in the eye of the leadership; Prescott saw Skinner as the grit in the oyster.

CHAPTER ELEVEN

Jobs

Jobs, jobs, jobs.
Neil Kinnock.

Easter 1985. Neil Kinnock launched Labour's 'spring offensive' as part of Labour's 'jobs and industry campaign'. It was to be the forerunner of Labour's showbiz campaigns. It had its own flashy logo, souvenir mugs, a souvenir toothbrush and balloons. And it had lots of razzmatazz.

The jobs and industry campaign featured a Labour-supporting folk-singer with an urban attitude called Billy Bragg. And Prescott's allies recall it was all BM – before Mandelson, the party's communications brainchild, arrived.

Bragg had the street cred to plug into 'yoof' culture. Bragg headlined a Jobs for Youth rock tour; there was a national poster competition on the same theme, a Jobs Festival, a Jobs Roadshow in key marginal constituencies, and an 'On Yer Bike' rally – a theme taken from Norman Tebbit's advice to the unemployed to follow his father who 'got on his bike' and went to look for work.

It was to be a test bed for Labour's ground-breaking 1987 general election campaign, culminating in Hugh (*Chariots of*

Fire) Hudson's party election broadcast on the Labour leader, which became known at Westminster as 'Kinnock – The Movie'.

The jobs and industry campaign, which ran from 1985 up to the general election, was born of Neil Kinnock's commitment that Labour would tackle mass unemployment. Labour strategists also believed that it was one of the key areas where the Thatcher government was vulnerable.

Unemployment had soared to over three million, and Prescott, Labour's shadow Employment Secretary, greeted every month's rise in the figures by accusing the Tories of fiddling the totals.

One of the campaign documents, 'Working Together for Britain', focused on the despair of the young, personified by the character Yosser Hughes in the TV series *Boys from the Blackstuff*. The litany of six wasted years was printed with an illustration of two unemployed teenagers and Yosser's slogan: 'Gizza job'.

Kinnock described unemployment as 'the biggest problem of all'. He wanted to see the jobs in manufacturing restored, and Labour winning the argument for 'real jobs'. The Labour leader's colleagues remember him repeating a mantra at every available opportunity: 'jobs, jobs, jobs'.

Kinnock was convinced that with rising unemployment, and the collapse of Britain's manufacturing industry presided over by the Thatcher government, a commitment to create jobs would have potent appeal, if it could be made to sound credible.

In 1981, Kinnock had helped to draft 'Economic Planning and Industrial Democracy', a joint Labour Party–TUC paper, which contained the commitment to reduce unemployment to below one million within five years. That pledge became one of the main battle cries of Michael Foot's doomed 1983 general election campaign. The trouble for Labour was that no one believed it then, and no one – least of all Kinnock – believed it now.

Kinnock was strongly advised it was no longer achievable for an incoming Labour government in the mid-1980s. Finding a more credible employment target became a priority in Kinnock's efforts to rebuild Labour for the next election.

Kinnock officially dropped Foot's target on 2 April 1985, at the press launch for Labour's jobs and industry campaign. He announced a new target: to reduce unemployment by one million in two years. It was intended as a headline-grabbing pledge to launch the national campaign on jobs, but those with the task of turning it into reality privately regarded this too as reckless, and more confusing than the old target. Labour policy advisers were unsure whether it meant Labour would create one million jobs or cut the unemployment figures by one million.

'It was a political decision, rather than an economic one. Labour had to move away from a commitment that had simply not been believed,' said Mike Craven, Prescott's adviser, in an unpublished analysis on Labour's mistakes leading up to the election.

It was over a year later, in May 1986, before a clear policy line to end the confusion was adopted at a private meeting by Hattersley; John Smith, then shadow Industry Secretary; and Prescott, the shadow Employment Secretary. They agreed that Labour spokesmen would say that the party would reduce registered unemployment by one million within two years. 'The discussion was not an economic one. Rather, it was felt that to argue for creating a million jobs would look like a climbdown,' recalled one source.

A secret paper called 'Target One Million', produced by a working party of trade union leaders and shadow Cabinet members code-named NEDC6 in January 1986, warned the leadership that a Labour government 'may need to create over 1.3 million jobs to reduce registered unemployment by one million as many jobs may be filled by unregistered female workers. (National Institute of Economic and Social Research suggest around 2m jobs will be needed.)'

The NEDC6 analysis of the cost made grim reading. 'Net increase in the PSBR of around £5.6bn in year 1 and £13bn in year 2 could reduce unemployment by 450,000 and 1.04 million.' It achieved the Kinnock target on unemployment, but at a cost that was more than double the sum allowed for by Hattersley.

No detailed work on how that commitment would be fulfilled, within those costings, was done until January 1987 – five months before the general election.

Prescott was engaged on a bigger project than producing figures to back up a headline target. He had embarked on a plan for 'full employment'.

The words 'full employment' carried powerful resonances for the Labour movement that echoed from the Great Depression years of the early 1930s. 'Idleness' was one of the 'Five Giants' which Sir William Beveridge sought to slay with his freelance paper 'Full Employment in a Free Society' and the coalition government's 1944 employment White Paper, which set the goal of maintaining public expenditure at a level to achieve 'a high and stable level of employment'. Prescott – like Margaret Thatcher – kept a copy of the Beveridge report to hand, and he listed the five 'evils' of want, squalor, disease, ignorance and idleness in his 1994 leadership manifesto. But what did 'full employment' mean? Some economists took it to mean an unemployment rate of 2.5 per cent of the workforce, roughly translated as a cut in unemployment of at least one million. Hugh Gaitskell, the Labour Chancellor, defined it in 1951 as 'a level of unemployment of 3 per cent at the seasonal peak'.

The post-Depression consensus over 'full employment' was broken by Sir Keith Joseph, Margaret Thatcher's mentor, in a speech in Preston in September 1974. Ignoring the debate over definitions, he set the defeat of inflation, not unemployment, as the political priority for the new generation of Conservatives. 'At each downturn in the economic cycle governments had tried to spend their way out of unemployment.'

Sir Keith said, 'It is perhaps easy to understand: our post-war boom began under the shadow of the 1930s. We were haunted by the fear of long-term mass unemployment, the grim, hopeless dole queues and towns which died. So we talked ourselves into believing that these gaunt, tight-lipped men in caps and mufflers were around the corner, and tailored our policy to match these imaginary conditions. For imaginary is what they were …'

The Labour government had accepted the new orthodoxy. James Callaghan, as Prime Minister, told the Labour conference in 1976, 'We used to think we could spend our way out of recession.' Chancellor Denis Healey – speaking from the rostrum in the days before the Cabinet had an automatic place on the platform – was booed for cuts in spending to meet the demands of the International Monetary Fund for a loan to bail out 'bankrupt Britain'. Healey imposed tight wage restraint, which led to the Winter of Discontent. Michael Foot, on the night the Labour government fell in 1979, in his last flash of brilliance in the Commons, warned the country that a Conservative government would lead to the 'naked laissez-faire policies of the Right Hon. Member for Leeds, North East' (Sir Keith Joseph). Foot had included a pledge to full employment in his 1983 manifesto – described (for other reasons) by Gerald Kaufman as the 'longest suicide note in history'. The depth of that defeat had shaken Labour's faith in its old songs.

One of the principal exponents of the Joseph doctrine was the Chancellor, Geoffrey Howe, whose lacerating resignation speech led to Thatcher's downfall. He later came to admit that his 1981 Budget, combining high interest rates and a high exchange rate – later coupled with spending cuts – might have been too tight. Howe was the master of understatement. It made the old smokestack industries more vulnerable to competition, and the leitmotif of the 1980s became the demolition gang's ball and chain. Factory chimneys seemed to be crashing all over the north.

Denis Healey in his many clashes with Howe – which Healey likened to 'being savaged by a dead sheep' – ridiculed the economic theories of Thatcherism as 'sado-monetarism'.

Keith Joseph's revolutionary choice of low inflation as the overriding priority still found its echo in the 1990s. Tony Blair, addressing a business dinner in New York on 10 April 1996, assured his audience that New Labour was 'moderate, realistic, committed to macroeconomic stability and will set a low inflation target in government'.

Not even the rioting in the inner cities in London and other areas of Britain in the early eighties, which had shaken the Thatcher government by its ferocity, could weaken the implacable conviction in monetarism in the Conservative camp. The favourite at Margaret Thatcher's court was TINA – There Is No Alternative. In a Budget debate on 21 March 1985, Prescott – sharing front-bench duties with Tony Blair – boldly declared that 'TINA no longer remains supreme', but few believed him.

Labour's answer to TINA, the AES – the alternative economic strategy – had been around since Foot's day, but there were growing disbelievers in the Labour ranks. Some of Kinnock's advisers appeared to regard Prescott as proving the adage that a little learning was a dangerous thing.

Armed with his Ruskin diploma, and his Hull degree in economics, Prescott was determined to prove them wrong. In his debut speech as shadow Employment Secretary, Prescott accused the government of deliberately creating unemployment, a charge they angrily rejected.

'It is a deliberate government policy to create mass unemployment to achieve the same object as in the 1920s – to discipline the labour force and reduce the wage level.'

His speech showed that he had taken painstaking care over its preparation. He compared Baldwin's approach in 1928 to Thatcher's tolerance of high unemployment; nothing had changed, he said. At its heart was Prescott's commitment to 'a high and stable level of employment' as defined by Beveridge.

'A Labour government will make it a central feature of government policy to get people back to work ... Unemployment will be a central issue at the next general election, with an electorate awakened to the government's indifference to the plight of millions of the British people. They will elect a Labour government committed to getting the people back to work.'

His remarks – winding up a debate on the Queen's Speech on 12 November 1984 – were brushed aside by his old adversary Norman Lamont, then Minister of State for Trade and Industry, who accused Prescott of repeating the speech he had made when they last crossed swords on the hustings in 1970. (Lamont would be remembered later for describing unemployment as a 'price worth paying' for economic recovery.)

Prescott also clashed two months later with Alan Howarth, the Tory MP who was to cross the floor spectacularly in 1995 to Labour. He accused Howarth of being 'one of the few Hon. Members to support the Government's policy on unemployment'.

Recalling Margaret Thatcher's words – borrowed from St Francis of Assisi – on the steps of Downing Street, Prescott said she had failed to bring harmony in place of discord. 'The Iron Lady, who is more concerned with resolution than charity, has no concern for the problems that we face. She is leading us to a society more divided between the north and the south, the rich and the poor. That is the result of the government's policies.'

He rejected the more emollient approach by Kenneth Clarke, then Paymaster General and understudy to Lord Young, as 'caring capitalism, the people's capitalism offering tea and sympathy instead of jobs'.

On 29 June 1985, Prescott gave the inaugural meeting of the Labour Party Economic Strategies Group at County Hall, the home of the Greater London Council, a taste of what was to come. 'Before the 1983 general election,' he told the private meeting, 'almost every issue of every journal on the left carried articles on the alternative economic strategy. Since the election, there has been a dearth of discussion on economic policy.

'The party failed to convince the electorate that our alternative economic strategy would create a million new jobs.'

He went on: 'If we are to achieve full employment in a more accountable economy, then we need much more than the simple reflation of the economy with a different order of public expenditure priorities. Our policies, central to our socialist conviction, make it essential that we achieve full employment with a redistribution of power, wealth and even jobs.'

Having successfully got the show on the road, Prescott decided to throw a party. He booked a Thames pleasure boat, and invited all his friends, his private office, MPs, trade unionists and party workers who had been involved in the jobs campaign.

'It was typical of the generosity of the man. Smith would never have thought of doing it,' said one of his friends.

Among those invited to the bash on board ship were a group of Labour-supporting cyclists who had ridden from Carlisle to support the jobs campaign. A buffet was laid on and beer was cheap. As the party was in full swing, Prescott approached one of the cyclists and asked whether he was having a good time.

'No,' said the cyclist. 'There's no vegetarian food.'

Prescott could not believe his ears. No vegetarian food? And he had laid on the whole show. For such ingratitude, there was only one answer.

'He suggested they should jump overboard if they didn't like it.'

One of the cyclists was so offended, he tore up his Labour Party membership card in Prescott's face. Fortunately, it did not come to blows, and the cyclist apologised in writing the next day.

But worse was to follow. When the boat docked back at Westminster pier, some of the revellers went on to the terrace of the House of Commons for an end-of-term party.

It was the dog days of July, when the Commons is hot and muggy; the MPs are listless and want to get away on their holidays; things happen.

One version of what happened next is that one of the women cyclists was taken ill, leaned over the terrace wall, lost her top, and was sick all over the security system. That started off the alarm bells and six plainclothes policeman then rushed on to the terrace, pistols at the ready.

TOPLESS LADY ON THE TERRACE was how most of the popular press reported the incident. The future deputy leader of the

Labour Party was not involved and one his closest friends said the whole story was a put-up job, but sometimes the myth takes on a life of its own.

Prescott had set about the fundamental task of redistributing 'power, wealth and jobs' by bringing together a cross-section of trade union contacts, local authority leaders and respected friends from university, including John Hughes, the principal at Ruskin College, who had been his tutor, to form his employment policy working group.

On the Sunday of the annual Labour Party conference in September 1985 – five months after Kinnock had made his jobs pledge – the shadow Employment Secretary published 'Planning for Full Employment'.

As with his regional policy paper which led to Labour's commitment to regional devolution, Prescott published it himself, because he did not trust the Labour Party headquarters research machine to publish it unamended. It carried a foreword by the Labour leader, but Kinnock's office had insisted on the phrase 'Options for a Modern Employment Strategy' being added to the title, to make it clear it was an 'options' paper, and not yet party policy. Prescott wanted a commitment to 'full employment' in the manifesto, but his document went much further.

'Planning for Full Employment' was to be Prescott's personal testament. Its packed 32 pages drew together a bewildering range of policy initiatives. Like his government White Papers that were to follow, Prescott threw everything into it: unequivocal support for a statutory minimum wage; intervention in economic strategy; new ideas for meeting Labour's commitment to Clause

Four nationalisation through 'social ownership' and share schemes; more wages councils to protect low-paid workers – harking back to Prescott's days as a commis chef; the repeal of the Conservative trade union laws; action on equal opportunities for women and ethnic minorities; a coordinated energy policy to rescue the pits from closure; and the main recommendations from his regional policy document from 1982.

At its heart was a commitment to demand-led economic planning. It was a broad sweeping vision for reviving the economy, and it was stuffed with Prescott's core beliefs: it reaffirmed his own commitment to the concept of 'full employment', it combined the thinking of the unions and Labour local authorities, and it spoke boldly of 'planned intervention':

'For socialists, there is no alternative to strong and direct involvement by workers and their representatives in partnership with a Labour government. Industrial and public sector planning and a strongly interventionist role in the economy can get Britain back to work,' it said.

These were strong Old Labour values, but they were enlivened by innovative ideas culled from other policy groups, typical of Prescott's scavenging mind. His paper still stands as a monument to his energetic thinking. The sheer volume of ideas thrown out in the document – too much to be easily digested – showed more clearly than any of his other papers how he was impatient for change.

It confirmed his socialism. 'A radical redistribution of wealth, power and jobs is required if this country is to make real economic progress.' But he returned to his earlier paper calling for a new allocation of resources between regions, 'accountable to local planning, as part of national economic planning'.

It gave a sideways nod to Kinnock's target, before it had been redefined, 'to create a million jobs within two years'. But it was vague on the figures. It said jobs would be created through local authority services, requiring higher public spending; 400,000 jobs would be provided at a cost of £1.5 billion in housing, roads and urban renewal; a further 600,000 would be created through other measures to boost demand, including a jobs subsidy.

And it sought to set 'full employment' in a new context. It marked the break from the idea that 'full employment' meant men in full-time jobs in factories. The document said: 'We mean by "full employment" useful work for all those able to make a contribution to society. Full employment will not mean the same in the 1990s as it did in the 1950s, 60s or 70s. Gone for ever are the days of one male breadwinner working forty hours a week for forty years supporting a wife and two children.'

Those were the same words he had used at the meeting at County Hall in June.

Echoing Beveridge, it also spoke about a minimum income level: 'We need also to set a minimum level of income within a new strategy for fair wages to ensure a decent standard of living whether people are at work or are in receipt of government benefits.'

Many of the detailed ideas are now accepted – some, including the minimum income level, were well ahead of modern Labour thinking, but the interventionist core proved too controversial.

He proposed a new public forum, the National Planning Council, bringing unions, government and bosses together to plan for sustainable economic growth to avoid another Winter of Discontent. It would be more interventionist than the 1970s National Economic Development Council (Neddy), and all sides of industry would agree a national economic assessment, with a five-year plan.

The centrepiece was the creation of a new Whitehall Department for Economic and Industrial Planning first proposed in 'Partners in Rebuilding Britain' in 1982, in which Neil Kinnock had a hand.

The Treasury would be responsible for exchange rates, interest rates and public sector borrowing, and setting taxes, but Prescott wanted the power of the Treasury to be challenged. 'The overall macro-economic stance and the short- and long-term growth strategy must be opened up to wider scrutiny in Cabinet and in the National Planning Council'.

The new ministry was to be responsible for a National Investment Bank and a new, recast National Enterprise Board, which would 'be provided with the resources and power to invest in industry and take public stakes'. The new ministry would move the centre of power in government away from the Treasury.

The document said:

> *The experience of past Labour governments with the Treasury has not been happy. The Department of Economic Affairs and the Wilson government's attempts to introduce indicative*

> *planning foundered largely as a result of Treasury power and influence. Its strategic position, the relationship to the Prime Minister, the control over not only the macroeconomic levers but of the whole public expenditure planning process give it the pivotal role in the management of the economy. The scale of the task facing the next Labour Government and the need for longer-term industrial planning, means that the role of the new Treasury will have to change …*
>
> *This will be more than a name change. DEIP should take over the strategic economic planning functions of the Treasury and responsibility for jobs-related public expenditure planning.*

The explicit aim of the DEIP – like George Brown's ill-fated Department of Economic Affairs in the Wilson government – was to wrest power from the Treasury, causing a seismic shift in Whitehall. It was something that the two rising stars of Labour, Gordon Brown and Tony Blair, would resist, and it was to be the cause of damaging friction between Prescott and Brown until they shared power together.

It would also cause Blair to distrust his future deputy's ambitions, for after winning the leadership Blair refused to give any commitment to Prescott to take on the same cross-Whitehall powers enjoyed by the then Deputy Prime Minister and First Secretary, Michael Heseltine, whose office had been dubbed 'Number 10A Downing Street'.

Kinnock's adviser was nominally on the production team for Prescott's paper, but Kinnock, in the foreword, emphasised it was 'compiled as a contribution to the public debates about the alternatives to unemployment, industrial contraction and social decay …'.

Its contents, therefore, could be quietly ditched, if necessary. Prescott hoped that if he got his draft in first, enough would survive in the rewriting to make it worthwhile.

Prescott's preface took the unusual step of absolving others from responsibility: 'I should make it clear as the Parliamentary spokesperson on Employment that I am responsible for the contents of the report. The people who participated in the group and the production of the report are in no way bound by its conclusions …' Prescott's momentous package was not intended to offer a specific target for growth in jobs. It was setting an agenda in which planning, cooperation between the unions and government, industrial intervention and Keynesian reflation could provide the climate for it to happen.

But there was a satisfaction in the Conservative camp that Labour was fighting past battles on unemployment. Even before the 1983 'Falklands Factor' election victory by Margaret Thatcher, Sir Bernard Ingham, Thatcher's chief press secretary, answered questions about the rising numbers of jobless by pointing out that there were more people in work than out of it. The Tories concentrated all their appeal for the coming general election on the vast majority who were earning, and paying taxes, and left Labour to pick up the votes of the unemployed, if they could.

It was a lesson Labour was painfully slow to learn. Prescott's adviser Mike Craven said after the 1987 election in an unpublished report that the old manufacturing base had gone, never to return in quite the same way. 'We live in a society where the multinational hamburger chain, McDonald's, employs more people than General Motors.'

That simple fact had a profound impact on Labour's support; the collapse of the smokestack industries had wreaked havoc with the solidarity of workers on the shop floor, who were now dispersed – if they could find work – to smaller light-industrial units. This phenomenon was described as 'Post-Fordism' by Martin Jacques in *Marxism Today*.

Yosser was soon to be followed by Harry Enfield's comic creation, Loadsamoney; his catchphrase, 'Show us your wad', captured the careless mood of the Lawson boom years. It was largely a southern-based boom. The north was still struggling to overcome the steel closures, and the rundown of the pits after the miners' strike. Some jobs were coming in the north in the form of inward investment by Japanese car-makers, and entrepreneurs such as John Hall were building new shopping malls, such as the Metro Centre on Tyneside. The old steel-rolling mills in Tinsley, Sheffield, close to where Prescott's father had worked, were transformed into the Meadowhall Shopping Centre.

Loadsamoney typified the get-rich-quick money-makers from the City, later to be associated with Nick Leeson and the £800 million collapse of Barings Bank.

It would have been easier to commit Labour to *creating* a million jobs than cutting unemployment by a million. Nigel Lawson, after the 1987 general election, created an estimated one million jobs in the Big Bang for the financial services. The

Labour Jobs and Industry campaign paper was a brave attempt to convince the electorate that Labour could create jobs at an affordable cost. Banking and accountancy, where the jobs were to be created in the Lawson boom, were placed near the bottom on Labour's leaflet, below refuse collection.

Kinnock's main concern was to get a watertight plan for his jobs target, which he believed Prescott's grandiose paper had failed to deliver.

On 7 and 8 January 1987, Kinnock held a special meeting of the shadow Cabinet at a trade union retreat at Bishop's Stortford to agree on the strategy for the general election. The centrepiece was to be a detailed plan on how Labour would fulfil its pledge to reduce unemployment by one million within two years of taking office. It was to mark the start of bad blood between the Labour leader and his employment spokesman, Prescott.

It was a two-day brainstorming session, responding to the challenge now presented by the Tories after their stunningly successful relaunch at their 1986 conference in Bournemouth. The Tories had turned around their fortunes by presenting their front-bench team as a Cabinet brimming with new ideas. Kinnock wanted Labour to match them. The key item on the agenda was economic revival, and the need for a properly costed, watertight package to reduce unemployment.

Prescott saw his paper, called 'Real Needs – Local Jobs', torn to shreds. The title of the paper was carefully chosen. Answering the union calls for 'real jobs', he tried to show that Labour could deliver its employment commitment by responding to needs with local jobs. It was in line with the thinking behind Prescott's 'Alternative Regional Strategy' set out two years earlier for 'bottom-up' solutions, rather than 'top-down' planning.

It was almost an afterthought to his main work, 'Planning for Full Employment', and was designed to meet Kinnock's target without conceding an inch to the party's PR men. But it crucially lacked figures. Looking back on the reasons for the failure of Labour's 1987 general election campaign, Mike Craven, Prescott's adviser, wrote: 'For almost the whole of the two years after Neil Kinnock set the target, no detailed work was carried out on how it might be achieved. Some limited assessments were made. For example, John Prescott published "Real Needs – Local Jobs" which was an (optimistic) assessment of the local authority contribution to the jobs package. But no credible figures were set out and it did not look at other areas of job creation.'

Prescott had gone back to some of his contacts in local government, and had drawn on the expertise of four local authorities and an enterprise board. The working group for 'Real Needs – Local Jobs' included a string of local authority leaders for whom Prescott had respect. Another whose name appeared in the credits was Tony Blair, then an opposition Treasury spokesman. They concluded that to do what Kinnock wanted – create more 'real jobs' in manufacturing – would take too long. Prescott and others on the team regarded it as an impossible target with an impossible timetable. In their view, no manufacturing-based programme could deliver on a scale of reducing unemployment by one million in two years; hence it was possible only if they created jobs in other ways. The quickest way would be through local authorities offering job creation schemes. Their report took examples from each of the four local authorities. Prescott was satisfied it was a 'bottom-up' exercise, in which the councils sought to meet local needs, and added up the jobs tally later, rather than being ordered from Whitehall to fulfil an arbitrary jobs total.

Its cost was clearly set out, but it is not hard to see why it failed to convince Kinnock and his ring of advisers who were obsessed with the 'cynical press'; he wanted a watertight, nationally costed programme for tackling his employment target. Kinnock, who at one time shouted at James Naughtie, the BBC *Today* presenter, that he did not wish to be 'kebabbed' on air, had no intention of being cremated over one of the main planks of his election platform.

The reliance on the local authorities guaranteed a hostile audience from the Tories, with some nervous sympathy among the right in the shadow Cabinet. It was the height of the Tory attack by Norman Tebbit, party chairman, on 'loony left' councils, and the Thatcher government was embarking on its policy of forcing local authorities to put their services out to private tender to cut their costs. Kinnock was haunted by the spectre of Militant activists in Liverpool, Lambeth and a string of other councils. Southwark Council, whose leader Anna Whyatt was on the Prescott working group, proposed expanding its workforce by over 3,000 in a jobs package which included 260 jobs in services such as arts for minority ethnic groups, women and the disabled. The total package would cost £136.4 million.

Labour's environment spokesman, Jack Cunningham, who would have to implement the policy, dismissed Prescott's paper as 'jobs on the rates'. The former Chancellor Denis Healey, whose London home was in the borough, pointed out that Southwark Council was 20 per cent under its own staffing complement.

Having invested his soul into the paper, Prescott was shattered by the rejection. As he brooded on the injustice of it, his office received a call from a researcher for the Sunday current affairs programme *Weekend World*, then being presented by Matthew Parris. They wanted Prescott on the programme to discuss Labour's plans for reducing unemployment.

The spin doctors said he should never have accepted, but Prescott was never one to duck a challenge, particularly from an adversary like Parris. His own policy paper had not received shadow Cabinet approval, and Gould was now in the driving seat, but it proved too great a temptation. Prescott wanted to explain his plans for an alternative strategy and cooperation with the local authorities, and to attack the Tories for allowing unemployment to rise unabated.

In the first week of February 1987 – a month after the Bishop's Stortford meeting – Prescott went on live television. 'It was an utter disaster,' said one of his friends.

'Parris kept asking how many jobs could be created through the public services. Prescott refused to answer because he didn't have shadow Cabinet approval.'

Initially, Prescott said he had a reasonable feedback about it. But there was consternation in the leader's team. On 10

February, after an ominous silence, Peter Mandelson, the party's director of communications, telephoned Prescott's office. A Prescott supporter recalls that Mandelson said he thought the programme had been appalling.

Ignoring the humiliation for his employment spokesman, Kinnock needed something more dynamic and handed the job to a fresh team of young junior shadow ministers, whom Prescott dubbed 'Kinnock's Colonels' – Tony Blair, Gordon Brown and Jack Straw – and put Bryan Gould, the articulate New Zealander, in charge. Gould was a new boy on the block, having gained a seat on the shadow Cabinet only a few months earlier as shadow Chief Secretary to the Treasury, the number two in Roy Hattersley's Treasury team. A former television producer, Gould was as ambitious as Prescott to modernise the party's thinking but in less interventionist ways.

Prescott, although the shadow Employment Secretary, was now not even part of the group; after his own paper had been summarily shot down, he was sidelined by Kinnock on the jobs project. Gould later said: 'Neil took one look at the draft and decided he could not allow it to go forward. It would, he thought, fail to carry credibility and, to the extent that anyone took it seriously, it would reveal the party as dangerously in hock to the public service unions.'

Prescott, forced to backtrack on his own ambitious strategy, was angry, and humiliated by the experience. He never forgave Kinnock, and it turned deteriorating relations between the Labour leader and his shadow Cabinet spokesman for employment almost into a blood feud.

The *Sunday Telegraph* reported that Gould had taken over Prescott's jobs package because the shadow Employment Secretary was 'exhausted'. Prescott, far from exhausted, was furious, and he was sure the bile was coming from the leader's office.

It had not always been like this. Prescott had nominated Kinnock for the leadership in September 1983 after Labour's disastrous election defeat under Michael Foot. A month later, Kinnock gave Prescott his first job in the shadow Cabinet as transport spokesman when, after years of standing in vain, Prescott was elected to the shadow Cabinet in sixth place with 88 votes. Initially, Prescott and Kinnock got on well. They were from similar backgrounds – working-class, rooted in the trade unions, and resentful about their perceived lack of intellect. Their chemistry proved explosive, however, and friends of both men would often privately observe, 'Opposites attract – likes repel.'

'They were too alike,' said one of Prescott's colleagues who saw the qualities of both men.

'Kinnock didn't know how to work with Prescott. Not like Smith; Smith knew how to deal with John and they were genuinely very close,' said another Prescott ally.

Kinnock had little respect for what he believed was Prescott's lack of self-discipline. Prescott summed up his attitude in an interview for a profile in the *Independent* in 1988, a month before the leadership election: 'Perhaps I don't like bosses … People have to earn my respect, they can't dictate it.'

By the time of the meeting in Bishop's Stortford, most of the early respect between the two had dissolved into bitterness.

After Blair became leader, Kinnock said, 'If John's vanity gland is working as it has done for many years it could be a real nuisance. It may be that Tony has got to do something important in order to squash him a bit, which will be a bloody nuisance ... As the election grows nearer all the tabloids and possibly one or two of the so-called heavies are going to be treating John Prescott as if he's a mixture of Lenin and the leader of the Waco sect. And that could be a problem.'

Gould was just as disenchanted with his task as Prescott. He felt he was set an impossible mission: he had to keep within a total spending ceiling of £6 billion fixed by Roy Hattersley, the shadow Chancellor; he had to deliver a detailed account of how Labour would get one million off the dole queues in two years; and it had to be done within three weeks.

Gould said the pledge to keep within £6 billion was 'always a ridiculous one'. He added, 'I eventually came up with a four-part package which relied at least to some extent on a boost in demand ... The package was, I think, as good an attempt as it could have been but it didn't cut much ice with the media.'

Prescott was also dismissive of Gould's efforts. One of the key findings of Prescott's paper was that manufacturing could not deliver jobs in time to meet Kinnock's target. That is why Prescott had argued that to stimulate demand was not enough. Yet Gould's plan proposed that 250,000 jobs would be created in manufacturing industry.

Mike Craven wrote to John Eatwell, then Kinnock's chief economic adviser, now a Labour peer, to protest that it was 'cobbled together at the last minute and was not the result of a detailed economic analysis. Nor was it tested on an economic model.'

It had been planned to publish the Gould paper early in March, but, as the row over jobs reached its climax, Labour lost the Greenwich by-election. Labour's candidate, Deidre Wood, had been portrayed as a hard-left activist, who had secured the seat by use of her power base as a councillor in Tower Hamlets and the Inner London Education Authority. She broke down in tears at one point during the campaign, but that did not help. She was seen as the unacceptable face of municipal Labour and was trounced by the cuddly Rosie Barnes, the SDP candidate. In the popular press, it was if Stalin's granny had been tripped up by Flopsy Bunny. On the day of Labour's by-election defeat, 26 February, Patricia Hewitt, Kinnock's adviser, later to become a Labour MP and Cabinet minister, penned a confidential note to senior colleagues in London, warning that polling showed that the Tory attack on the 'loony left' in London was hurting Labour. 'The gays and lesbians issue is costing us dear among the pensioners, and fear of extremism and higher taxes is particularly prominent in the GLC area,' she said. It was true, but it was leaked to the *Sun*.

An internal inquiry into how the Hewitt memo came to be leaked drew a blank, but there were plenty of conspiracy theories including the Machiavellian possibility that it was leaked from Kinnock's office, finally to nail the London left.

The cloud of warm air which gently wafted the SDP upwards in the opinion polls after the Greenwich result forced Labour to postpone its jobs package until 10 March.

The stage was set for Kinnock's cast-iron, costed commitment on jobs to be unveiled, one year and eleven months after it was first made. With 24 hours to go, Prescott – still bristling with anger – bumped into the affable James Callaghan, the former Labour Prime Minister, in the members' tearoom of the House of Commons.

Labour, at that time still wedded to its policy of unilateral nuclear disarmament, was officially committed to cancelling Trident, the replacement for the ageing Polaris nuclear submarine system. But Callaghan had used a speech in the Commons the night before to call for Trident to be retained. Callaghan, a die-hard multilateralist, had said before the 1983 election that Labour should retain Polaris. The late Labour leader was being consistent and so too was Prescott, who, in the post-election inquest in 1983, had accused Callaghan of helping to sabotage Labour's campaign. Over the tea and toast in the members' tearoom, Prescott chided 'Sunny Jim'. 'You've lost us two elections in a row … You are leading us like lambs to the bloody slaughter.' In Prescott's book of parliamentary insults, it amounted to no more than jovial banter. Prescott had spoken to Callaghan before his speech in the Commons the night before and had no reason to be angry with him.

But the Tories used it to damage Labour. Gleeful Tory MPs ran to inform the press of the 'tearoom tiff'. The next day, 10 March, the news of the 'furious row' in the tearoom between the widely respected former Premier and the Bull from Hull was all over the front pages.

Prescott had made few speeches on defence, and was not

noted for unilateralism – unilateralism is not a concept that comes easily to boxers. Prescott was listed in *Sanity*, the CND paper, as being a member of parliamentary CND. But then so was Tony Blair. He was more upset that Callaghan, the elder statesman, should get away with disowning conference-agreed party policy, while Prescott was constantly accused of rocking the boat.

The next day, Kinnock's aides were desperate to keep Prescott off the platform for the launch of Gould's jobs package, but Prescott insisted on being there. He was, after all, the shadow Employment Secretary. It would have been an unbearable humiliation for him not to be on the platform for such an important statement of policy. It could have forced his resignation. Coming within months of the general election, with the Tories rebuilding their support, it had all the potential to turn a crisis into a catastrophe. Kinnock decided to allow Prescott on to the platform, provided he kept his mouth shut.

Like a naughty schoolboy, Prescott stayed silent. Patricia Hewitt passed him a note. It said, 'For God's sake, smile.' Prescott smiled, but he never forgot. And he certainly did not forgive.

On Friday, 13 March, *The Times* reported that a sequel to the tearoom tiff had happened in the tearoom, when Prescott had confronted one of the Tory MPs he suspected of spreading the earlier story, a moustachioed northern lawyer called Ken Hind.

> *According to Mr Hind, Mr Prescott approached him in the tea-room and said, '"Are you Hyde?" He replied, "No –*

> *Hind." … I even spelled it out for him.'*
>
> *'He said, "Were you responsible for leaking stories about the incident in the tea-room?" I looked at him, and he looked quite aggressive. I didn't want any trouble.'*
>
> *Asked if he was the source of the original report, Mr Hind said: 'I was one of fifteen or sixteen members in the tea-room.'*

The Times had a livelier account: 'Mr Prescott said that Mr Hind had admitted that he was responsible for relaying the conversation with Mr Callaghan.'

'I said to Mr Hind, "Then you are a bastard." What was I supposed to do, kiss him on the cheek?' said Prescott.

Prescott also never forgave Gould, whom he saw as one of the new breed of technocrats who put personal ambition above the party. If anything, Gould was a forebear of New Labour. When Gould later resigned to return to an academic career, Prescott said in the *Daily Telegraph*: 'Everyone knew Bryan would move on once he had made his play for the leadership. He said it was Labour's lack of radical economic policy. He is just hacked off with his own career. I came into politics as a seaman, wanting to change laws that affected shipping. People like Bryan come in a different way. They have a career in the Foreign Office, a career in the university, dabble a bit in politics, find they haven't become Prime Minister, and decide to go somewhere else.'

Gould went back to New Zealand. Prescott stayed, to fight on. 'My movement has taught me that, if you get beat democratically, you carry on doing the job. I am now concerned to find ways to get three million people back to work. I don't take my ball home and run away,' said Prescott.

After the rows over the employment paper, and the 'tiff in the tearoom', Mandelson kept Prescott out of the limelight for Labour's 1987 election campaign. He was seen by the Kinnock camp as an unguided missile that was to be used only with extreme caution. In Prescott's view, it was the campaign of 'warm words'; he was kept out of the party election broadcasts; other more telegenic faces, such as Harriet Harman's, were hand-picked to present Labour's image to the southern voters; Prescott was largely kept off the platform in London, where the morning conferences were held with the seasoned lobby journalists. Instead, he was allowed a few walk-on parts in the regions. These included the humiliating task of presenting the Gould plans for reducing unemployment at a press conference at Manchester Airport at the start of Labour's general election campaign.

Prescott appeared in front of a blackboard on which Labour's plans for reducing unemployment by a million – with 'real jobs' in the manufacturing industry – were pinned up. As he faced the press, the figures fell to the floor behind him. 'There you are – even the bloody notice board doesn't believe it!' said Prescott.

In 1989, describing his relationship with Kinnock, Prescott remembered that incident with more than a hint of remorse for the way he feels his irrepressible humour can sometimes let himself and his party down. Speaking of Kinnock, he said, 'He's not overfond. The worst brick I dropped was when I was pinning up a notice about the million jobs he and Hattersley were going to find from nowhere. When the notice fell on the floor, of course I had to say: "There you are – even the bloody notice board doesn't believe it!"

'That sort of thing damages the party, I know it does, but it's me who has to speak his mind if I know it's right.'

CHAPTER TWELVE

Round One

All that's changed is the scenery. I'm still in the corner, taking the world on.
Prescott profile, the *Independent*, 3 September 1988.

When Neil Kinnock and Roy Hattersley ran on to the platform together at London's QE2 Centre to launch the 1987 general election manifesto they clasped hands. It was intended as a show of unity for the cameras, but it was perfectly described by Michael White in the *Guardian* the next day as the celebration of a gay wedding. In some respects it did resemble a marriage – Hattersley stayed at home, knitting together his beautiful prose in 'Aims and Values', while Kinnock was out slaying the enemy, in the form of Militant Tendency. They found a way of operating together in harmony; Hattersley swallowed his personal disappointment after being defeated for the leadership by Kinnock in 1983 and played the subservient role. And, like a couple devoted to making their marriage work, they kept their tiffs within the privacy of the four walls of the leader's office, most of the time.

By late 1987, it was a mature relationship. They understood each other, and knew each other's failings. When Kinnock was away, Hattersley could shine at the Despatch Box, frequently besting Margaret Thatcher, showing what might have been had the block vote in the electoral college swung the other way.

The shock of defeat on 11 June 1987 led to inevitable recriminations against the leadership and particularly against the shadow Chancellor, whose figures on taxation had unravelled as journalists picked away at the promises that Labour would not raise taxes for those on modest incomes. They smelled blood when it became clear that National Insurance contributions – a tax by any other name – would go up with the abolition of the married man's tax allowance, hitting those on less than the average wage. Roy blamed Neil. Neil blamed Roy. Mike Craven recorded: 'It was incredible to argue both that a Labour government would not increase taxation for anyone earning less than £500 a week and, at the same time, claim to want to abolish the married man's tax allowance.'

After the general election defeat, Prescott had his best ever result in the shadow Cabinet elections on Wednesday, 8 July, coming second behind Gould with 130 votes to Gould's 163. It was achieved by the combination of the Tribune Group slate and the hard-left Campaign Group holding together, the only time this was managed. The previous year, Prescott had mustered only 89 votes. Nine out of fifteen elected, including Prescott, were on the Tribunite slate. The centre-right Solidarity Group saw four of its members lose their seats. The elections proved a watershed, marking the departure of some of the old guard, and the arrival of some of 'Kinnock's Colonels'. Denis Healey did not run; out went Giles Radice and

Peter Shore; Gordon Brown was elected to the shadow Cabinet for the first time with 88 votes. Another rising star, Blair, failed to get on with 71 votes, but was clearly knocking on the shadow Cabinet door. Jack Straw scraped in for the first time with 84 votes.

Prescott's employment portfolio was given to Michael Meacher, who came third in the ballot with 127 votes. Meacher was regarded as one of the so-called 'cuddly left', who broadly followed the leadership's modernising project. Prescott wanted an economic portfolio. Prescott's friends said he wanted the trade and industry portfolio – to fulfil the ambitions of his earlier policy paper, 'Planning for Full Employment' – or environment, to carry out job creation with the councils. Kinnock had no intention of rewarding Prescott for gaining the support of the Campaign Group. Kinnock gave trade and industry to Gould and made a point of sending for Prescott last. He offered Prescott transport.

'I said, "No, I'm not having it. Give me defence." Kinnock said, "You'll burn your fingers." I said, "You've not done too badly at that yourself."' There was a shouting match in the leader's room, and Prescott left with the offer of the energy portfolio. After the miners' strike, that was fairly safe and undemanding – or so it seemed.

It took 24 hours of public soul-searching before Prescott accepted.

Kinnock rang Prescott at home and suggested they should get together for a drink.

'Don't give me any of that shit for Christ's sake,' said Prescott.

'You've done what you've done. Now get on with it. Don't give me any crap about how nice it is.'

A year later, when the government began the serious business of privatising the electricity-generating industry, he removed Prescott from energy and gave that job to Blair.

At the September 1987 conference of the TUC, the springboard for Labour's conference a few weeks later, Prescott decided to turn his dissatisfaction with Kinnock's leadership into action by announcing that he was going to run for the deputy leadership of the party over a cup of tea in the Winter Gardens with a few friends, including Dick Caborn, and Robert Taylor, then of the *Observer*.

Taylor broke the story on Sunday, 13 September 1987, under the headline PRESCOTT'S THREAT TO HATTERSLEY. 'The pugnacious left-wing MP for Hull East', the story read, 'believes Mr Kinnock's deputy should play a more active, campaigning role, mobilising support for Labour in the unions and encouraging a larger individual mass membership.'

'We discussed what we should do – all this organisation stuff – and we came to the decision that we ought to throw the cap into the ring, and get the debate going,' Caborn recalled.

Alarm bells around the leadership were already ringing. A Hattersley aide was quoted in Taylor's report as saying: 'The last thing the party wants is to be plunged into a damaging deputy leadership contest when Labour is trying to get into shape for the next election.'

Prescott threatened to raise the issue of the deputy leadership at the forthcoming annual conference of the Labour Party, but he was blocked. Determined not to be fobbed off, Prescott called a group of journalists to a briefing as the party conference approached to raise his rebellion against the leadership. They included Alastair Campbell, later to be Blair's press secretary, then of the *Sunday Mirror*; Jill Hartley of the *Sunday Times*; and Donald MacIntyre, then political editor of the *Sunday Telegraph*. Remarkably Andy McSmith, then a Labour press officer, was allowed to sit in on the meeting at Prescott's invitation. It was held in his office at Norman Shaw North. There were potato crisps for the journalists, and glasses of wine were handed out.

Prescott opened by saying he did not do much press briefing on lobby terms, and it was time that he did. It was supposed to be a briefing about electricity privatisation, but Prescott began by saying he knew they were only interested in the deputy leadership story. He proceeded to brief them on his intentions, leaving McSmith decidedly uncomfortable: he had to make a quick calculation over whether to resign his job and join the Prescott campaign, or loyally report back. He chose the latter course.

Prescott told them off the record that he believed the deputy leader should have more of a campaigning role, that Kinnock should not have to spend time dealing with building up the mass membership, or tackling problems, such as Ken Livingstone.

The impression Prescott had wanted to give was that he would be a 'friendly candidate' for Kinnock. He gave a clear hint that he would run against Hattersley, but he asked them to delay publishing the story until the following week. McSmith, not bound by any such embargo, said he would have to relay it to Kinnock. After leaving the private briefing, McSmith saw Ann Norris in Kinnock's office and took her for a drink; he wanted a witness so that it was out in the open, to make it clear that he was being loyal to the leadership, and was not engaged in a plot behind Kinnock's back.

Word quickly got back to Mandelson, via Charles Clarke. The next morning at the monthly meeting of the NEC, McSmith met Kinnock in the lift in the party headquarters in Walworth Road and mentioned the briefing. Kinnock went 'into orbit'. He ordered McSmith to produce a full note of the meeting and what had been said by Prescott, which he did.

Prescott was called into Kinnock's office after the NEC and the leader presented him with McSmith's note. Kinnock asked if it was true. Prescott said it was. Those who were nearby recall a fantastic row behind the locked doors of the leader's room. When he emerged, Prescott was fuming.

Kinnock privately told aides about Prescott, 'If he thinks he's had trouble in his life, it's nothing to the trouble he's going to get now.'

Kinnock issued an ultimatum to Prescott at the party conference in October. Warning him that his challenge for the leadership would be a damaging distraction from his efforts to rebuild Labour after the election defeat, Kinnock gave Prescott four weeks to stop 'playing the fool', to put up or shut up.

The Labour leader then moved the trade union big guns to try to make Prescott shut up. Sam McCluskie, leader of

Prescott's union, the NUS, and a close friend of Prescott's, who initially had agreed to back him, now joined the trade union heavyweights, including Ron Todd of the TGWU – Kinnock's union – to put heavy pressure on Prescott not to go ahead with his challenge. McCluskie, treasurer of the party, told Prescott in a series of telephone calls that a contest would reopen the old wounds caused by the Benn–Healey battle, which had split Labour in 1981.

Prescott doggedly stuck to his belief that the way to rebuild the party was from the grass roots, by creating a mass party. And that required a campaigning role for the deputy leader. In desperation, Kinnock called Prescott and Hattersley to a meeting in his office at the Commons to try to persuade Prescott to relent. Hattersley accused Prescott of threatening to 'sabotage' the party. Kinnock's aides accused Prescott of 'sheer bloody-mindedness'.

The striking thing about his threat of a challenge was that there was no evidence that it was driven by any left-wing ideology. Prescott was driven by his personal conviction that organisation – as well as ideas – would bring about a revival in the party.

As the party began to shake off the depression of losing the 1987 election, Prescott had produced a pamphlet calling for a mass membership drive, which was part of his strategy for the deputy leadership.

In this, Prescott anticipated by nearly a decade the Blair drive for mass membership that saw Labour's membership figures rise while the Tories' plummeted. Much of Labour's progress was due to Blair's wider appeal, which Prescott was ready to acknowledge. But Prescott believed it was also due to wider participation in decision-making, the power of the ballot, and one-member-one-vote democracy, which Prescott helped to champion.

The mass membership pamphlet was produced as a discussion pamphlet by the Tribune Group of Labour MPs but it was Prescott's document. Dick Caborn, a close friend of Prescott's, had it printed in Sheffield. It said the party had only 297,000 members, of whom only 100,000 were trade unionists. Affiliated members, or levy-payers, could not attend local party meetings or act as delegates.

The plan was simple: to attract more members, the £10 party subscription for trade union members who already paid a levy would be cut, enabling them to take a more active role in the Labour Party for a nominal additional fee, called 'levy-plus', of £1 or £2.

It was supported by trade union leaders and endorsed by Blair and Brown, as Tribune members, but Kinnock and the party leadership feared it would not work, and risked cutting the party's income. 'The only one who bounced it out was Kinnock,' said Caborn. Prescott told Tribune: 'It is a disgrace that our party membership is only 300,000 or one in 170 votes ...' By February 1993, membership had slumped to 90,000 according to an internal report produced in support of John Smith's drive for one-member-one-vote democracy in the party. Prescott complained, 'The Labour Party is the most difficult institution to join in Britain. Our target was to get a million people. The objective of our exercise was to empower people; to get people into the party to start making the decisions.'

Kinnock's response was to launch a 'Labour listens' campaign on 18 January 1988. However, after Gould and Smith announced they would not be standing in any leadership election, Prescott said he would be seeking the backing of his constituency to announce his decision to stand for the deputy leadership on 19 January, the day after Kinnock's launch.

'Kinnock put pressure on the constituency party to persuade John not to stand,' said one of his aides. 'There was a row but they backed him. *Newsnight* showed him being driven away from the school where the constituency party then met. He was in the back of Dave Taylor's [his adviser's] Ford Granada. Dave was frightened that his bosses would notice he was driving the company car.'

When the pressure failed, Kinnock called Dick Caborn, Prescott's most trusted ally, into his office, and asked Caborn whether he could persuade Prescott to withdraw.

'I said, "No, I doubt it,"' said Caborn. '"Let me tell you this, Neil – he's not challenging you. What he is saying is there is a position in the party which is under-utilised. It is the only position outside yours and the treasurer that commands the whole support of the movement because it is voted on by the whole of the movement."

'I said, "You know what he is like – he will row with you all the way to the Cross, but he will never stab you in your back." I said in my view the party did need reorganising, it did need changing into a mass party. It was the politics of organisation.'

Kinnock said, 'I can't agree with it.'

The pressure on Prescott from the union leaders not to mount his challenge was becoming unbearable. Sam McCluskie, with a foot in each camp, sought a face-saving way out. With two other trade union leaders who were trusted by Prescott, he went to Kinnock to persuade him to agree to a formula that would give Prescott what he wanted without a challenge to Hattersley for the deputy leadership.

Ron Todd, Rodney Bickerstaffe, general secretary of NUPE – one of Prescott's closest friends – and McCluskie got Kinnock's agreement for a form of words for an NUS resolution, to be moved by Prescott, for the 1988 party conference, giving a new campaigning focus for the deputy leader.

It was published in *Fighting Talk* for the first time.

The draft, covering a full sheet of A4 paper, began with a general statement, welcoming the increased commitment to campaigning by all sections of the party. It went on:

> *Conference believes, however, that it is now time to examine how the various campaigning activities of the party can best be coordinated and developed at national level. In particular, consideration should be given to ways in which initiatives to increase party membership can be effectively introduced and implemented. In addition, there is a need to ensure that the party's members and supporters are fully equipped with the arguments and ideas needed to promote Labour's policies with the electorate.*
>
> *As the Deputy Leader is both a member of the Shadow*

> *Cabinet and the National Executive Committee, conference recommends that he or she should be given formal responsibility to coordinate the party's campaigning activities. The Deputy Leader would therefore draw together the work undertaken by the Shadow Cabinet, MPs, the Campaign Strategy Committee and the Organisation Committee of the NEC. In addition he or she would work closely with affiliated trade unions and constituency parties.*
>
> *While in opposition, the increased organisational and campaigning duties to be allocated to the post would be such that conference believes that it would be inappropriate for the Deputy Leader also to carry a major parliamentary departmental responsibility.*

In his own handwriting, the Labour leader added the words: 'In future, candidates for the posn of DL should regard themselves primarily as candidates to fulfil the co-ord and promo activities above.'

Armed with that assurance in Kinnock's distinctive spiky handwriting, Prescott called a press conference on 20 January in room WI off the Great Hall at Westminster to announce he was pulling out of the leadership contest. Prescott said he was 'delighted and assured' that a debate on the role of the deputy leader would take place at the October party conference. Prescott was to be made a delegate of his union, the NUS, so that he could move the resolution for the debate. His press release carried a statement from McCluskie saying he had received assurances from other unions that they would support a debate and his union would be submitting a motion which would 'cover the views expressed by John Prescott'.

Within minutes, the Labour spin doctors were spinning a different story. Journalists at Westminster were told that no such deal had been hatched, and that Prescott had pulled out because he feared he would be humiliated by the size of his defeat.

David Hill, the party's press officer and a long-term close friend of Hattersley, was sent to brief lobby correspondents with his partner Hilary Coffman, from Kinnock's office. Prescott blamed Mandelson, souring their relationship for years, but Mandelson denied he was involved.

Kinnock reinforced the 'spin' with his own terse press release in which he made it clear that a deputy leader with nothing else but a campaigning role would be created over his dead body.

Journalists were handed the following statement on notepaper headed 'the Office of the Leader of the Opposition':

> *Statement from Neil Kinnock following John Prescott's decision today that he will not stand for election as deputy leader of the Labour Party:*
>
> *'It's good that John Prescott will not provoke a diverting contest – the pity is that we've had any distraction.*
>
> *'My view on the idea of excluding a Deputy Leader of the Labour Party from a major parliamentary portfolio is well-known – I'm completely hostile to it, like, I think, just about everybody else in the Trade Union and Labour movement. I've already turned the idea down flat.'*

The clear impression given to the press by both the spin doctors and by the press release was that Prescott had pulled out, not because he had secured what he had wanted from Kinnock, but that he was running away from the fight because he was scared of losing. Kinnock's aides also cast doubt on whether the issue would even be aired at the party conference.

The Times's headline the next day read: KINNOCK EXPLOITS PRESCOTT RETREAT. 'Mr Neil Kinnock last night publicly humiliated Mr John Prescott after he had announced that he was not after all forcing a deputy leadership contest this year,' the story read.

One of Prescott's campaign managers said, 'I walked out of WI and John Cole [then BBC political editor] said, "Look at that." I looked at the thing; it said how pleased Kinnock was that he had pulled out, never going to win ... blah, blah, blah.

'Prescott went absolutely wild because he didn't refer to any of the stuff in the statement we had agreed. We didn't put any of that in the statement we issued. We just said John was withdrawing. And we had got this deal with Kinnock which had been brokered by the trade unions, and then he had reneged on it.

'That's when there was hell on.'

Some on the left were extremely angry with Prescott for pulling out. They wanted the recriminations after the leadership contest to come out, and would have preferred them to do so behind Prescott's campaign banner. His retreat from the race forced their hand. Benn, whose high-water mark of support came when he narrowly lost to Denis Healey for the deputy leadership, was now an old warhorse of the left, but he decided to run again, this time with Eric Heffer, the Labour MP for Liverpool Walton. The right called it the 'nightmare ticket'.

They consulted the left-wing Campaign Group of MPs, before announcing they were standing for the leadership and deputy leadership respectively.

That was the trigger for Prescott to return to the fight. 'When Benn and Heffer entered the field, Prescott said, "All bets are off now." To be honest, he was looking for all bets to be off by then because of the way he had been treated by Kinnock,' one of his campaign team said.

The key planks in Prescott's campaign were to become familiar – full employment, mass membership and a campaigning role for the deputy leader.

Prescott had allies in unusual places. Alan Clark, Tory toff and Thatcherite Minister for Trade, was one of the first to urge him to stand on the grounds that he was a conviction politician and might do for Labour what Thatcher had done for the Tories in the wilderness years. He recalled in *The Alan Clark Diaries* bumping into Bob Cryer in the division lobby on 14 January. Cryer, a likeable left-winger, was the MP for Bradford South until his death in a car accident. 'Speaking as an historian as well as an old mate, I told him Prescott *must* stand. He became very enthused, said Prescott was checking with his Exec Committee, and certainly would. Bob agreed completely with my analogy with the Tory Party in 1976, and how we recovered our confidence when Mrs T. gave us a bit of conviction. The Labour Party is full of "idealists" (sic), it depended on ideals. "That's right," I said. Stirring.'

Prescott had a sneaking respect for Thatcher. 'As an impetus for change in what is largely a conservative country, she's produced more change than anyone since Attlee, and he only succeeded because it was after the war,' he told the *Independent* on 31 August 1988. There was a subtext, however – Thatcher had dictated the political agenda by her radicalism; he feared that Labour was surrendering it, because it was too mealy-mouthed on the central issues of taxation and spending.

Typical of Clark, he had mischief in mind. When I asked him whether he really had compared Prescott with Thatcher, Clark said there were parallels in conviction politics, but he also hoped Prescott's election as deputy leader would foment dissent within the Labour Party ranks. 'As always in politics, the motives were nothing other than mixed. I thought it would be a way of getting dissension going.'

But Clark did respect Prescott's conviction as being as honest, in its way, as Thatcher's. 'I still think he's terrific. He is a politician who rules by instinct. And I like that.'

Like Prescott, Clark had little respect for 'spin doctors'. In his *Diaries* he added, 'I get on well with the Labour Party. The MPs, that is, not the functionaries who hang about in the corridors, still less those crazy hyped-up "researchers". There's that dreadful little tick with curly hair and glasses, four foot six or thereabouts, I've never seen him smile [Dave Hill, communications director, Labour Party].'

With 'friends' like Alan Clark, Prescott hardly needed enemies.

Frank Dobson, with whom Clark recalled exchanging ribald jokes, used to run the Tribunite slate, and Prescott had been hoping that Robin Cook, a fellow Tribunite, would support him against Hattersley, especially as Cook had criticised Hattersley's 'Aims and Values' document. It came as a blow to Prescott's campaign – and a pointer to the result – when Cook announced on 31 March 1988 that he would be acting as campaign manager for Kinnock and Hattersley, with John Smith. Cook had acted for Kinnock when he beat Hattersley for the leadership in 1983. Prescott continued to respect Cook's talents as a politician and share many of his opinions, particularly over the need for a bolder cutting edge for Labour, but it was a personal letdown he never forgot.

Kinnock staked his authority as Labour leader on Hattersley's winning, and firmly shut the door on Prescott. 'I will be voting for Roy Hattersley as deputy leader and myself as leader. As far as I am concerned there are no other tickets.'

The decision by Benn and Heffer to force a contest – which allowed Prescott into the ring – caused a split in the left-wing Campaign Group with long-term consequences for the leadership under Blair. It led to some MPs on the left finally breaking with the activist Campaign Group, including Margaret Beckett, Clare Short and Jo Richardson. Dawn Primarolo, who also opposed the Benn–Heffer challenge, stayed in the group, but became Beckett's campaign manager in 1994. Beckett for the moment backed Prescott, along with Alan Meale, the Campaign Group secretary, who became part of Prescott's team as his parliamentary Private Secretary. Meale had been running the Campaign Group slate, known as the 'Meale ticket'.

Opposing Benn's challenge, Short said, 'This is not the way to change the Labour Party. This contest will be a waste of time and energy. It's sort of old-fashioned.'

The Benn–Heffer campaign took to the road, and provided genuine warmth and entertainment, with Benn's sparkling wit turning them into Old Time Music Hall for Militant or Campaign Group supporters who turned out in their thousands to see them. For all the impact they had on the party as a whole, they might have been at the end of Brighton pier.

The efforts by the leadership to get Prescott to back off underlined the real fears that Prescott could win. The *Sunday Times* said: 'Hattersley – patronising, altitudinous, wine-wise and rather slack boulevardier – is horribly vulnerable.'

The railway union ASLEF and the NUM backed Prescott in June. NUPE, led by his close friend Bickerstaffe, kept up the momentum by backing him in July. Prescott's attempt to keep it a friendly contest wore thin when his side issued a newsletter with an article from Tribune in which Prescott complained that Kinnock could not match Thatcher's control of the party, because he had sought to do it by patronage rather than political agreement. 'Those who dissent are either marginalised, ignored or taken on one side and pressed to mend their ways.' It caused ructions in the Kinnock–Hattersley camp. One of Prescott's team said, 'It was almost like they were trying to force John into having a damaging dispute, when he was not prepared to have one. That was a difficult period.'

By the September TUC conference, after months of speculation about the result, the TGWU finally decided to swing behind Hattersley, and sank Prescott's campaign. After that, a

Kinnock–Hattersley victory was a foregone conclusion for the party conference in October. Ron Todd implied there was a price to be paid for rescuing Kinnock with his 1.5 million block votes, in not pushing too fast with the modernisation of policy, particularly on unilateral disarmament, to which he was passionately committed.

The electoral college comprised 40 per cent for the unions, and 30 per cent each for the constituencies and MPs. Hattersley took 66.8 per cent overall; Prescott 23.7 per cent; Heffer 9.5 per cent. Kinnock won 88.6 per cent and Benn took 11.4 per cent. The surprise was that Hattersley did well among the constituency supporters, taking 367 constituency parties, or 18.1 per cent of a maximum 30 per cent for the constituency section.

Hattersley's success in the constituency section was due to the innovation of balloting among many of them. In a clear pointer to the impact one-member-one-vote (OMOV) democracy might have on the hold of the activists, it showed that, where ballots took place, the constituencies invariably voted for the party leadership. Of the 327 constituencies which balloted their members, Hattersley won 250 – 76.5 per cent – of their votes, compared with only 18.6 per cent for Prescott and 4.9 per cent for Heffer.

Prescott won the votes of 53 MPs, including two members of the shadow Cabinet, Michael Meacher and Jo Richardson; others who voted for him included Beckett and David Blunkett, his campaign managers, Peter Snape and Dick Caborn, Graham Allen, Paul Boateng, Ann Clwyd, Frank Cook, Ron Davies, Terry Davis, Don Dixon, Stuart Holland, Doug Hoyle, Eric Illsley, Terry Lewis, Bob Litherland, Tony Lloyd, Tommy McAvoy, John

McAllion, Ian McCartney, William McKelvey, John McFall, Bob McTaggart, Alan Meale, Austin Mitchell, Elliot Morley, Terry Patchett, Ernie Ross, Joan Ruddock, Clare Short, Chris Smith, Gerry Steinberg, Joan Walley, Alan Williams, and David Winnick. Peter Shore, his old boss, refused to vote, and his flatmate, Skinner, voted for Heffer.

Prescott wrote a letter to his supporters afterwards.

> *Just a short note to thank you for your support in the deputy leadership election. I'm sorry that I wasn't able to repay your support by winning, but in the circumstances, I think that we put up a good showing. The election was a good exercise in democracy and I hope it has killed the myth that you cannot have a contest in the Labour Party without conflict and bitterness.*
>
> *Our campaign succeeded in making the need to build a mass, campaigning Labour Party a political priority.*

Benn secured 38 MPs' votes for the leadership, mainly the Campaign Group.

Kinnock hoped to use the endorsement of his leadership with Hattersley as a mandate to revive his vigorous campaign to renew the party, a campaign that had been put on hold for six months. On the day, it was overshadowed by a Labour Party conference cock-up in which the party was left facing both ways on nuclear deterrence.

One Labour source said, 'Prescott would have been a disastrous deputy to Kinnock. They were too alike. I've heard

Prescott say of Kinnock, "Courage is not enough. You have to bring the party with you. His trouble is that he hasn't got a good university degree; he's insecure; he feels inferior; he's got this trouble with his language." It all sounded just like Prescott on himself.'

Prescott believed he could act as a foil for Kinnock. 'I think we all need standing up to. I'm a similar personality to Neil Kinnock and I readily accept that. But I know that I need to listen to independent advice. Strong-willed people have to remember that.'

It was not a view shared by Kinnock. However, Kinnock said before the vote there would be no victimisation.

'John has got to run for election like everybody else in the Shadow Cabinet. But there is no question of me trying to victimise him.'

A month later, the *Daily Telegraph* reported: PRESCOTT PAYS PRICE FOR DEFYING KINNOCK when he was stripped of the high-profile energy portfolio and was given transport instead. Energy – now of vital importance because of the privatisation of electricity – was handed to Tony Blair, one of Kinnock's most trusted protégés. Prescott's vote had dropped in the shadow Cabinet elections from 130 to 94 and he was third from bottom, largely because some on the centre-left had decided to punish him for the disruptive challenge against Hattersley. The leader of Kinnock's young colonels and shadow Treasury spokesman, Gordon Brown, saw his stock soar from 88 votes to top the poll with 155, beating his 'boss', shadow Chancellor John Smith, into second place. Smith had suffered his first heart attack but was expected to make a full recovery – he lost weight, and to keep fit returned to bagging 'Munroes', the mountains in Scotland over 3,000 feet high. Blair got in for the first time with 111 votes, in ninth place, one behind Bryan Gould.

Prescott accepted his 'slap on the wrist' with good grace. John Fallon, his adviser, was sent round to Blair's office with a 'present': he handed over all Prescott's files on energy and the privatisation of electricity which Prescott had intended to use.

'Transport is now a vital political issue. Britain has one of the worst transport systems of any developed economy. Deregulation and a lack of public investment have brought chaos to our road and rail network. There is a lot to be done,' said Prescott.

The Times reported that transport was soon to be given a higher profile. Neither Kinnock nor Prescott knew just how high it would rise.

CHAPTER THIRTEEN

Disaster Strikes

Don't worry, there will be another one along in a minute.
John Prescott on Tory transport ministers.

Almost from the moment Prescott took over the transport portfolio, Britain was hit by a series of major transport disasters. The roll-call of tragedies was horrendous: King's Cross, Clapham, Purley, Lockerbie.

As MPs were packing up for the Christmas break with a desultory debate in the House of Commons, news began to filter through the Palace of an air disaster – Pan Am flight 103 from Frankfurt to America had crashed on the small Scottish town of Lockerbie. TV crews produced late-night coverage of the nightmare after the jumbo jet crashed on the town, and of the devastation wrought by the fireball it caused. The unspeakable horror of a plane breaking up in flight was reinforced over the coming days by ghoulish photographs of the impact marks on the fields around the small Scottish town where bodies had crashed to earth and bounced; in a macabre touch, the buckled nose cone containing the flight deck, and the bodies of the pilot and crew, was found in a field, largely intact.

Paul Channon, then Transport Secretary, put the wheels in motion for the statutory inquiry, and went on holiday. It was a mistake from which he never recovered. Newspapers carried photographs of Channon arriving in Barbados, en route to the exclusive sun and society island of Mustique. Channon was pursued halfway across the globe to the Caribbean by Prescott's condemnation for leaving his desk.

'It is unbelievable, intolerable and insensitive for him to leave on holiday within 48 hours of Britain's worst aviation disaster and when bodies are still being retrieved and a major security review is under way,' said Prescott.

Within a month of replacing Bob Hughes, a likeable but lacklustre Labour frontbencher, Prescott had stamped his authority indelibly on the transport portfolio. Over the winter and well into the spring, Prescott was fired into the news by successive disasters, always harrying Channon. He was a well-liked Conservative of the old school, the son of the dilettante diarist and MP Henry 'Chips' Channon, and heir to the Guinness fortune. The Southend constituency was also part of the family 'inheritance', 'bequeathed' to Paul by his father in 1959. Eton- and Oxford-educated Channon was no match for the brawler from Hull.

These were no 'Acts of God'. There was a single thread running through all the disasters and loss of lives – human failures over safety in Prescott's view; on British Rail they were caused by cutbacks in preparation for privatisation; on Pan Am 103 it was the failure to carry out adequate bomb checks on through cargo at Heathrow. If there was one thing Prescott knew something about it was safety. Transport safety had been his specialist subject when he first became an MP. Prescott was in his element, and Conservatives accused him of exploiting the human tragedies. He had gained a reputation for blaming the government for everything from rising unemployment to the *Herald of Free Enterprise* ferry disaster in July 1987, but now the blame began to stick. He was hurting the government more than any other shadow minister.

By the end of 1989, Tony Blair was in Prescott's old employment post, hardening Labour's attitude towards the unions. Lawson and Thatcher were engaged in their fight to the death over exchange control policy, but Kinnock and Smith found it difficult to draw blood. Robin Cook, Labour's most lethal debater, was sidelined in the health portfolio, leaving Prescott on a roll.

Prescott believes one of the key factors in his battle with Channon was that Prescott was one of the first to install a mobile phone in his car. It was constantly in use. Before driving and using the mobile phone was banned, one journalist got a call from Prescott driving up the M1, with one hand on the steering wheel and the other on his phone, only to hear a strangulated cry from the shadow Transport Secretary: 'I've missed my bloody turning ...'

After suffering Prescott for nearly a year, Channon was dropped from the Cabinet by Thatcher, and replaced by Cecil Parkinson, in the second flush of his political career. The matricide in the Tory Party in 1990, which brought Major to power, also ended Parkinson's second ministerial career in the

Commons. He was replaced by the more studious Malcolm Rifkind and, a year later, elevated to the Lords. Prescott held the transport portfolio for five years, and saw them all off.

Surveying the wrecks of the ministerial careers around him in 1993, Prescott said, 'No, I don't hate them. I just have contempt for them. Channon's heart was in the right place, but he didn't have the head to match it – spent the whole time wringing his hands.

'Parkinson was just a smiler: no great ability. That's what he did in the Falklands: the troops did the fighting and he did the smiling.

'Malcolm Rifkind's great claim was that he caught the sleeper to Scotland. He actually went on a train. He explained to Thatcher that if you slept all the way, it's not too bad.'

But elections were not won on blaming the government for crashes. In 1992, after the fourth successive Conservative general election victory, John MacGregor, a former Treasury Minister, was put into the transport department by Major. It was to be his last ministry. MacGregor was brought in by Major to make sense of the rail privatisation proposals. Channon was patrician, Parkinson had charm, and Rifkind brains, but MacGregor – the Captain Mainwaring of the Cabinet – was a banker, with little time for Prescott. The feeling was mutual.

'He's a shitty little bastard,' said Prescott. 'He's a man of no courage. He won't even appear on TV with me. He is a little man, with a little mind concentrating on little problems, who cannot see the scale of things. It is a tragedy we have got him in Transport.'

Matthew Parris observed one clash between Prescott and MacGregor in the Commons, cruelly noting how Hansard had cleaned up Prescott's lack of syntax in defending his proposal that British Rail should be kept in the public sector but allowed to invest with private finance. In one column, Parris published what Prescott had actually said; in another, what Hansard reported he had said.

Thus:

> *I mean that's an example of this government that believes in the private sector and is in fact damaged the public sector's handling within the public sector in a number of these areas and you can go on with them in another areas.*

Became:

> *The government's insistence on private sector terms has damaged the public sector.*

And:

> *So I think the basic point that it is necessary in order to have private capital in our industries to get the extra resources that we do want that you have to be privatised is not borne out by the facts in other countries and neither we should we have it here also and if he's any doubts about that go and have a look at the reports that talk it.*

Became:

A blank. Parris said Hansard gave up.

Prescott may have had problems with his syntax, but he did have a wider vision for transport. It was his political home. His first front-bench post had been in transport, as merchant shipping spokesman in 1972–4; when Labour were next in opposition in 1979, he was the deputy transport spokesman to Albert Booth. Their researcher at the time was Peter Benjamin Mandelson, a bright former whizz-kid from the TUC's economic department who was also at the time the chairman of the British Youth Council and a Lambeth Labour councillor. Mandelson, educated at Hendon Grammar School and St Catherine's College, Oxford, where he gained a PPE honours degree, was the grandson on his mother's side of Herbert Morrison; in 1982, he left politics for the wider experience of television, joining LWT as a producer for the *Weekend World* programme. It was fronted by Brian Walden, the former Labour MP, and in those days a fearsomely incisive interviewer; but Mandelson was responsible for the political knife-work behind the scenes until returning to work for the party as its communications director in 1985 with a reference from Prescott. Prescott credits himself with giving Mandelson 'a reference for his first job in this spin-doctor world … and there are times when I have wondered about that, but I can't doubt his skills.' Larry Whitty, then General Secretary, confirmed that Prescott's reference for Mandelson was decisive in swinging the NEC vote for Mandelson to get the job.

After Michael Foot made Prescott the regional affairs spokesman, Prescott was shadow Transport Secretary in 1983–4, before taking over the employment portfolio, and then had his brief spell as energy spokesman. He was under a cloud of resentment from the leadership and the left of the party, when he took the transport portfolio for a second time in 1988.

It could have spelled his own disaster. He was slipping down the shadow Cabinet poll; Kinnock had punished him for running for the deputy leadership by dumping him in a political backwater; and, with the younger modernisers in the ascendancy, he could have sunk without trace. Instead, it proved the making of Prescott.

At the end of 1989, Prescott – for years regarded as the 'Mouth of the Humber' – was presented with the Debater of the Year award at a lavish *Spectator* awards ceremony in London. 'Transport … was meant as both demotion and a railway siding … The trains have been running pretty smoothly out of that siding, almost on the hour; the Opposition job is well enough done. The man himself is a worker who will never be caught under-read for a debate. There are people – the fervent and dim Michael Meacher and the sloppily bonhomous Frank Dobson – who do not fit in a modern-minded Labour front bench. Prescott, on intelligence and serious purpose, emphatically does,' Ed Pearce wrote in *The Shooting Gallery*.

The other winners included John Smith, Parliamentarian of the Year; Nigel Lawson, the former Chancellor, Speech of the Year, for his coruscating nine-minute resignation speech; Eric Heffer, Backbencher of the Year; and Neil Hamilton, Wit of the Year – he told the Commons that, when he was informed he was being given an award for being a shining wit, he assumed it was a spoonerism.

But there was a bigger prize for Prescott. A seat on the National Executive Committee.

Prescott fought on the issue of reforming the party's campaigning machinery, on which he had contested the leadership, and was voted on to the NEC at his first attempt, in the constituency section. Ken Livingstone was knocked off the NEC in the constituency section after many constituencies balloted their members.

Few had seen the possibilities that Prescott produced from the transport portfolio, and his vision for the subject has stood the test of time remarkably well.

In common with almost every front-bench job he has taken on, Prescott got to work in producing a major policy paper. It was called 'Moving Britain into the 1990s'.

There was one big new idea, buried in its 25 pages: private finance for investment (PFI) in British Rail. It said: 'Labour will encourage joint projects using public and private finance.'

Taken with a pledge to release the tight Treasury constraints on BR's rate of return, which were proving a straitjacket for investment, it was to be the pioneering idea which more clearly than any other demonstrated his willingness to challenge party orthodoxy.

Prescott has claimed, with some justification, that he was the first to promote PFI for railways. 'I made the case for private sector involvement in public investment,' he said.

The idea of private finance for BR occurred to Prescott when he was a junior Labour spokesman on shipping, when Sealink – then part of British Rail in the public sector – complained that they could not update their cross-Channel ferries, because, unlike their private competitors, they were not allowed by the Treasury to borrow money. His predecessor, Bob Hughes, staked a paternity claim to the idea of private finance for British Rail; his paper, 'Fresh Directions', promised to relax the profit targets on BR, with 'far greater flexibility' in financing, but it did not spell out the private finance proposal.

The Tories dispute his claim. John Major, then Chief Secretary to the Treasury, also proposed scrapping the Ryrie rules in 1989; but it did not come fully to fruition until 1995 – and the government still refused private finance for the Royal Mail. (The Ryrie rules were drawn up by a committee under a civil servant called Ryrie, and were interpreted to mean that private finance for public schemes, such as the building of the Dartford Bridge, should be treated as part of the public sector borrowing requirement – subject to the same spending controls – and allowed only where the money was cheaper to borrow than from the government; the last rule made it almost impossible.)

Prescott's determination to break these constraints showed the flexibility of his approach to old shibboleths like Clause Four of Labour's constitution, committing the party to public ownership. It was forced on him by a determination to sidestep the restrictions on spending imposed by Margaret Beckett, then shadow Chief Secretary to the Treasury, who was imposing a financial discipline on shadow spending commitments as rigorous as that of any Thatcherite.

'It was borne out of John's frustration with the shadow Treasury team,' said one of Prescott's allies. 'Margaret Beckett was chief secretary. Everything came back with "as resources permit" written on it. There was a major infrastructure crisis and private finance was his way of dealing with it.'

Beckett had taken over from Gordon Brown as the shadow Chief Secretary to the Treasury. Brown had resisted Prescott's expenditure plans in their draft stages. Now Beckett carried out a spending review as if she was in government, and enforced her iron will on Prescott and the other shadow ministers to stick to the discipline. John Marek, a junior Labour Treasury spokesman, was given the task of laying down the law to the Prescott camp in a meeting with Peter Snape, Prescott's transport deputy – a former signalman steeped in public transport. Marek told Snape that the Treasury team would not accept a hypothecated tax earmarked for improvements to public transport. Snape reminded Marek that Beckett represented the railway town of Derby; it was difficult to believe she would oppose a plan that could hit orders and jobs in the railway carriage works, but she was resolute.

The Labour policy document 'Meet the Challenge, Make the Change', the final report of Labour's policy review in 1989, steered around the subject. It promised to relax the Treasury's demands for British Rail to make a high rate of return on its investment, but omitted any specific mention of private finance. By 1992, Prescott had won his argument. The Labour manifesto said: 'Within six months, we will review the roads programme and mobilise private capital for large-scale public transport investment.'

On the day that John Major called the election, Prescott met the head of British Rail InterCity and other senior BR managers about private finance being used to modernise the network of main lines under a Labour government. It was overtaken by the drive towards privatisation after the election, but Prescott kept up the momentum for the concept, and in February 1994 – before the leadership election – he got the backing of Gordon Brown and Robin Cook, then DTI spokesman, for 'Financing Infrastructure Investment – Promoting a Partnership Between Public and Private Finance', setting out the new approach. Prescott was against toll roads, but saw no problem with private funds for the NHS, in spite of earlier protests by Harriet Harman that the government's private finance initiative was a 'privatisation initiative' on the health service.

When it was published, 'Moving Britain into the 1990s' caused controversy, not because of private finance, but because of Prescott's attack on Thatcher's 'Great Car Economy'.

In his policy paper 'Moving Britain into the 1990s', Prescott recognised the growing importance of the green lobby with two pages on environmental issues – including a promise 'to review road taxation to promote greater energy efficiency and environmental improvement'. It also promised to 'reshape taxation' on cars and coupled that with a range of new consumer protection measures for car-owners, including anti-clocking laws to stop Arthur-Daley-style second-hand car dealers cheating on vehicle mileage. 'Our aim is not to discourage people from owning cars, but to encourage their more sensible use.' But it still explicitly maintained the policy of using tax as a lever to reduce car use, not merely to cut lead emissions. 'We will encourage a significant and continuing shift from use of the private car to public transport …'

Prescott again encountered resistance from Smith and Beckett, the Treasury team, about the implied tax and spending commitments in his paper. There were wider worries about his proposals for cars. In addition to reducing the general motorway speed limit to 50 miles an hour at peak times and lowering the alcohol limit for the breath tests, Prescott proposed giving police the unequivocal power to carry out random breath tests, an issue he had first raised in 1984; Labour's left wing led by Tony Benn – not usually seen as the 'motorist's friend' – objected that the police might use the powers to stop young blacks for no reason, like the 'Sus' laws. That idea was dropped.

There were also battles in the shadow Cabinet and the NEC over the policy on cars. By 1991, with 'Opportunity Britain' – the forerunner of the 1992 manifesto – Labour under Kinnock had gone full circle. The tax review was still there, but it said: 'We are not "anti-car". We value the mobility which car ownership provides and want more people to benefit from it.' Tax was no longer to be used to balance car use with public transport. It was to be used to encourage 'greener' use of fossil fuels. 'It's Time to Get Britain Working Again', the 1992 election manifesto, said: 'We will reform transport taxation in order to encourage smaller, cleaner cars and the use of catalytic converters.'

Given the effectiveness of the 1992 Tory election campaign posters warning of 'Labour's tax bombshell', Kinnock, Smith and Beckett understandably were wary about taxing motorists off the roads. But Prescott felt their caution stifled the enterprise of ideas. Another plan, to tax employers to pay for new Tube lines and high-tech trams for their workers, had been tried in Paris and was proposed by Prescott in 'Moving Britain into the 1990s', but was quietly consigned to the waste bin by 1992. Chancellor Kenneth Clarke had no such worries: he imposed an additional 5 per cent on unleaded fuel duty without a squeak of protest.

Prescott's authority as shadow Transport Secretary was somewhat dented by his own driving on the M1 between Hull and Westminster. In spite of advocating lower speeds, Prescott was prosecuted in 1991 for his third speeding offence. The court was told that Prescott was driving his eight-year-old blue A-registration Daimler along the southbound carriageway and was doing an average of 105 miles an hour. Prescott was not in court, but his solicitor said the shadow Transport Secretary travelled more than 30,000 miles a year. He had two previous speeding convictions in July 1988 and March 1989 – so the court had little option: the shadow Transport Secretary was banned from driving for 21 days and fined £200. In 1995, Prescott and his car were again in the news, when his Jaguar XJ6 mysteriously disappeared from a street near the Commons – and Tory Central Office – where it had been parked. David, his son, drove him around the streets at 1 a.m., but they failed to find the car, which later turned up in the police pound, having been towed away from where it was parked, a few streets away. Prescott, convinced it had been stolen and dumped, could see the funny side, in spite of a bit of ragging in the press. 'The first thing I'll do is look at the membership forms in the boot – to see if they have been filled in.'

'Meet the Challenge, Make the Change' did go further than Prescott's own statement in one respect, however: it gave a cast-iron commitment to provide public finance to complete the high-speed link to the Channel Tunnel and the cross-London rail links. As a merchant seaman, Prescott had been a critic of the 'Chunnel', but, once it became a 'large hole' under the English Channel, he became a firm believer in a dedicated high-speed link to the Tunnel. He won Smith's permission to make the high-speed link a firm pledge in the manifesto; the government's failure to do so, and difficulty in agreeing a route, opened Malcolm Rifkind and John MacGregor to criticism, and Britain to continuing ridicule about the slow trains that didn't speed up until they got to France.

John Major's vision for the privatisation of British Rail was to revive the glorious days of pride in our railways. He spoke movingly of the coffee and cream livery of the Western region, which as a child he might have seen at Paddington. It was clear that his original concept was to privatise the railways by regions. That idea was gradually torn apart by the policy advisers at Downing Street and think tanks such as the Adam Smith Institute. InterCity was the money-spinner and the regional companies each wanted a slice. His approach was unworkable, he was told. British Rail had been split into different business sectors. It would make more business sense to hive off those sectors separately. Major's romantic sepia vision of the railways was replaced by a business hybrid, combining the sale of the track with franchising of the routes, supported by the taxpayer through continued public subsidies.

Prescott was opposed in principle to rail privatisation, but the muddle produced by policy committees under MacGregor made his job easier. Labour went into the 1992 general election firmly committed to stopping it. 'We reject Conservative plans to privatise British Rail. Instead, we will modernise setting clear performance targets to improve the quality of service and shift more freight from road to rail.'

There was just one blot on the horizon for Prescott: Kinnock.

Relations had got worse, not better, in spite of Prescott's success with the transport portfolio. As Britain prepared for war in the Gulf in February 1991, news leaked at Westminster of a small group of highly placed Labour frontbenchers, including Prescott, who had met in secret to discuss their objections to Labour's official strategy for the war. The group called itself the Supper Club.

The Supper Club met at the Red Lion (a pub near the Cenotaph), in committee rooms at the House of Commons and in a private room above a real-ale pub, the Westminster Arms. They were born, according to one of their number, out of frustration with the 'sterile' debates in the Tribune Group, which had become an 'election machine' for the annual shadow Cabinet beauty parade. 'Lots of new members were desperate to have a dialogue about the real issues of the day. It was not a meeting of plotters. It was a wide spectrum of people. We all stuck a fiver in for the buffet and we got stuck into a subject.'

Kinnock was furious after a copy of the minutes challenging Labour's Gulf War policy circulated by Mark Fisher was found by other Labour MPs and leaked to the press. It was pointed out that Eton-educated Fisher had failed the two guiding rules for plotters: don't get caught; and don't commit anything to paper.

In 1982, Prescott had dissociated himself from the NUS over its policy in support of sending the British armada to fight for the Falkland Islands. He told his union's annual conference: 'It would be a long and bloody road, and we cannot maintain a force down there even if we take [the islands].' Denis Healey took a similar view. A decade later, Prescott had reservations about going to war in the Gulf.

Prescott had not made his own views on the Gulf War a secret: in mid-January, he had told a meeting of the shadow Cabinet that Labour should not support any moves by the government to widen the war aims to include toppling Saddam.

But Kinnock was outraged to have a group apparently meeting in secret to challenge his authority. They included Joan Walley, who was close to the leadership; when she was challenged in the members' tearoom by other MPs about the discovery of the minutes the colour was said to have drained from her face.

There were plenty of 'supper clubs' on the Tory side: Nick's Diner, the Lollards, the 92, No Turning Back, One Nation. But Kinnock was not tolerant towards this challenge to his leadership. Fisher, the public-school boy, was summoned to the leader's room. Presented with the evidence, the bald, mild-mannered Fisher was said to have 'turned white as a sheet'.

The minutes showed that the group was planning to oppose a motion tabled for a PLP discussion on the Gulf War by Kinnock and Gerald Kaufman, the shadow Foreign Secretary, which, in addition to giving full backing to British and Coalition forces to secure fulfilment of UN resolutions on freeing Kuwait, also called for the 'restoration of international peace and security in the area'. Fisher said that appeared to be going beyond the UN resolution to liberate Kuwait.

The minutes said:

> *After an hour's discussion of various options … we agreed a) individually to seek out Gerald [Kaufman] today to stress our worries and urge him to make clear in his speech that this phrase did not, and would not, be used to widen the war aims. b) to attend the PLP if possible and try to speak, to voice these fears/warnings, c) put down a motion for next week's PLP clarifying the commitment … d) to use the next week to lobby support for such a motion.*

Fisher said Joan Ruddock, another member of Prescott's team, and the former leader of CND, would draft the motion.

> *With regard to potential support, I've trawled through the votes on the three debates and can identify just over 100 colleagues who, either by abstaining, voting against the leadership's line, or by belonging to Campaign or this group, can be said to have grave reservations about the present position.*
>
> *I've tried to avoid double counting, optimism etc. but that's the sort of level of concern, and doesn't count the (several) who've voted with the leadership on each occasion but who have real worries and reservations.*

Ruddock's PLP motion, with the benefit of hindsight, seems naive. It wanted offensive action to stop at the Iraqi border. It said the UN resolution would be fulfilled 'when complete control of Kuwaiti territory is achieved by the Allied Forces [and] no further offensive military action is taken and only such defensive military action as is absolutely unavoidable in the event of Iraq continuing hostilities ...'

It failed to anticipate Saddam's deception in concealing the Super Gun, the speed with which the Iraqi conscript army would be overrun, and the ruthless tenacity with which he would hold on to power after his defeat. And it failed to recognise the military needs of a wide sweep into Iraqi territory to smash Saddam's forces from behind. But the anxiety about Labour's line was shared by nearly half the PLP and borne out in 2003 after the second attack on Iraq, this time to overthrow the dictator.

Fisher referred to a Consolidated List of the names of all the MPs who had abstained in the Gulf War debates on 11 December 1990 and 15 and 21 January 1991 as potential supporters for the Supper Club amendment with the names of Labour MPs who had at any time voted against the leadership line on anything. When Campaign Group members and the Supper Club – calculated at 36 votes plus Bryan Gould – were added together, they came to 103 MPs, including four shadow Cabinet members, and ten other frontbenchers.

The Supper Club's days were numbered by this exposure; the end came when a photographer and reporter from the *Mail on Sunday* burst in on a meeting in the upstairs room at the Westminster Arms. Ian McCartney recalled that the reporter tripped over in her rush to get in, and the snapper fell over her. It was chaos. Some Supper Clubbers thought they were about to be shot by an armed gang of terrorists.

The snapshot showed Prescott leaning back with his finger pointing, as if in mid-sentence, Clare Short looking at the camera, Michael Meacher turning to see what the commotion was about, and Joan Walley with a startled look of consternation on her face. Others identified at the meeting were Leo Beckett, Joan Ruddock, Dick Caborn, Margaret Beckett, Frank Doran, Mike Watson and Jim Cousins.

The clandestine appearance of the meeting made them look like a plotters' society. Kinnock was furious to discover that three members of his shadow Cabinet – some said they would not admit Robin Cook – were continuing to meet behind his back, after the Gulf War leak.

McCartney, who signed himself 'the head waiter', sent round a note for the next meeting saying, 'Those of you who applied for a rebate on the grounds that your photograph did not appear in the *Mail on Sunday*, I have to inform you that your appeal has been rejected. All future claims for such rebates to be directed to Comrade Fisher (but not in writing)!'

Kinnock told McCartney: 'It's the Last Supper Club.'

He was almost right. It folded before the general election.

Kinnock was convinced that it was a vehicle for Prescott's next leadership campaign. In that he was wrong. While there were overlaps with its members and his campaign team, a number who joined failed to back Prescott when he ran for the deputy leadership a year later. They included Margaret Beckett, who beat him.

CHAPTER FOURTEEN

Round Two

> *Went down smiling …*
>
> Prescott campaign medal.

Nothing seemed to go right on election night in 1992. Prescott had bitten into a Cadbury Roses chocolate and cracked a tooth. (Pauline keeps the chocolates in the refrigerator and it had been frozen when he bit into it.)

The shadow Transport Secretary had been kept out of the limelight for most of the campaign by the party's spin doctors but he was allowed on to *Election Night* on television after the polls had closed. The spin doctors need not have worried. In spite of the pain of his cracked tooth, Prescott was on his best behaviour. He floored a television interviewer by defending 'designer socialism'. He said Labour was nearly dead as a party when designer socialism helped to revive it.

The spin doctoring was maintained to the end.

'We were all sent our common message, what to say when the results came through. It said the first [point to make] is "moral victory for Labour"; the second thing to say was "best since World War II"; and the third one was to say Neil Kinnock was a great leader. They all said exactly the same thing through the night until it became clear that the Tories were going to get a majority. Then nobody would go on after two o'clock. I was the only one on television,' said Prescott.

Prescott had been a member of the leader's general election strategy committee, but effectively had been frozen out of the campaign. There were only three meetings of the leader's committee and they were to rubber-stamp decisions that had already been taken. He had no idea who some of its members were or why they had been drawn into the campaign team.

He was staggered to see they had recruited Patricia Hewitt, the former policy coordinator in Neil Kinnock's office, who had written the leaked memorandum about the 'loony left' before the 1987 election. She was the director of the centre-left think tank the Institute for Public Policy Research. What was she doing there, he wondered. And Lord Hollick, a wealthy Labour backer, was also there. What was going on?

Prescott was appalled to find that some of these imported advisers, who had never been elected, were involved in filleting the manifesto before it was published; it was another example in his view of 'aides' influencing policy in the most arbitrary fashion.

They left out a key phrase, qualifying all Labour's spending commitments with the rider: 'We will not spend, nor will we promise to spend, more than Britain can afford.' It may not have prevented the damage that was to come with the Tories' 'tax bombshell' charge, but the omission left Labour more vulnerable to the central attack on spending by the Tories.

Every morning, Labour held a press conference in an ice-cold white set – relieved only by the red of a bowl of red roses and the red rose logo – at 4 Millbank, a stylish office complex with atrium and basement health club where the BBC, ITN, Channel Four and regional channels had their Westminster television studios. The shadow Transport Secretary had no more than a walk-on part when transport was the issue of the day.

Prescott was determined he was not going to be packaged into silence. With the first week of the campaign over, he slipped through the spin doctors' net on to satellite TV, and went on Sky's *Election Call.*

Prescott was asked to admit that the minimum wage, which he had supported since the 'Full Employment' document in 1985, could mean job losses. To the horror of the 'aides', he decided that honesty was the best policy.

'I think you have to accept there may be some shakeout in some of the jobs in certain areas, but generally it will be beneficial to the community,' he admitted.

Labour aides criticised him for his remarks. 'I was told by the spin doctors that we're not saying that.' But Prescott was not being dictated to by soundbite salesmen. He fought back. 'Who's not saying it? The party policy's clear about it …' he said.

A month after the election, he justified his honesty in typical Prescott fashion. 'On the minimum wage, I was the one that first brought it in with the Low Pay Unit, in my policy document "Planning for Full Employment". And I knew the consequences were that there'd be some shakeout, any silly fool knew that, and it was in our documents that would be one of the consequences …'

Prescott the fighter learned, however, that leading with the chin was not wise. In June 1996, he changed his approach. 'Several years ago I worried that a minimum wage would lead to a shakeout of jobs. I must say the evidence I have seen over the past few years has convinced me that we should have no such fear.'

It was a hostage no one was interested in at the time, but his quotes were diligently stored on the Conservative Party headquarters computer to be used against Labour at the next election. For now, the Tories had bigger targets – tax, tax and tax. Prescott, arguably one of Labour's best campaigning assets, was left to tend his constituency.

In previous elections, Prescott had led a motorcade through Hull East, which had become his adopted home. He was well known, and well liked. Going out to the chip shop or the pub, he would be instantly recognised, and shown genuine warmth. 'He's like a big soft uncle to them,' said one of his relatives. On one occasion, not realising his mike was switched on, he had a swearing match with an official, which was broadcast to his loyal voters as he toured the streets.

Harry Woodford, his agent, advised him that his majority would look after itself in East Hull. He told Prescott to get on the road again, and put his campaigning energy to good use in the marginals. That is what he did.

'He had 90 places where they wanted him to speak,' said Woodford. Prescott had a majority of 23,692 in 1979 when he ran against Mr Bean, the Tory candidate; that was reduced by boundary changes to 10,074 in 1983. It had risen to 14,689 in 1987 with 27,287 votes. Woodford was right. In 1992 Prescott's majority went up to 18,719 with 30,092 votes – 62.9 per cent of the poll.

Unfortunately for Labour, the pull of Prescott was not felt in places like Basildon, the home of 'Essex Man', where Labour needed to win back blue-collar Tories to regain power. The opinion polls that showed Labour in a three-point lead when Major called the election for 9 April mesmerised the media and the campaign teams. The triumphalist Kinnock rally in Sheffield a week before polling day struck the wrong note. Like the rest of the shadow Cabinet who trooped on to the platform like rock stars, Prescott watched as Neil Kinnock became Meatloaf for a moment. Met by the wall of noise from cheering supporters, the Leader of Her Majesty's Opposition, in a mid-Atlantic-meets-Rhondda accent, shouted: 'Awright …'

The show overran and almost missed the BBC's nine o'clock news. 'I had to do a live interview … against competition from rock music, exploding fireworks and assorted mayhem,' John Cole recalled.

The rally was criticised with the benefit of hindsight because it looked like a victory parade. But that was not the problem. It was on an epic scale. Huge flags fluttered in a breeze made by wind machines on the platform. The visual image for television viewers – the undecided voters who anonymously slipped out to vote for John Major a week later – was not so much of Kinnock the Rock Star as Gorbachev addressing the last Soviet Presidium.

In response, Major brought out his soapbox.

The Tory campaign had been universally criticised as lack-lustre, and Major was patronised by the press. 'As the third week of campaigning drew to a close, it was hard to believe that the Prime Minister's grasp on reality was entirely secure. Did he really imagine that in this series of bleak photo-opportunities and stage-managed rallies, he had touched the pulse of the nation?' wrote Isabel Hilton.

But the Tory campaign came alive when Major took to the soapbox, first in Luton, and then around the country. Prescott felt that Major's simple honesty had out-campaigned all Labour's flashy public relations.

'And there are all of us laughing at him, appearing at our press conferences with our bowl of roses and the proper sound-bites, and looking nice. Both are needed but we've been obsessed with the form. I'm interested in the substance,' said Prescott.

On the road with Major, it was impossible not to be impressed by his guts. In the face of all the polling evidence he kept saying he was going to win. There was a serious wobble halfway through the campaign at Manchester Airport on 1 April when – with the press pack waiting on the tarmac for the flight to London – news came through that Labour had extended its poll lead to 7 per cent. The next day, Labour held the Sheffield rally. The polls were right, up to a point; but they could not second-guess voters' real intentions. The voters felt bad about the government, but, when it came to what Major calls 'the stubby pencils' in the polling booths, they would not trust Labour and Kinnock.

In the midst of his campaign, Prescott criticised the Labour election crusade for being too cautious. 'Playing safe hasn't done us very well, has it? All the individuality, the chance, the difference has been taken out of our politics, and the electorate doesn't trust it.'

He was disappointed that Labour had not given more prominence to the training levy and full employment. 'It's the fourth election we've lost running under, as I understand it, these people – I call them the beautiful people – who have, in fact, run the elections the last two times and we've still lost.'

The frustration extended to Glenys Kinnock and Ann Clwyd, a Labour frontbencher. Clwyd was returning by car from the Sheffield rally when she was informed that a press conference with Glenys Kinnock on Third World aid had been cancelled. It was later held on a Sunday, with little notice. Clwyd, like Prescott, resented the power of the young magic circle and later clashed with David Miliband, one of Mandelson's friends, later to head Tony Blair's policy unit and become a Cabinet minister in Prescott's Office of the Deputy Prime Minister. 'Some of us have been around this place longer than you,' she told him.

From the Labour bunker, it hardly felt like 'playing safe'. John Smith's shadow Budget offered to raise the upper rate of tax to 50p, and abolish the ceiling on National Insurance contributions, hitting millions of taxpayers. In return, it promised to raise child benefit and state pensions, but Labour's pledge to increase taxes was the message that lingered longest. The Tories saw to that with the 'tax bombshell' poster campaign. It had been wheeled out by the Tories in two previous campaigns, and looked outmoded when it was tried again. The bomb depicted in the posters was no high-tech guided missile of the type used in the Gulf War. It was an old-fashioned, World War II block-buster with big rivets, the kind of device seen by younger voters only in black and white war movies with Jack Hawkins and Richard Attenborough.

But it landed bang on target.

The power of the Tories' tax weapon – in spite of their own increases in taxes since 1992 – continued to keep Labour's leadership on the defensive into 1996, adding to Prescott's frustration at the caution displayed by Labour out of fear of another attack.

The 'Kinnock factor' was also exploited mercilessly by the Tories. A couple of floating Tory voters in Bath were typical of the problem. As Major's campaign bus rolled through the city centre, they said they would not be voting Conservative. 'Not even if it let in Kinnock?' they were asked. Put that way, they were don't-knows. Chris Patten, the Tory chairman, lost his Bath seat to the Liberal Democrats. Tory advertising, hitting tax and Kinnock, reinforced by a willing press, targeted with pinpoint accuracy the two fears about Labour in voters' minds. Patrick Rock, Chris Patten's adviser, had kept predicting the appearance of 'that tardy Russian', and on polling day 'Late Surge' galloped to Major's rescue.

By 4 a.m. on Friday, it emerged that Major had won a working majority with 14.2 million votes, the biggest popular vote for any government since the war. Within 24 hours, as Major prepared a Cabinet reshuffle at Number Ten, Kinnock, in a mood of bitter disappointment for the party as well as himself, privately made it clear he had decided to resign. His likely resignation was the main lead in the *Independent* on Saturday, 11 April.

The speed of Kinnock's departure pitched the party into a fresh round of recriminations. Trade union leaders, with astonishing ineptitude, began jockeying for position to endorse John Smith, the shadow Chancellor, as the next leader of the Labour Party before Kinnock announced he was standing down. They were led by John Edmonds, the leader of Smith's own GMB (general workers') union. There was also speculation that the union barons wanted Margaret Beckett as his deputy for a 'dream ticket'.

Clare Short protested that Kinnock appeared to be engineering events by the timing of his departure so that Smith could be crowned before the annual party conference in October. Colin Byrne, a former Labour Party press officer, wrote an intemperate letter to the *Guardian* disclosing that he had quit the party in protest at what he believed was a conspiracy to make Smith the leader if Labour lost the election. Byrne was married to Julie Hall, Kinnock's press officer, who had dramatically burst into tears during the campaign in front of the cameras at a campaign press conference when she was forced to defend her family for using private health care. Byrne felt that the whispering campaign had undermined Kinnock to make Smith his natural successor. Now it seemed to be coming to pass.

The 'nod and a wink' contest to put Smith and Beckett into office also upset Prescott. 'What the election seems to have been based on is the idea that we can get two candidates and perhaps have no need for any election at all,' he said. 'People are getting angry about it, particularly in the constituency parties ... that somehow it is being settled before even the MPs have met.'

On Monday, 13 April, Kinnock with his wife, Glenys, and his parliamentary aide, Adam Ingram, called a press conference to announce he was standing down 'in the best interests of the Labour Party'.

'The decisions which I have made will require rapid change. Those decisions have not, however, been taken hastily. They result from rational consideration which I have given over a period of time to the future of the Labour Party.'

It had been a long, hard road for Kinnock, who took over a shambolic Labour Party from Foot in 1983, took on Militant, and made Labour into a fighting machine. It was not a fit of pique – 'the action that I am taking is an essential act of leadership' – but he could not go without a final sideswipe at the Tory press who had pilloried him. He quoted Lord McAlpine, former Tory Party treasurer, who said the heroes of the campaign were Sir David English, editor of the *Daily Mail*; Sir Nicholas Lloyd, editor of the *Daily Express*; and Kelvin MacKenzie, editor of the *Sun*.

'I make, and I seek, no excuses and I express no bitterness when I say that the Conservative-supporting press has enabled the Tory Party to win yet again when the Conservative Party could not have secured victory for itself on the basis of its record, its programme or its character.'

His warning was felt deeply across the party. It increased the belief of the modernisers waiting in the wings that, in order to win, abandoning the 'safety first' strategy was not the answer: it had to be reinforced.

Roy Hattersley also confirmed he was standing down as deputy leader.

The other candidates now rushed to the starting line.

Bryan Gould, who had been Labour's campaign coordinator for the general election, was the first to announce he was standing. As a journalist, 'one of us', Gould was well liked by the press for his frankness. He did not disappoint. In his memoirs, Gould's bitterness spilled out, accusing Mandelson of running 'The Mandelson Project' before the 1992 general election to get Gordon Brown – or Tony Blair as a fallback – eventually elected when Kinnock stood down, by undermining others, including Gould, Cook and Prescott.

Mandelson, who had transformed Labour's campaign machine behind Kinnock for the 1987 election, protested to the *Observer* after one Prescott interview that he was not to blame for Prescott's isolation; in 1992 Mandelson was fighting for his own seat in Hartlepool and was not in charge of the election campaign strategy.

Gould launched his campaign by attacking Smith's shadow Budget, which was held, in retrospect, to have sealed Labour's defeat. Kinnock had tried – at a notorious off-the-record lunch at Luigi's, an Italian restaurant in Covent Garden – to ease its impact by saying the lifting of the National Insurance contributions ceiling would be phased in; Smith went nuclear and stubbornly insisted it would not. A long-term Euro-sceptic, Gould also tore apart Labour's most obvious election deception, that Labour would not have devalued the pound, and openly advocated devaluation of sterling within the Exchange Rate Mechanism. Without it, Britain could not reflate the economy, a view Prescott strongly supported. And he called for the ending of the trade union block vote. That set the tone for the election campaign.

Clearly he could not be endorsed by Smith. Backed by his campaign manager, David Blunkett – one of the architects for change behind Kinnock – Gould set out to capture the modernisers' votes. His campaign leaflet said: 'A "safety first" approach and waiting for the Tories to lose won't produce election victory. We'll have to reach out to those voters who felt unable to trust us. We need to get ahead of the game, no longer trailing along behind the voters, but thinking our way through to where their aspirations will take them.'

Gould reinforced the point in a letter to MPs. Labour had failed to break through in the south, he said, because 'our policies appeared to set a cap on the aspirations on the voters we need to win.'

Apart from the anti-European tone, it was pure Blairism.

In fact, the Tory strategists told me as the Labour campaign began, the man they feared most was Blair. But Blair judged it was too soon. He was not standing. Gould's result proved him right. Kinnock advised Gould not to stand because 'Smithy has got it all sewn up … He won't last the course. It's important that you're there to pick up the pieces.'

Prescott's team felt Gould had effectively tripped himself up before the gun was fired by announcing he was running for the leadership and the deputy leadership. On Monday 14 April, Prescott made it clear he would stand, but only for the deputy leadership.

Smith feared that Gould might win the deputy leadership, and felt that Gould's attack on his Budget strategy had made it impossible to work with him. That forced Beckett, Smith's deputy in the Treasury team, to show her hand. On 15 April, she announced she was standing for the deputy leadership against Gould and Prescott.

Prescott would have had to reconsider if Beckett had announced her intention before him, but not for long. He supported women's quotas – much to the amusement of his constituency, which did not – and he made great play of the fact in his campaign that half his shadow transport team were women. Beckett would give women a voice at the centre, but she was not standing on his platform for constitutional change. And it is unlikely anything would have stopped Prescott from standing. One of his supporters had telephoned Beckett over the weekend to ask whether she would stand. She was waiting to see whether Blair would run as deputy.

Blair spent the weekend calculating. To go for the deputy leadership now, and to win it, would have a serious downside for the young pretender. It was a job which nobody with serious ambition to be leader really wanted; Brown, Healey and Hattersley all took it as second best. Blair did not want to be cast as the deputy while Gordon Brown eventually succeeded to the leadership when Smith stood down. Smith was 54 – the possibility that he might be too old was part of a black-propaganda whispering campaign from the start of the contest. He had already suffered one heart attack, and would be 59 by the time of the next general election. Blair decided to watch, and wait.

Beckett's 'Modernisation Manifesto' – its title chosen to show that, in spite of her left-wing roots, she wanted the votes of the Blairite modernisers – was a wide-ranging policy document, calling for reviews on tax and social insurance, poverty and state funding of parties. She also supported Prescott's line on widening membership through union political levies. However, while she defended the link with the unions, she wanted to think 'long and hard' about one-member-one-vote democracy.

Margaret Beckett had many detractors. She had been on the left of the party in the 1970s and early 1980s, when the left was in the ascendancy – excoriating Kinnock to his face at a Tribune rally; Joan Lestor tartly reminded the activists at the rally that, when she had resigned as a Minister for Overseas Development in the Callaghan government, it was Margaret Jackson (before she married Leo Beckett) who jumped into her seat. As a 'retread', in a new constituency, she had returned to the Commons determined to rebuild a formidable reputation as a hard-headed politician – no mean feat for a woman in the Commons – with real influence on the leadership, not on the sidelines criticising it. Like Prescott, she had from time to time proved incapable of supporting Kinnock on the NEC, voting with the left in favour of cuts in defence spending at a tense NEC meeting at the party conference in 1990. But she was one of the strongest supporters of Smith's economic orthodoxy. As shadow Chief Secretary to the Treasury, she had been responsible for

'Beckett's Law' – limiting spending commitments by Labour to child benefit and state pensions. Her campaign manager was Gordon Brown, who was later appointed shadow Chancellor by Smith. She was seen as Smith's running mate, and ran a clever but cautious campaign, distancing herself when necessary from Smith, by reaffirming her support for CND.

On the same day as Beckett, Prescott drew around him his close friends at Westminster, and launched his campaign on 15 April 1992 – less than a week after the shattering election defeat – at a press conference at Westminster.

'In view of the encouragement and messages of support that I have received from my friends and colleagues, I announce that I am standing as a candidate for the deputy leadership of the Labour Party.'

The main themes of his campaign, he said, were decentralisation of power and government, full employment and a coordinated transport policy. But he believed the campaign was not about policy. He fought it on the narrow issue of organisation. 'My main priority will be to lead the revival in the Labour Party's organisation, membership and finances, which is vital to our success at the next election …'

He had a dig at the party spin doctors for excluding him from the election campaign team. 'We have learned that elections cannot be won by simply relying on a highly centralised campaign and mass communications …'

And he set out what was to become his successful stall for the 1994 leadership election campaign. 'I believe the deputy leader should relieve the pressure on the leader by not taking a major parliamentary portfolio. Instead, the deputy should devote all their efforts and energy to building the organisational strength of the party.'

He was two years ahead of his time, but his ideas had their own gravitational pull. As Prescott's campaign began to roll, the other candidates had to respond to his strategy for a mass party, first outlined in his paper in 1988. 'At least the ideas I put forward in the 1988 campaign to rebuild our organisation have now been adopted by the other candidates in this election.'

Prescott's case was supported by academic evidence by Patrick Seyd and Paul Whiteley, who studied the 1987 results and concluded that local activism had a very important influence on the Labour vote at constituency level. 'These results show, for example, that if the Labour Party had been about one-third larger than it was at the time of the election (1987), it would have received nearly 5 per cent more of the total vote than it actually did receive,' they concluded in *Labour's Grassroots: The Politics of Party Membership*.

Anthony Bevins, the assiduous political editor of the *Independent*, reported that, in spite of Major's overall vote, there were wide regional disparities in voting patterns, and the Tories' victory was achieved with very narrow margins in many seats; if 1,248 voters in eleven marginals had voted differently, Major would not have had a Commons majority.

A miss was as good as a mile, in soccer manager's terms, but the message was driven home for Prescott's opponents. Prescott had a point. Better organisation could have tipped the balance. And, if Prescott was good at anything, it was organising votes.

From his earliest days on board ship, he had coupled his rabble-rousing with canvassing for votes. In one shadow Cabinet election, the leaders of all the big transport unions, attending an international transport conference in Madrid, personally telephoned their union-sponsored Labour MPs at Westminster to canvass in support of Prescott. His support duly shot up.

The acrimony with Kinnock had gone, but the wounds were yet to heal. Prescott's campaign leaflet carried an article from the *New Statesman* in which he had taken a swipe at Kinnock. 'It is unfortunate that the leadership contest was called immediately after the general election. We are still unclear about why we lost, and there are two reasons why we should not rush to conclusions. First, flawed analysis will lead us in the wrong direction; and second, candidates making snap judgements today may discover that, if successful, they may not be able to retract hasty conclusions tomorrow. We need no more "back me or sack me" decisions.'

Labour had lost many of its core voters. He promised a detailed post-mortem into the election defeat, but said, 'We should not destroy the historic link between the unions and Labour.' It was not only a philosophical view. As ever, his politics were driven by pragmatism. 'Their financial support is essential for a country bereft of state finance for political parties.' He returned to the drive for a million members he had wanted in 1988, and said the party should look at introducing a 'levy-plus' system where a nominal sum in addition to the political levy would grant full Labour Party membership rights.

Prescott's campaign manager was Dick Caborn, his long-standing ally from Sheffield. On the management team were Peter Snape (his deputy in the transport team), Simon Buckby (his press officer), Joyce Matheson (office manager), Rosie Winterton (his adviser) and Ian McCartney (the 'head waiter' from the Supper Club and MP for Makerfield in Lancashire).

McCartney's strength was in organisation and attention to detail. McCartney was made campaign coordinator and issued the campaign team with its marching orders. The campaign writers were Phil Murphy, then with the *Yorkshire Post*, later political editor of PA News; and Andy Fox, a former Labour press officer. Caborn and two MEPs, Brian Simpson and Roger Barton, were to recruit regional groups of MPs and MEPs. Sam McCluskie, leader of Prescott's RMT union, was to lead the campaign in the unions. McCartney's memorandum said Rosie Winterton and Joan Walley (on Prescott's transport team) were to 'develop strategy of positive image and counter "gender factor" campaigning by Smith/Beckett, recruit key women supporters.'

McCartney said, 'To achieve our targets, we shall require a highly disciplined and motivated management structure to implement our twin political and organisational strategies …'

If Prescott had a 'Mandelson' figure, it was Alan Meale. He was always in the background, quietly organising votes, pulling in trade union support, backing Prescott to the hilt. Meale, ten years younger, first came across Prescott when Meale was a seaman, serving on cargo ships and tankers in the sixties for companies such as Pacific Steam Navigation. Prescott had been a rabble-rouser during the 1966 NUS strike and Meale had been bowled over by his ability to connect with a crowd.

'You could see there was an ability there. He could lift a crowd; he believed in what he was saying, from the bottom of his boots.'

Meale, from Bishop Auckland, had been educated at Ruskin, before a university course at Durham; he became an assistant to Ray Buckton, the general secretary of ASLEF, the rail union, before working as political adviser to Michael Meacher, a candidate for the deputy leadership in 1983. In 1987, Meale secured the rock-solid Labour constituency of Mansfield. Quiet and astute, he became so good at delivering the Campaign Group slate at shadow Cabinet elections that it became known as the 'Meale ticket', and one of those to benefit was Prescott. He played a key background role in all three of Prescott's campaigns for the deputy leadership, and in 1994 was appointed his parliamentary Private Secretary. Like most of those around Prescott, he was loyal, and trusted by Prescott.

The campaign team threw themselves into a storm of speeches, leaflets and canvass returns. There were speeches by someone from the Prescott team somewhere, almost every night. Caborn's campaign diary for 2 June 1992 records: 'House back – 9 am Institute of Corrosion – opening speech'; on 4 June – '"Clive Anderson Talks Back"?' On 12 June they were in Aberdeen, the next day in Edinburgh.

The endorsements included that of Joan Lester: 'He's a fighter – a campaigner who gets things done.'

Lists of MPs were ticked off, region by region, supporting, not supporting, maybe supporting. On one canvass sheet,

Caborn scribbled in black ink his guesstimate of the nominations for the deputy leadership: Prescott 64, Beckett 89, Gould 64, Grant 15. And he circled the Gould votes – they were vital if Prescott was to gain on Beckett. His guess was not far out. Ann Clwyd dropped out after an acrimonious battle over the rules.

On 7 May, the parliamentary Labour Party was told the following nominations had been received from MPs: leader – Gould 62, Ken Livingstone 13, John Smith 163; deputy leader – Beckett 88, Gould 70, Bernie Grant 14, and Prescott 65. Grant and Livingstone failed to reach the required threshold and dropped out.

The unions held 40 per cent of the votes in the electoral college; the MPs and constituencies, 30 per cent each. The candidates spoke at union conferences up and down the country; Caborn carefully listed the union support, as their executives made recommendations, and membership ballot results came in. Nobody was overlooked, not even the Loom Overlookers' union, whose share of the poll was 0.008 per cent. By early June, the picture was pretty clear: most of those who had supported Hattersley for the deputy leadership in 1988 – including the TGWU – were solidly backing the Smith–Beckett ticket. A few, like the Bakers and BECTU, were supporting Smith–Prescott; some, like the clerical NCU, had switched from Prescott in 1988 to Smith–Gould. Prescott had SOGAT, the NGA – left-wing printworkers' union – the miners' NUM and NACODS, and NUPE, but it was not enough. Beckett was sailing home.

Some members of Prescott's team said that in the first

campaign they issued completely phoney canvass returns showing Prescott well ahead of Hattersley, after bending the data fed into the computers. It was known in the team as flying 'paper aeroplanes'. Prescott asked one of his aides what they could do now to boost the campaign for the last few days. 'Try the paper aeroplanes,' he was told. If they were going to lose, they were going to have fun in doing so.

There was a brief hope that he might force Beckett into a second ballot, but by early July it was all over bar the shouting.

On a sunny day on 18 July 1992, Labour's electoral college – constituency delegates, MPs and union leaders – gathered at the Royal Horticultural Hall in London to elect Smith and Beckett. The mood was a 'love-in' – Beckett in her victory speech praised Prescott and Gould for the 'excellent spirit' of the campaign, and Gordon Brown. 'No one ever had a bigger slave-driver as a campaign manager.' And she praised Kinnock for his 'courage, vision and dignity'.

The results were: leader – Smith 90.9 per cent, Gould 9.1 per cent. Deputy leader – Beckett 56.8 per cent (19 per cent from the CLPs, 12.8 from the MPs and 25 per cent from the unions), Prescott 28.4 per cent (7, 9.4 and 12), and Gould 14.7 per cent (4, 7.7 and 3).

The speed with which the union barons appeared to adopt the 'dream ticket' of Smith and Beckett had accelerated the demands from the grass roots for more say in the decisions of the party. That meant reducing the power of the trade union block vote by replacing it with greater democracy, based on the principle of one member, one vote.

As Smith and Beckett posed for the cameras, and the hall began to pack up, Tom Sawyer, the deputy general secretary of NUPE, spoke to me. He had a grizzled grey beard, and a quiet manner, but was one of the most astute players behind the scenes in the Labour Party. As chairman of the NEC home policy committee, Sawyer was a shrewd operator, who had quietly helped Kinnock modernise the party with minimum fuss from the unions. He suggested I should keep an eye open for an idea that was coming up for something called a 'supporters' club' in which payers of trade union political levies could hand over an additional supporters' fee to join the Labour Party and take part in its votes. It was a variant of Prescott's 'levy-plus' idea, and it was clearly on the agenda now the leadership election was over.

As the results were read out, Meale told Prescott to smile. And he did so. It was like the sun coming out. Mr Angry had gone. In his place was a candidate who, though defeated, could live to fight another day without rancour or bitterness. It was a piece of advice that proved crucial to his next assault on the leadership. Prescott struck a medal for his defeated campaign team, which summed up the mood. The medals bore the legend: 'Went down smiling'.

PART TWO

CHAPTER FIFTEEN

OMOV

If he does nothing else in his life, that speech had everything.
Pauline Prescott.

John Prescott made the speech of his life at the Labour Party annual conference in October 1993. It was a passionate appeal for the party to back John Smith, then Labour leader, for the introduction of one-member-one-vote (OMOV) democracy in the constituency parties. It was a cry from the heart from one of the strongest guardians of the Labour Party's links with the trade unions to support a move that would weaken trade union power. Prescott and Smith narrowly won the vote, and the Labour Party embarked on the first radical step towards the modernisation to which Tony Blair has committed his party since winning the leadership.

Those who were in the lofty Brighton conference centre to hear Prescott's speech will never forget it.

'There's no doubt this man, our leader, put his head on the block when he said he believes, because he fervently believes, of a relationship and a strong one with the trade unions and the

Labour Party. He's put his head there; now's the time to vote, give us a bit of trust and let's have this vote supported.'

The words tumbled in a torrent, but people knew what he meant, and they gave him a standing ovation.

Smith had warned Prescott that if he lost he would resign.

Some observers said that, by then, the votes had already been decided in caucus meetings around Brighton, and that Prescott's speech, though moving, did not tip the balance. There is evidence to suggest that it was more than mere folklore.

David Hill, Smith's press officer, says that Prescott's intervention was crucial.

Hill was told late on Wednesday morning that the support among the constituency parties appeared to be slipping. Sally Morgan, the official advising the conference arrangements committee, was responsible for the idea of putting Prescott in. Prescott had done his transport speech two days earlier. Sally Morgan had said, 'Why don't you ask John to wind up?'

Beckett would have been the natural choice, but on Tuesday, the day before the vote, she had failed to give her wholehearted support to the leadership line in a BBC interview. Pressed whether she hoped Smith would win, she said, 'I very much hope that we will be able to reach a decision.'

Prescott was on the platform on Wednesday morning with Sally Morgan and David Hill when he was summoned to see Smith in the leader's room, an anteroom at the back of the conference platform. Murray Elder, Smith's adviser, was also there. Smith was blunt. 'John, I am going to lose this vote. I am going to lose the MSF [Manufacturing, Science and Finance Union].'

Prescott takes up the story. 'He said, "Would you do the debate?" I said, "Yes, if you are asking me to do it, I will do it. The first thing you need to do is square it with Margaret [Beckett]. I don't want to be getting up there without knowing that Margaret is on board." And I said, "What about Larry [Whitty, party General Secretary]?" He was due to wind up the debate. Larry was brought in and agreed. John was going to a *Daily Mirror* lunch.'

David Hill recalled: 'We had taken soundings and they showed that we could lose support among the constituency parties. Prescott's speech stopped that support draining away.'

Caborn confirmed this account. 'It was eleven o'clock in the morning when Smithy spoke to him. He had to pull half a per cent, or 1 per cent. It was the MSF. He was called up but he would do it only on one condition, that he didn't usurp Margaret Beckett's authority [as deputy leader]. He told John [Smith] that, "Look, as far as I am concerned, I'll do it, but you must clear it with Margaret." Margaret said, "Fine." So he went away and scribbled some notes together and then did the impromptu stuff.'

At lunchtime, Prescott was due to address a fringe meeting, organised by Rosie Winterton, his former aide, who was then with Connect Public Affairs, a PR company handling the campaign to build a dedicated rail link to the Channel Tunnel with access to the north of England.

The night before, Rosie, later to rejoin Prescott's office as a key adviser, met Tony Blair in one of the parties around the conference. Blair told her there was trouble brewing over the

OMOV vote and in his view, the only person who could sort it out was Prescott – a view that would be repeated when Blair, as leader, decided to rewrite the party's commitment to Clause Four, concerning public ownership.

Prescott, in spite of the pressure now on him to deliver the closing speech in the OMOV debate that afternoon, went to the fringe meeting to apologise to Rosie that he could not address them as he had planned. 'He said, "I can't do it because Smithy's asked me to a meeting."' He had been asked to a lunchtime meeting with John Smith to discuss the speech he would make that afternoon.

He made a brief speech in support of the Channel link, and told his audience, 'I cannot tell you why I have got to go …'

The Prescott text was quickly scribbled out over lunch in consultation with Smith, but it hardly mattered. Prescott knew what he had to say and did so without notes. It was here that, during the course of their private meeting, Smith told Prescott that, if he lost, he would resign.

'I said to him, "Have you looked at all the possible compromises?" And he said, "Yes, but there's no time for compromise now – I have to make my position clear. I've made it, and I'm going to fight for this principle." And he then indicated that if he lost he would resign. I was quite appalled by that, but this was the measure of this man. He had reached this stage; he had listened to the views; he'd made his mind up. Now was the time to make clear his view and his party could come along with him or not.'

Prescott told Smith he could not resign, but Smith was adamant.

However, Smith had a fallback position, which has not been told before. Smith told Prescott in their private meeting that, if he did lose, he would go to the executive and ask it to back him. Then he would go back to the conference and seek to reverse its vote. He would resign if that failed. John Edmonds, the GMB general union leader, was ready to move a confidence motion for Smith the next day, if he lost.

Prescott told him point-blank, 'You cannot ask the conference to stand on its head. They won't do it.'

He warned Smith that, if he took that course, Prescott would oppose him. Smith did not argue. He was intent on winning the vote at the first go. Prescott also warned the party leader that if he won the vote it would be Prescott who would be the hero of the hour. Smith shrugged at that prospect.

'If I win, I will live with that problem.' Smith smiled.

That lunchtime, as Smith and Prescott talked, there was frantic activity among the delegations around the bars, chip shops and restaurants on the seafront at Brighton. The Manufacturing, Science and Finance Union formerly led by Ken Gill, bizarrely, had chosen the Brighthelm church hall for their lunchtime delegation meeting to dodge prying eyes. Figures worked out on the back of countless fag packets, including those of the media, that lunchtime showed that with the big guns – the TGWU and GMB – against the change, the MSF delegation could turn the vote, one way or the other. When word got out where they were holed up, the chapel was besieged by an agnostic press.

Gill's position had been made clear during the Labour Party leadership election in April 1992, after Gould and Smith had both come out in favour of abolishing the block vote for the electoral college. 'It would be an unmitigated disaster to do anything to exclude the trade unions. That does not mean to say you may not decide to change the proportion of the influence the trade unions have – that is legitimate.'

Smith had gone to the MSF annual conference at the Pavilion Theatre, Bournemouth, in the midst of his leadership campaign to seek their support and had tried to reassure them about OMOV. 'In reforming the block vote, and in extending the principle of one member, one vote, I believe that the trade unions have more to gain than lose.'

Prescott won the hustings battle for the MSF vote in the deputy leadership contest against Beckett after telling them, 'It is a sad reflection of the political climate in Britain today that it is necessary for me to say that I am proud to be a trade unionist ...'

Prescott strongly shared Gill's position, that the union block vote needed changing but not ending. His presence on the platform that afternoon in October 1993 may have reassured the doubters in the delegation that they were doing the right thing.

The delegation was committed to voting against OMOV and levy-plus, and, unless it changed its mind now, Smith would resign. However, the conference arrangements committee had cleverly bound the OMOV vote to a quota system for women, requiring half of all winnable seats with no sitting Labour MP to choose a woman candidate. The MSF delegation supported that. Hilary Armstrong, Smith's parliamentary aide, and Judith Church, an MSF organiser, an MP close to Blair until she left the Commons in 2001, wisely decided that because they were known modernisers it would be counterproductive for them to speak. Another woman on the delegation, Ann Gibson, a powerful campaigner for women's rights, put the argument that in effect the two positions cancelled each other out; they should abstain. She warned the men they would be accused of a sell-out if they betrayed the women now. It was narrowly agreed by 19 votes to 17. In the conference hall, the MSF had 4.5 per cent of the block vote. Smith won with a margin of 3.1 per cent.

The atmosphere was electrifying when they reassembled. Smith had already heard the good news from Armstrong that the MSF would abstain. 'I told him not to smile but he'd won,' said Armstrong. Smith's beautiful daughters were smiling at him from the front row, in the belief that Daddy would scrape home. It was far from certain he would. Smith had made his keynote leadership address the day before; now he left no one in any doubt about the importance of the vote. 'As leader of our party, charged with the responsibility to secure that victory, I say to this conference that the changes I propose today are vital – absolutely central – to our strategy for winning power. And I ask you to unite behind them.'

The stage was set for Prescott's final appeal.

Caborn gulped when Prescott said Smith had put his head on the block. Caborn had not been told that Smith would resign, and thought Prescott had gone over the top. Prescott was not intending to invite the conference to go for the chop. He was speaking in more general terms, meaning Smith had gone out on a limb for his party. But he had no doubt that limb was Smith's neck. 'All I was doing was giving them an excuse to vote for the resolution. My speech was designed to encourage them to go back to their constituencies and say why they had changed their vote.'

He was quite conscious of what he had to do. It was like the old days at union rallies. 'I had to ask them to break the mandate. I had to whip up an atmosphere to make them feel there was such a moment, they would go back and say, "When John spoke I had to do it." I had to reach that moment that would allow them to vote like that. I had to turn it into something which was about emotion, that they would feel safe about going back to their constituencies. It was the theatre of politics.'

Pauline Prescott sat watching from the CLP seats directly opposite the platform, and where, even in a sea of faces, he could not miss her. After it was over, she said to Alastair Campbell, 'If he does nothing else in his life, that speech had everything. No one can take that away.'

One effect of Prescott's speech was to put autocue out of fashion for the Tory conference the following week.

He may have taken the stage by storm, like Pavarotti at La Scala, but it was a fortnight before he could bear to look at himself in the television video of his speech. Matthew Parris, in *The Times*, reported that Prescott had gone several rounds with the English language and had 'left it slumped and bleeding over the ropes. Among the collateral damage were thousands of Mr Smith's critics, many trade union dinosaurs, several big composite motions and Margaret Beckett's political career. And all this in quarter of an hour ... The very thought of a Prescott transcript is laughable ... Any transcript would be gibberish – nouns, adjectives, and unattached parts of speech lying among the verbal wreckage like a rose garden after a bulldozer. Yet, somehow, everybody guesses what he meant.'

In spite of all the adulation, that hurt. 'Everybody was telling me it's marvellous and one of those things that will go down in the history of conferences, but I couldn't watch it for a fortnight because I had been so intimidated – perhaps I shouldn't admit this – by all those who said it hadn't got any syntax. The *Guardian* snobs said it was a parody of how I would say something. It's an expression of class, all that, isn't it. You know: "I was educated properly; he wasn't."'

Why had the party nearly lost its leader over the simple device of offering one vote to every member? OMOV combined all the fears and conspiracies of a party in deep introspection after its fourth electoral defeat in a row. The trade unions, whose block-voting power would be weakened by OMOV, were reluctant to give up their influence over the choice of candidates in constituencies, as well as policy at conference. Moreover, some on the right feared that, although the left was subdued, the unions represented a bulwark against a future resurgence of the 'loony left'; once that was gone, the lunatics might take over the asylum. The left suspected that it might be a conspiracy to turn the Labour Party into the SDP, sanitised and shorn of any trade union link to make it more acceptable to the voters.

There had also been dangerous talk, in the despair of defeat in April 1992, of the need for a realignment in British politics and pacts with the Liberal Democrats. Dennis Skinner dismissed such talk saying, 'I've been fed up this last decade listening to Dr Death and Shirley Poppins and Woy of the Wadicals and this Paddy Backdown … It's time we represented our class.'

Smith and Prescott ruled out pacts during their election campaigns, but on OMOV Smith was in the middle, believing, like Prescott, that change was inevitable, but keen to preserve the links with the unions.

Prescott had been against one-member-one-vote democracy like others on the left, including Robin Cook, when it was put forward by Kinnock in 1984 for the reselection of Labour MPs, but Kinnock had succeeded in pressing forward with the change and had secured agreement that the block vote in the conference should go down from 90 per cent to 70 per cent by the autumn 1993 conference. Smith had said in his leadership manifesto, 'New Paths to Victory', that he did not believe it was acceptable any more that the members should have only a tenth of the votes at the party conference over the election of the leader. He put forward an alternative: the MPs should have 50 per cent and constituency parties should have 50 per cent, but their votes would be cast following a ballot of all the constituency members. He later reneged on that plan, under pressure from the unions including his own, the GMB, alarming the modernisers with his backsliding.

Alastair Campbell, political editor of the *Daily Mirror*, later to become Blair's press secretary, described the split between those frantic for change and those happy to play a longer game. The 'frantics' included Tony Blair, Gordon Brown and Jack Straw.

The 'long gamers' included Smith, Beckett and Prescott.

Prescott saw Labour's link with the trade unions as a marriage; he was against a divorce, but he was prepared for a more open relationship to breathe fresh life into it. Prescott said: 'Do we go through this kind of divorce with all the attendant problems that would come from that or do you begin to argue there is some justification for it, but let's democratise its context and its influence on the Labour Party?'

After winning the leadership, Smith had appointed Prescott to a Union Links Review Group to find a way out of the OMOV maze. Smith wrestled with various compromise options including abandoning total OMOV in the selection of candidates for equal votes for unions, MPs and members. Blair attacked that plan as a 'disaster'. Blair also opposed the unions' compromise for a 'supporters' club' of affiliated trade union members. 'I believe it should be one member, one vote ... There should not be two classes of membership,' Blair said on the BBC's *On the Record*.

Prescott came up with the plan, based on the levy-plus system of increasing trade union membership of the party, that he had put to Kinnock years before. This was to provide the way out. He did so with Tom Sawyer, the deputy general secretary of NUPE and number two to Rodney Bickerstaffe, Prescott's closest ally in the union movement. Bickerstaffe – a Buddy Holly lookalike – had been a NUPE official in Doncaster, South Yorkshire, and they had come up together. Sawyer had, like Prescott, bluntly told the leadership that cutting the unions off from all influence in the Labour Party was not wise. They were, after all, the party's financial backers. 'No say, no pay,' Sawyer had said at his own union conference. The compromise was to have a lasting impression on Blair. 'While Prescott and Gordon Brown remained on prickly terms, he and Blair began to develop a relationship of mutual respect,' said John Rentoul in his biography *Tony Blair*. Prescott felt Brown would not engage with him, but Blair listened to his arguments and he warmed to him for that reason. Prescott also had changed his mind about their relative strengths, feeling that Blair had become the stronger of the two, replacing Brown with his own vision. He was also pleased when Blair hired Alastair Campbell, the *Daily Mirror* political editor, as his press chief, because Campbell like Prescott was tribalist about Labour.

The union leaders, including John Edmonds, leader of Smith's own union, the GMB, refused to accept it. But Smith drove through the compromise plan at a meeting of the Union Links Review Group at Westminster on 14 July 1993. It proposed OMOV with levy-plus for the selection of parliamentary candidates; equal voting power – one-third for MPs, one-third for members and one-third for unions (who would ballot members) – for the election of the leader; and changes to the block vote at the conference. In a bravura performance, Smith ended the meeting by telling the press there had been an agreement. There had been no such thing. There was no vote. New Labour was, in fact, born in an old-fashioned stitch-up in that cliché of intrigue, a smoke-filled room.

Blair was anxious for more change, and in 1996 put the manifesto out to a vote of the entire membership in a consultation exercise that pointed clearly to further reforms.

Prescott had come to broadly the same conclusion as Blair from the opposite direction. Blair saw it as an inevitable consequence of the intellectual modernisation of the party. Prescott, ever the pragmatist, had been convinced of the need for union ballots when he was in the NUS as a Cunard steward 30 years earlier because it was impossible to hold mass meetings at sea.

'That process cannot be carried out in all trade unions. Members of the National Union of Seamen, in 800 ships around the world, cannot be convened in that way. It has to rely on ballots.' Prescott wanted free postal ballots for all unions.

OMOV also tied in with his one-man campaign for a mass party and belief in decentralisation of power; if they attracted more members, they needed to spread the power out. The levy-plus system, which he had advocated in 1988 with his leaflet on mass membership, would increase the number of members, and could also provide the answer to the OMOV riddle: by getting more union members into the party, the unions would retain influence, but could reduce the block vote.

There was another attraction for Prescott. It reduced the power of the leader. 'In the little confines of a few people, a few phone calls are made to try and get the support of one or two general secretaries. I am bound to say that is not a very satisfactory way of making decisions. We're in trouble because we've done that before,' he said.

When the conference debate was all over, Prescott persuaded Rodney Bickerstaffe to do a sketch with him at the Red Revue that night. Prescott was thinking of having some fun with a dustbin, with himself being 'rubbished', but he dropped the idea. Instead, he play-acted, in a wholly self-deprecating way, the drama of the morning, and his phone call from Smith. Bickerstaffe played Smith, telephoning Prescott, who made a farce of his total disbelief. 'Not *the* John Smith? My party leader?' As with all farce, there was a grain of truth in the jest. 'Prescott was not exactly *persona non grata* but even with Smith he was not quite in the inner circle.'

For the second time that day, Prescott brought the house down.

CHAPTER SIXTEEN

Bambi and Thumper

'What is his name?'

'Bambi,' answered Mother Deer, better known as Mo.

'That's nice,' said the rabbit. 'My name is Thumper.'

Around midnight on 11 May 1994, John Prescott telephoned Pauline in high spirits. He had been to a celebrity fund-raising event for the Labour Party, a £500-a-head banquet at the Park Lane Hotel, London, and John Smith had been the life and soul of the party.

'John rang me about midnight. He said John Smith was in really good form, laughing and joking with everyone. Everyone was really enjoying themselves, in really good spirits.'

At 9.15 the next morning, Smith was declared dead at St Bartholomew's Hospital in the City of London, after suffering a heart attack at his London flat in the Barbican. He had collapsed in the bathroom of the flat on the 35th floor of the modern tower block at about 8.05 a.m. Having survived an attack before, Smith – and his family – had dreaded a recurrence. His wife Elizabeth desperately tried in vain to resuscitate him. A paramedic on a motorcycle arrived at 8.16 a.m. and an ambulance arrived a minute later. They tried a defibrillator but found no heartbeat, and rushed him to hospital, where he was pronounced dead.

The party was shattered, but Prescott took his death as a personal blow.

On the afternoon of John Smith's death, Steve Hardwick, Prescott's assistant, walked into Prescott's office, the turret overlooking the corner of Parliament Square. Prescott had his back to him, looking out of the window. He was staring into space across Parliament Square. When he turned, Hardwick could see that the big man had been crying.

Prescott and Smith had been close, and Prescott felt his death dreadfully.

'John Smith has got a bit of fundamentalism, hasn't he – the Christian spirit, a basic fairness about life? He's a guy you can trust ... I like people to believe in something. The great problem of the past few years is that people weren't sure what the hell the Labour Party believed in ... People wondered what the hell we stood for ... That's not the way with Smithie,' Prescott had told the *Guardian*.

They were of the same generation. Prescott was three months older than Smith. They came from different backgrounds, but Smith had the confidence to handle Prescott without feeling threatened. They had their differences over Smith's cautious approach to tax and spending, exemplified by his shadow Budget before the 1992 election, but they had a relaxed relationship of mutual respect. Prescott knew where he stood with Smith.

Now the uncertainties returned.

While others were preparing their next move, Prescott was grieving. Another shadow Cabinet colleague had said to Prescott, 'What are you going to do?' He replied, 'Go to the funeral – what else?'

He had reached an understanding with Smith, and felt Smith's respect, which he had not felt before from a leader of the party. Smith was deeply religious, but he wore it lightly, and swore like a squaddy; he was earthy, and a man of the party, down to his roots. All this Prescott felt he had in common with Smith.

'I like John because he's straight.' On 20 February 1994, clearly at ease with himself and the leadership for the first time in years, Prescott posed for portrait photographs in a big armchair for the *Mail on Sunday*. It was just three months before Smith's death. This was the smiling face of Prescott, confident and happy. 'I don't hate Neil any more. I don't feel any warmth for him, but he paid a hell of a price for all he did.'

He had even softened his view of the 'beautiful people'. 'I don't use the term that much now, you know. If anything, people might look at me now as a beautiful person.'

The rapport he had with the Labour leader was genuine, and lasting. Smith saw himself as a 'doer'. That is how Prescott's closest friends describe Prescott. Although Smith was a barrister from Scottish nonconformist stock, he had Prescott's love of a fight, and a readiness to go for the jugular. Smith had built his Commons reputation on claiming the scalp of Leon Brittan for the leaking of the Solicitor General's letter at the height of the Westland affair in 1986. Using forensic skills, he had carved up

Brittan in a late-night clash across the Despatch Box in a piece of Commons drama which was unforgettable for anyone who witnessed it. Prescott rated Smith for that, and for his commitment to his brand of socialism. He also liked him as a man. Smith had once been a short-order chef on the Clyde 'puffers', the ferryboats, while waiting to go up to the university, and had that experience in common with Prescott. Smith, in return, respected Prescott, and knew he could trust him. After the troubles with Kinnock, Prescott felt Smith was like a brother to him. 'He loved the man,' said one of Prescott's close friends.

At the TUC conference Smith had told the trade union leaders and their rank and file that he would use every economic lever at his disposal to deal with unemployment. For Prescott and his close allies, who were in the hall, it connected like a bolt of electricity. 'It went right to the core. We saw how well that went down. We played on that for his campaign.'

Smith created a 'Q' committee of key economic shadow ministers comprising Prescott, Margaret Beckett, Robin Cook and Gordon Brown. Although Brown was Smith's shadow Chancellor, Prescott felt he had Smith's ear, and Prescott's friends believe Brown was feeling uncomfortable with that influence. Blair was not in the team. Prescott felt that his alternative economic strategy now had a real chance of being implemented. On the day before Smith died, the Labour leader had approved an ambitious policy statement by his shadow Employment Secretary called 'Jobs and Social Justice'. It was buried with Smith on the lonely island of Iona, or so it must have seemed to Prescott. Beckett, who took over the leadership, told him it would have to be shelved, at least for the duration of the European elections, which were due to be held in mid-June. Prescott disagreed but accepted her decision. 'You're the leader,' he told her.

Those around Prescott are convinced that Smith would have won the next election; but, while he was alive, Smith's leadership was seen as too conservative, too old-fashioned – too Scottish – to carry the south of England with Labour. And while he was alive, in spite of OMOV, he held at bay the modernising tendencies of the Blairites, who wished to 'Clintonise' the party. That agenda could now be put into action.

Blair and Brown shared the sense of personal loss, but within hours, they were planning their next moves for the leadership, and Prescott, too, was having to consider his future.

Beckett filled the gap as leader with grace and natural authority. She is not someone who is constantly in the press, preferring not to issue a blizzard of press releases like her colleagues. A holiday caravan enthusiast, Beckett quietly – for some too quietly – got on with the chores of leadership, competently dealing with John Major at Prime Minister's Questions and with few ructions around the shadow Cabinet.

But it was not enough. There had to be a leadership election, and she would be challenged. Brown and Blair could both have run, but they knew to do so could let in Prescott or leave Beckett in charge. Peter Mandelson sought to avoid being too closely associated with either of the camps, but remained a figure in the background (at Blair's subsequent victory party, the new Labour leader would thank 'Bobby' – the Bobby Kennedy code name the Blairites had used for Mandelson).

The Prescott camp had no illusions that Blair had, with Mandelson's assistance, set his sights on the leadership before Smith's death, 'but it came sooner than he had thought. Brown had peaked,' said one of Prescott's supporters.

'Gordon was seen to be very restrictive on the ideas as far as the Shadow Cabinet was concerned. That was against him. The other thing was that Mandelson set his stall out – an article [not by Mandelson] in the *Evening Standard* was all about why Blair should be leader. He got Blair up and running, and totally outmanoeuvred Brown. The rest is history. A deal was done, and what that deal was nobody else knows, and nobody will know other than Brown and Blair. What the long-term future is we don't know,' the supporter added. Mandelson strongly denies that account.

Prescott's camp believed the Blair–Brown deal, agreed over dinner at an Islington restaurant, Granita, was to give Brown total control of the economic strategy, keeping Cook and Prescott firmly out.

On Wednesday, 1 June, Brown issued a press release announcing he would not be standing, and that his decision not to stand had leaked out. I was responsible for one of the 'leaked' reports, which was prompted by a telephone call from a source assumed to be a Blair supporter. It went into the *Independent* a day before the Granita supper to decide which of the two would run. The next day, Brown formally pulled out. I have no doubt in my mind that it was done to force the issue on Brown and Blair. The manoeuvrings were the cause of continuing suspicion and bitterness. On 11 May 1996, *The Times* reported that Brown and Mandelson had hardly spoken to each other for eighteen months.

Once Brown gave Blair a clear run, it was clear that the race was for second place, and, in that, Prescott was quickly ahead of Beckett, who ordered her team not to campaign for the deputy leader's job. She was only interested in the leadership she had held so briefly but so well after Smith's death. There was one interesting footnote to the nominations: a sole Constituency Labour Party had nominated Brown for the deputy leadership. As he was not running, it was ruled out of order. It was from Hartlepool, Peter Mandelson's constituency. However, Mandelson, when the votes were cast, plumped for Prescott for the deputy leadership.

The contest was remarkable for its good nature, and it enabled Prescott to see Blair at close quarters, but it was not until it was over that the leader and the deputy leader had a heart-to-heart conversation to thrash out a working relationship, in the privacy of Prescott's Jaguar. It was the day after the elections when Blair went to a celebratory party for Prescott in his Hull constituency. 'At the end of the journey,' said a Prescott aide, 'Prescott said there were things that he didn't agree with Tony on, but he won his respect. That was the most important thing. He got to know him better on that drive. That was the breakthrough, really, in their relationship.'

They were from different backgrounds, and different generations, but Blair recognised that Prescott, in spite of his image, was a pragmatic politician with vital links to the trade union movement, and above all, he was loyal. Bringing them together was a tricky task. A Labour MP, Ian McCartney, took on the role of go-between almost as soon as Smith had won the leadership.

McCartney had two things in common with Blair: a friend and an enemy. McCartney was friendly with Tony Booth, Cherie Blair's father, who lived on Merseyside; and as a constituency secretary to Roger Stott, the Labour MP for Wigan, McCartney had also helped to defeat the left-winger Les Huckfield when he made a bid for the Wigan seat – before Huckfield fought Blair for Sedgefield. When McCartney entered the Commons in 1987, Blair was on the front bench and asked him to do some backbench Bills on his behalf. McCartney also became chairman of the Labour backbench employment committee, when Blair was put in charge of the employment portfolio; they worked closely together. It was a friendship he had in parallel with Prescott. Like Prescott, McCartney had been a cabin boy in the merchant navy. Prescott had entered the House in 1970 with McCartney's father, Hugh, the MP for Dunbartonshire Central. Prescott had first met Ian, a diminutive Clydesider with a tenacious talent for employment statistics, in 1971 when McCartney was the party's youngest official.

McCartney attempted on several occasions to 'tie the knot' between Prescott and Blair without success. On the night that Smith appointed his first shadow Cabinet, McCartney was in Prescott's turret. Two floors below, Tony Blair and Gordon Brown were celebrating having been made shadow Home Secretary and shadow Chancellor respectively.

'I went down and said, "John's upstairs. I think we should get together."'

Prescott went downstairs to join the celebrations. Over champagne, Prescott and Blair discussed the future under Smith. Blair and Prescott kept up the contact. When it became clear that they would both run in the election after Smith's death, McCartney again acted as a go-between. He went to Blair and said he thought it was critical for the future of the party that he should become leader with Prescott as his partner. Even some in Prescott's own constituency supported that view, although Hull East nominated Prescott for both leader and deputy.

Prescott, in spite of his image as a 'traditionalist', was a moderniser, and shared with Blair a vision about the need to reform party policy. But there were clear differences, particularly over the unions. Prescott had grown to respect both Blair's judgement and a quality completely missed by the popular portrayal of him as Bambi: Blair's ruthless instinct for leadership. Blair was later to complain to the party conference that he had gone from Bambi to Stalin in one leap.

Prescott poked fun at the Bambi image – together with the other major players, Mo Mowlam, Gordon Brown, Robin Cook and Margaret Beckett – at a dinner at the Café Royal. It is the only recorded time when Prescott has broken into the Wonderful World of Walt Disney:

> *One day, as the sun rose, there was great excitement in the forest.*
>
> *A new prince had been born.*
>
> *A little fawn, son of the great Smith. All the animals and birds and press hacks proclaimed the new prince of the forest.*

A young rabbit asked, 'What is his name?'

'Bambi,' answered Mother Deer, better known as Mo.

'That's nice,' said the rabbit. 'My name is Thumper.'

And Bambi's friends said, 'This is the future leader of the forest.' Bambi issued a denial.

Suddenly, a small black nose poked out of the flowers. 'Flowers?' asked Bambi.

'No, no,' laughed Thumper. 'That's Robin, a skunk.'

'He can call me Flower if he wants to,' said Robin.

Bambi had found another friend, simply by showing love and kindness.

Then came the sound of running feet and the stags burst into the woods shouting, 'Beware of the Gordon Prince.'

Bambi and his mother trembled with fear as they heard shouts: 'We will not spend more than we can afford. We will not tax unnecessarily.'

'That man,' said Mother Mo, 'carries sound bites that can kill you. He means danger to all in the forest.'

Suddenly, Bambi found another deer beside him – a beautiful doe. 'Do you remember me, Bambi?' she asked. 'I'm Margaret.'

And they went down the path, safe in each other's embrace, to start their life together. The forest was now beautiful, a green and pleasant land at ease with itself. A Christian Socialist forest.

Thumper was so pleased that he hung out the red flag. Then he was expelled by the constitutional committee for bringing the forest into disrepute.

Prescott drafted it himself from a Bambi nursery book. A closer analogy was from another nursery story: the tortoise and the hare. They were heading in the same direction at different speeds. There was no doubt who was playing the tortoise. Blair was impatient for change. Within 24 hours of being 'crowned', Blair raised one of the most sensitive issues involving the Labour movement when he declared the unions 'will have no special or privileged place within the Labour Party. They will have the same access as the other side of industry'.

This was intended as an assurance to the voters who had rejected Labour at the 1992 election, but it sounded alarm bells through the unions and the left. Prescott was asked on *Breakfast with Frost* on Sunday, 24 July – two days later while Blair was still with him in Hull – whether he was annoyed by Blair's remarks. He could hardly say yes. He wryly noted that the 'honeymoon' between the media and the new Labour leadership had not lasted very long. He then did his best to reconcile his leader's words with his own views, but it sounded lame.

'What we are saying, of course, is they're entitled to have a say in the major decisions that go on in this community, as other interested groups have, and we would restore that along with other bodies. But no special relationship in the sense of saying well that has to be the position and we have to accept it because the trade union said it.'

Blair's conviction that Labour had to change its outright opposition to changes in trade union laws crystallised on 29 November 1989, when he was ambushed in the Commons by Norman Fowler, then Employment Secretary, with a clever trap.

If Labour signed up to the European Social Chapter, in all its facets, it meant Labour also supported 'the freedom to join or not to join' a trade union. And that meant ending the closed shop, said Fowler.

'Is that Labour's position?' asked Fowler. Fowler, an old hand, who was one of the few surviving ministers from Thatcher's first government, knew the answer was no. Labour had been committed to the closed shop. But it could not continue to be so, unless it disowned part of the Social Chapter.

Blair had to bluster his way out, but in the month that followed he took decisive action to abolish Labour's adherence to the closed shop. He faced an angry backlash from the left wing at a meeting of the parliamentary Labour Party, but when he got to the shadow Cabinet he found to his surprise he was supported by Prescott.

Prescott, as a former employment spokesman, had already come to the same conclusion as Blair on the closed shop, but from a different direction. Prescott rejected the view of most on the left that the law had no role in trade union relations. Prescott believed in trade union rights, and 'that implies the right not to join'. His belief in 'rights and responsibilities' was well documented. Prescott disagreed with Blair over implementation, being in favour of sweeping away the Prior–Tebbit–Fowler legislation. 'Labour is right to commit itself to repeal all the Tories' anti-trade-union legislation.' A year later, he reinforced that view. 'We shall repeal all of it. There's no little bits you can keep of it. There is nothing you can keep of this legislation … It has all got to go.'

Blair, in a stand that was to show he had backbone as well as charm, was determined to retain parts of the Tory trade union legislation.

Prescott accepted the need to retain secret strike ballots, writing in the *Guardian* on 29 August 1986: 'The only requirement will be that the decisions relating to strikes and the method of elections of union executives shall be based on a system of secret ballots.'

The Tory requirement for pre-strike ballots was a problem, but Prescott said there would be loopholes to allow immediate withdrawal of labour where, for example, an employer took unilateral action to change accepted working conditions.

The niceties of dealing with trade union law were only part of the question. The big issue was over Labour's relationship with the unions. Under Kinnock's and Smith's democratisation, the block vote was reduced to 70 per cent but Prescott was against going down to 50 per cent as the modernisers wanted. 'I don't like that idea – I like the principle of getting a fair balance,' he said. Prescott was holding the ring between the Blairites and the traditional supporters of the Labour Party, but on 1 October 1995 in a lengthy BBC *On the Record* interview at the start of the annual party conference, he conceded that the block vote could go down if the number of trade union levy-payers fell. 'Here again I had a difference. I always thought this relationship of the vote should be tied to how many members that trade unions have paying political levy but I was in a minority. Funnily enough Tony agrees with me on that, but we've always been in the process of change.'

The spin doctors tried to make a virtue out of the differences between Prescott and Blair – working-class and middle-class, traditionalist and moderniser, working in harmony; but suspicions remained in the Blair camp over whether Prescott was mentally agile enough to cope with the changes ahead. The whispering continued: was he up to it? In fact, Prescott had been arguing for mass membership of the party – and greater democracy – for years. He also wanted to reform the voting system of the trade unions which in the Wilson era, when Prescott was rising through the ranks, gave power to right-wing trade union barons over the constituency activists. For Prescott, reform was a question of balance between the unions and the rank-and-file membership. 'It's about time we stopped ringing up one trade union leader and another to say, "Do you agree with this? Can I get this through? Will you give me the votes?" The constituency parties, the trade unions and everybody else, they make the policy in our party,' he said.

Blair confided in Prescott that he was worried that he was 'in the dock' over the unions. 'As somebody who has been in the dock all my life, I urged him to keep on arguing. The Labour Party should always have people prepared to argue against the conventional thinking. I said to Tony, "This movement will respect people who argue their case. You should do that."'

CHAPTER SEVENTEEN

Knock-Out

If I can get across to enough people, I will become Leader and Prime Minister and that will shake a few people up in this country.

John Prescott was in University College Hospital, detained overnight after a thump on the head caused by an accident in a London taxi, when he was told by Margaret Beckett over the public telephone he had commandeered that she had decided to run for both the leadership and deputy leadership of the Labour Party. The effect was like an injection of cocaine with a horse syringe. Prescott was out of the starting gate like Red Rum on crack.

He would have been hobbled if Beckett had decided to let Blair, Prescott, Brown, Cook and any others fight it out for the leadership. She had until October, when she could have expected to be returned as deputy leader at the party conference without a challenge, as recompense for the dignified way she had steered the party from Smith's death, through the European election victories, and the leadership election. Prescott could not then have contested the deputy leadership in those circumstances.

In October 1993, a few months after his second defeat, he was asked on the BBC's *Breakfast with Frost* whether he would stand against Beckett again. 'No, no, no, those decisions have been taken by the party. I'll get on with doing the job that I've got now.'

Pressed further whether he was ruling himself out, Prescott said, 'Well, who knows what might happen to Margaret Beckett?'

The moment she decided that she was going for the leadership, the field was open.

An approach was made to Blair's camp to endorse a Blair–Prescott ticket as leader and deputy leader. 'Blair would not wear that,' said a Prescott supporter. It meant that Prescott would have to run for both the leadership and the deputy leadership, while Blair ran solely for the leadership.

Brown quickly came out in favour of Beckett for the deputy leadership, underlining his differences with Prescott. But Blair made sure that Mo Mowlam, number two in Blair's campaign team for the leadership, countered Brown's move by announcing she was supporting Prescott for the deputy leadership.

After his second unsuccessful campaign, when Beckett won the deputy leadership, Prescott had told his supporters that there would be no 'three times lucky', but he pulled together the nucleus of the team he had used on the two previous occasions. Caborn was the campaign committee chair and McCartney the campaign coordinator, but there was a large cast behind them including Alan Meale. Rodney Bickerstaffe, Prescott's closest friend in the union movement, was an important ally for the campaign, but other union leaders quietly gave him support.

With all the expertise of a professional shop steward, Prescott had drawn up canvass lists of MPs by region, and allocated minders to lobby each of them; an exhaustive campaign diary was worked out, with meetings every day between the Northumberland miners' picnic at Ashington on 11 June and the Tolpuddle Martyrs' rally in Wiltshire on 19 July. The contest coincided with the summer conference season for the main trade unions, and so involved trooping round the country like an end-of-the-pier show to resorts all over Britain. Even the D-Day commemorative service was pencilled in for 15 June.

It would not be like the previous campaigns: it would not be rancorous, like the first; and it would be more serious than the second. He needed to avoid the mistakes of the bitterness of Bryan Gould's challenge to Smith – one of Meale's sayings was 'Remember there is a life after death' – and to set out a policy agenda that would not only steal a march on both Blair and Beckett, but would lay down important markers for the future. He set out to make it impossible for Blair to reverse his policy advances, if he could stake out the ground clearly enough. It was a difficult line to walk.

Ian McCartney, Rodney Bickerstaffe and Prescott were sitting up into the small hours thinking of a theme. 'It was about three o'clock in the morning,' said McCartney. 'We could have cried with tiredness. Then we came up with the phrase "traditional values in a modern setting".'

They were considering how they could encapsulate that idea without losing traditional support, and came up with the phrase 'the politics of ideas and the politics of organisation'. These were hardly catchy enough to earn them jobs in advertising soap, but they were right for the market – the unions and the constituency parties. It became clear that the most likely scenario would be that Blair would win outright victory. As a result, it was decided that Prescott's best plan would be to make sure he was on the inside track after the leadership election to keep the balance of the party.

'That meant convincing not John but some of the people close to him that it should not be an all-or-nothing campaign for the leadership,' said McCartney.

The strategy required two things: Prescott had to stand on a positive range of policy issues (it was not good enough to be negative); and he also had to appear credible as an alternative leader, should Blair fall under a bus.

'The party needed to be transformed and John Prescott had a long history of that – one member one vote, mass membership, a new relationship with the trades unions, an effective role for the PLP, things that the constituencies wanted,' McCartney added.

Prescott's advisers warned him there was a problem of perception. Some of the 1987 intake arrived when Prescott was engaged in battles with Kinnock; they saw him as a man who shot from the hip and asked questions later; they questioned whether he could work with Blair as a deputy to bring about a Labour victory. That had to be tackled. An 'A-team' of Labour MPs who supported Prescott was given the task of putting that right – Peter Kilfoyle, Don Dixon, Bill Olner, Keith Bradley, Kevin Hughes, Joan Walley, Bridget Prentice, Janet Anderson, Helen Jackson and Jane Kennedy.

McCartney felt his best role was to try to bring about a closer relationship between Prescott and Blair during the campaign. He set out his strategy to Blair; Blair was less open about his own plans for the leadership contest, but they developed an unofficial commitment that whatever happened during the campaign it should not undermine the party. Blair made it clear he was not going to stand for the deputy leadership, leaving Prescott free to set out his stall.

McCartney acted as an unofficial go-between for the Blair and Prescott camps throughout the campaign. On one occasion, he advised the Blair camp that their 'cold' canvassing of Labour members by telephone – something they were not supposed to do – was in danger of backfiring. Prescott's camp had had a number of complaints. Prescott's camp could have used the information to damage Blair, but instead McCartney decided to warn Blair's team before it got into the press.

McCartney personally shunned any publicity, staying in the background, acting like the tea boy to Prescott's team. 'The key thing was that Tony would not criticise John and John would not attack Tony. That was the overriding point in the campaign in a way,' said McCartney.

Prescott's strategy was to set the pace. 'We had a clearly worked-out strategy. We wanted to show that John had a record of being prepared to think about change. The one person who had evidence in the bank was John Prescott. In the Shadow Cabinet, he was in intellectual terms the most productive, despite all the problems of keeping his position under Kinnock.'

What the Prescott camp lacked was resources. They feared

Blair's team would be able to send out glossy brochures to thousands of supporters. They had to win the battle in the media. By pitching for full employment, Prescott was able to sound credible – his commitment was well known – and it left Blair and Beckett to pick up the gauntlet he had thrown down.

'We had to start thinking what happens after the contest is over,' said McCartney.

The alarm bells sounded in the Blair camp in the middle of the campaign when Prescott told *The Times*: 'I do not agree with many of his views, quite frankly.' Gordon Brown was also furious with Prescott for challenging his safety-first strategy on taxation. 'If everybody is going to make an effort to get our people back to work, that will involve tax payments as well as the new forms of borrowing,' said Prescott. There were angry telephone calls between the Blair and Prescott campaign head-quarters, but Prescott was never afraid of a stand-up fight with Brown. It was one of the few serious wobbles in an otherwise friendly election.

There was an inauspicious start to Prescott's campaign at 11 a.m. on Friday, 10 June, in the packed and sweaty Jubilee Room off Westminster Great Hall. He got the pages mixed up for his opening remarks at the press conference and tripped up over his text. 'This will be an election about Labour's values, approach, style and direction as we move towards the twenty-first century' became 'as we move towards the twentieth century'. He laughed off the slip of the tongue, but he made no apology for looking back to 'embrace the spirit of 1945', of which he wanted a cultural renaissance. He set out the themes of his campaign: full employment and social justice with a reminder that he was building on the policy initiatives set in train by John Smith. 'Labour Party members in this election will want to choose a leadership team which will maximise our appeal to the electorate. That has been my overwhelming consideration in my decision to contest the leader and deputy leader vacancies.

'Campaigning in the country for the party is a role that I relish. Injecting a new enthusiasm for Labour from Land's End to John O'Groats and motivating tens of thousands of Labour supporters to join the party is a task that needs to succeed.'

His campaign leaflet, 'Building on Success', carried a smiling, authoritative portrait of Prescott on the cover with the eight policy documents that had been the signposts to his career – from the one outlining his alternative regional strategy in 1982 to that which put forward his proposals for jobs and social justice, which was at last published in the midst of the campaign on 13 June. At its heart was the proposition that wealth creation finances the safety net that social justice provided for the less fortunate. It could not be delivered by market forces alone, he said. His manifesto, 'Policies into Action', was the last of the three to be published and was delayed until 4 July to maintain the policy momentum. At its core was the promise to tackle the five evils identified by Beveridge: want, squalor, disease, ignorance and idleness. And he proposed a partly un-Blairite solution:

> *To secure full employment, it is no longer sufficient to manage demand. Failure of demand can still lead to a recession and hinder a recovery. But a failure of supply –*

> *investment in training and education, capital stock and infrastructure – can cause chronic economic weakness and high levels of unemployment. I want to see demand management to compensate for cyclical failures of demand and supply-side reforms to remove or reverse structural deficiencies.*
>
> *Government must be a facilitator of change, providing opportunities for people, industry and commerce to respond to new challenges. I know that the free market alone cannot deliver.*

Drawing on his previous policy documents, he proposed a commission for full employment to define full employment and achievable employment targets; audits for skills and jobs; decentralisation; and private finance in public schemes. It was uncosted but it called for 'a more progressive tax system, a fairer distribution of work and a fairer distribution of power'.

The campaign strategy was to focus on a few key issues – the campaigning role of the deputy leadership; a commitment to full employment; links with the trade unions; democratic accountability; and constitutional reform, including the House of Lords. They never got on to the fourth and fifth items.

'We stuck to the campaign. It got a bit wobbly in the middle where people said you have to widen it out. We said no we're not going to widen it out. We are going to stick to the issue of full employment,' said Prescott.

The first televised hustings gave Prescott the boost from which he never looked back. The Norbreck Castle Hotel, Blackpool, a grey edifice on the northern limits of the resort, was the annual conference hotel for the GMB union and the location for the first televised debate by the three candidates, organised by the BBC *Panorama* programme in front of the union audience. The three candidates were in separate rooms when their 'seconds' were offered the chance to draw straws to decide who went first, and where they would stand. Caborn refused. He said Beckett could go in the middle; the organiser insisted they should draw straws. Caborn drew the middle one.

He told Prescott, 'You've got to smile. If you're in the middle, you're the kingpin. And at the end of it, no matter what happens, you've got to shake hands.' Caborn said Prescott 'went down an absolute bomb. It set off our campaign like a rocket. He told a few jokes, and set out his stall.' Above all, he looked like a leader. At the end, he followed the advice, shook hands with the other two candidates, and smiled for the viewers at home.

In fact, you could almost time Prescott's more cuddly approach from a BBC *Question Time* programme he did in 1989. That had been a turning point for him, as he conceded in an interview with David Dimbleby at the Labour conference on 3 October that year. 'I think I was making a certain amount of mistakes. My view, you should come and ask me, and I'll tell you – right? Then it was done with a rather aggressive style … Funnily enough, the Robin Day *Question Time* when I started to smile, people were writing to say, "Ooh, isn't it marvellous? You can smile." I learned some lessons from that. It's not only about putting the policy across. It's a certain amount of presentation.'

Prescott certainly managed to put full employment on the agenda. It produced the striking spectacle of David Hunt, the Employment Secretary, uttering the words at the annual conference of the TUC – albeit to warn against short-term solutions to achieve full employment. Blair included full employment in his manifesto, 'Change and National Renewal', but he sounded more like Hunt than Prescott. Blair's target was 'high and stable' employment with no fixed target. 'My position is exactly the same as John Smith's. I don't favour putting targets on it,' said Blair. Nor would he pin himself down to how fast it would be achieved.

Beckett played on her laurels as leader; her manifesto, 'The Leadership to Win', highlighted her achievements including 'dealing with the Prime Minister at Question Time', and 'successfully taking on the Liberals' although the Tories lost the Eastleigh by-election on 9 June to the Liberal Democrats. It also contained a colour photograph of Beckett with the US President, Bill Clinton – coupling stature with a modernising connection – but the manifesto was unashamedly designed to appeal to the traditional Labour voters in the unions and the constituencies. Her campaign supporters complained of a male chauvinist stitch-up, but she accepted defeat without rancour or recriminations.

Prescott scrubbed out a reference to the lack of recriminations in his acceptance speech. On a gloriously sunny day on 21 July, it would have spoiled the party atmosphere. After a moving speech by Blair, with his voice breaking at points, Prescott praised the victor. 'He commands moral authority and political respect. He has the energy and vitality to win people over to Labour. And he scares the life out of the Tories. And me.'

Prescott was particularly pleased at beating Beckett, who had beaten him two years before for the deputy leadership. Blair won the leadership with 57 per cent of the 952,109 votes that were cast; Prescott got 24.1 per cent for the leadership; Beckett came third with 18.9 per cent. For the deputy leadership, Prescott won with 56.5 per cent to Beckett's 43.5 per cent, coming ahead in all three sections of the electoral college for unions, MPs and MEPs, and constituencies. Of the unions, Beckett beat Prescott for only one – the TGWU, her own union (54 per cent to 46 per cent); in the rest the main union votes were RMT (Prescott–Beckett) 72–28; GPMU 70–30; MSF 59–41; NCU 67–33; GMB 57–43; and UNISON 55–45. It is worth noting that the RMT – Prescott's union – and the GPMU supported Prescott over Blair for the leadership.

Among the MPs who voted for Prescott for the deputy leadership were Hattersley, who had changed his mind about this troublesome seaman; Gerald Kaufman, credited with saying 'the bull has withdrawn from the china shop' when Prescott pulled out of his first challenge against Hattersley; Mandelson; Robin Cook; and Michael Meacher. Prescott's old friend Dennis Skinner voted for Beckett, like most of the Campaign Group. Three MPs – the *Guardian* reported it as 'more than ten' – who nominated Beckett were among the 143 who voted for him. Those prominent MPs who voted for Beckett for the deputy leadership included Neil Kinnock, Glenys Kinnock (as an MEP), Harriet Harman, Donald Dewar, Chris Smith, Frank Dobson, George Robertson, Ann Taylor, Jack Cunningham, Clare Short and Gordon Brown.

Afterwards, Prescott held a celebration on board his campaign headquarters, appropriately the former Humber ferry, the *Tattershall Castle*, which was moored on the Embankment near Charing Cross pier. Even the non-appearance of Tony Blair failed to dampen the party. Blair's camp said it was a simple cock-up but others said it was the idea of Blair's advisers to show who was boss. The invitations carried a Garland cartoon of Prescott as a trapeze artist flying through the air from one trapeze marked 'leader' to another marked 'deputy leader' with Blair as the ringmaster and Beckett as a monocyclist looking on from the ring below. It summed up the campaign neatly in one image. Prescott had provided the spectacle, but Blair was always going to end up in charge, once it had been agreed that the contest would be held in July.

Had it been held in October, Prescott's team remain convinced that their man could have won. At the opening press conference, a *Sun* journalist challenged Prescott over a remark he had made to *Esquire* magazine, just before John Smith had died. When asked whether he wanted to lead the party, he said, 'Naah. If all the likely candidates were run over by a bus, I would do it to the best of my ability and probably make a good job of it. But I am out of that league really.'

Asked why, in that case, he was running for the leadership, Prescott answered, 'Well, times change, don't they.'

One of his campaign team has no doubts he has an ambition for the top job. 'When you get in the race, you want to win, don't you.'

CHAPTER EIGHTEEN

Clause Four

On Clause Four I had real doubts ... I was wrong.
John Prescott.

The old Clause Four, carried on membership cards, committed Labour to 'secure for the workers by hand or by brain the full fruits of their industry and the most equitable distribution thereof that may be possible upon the basis of the common ownership of the means of production, distribution and exchange, and the best obtainable system of popular administration and control of each industry and service.'

The New Clause Four, six times longer, says:

> *The Labour party is a democratic socialist party. It believes that by the strength of our common endeavour, we achieve more than we achieve alone, so as to create for each of us the means to realise our true potential and for all of us a community in which power, wealth and opportunity are in the hands of the many not the few, where the rights we enjoy reflect the duties we owe, and where we live together, freely, in a spirit of solidarity, tolerance and respect.*

> *To these ends we work for:*
>
> *A dynamic economy, serving the public interest, in which the enterprise of the market and the rigour of competition are joined with the forces of partnership and cooperation to produce the wealth the nation needs and the opportunity for all to work and prosper with a thriving private sector and high quality public services, where those undertakings essential to the common good are either owned by the public or accountable to them …*

When Tony Blair asked John Prescott to go along with his plan to reform Clause Four of the party's constitution, his newly elected deputy said no.

Clause Four public ownership, in Prescott's view, went to the heart of Labour's philosophy, and it would be a mistake to meddle with it in the run-up to the general election, and would cause bitter division as on the last occasion under Gaitskell.

Like most party members who bothered to study their membership card, Prescott felt the wording, drafted by Sidney Webb in the year of the Russian revolution, was an anachronism, but he told Blair he was wrong to tear it up. Blair would not be deflected.

One of the first people Blair told of his plans was Alastair Campbell, the political editor of the now defunct *Today*. He told Campbell in early August 1994 when he asked him to become his press secretary.

Campbell was enthusiastic, but, before agreeing to do the job, he went on holiday with his partner, Fiona Millar, and their children, to think it over. They had rented a cottage near Avignon in the south of France, with Neil and Glenys Kinnock, who were close friends.

It was as a friend that Neil Kinnock tried to talk Campbell out of taking the post with Blair during their holiday together. Kinnock told Campbell that the demands of the job – Kinnock had been scarred by the press – would ruin his life.

During the holiday, the Blairs arrived at the Campbell–Kinnock *gîte*. Blair said he had been staying nearby and thought they would drop in. It gave the Labour leader the chance to persuade Campbell to take the job against Kinnock's advice; he also wanted to discuss more closely his ideas for relaunching the party with a new Clause Four. That was the moment that convinced Campbell he was right to leave *Today* and take his high-powered, high-anxiety job with Blair. 'If Blair was going to try to get rid of Clause Four, win or lose, he rationalised, he wanted to be part of it.'

Campbell advised Blair that Prescott would be against the idea at the outset, and would take some convincing.

Prescott had to be brought in at the earliest opportunity. 'Prescott could have blocked it at any time,' confirmed one close ally of Blair.

Prescott's support had not only to be secured but he had to be positively in favour if it was going to work, said a Blair source. Gordon Brown, no friend of Prescott's, advised Blair to get Prescott on board.

In fact, Blair broached the subject with Prescott in July 1994, when he said he wanted to raise constitutional changes. Prescott asked him then whether he meant Clause Four. And if he did, said Prescott, he did not agree with him.

'Prescott was anxious to begin with,' a Blair aide told me. 'He was persuaded that there was additional strength to be gained in having in the constitution something that people actually believed in.'

Campbell's first discussion with Prescott about Clause Four reform was two weeks after the leadership election. Prescott had already been fully briefed by Blair on what he wanted to do.

The deputy leader maintained his opposition right up to seeing the first drafts of Blair's speech for the conference. Then, like a reluctant craftsman, drawn into a project to make it work, Prescott relented. Prescott recognised that Blair needed Clause Four reform to show the public that he could stamp his own authority on the party.

He advised Blair that he had to bring the party with him, and the best way to do that would be to talk first about socialism, and public ownership of the railways. 'They will be so made up with socialism and public ownership that when you come to make the speech, you can then move on.'

Blair asked Prescott to go on the platform for the speech. Prescott said, 'No – I'm not going but I will not go against it.' He appeared at his most Bevinesque, acting as the ultra-loyal deputy to Blair's Attlee. 'I have done all I can to stop you, but you have been elected leader,' Prescott told Blair.

'What you have to understand about John', said one of Prescott's allies, 'is that, even though he is totally committed to the party, he believes the leader has to make certain decisions about how they want to lead, about the direction they want to go in. He believes Clause Four was part of the process of turning round Blair's "family image" to show he was a really serious politician.'

There was a serious downside for Prescott. He had won a leadership election with the support of the left of the party, and the trade unions, including those representing millions of public-sector workers, such as UNISON, who remained of crucial importance to the Labour Party. He knew he would blow his credit with the left if it went wrong.

Prescott insisted on the right to reject the new wording of Clause Four as one of the conditions of his support.

Blair's speech announcing the review of Clause Four was drafted in conditions of high secrecy before the conference, but 'virtually every phrase' was seen and approved by Prescott before it was put into the speech.

On the eve of the leader's conference address, Prescott was given the relevant page with the announcement in it that Clause Four would be reviewed. It was the early hours of the morning when the drafting was nearly complete.

With the final draft agreed, they collapsed back into their hotel beds, to await the trials of the next day. In the morning, before Blair left the Imperial Hotel for the Winter Gardens in Blackpool, Campbell phoned Prescott with a final revision. It was agreed and Blair went to the conference hall.

Shortly before it was delivered, Murray Elder, a Blair aide, and David Hill, the party's chief press officer, were told about the details.

According to Blair aides, it was too enigmatic for Prescott. In their accounts, which he denies, he had said, 'If you are going to say it, say it.' Prescott rejects this account, and it does not fit with the facts. Blair had wanted to be more specific about his plan to change Clause Four and Prescott helped to persuade him in private talks to be less explicit. The final speech was so enigmatic its significance passed most people by in the conference hall. George Robertson, the canny shadow Scottish Secretary, told me afterwards that the only sound you could hear was that of pennies dropping.

The last three pages of Blair's conference speech had been held back from the press to preserve the secret until the last moment. Political editors were briefed as the speech was being delivered that Clause Four was about to be abolished. Word of the announcement passed like a breeze around the back of the conference hall, and around the balconies, where the camera teams had makeshift studios, as the message was relayed by the press, by word of mouth. I was standing by the VIP section, including Lord Hollick and David Puttnam, the *Chariots of Fire* film producer, looking down on Blair from the gods. As he approached the key paragraphs, Blair promised there would be 'no more ditching, no more dumping. Stop saying what we don't mean and start saying what do we mean …'

The approach, suggested by Prescott, was working. That was the signal for the changes to come. 'Start saying what we do mean' would be used again and again by Blair in the coming months to convince the party that the newly worded Clause Four was something on which they could all unite.

The crux to the speech never mentioned Clause Four. 'It is time we had a clear up-to-date statement of the objects and objectives of our party. John Prescott and I, as leader and deputy leader, will propose such a statement to the NEC. Let it then be open to debate in the coming months. I want the whole party to be involved ...'

There were suspicions that the text had been left enigmatic for reasons of deniability. If Blair got booed, the Blair aides could deny it was an attempt to change Clause Four. But Blair's aides rejected the conspiracy theory; their briefing while the speech was going on was too strong to deny it now. Blair was risking his leadership as decisively as John Smith over OMOV, and again the support of Prescott was crucial. Robin Cook knew at 9 a.m. and went to see Prescott in his hotel room. He was 'clearly not happy', but Prescott had set his course and would not be driven off it.

Puttnam was delighted by Blair's boldness, when I told him what it meant. Arthur Scargill was livid, and went upstairs to explode in front of the cameras. That suited the spin doctors. If there had been no reaction from the 'dinosaur' tendency, the floating voters might have doubted Blair's sincerity. He had carried the audience with amazing ease.

Afterwards, with his aides running high on adrenalin, he seemed remarkably cool about the whole thing, oblivious to the fact that it could have destroyed his leadership.

Kinnock walked into the leader's office at the back of the stage to congratulate Blair on his courage and his vision. Blair was meeting with Prescott and their aides. During the conversation, it was decided that the party needed a clear signal that the leader and the deputy were at one in supporting the policy.

Blair and Prescott were persuaded to go out again on to the platform, and to stand together at the podium for the benefit of the cameras. They went out, and to their dismay found that the podium had gone.

What followed was a spin doctor's nightmare. Blair and Prescott made a triumphal march around the hall, not quite knowing what to do next.

'It was totally chaotic,' confessed one of Blair's aides. When they did find a film crew, it was French.

Prescott's week was not over. He still had to deliver his own speech as deputy leader to wind up the conference. There had been a long period when Prescott was suspicious of Campbell but now he was one of Prescott's close friends. He was in on the drafting of the deputy leader's speech to the conference.

It was after midnight in the Imperial with the windows wide open, and a strong breeze blowing off the Irish Sea. Pauline had gone to bed, leaving John, in his vest, and a couple of advisers, including Campbell, to declaim his own conference speech through the open window, at the wind, the wagging illuminations, and the crying of the gulls. Many a true word has been spoken by Prescott in a vest. It is his way of relaxing.

'It's been a great conference for a great party …'

He delivered it on Friday as a rousing finale.

'The Tories think they have a secret weapon for winning the next general election. It's me. They have got a whole department inside Tory HQ. Last year, I did a star turn at their party conference. They played a film of my OMOV speech. Backwards. My wife says she understood it better that way.

'Now, there's one of Major's men who follows me around. Day and night. Hanging on every word I say. You've got to feel sorry for him. I'm going to spell it out in sentences that even I can understand:

'We have had it up to here with the Tories.'

The core of his speech was his commitment to boost the membership of the party with a 'recruit a friend' campaign. And he warned that Labour would not win by default. 'We will win it through the force of our ideas and the strength of our argument' – words he echoed in an interview in the *Independent* in August 1996, when he said Labour's campaign had to be based on 'substance not soundbites'.

The troops went home surprisingly happy given the changes they had been asked to endorse.

Blair's approach to Clause Four sharply delineated the difference between his leadership and that of John Smith. 'Smith's approach was … to put the Left to sleep and allow people to forget about them, whereas Blair's was deliberately to open Pandora's box to let out more dragons to slay.'

Smith had intended to supersede Clause Four, not by scrapping it, but by issuing a statement setting out his own Christian socialist beliefs for adoption by the party conference in 1995. He planned to issue it in June 1995. It was one of his last plans before he died.

Dennis Skinner argued in the NEC with considerable force that the Tories would dismiss any New Clause Four as not going far enough, and Blair would be upsetting the rank and file for no public-relations advantage. Prescott shared that concern, but later admitted he was wrong. 'On Clause Four I had real doubts that we should go along this road for what it might do to the Labour Party. I was wrong. The Labour Party dealt with it in a most mature way …'

How it was achieved was a credit to Blair's leadership. He had come under withering attack from the left-dominated Labour Group of MEPs, and decided in January 1995 to go out and win the hearts and minds of the rank and file for the change. The CLPs had grown by a third since he became leader, as membership soared to over 300,000. They were mostly relaxed meetings in small gatherings of about 500 supporters, Blair in shirtsleeves, looking young, and confident, and convincing. Above all, they were happy meetings. Blair played them almost like a stand-up comic, flashing the intelligence, and that smile. The party members had voted for Blair as their leader, but the Clause Four campaign gave him the chance to get to know his party for the first time, and them to know him. It was an extraordinary bonding exercise, which showed Blair's skills at mixing self-effacement with a strength of leadership which was infectious. During his tour, Blair kept returning to the point that nobody really expected Labour to spend billions in buying back the shares of private investors who had responded to the government's campaigns, such as 'Tell Sid'. 'Say what you mean and mean what you say …'

He had been planning this for a long time.

He had been working on the project from the moment he became leader, and had discussed it with Gordon Brown as early as 1992, in the aftermath of the 1992 general election defeat. In Blair's view, the public would not trust Labour while the old attachment to Marxist theory remained in place. For Blair, scrapping Clause Four was the Labour Party's journey to Bad Godesberg. In 1959 the German socialist party, the SPD, broke away from its Marxist past at a conference in the German town, and became a new, social democratic party. That was Blair's vision for New Labour. It was achieved at the special Clause Four conference on 29 April 1995 at the Methodist Central Hall in London – the place where Clause Four was adopted during World War I in 1918. Rodney Bickerstaffe, the leader of the public workers' union, UNISON (which was formed of his old NUPE, along with NALGO and COHSE), was worried that Prescott was conceding too much ground and spoke against Clause Four revision at the special conference.

The result was never in doubt once the process was started; it was portrayed as a victory for Blair's leadership over the Bennite old guard, but of largely symbolic importance. Prescott ensured there was a reference to public ownership in the final wording. 'I was not happy about changing Clause Four. But I am quite happy on the wording now. Clause Four still emphasises public ownership.'

Ditching the old Clause Four was seen as much more than a cosmetic exercise by the modernisers who were behind the project. 'More than anything else, this change demonstrates that Labour rejects its past as a seemingly anti-private-sector, class-based, trade-union party …'

It did more, and they knew it. It finally buried the theoretical support for Marxism, over which Labour had always been in two minds. The explicit commitment to 'equitable distribution' of wealth in the old Clause Four was replaced by a commitment to equality of 'opportunity', about which few Tories could complain. It was a framework that enabled Gordon Brown, as shadow Chancellor, to set out new principles, including a commitment to the Employment Policy Institute not to tax for taxation's sake, which he made on 25 June 1996. 'We do not and will not seek tax and spending increases for their own sake.'

Redistribution of wealth was still part of the New Labour agenda, but it was at the margin, where the taxpayer was being ripped off by 'fat cats'. Labour's new driving principle was fair taxation, not equality of misery. 'New Labour's belief in the dynamic market economy involves recognition that substantial personal incentives and rewards are necessary in order to encourage risk-taking and entrepreneurialism. Profit is not a dirty word – profits are accepted as the motor of private enterprise.'

The Clause Four debate was, however, dominated by the debate on public ownership. On the first day of the leadership campaign, Blair said it was not one of his priorities to drop Clause Four, but he went on to abandon Labour's 1992 manifesto commitment to take back into public control the privatised water industry.

'The reality is [that] the likelihood of having sums of money of that nature is fanciful ... The public would not respond very kindly if the Labour Party spent its money on repurchasing private share capital instead of improving public services,' Blair said.

That was a view which Prescott perhaps surprisingly shared.

Prescott had always taken a pragmatic view towards Clause Four public ownership. 'I don't let ideology get in the way of common sense.'

Prescott had fought against the privatisation of the bus services in the early eighties, but rejected the demands of Labour's left for a commitment to renationalise the buses on the ground that he would not use taxpayers' money to buy back a load of 'knackered' buses from the privateers.

In 1994, when the Tories were still trying to claim that Tony Blair was an old-style socialist underneath the public relations paint, Conservative Central Office published its own dossier in a pale pink cover, called 'Shadows from the Past', containing the 'damning' quotes on public ownership. The longest list belonged to Prescott:

- *It is essential that the Labour Party has always believed that public ownership is part of our philosophy … Public ownership is a distinguishing feature between a left of centre party and a right of centre party.*
- *I believe in Clause IV. I think there is a role for it.*
- *An interventionist approach, a socialist approach, will starkly illustrate the fundamental difference between Labour and the Tories.*
- *The public utilities should be returned to public ownership and there should be state intervention elsewhere where capitalism fails.*

Oddly, the CCO file did not record the occasion when Prescott joined Skinner in a backbench bill for a socialist programme three years after he became an MP.

The docks strike, he said, could be solved 'only by a socialist policy, because a socialist policy involves taking over the means of production …'

They could have added this quote from Hansard to their list:

> *'There is a good case for public ownership which is embodied in Labour's Clause Four – which I am happy to accept …'*
>
> Hon. Members: *'Oh.'*
>
> *'I do not see why that should be so staggering … I do not know where regulators fit into Labour's Clause Four but it is about intervention, controls, and judgement in the community as to the price mechanism and investment levels. That is as at home in America as it is here.'*

And he reminded the Commons that in Hull they still had their own publicly owned telephone service.

Compensation had been the unresolved problem for the left. Tony Benn was sacked from the Labour front bench by Michael Foot for threatening renationalisation of oil without compensation. Flouting the left fashion of the time, Prescott had the guts to speak out in the *Guardian* against nationalisation without compensation before the 1981 party conference. 'There are very important political principles with electoral consequences to be considered about the justifiable use of the state's power to confiscate,' he warned. One reason for his stand was that the unions' pension funds had invested heavily in privatised stock. Another reason he gave was that the workers themselves had bought the shares in privatised companies such as British Aerospace. The NUR, the railwaymen's union, had bought shares in the privatised British Rail Gleneagles Hotel as protection for the workers, pending the return to power of a Labour government.

But, having accepted the principle of compensation, Prescott and the Labour leadership had to work out how an incoming Labour government could afford to take the utilities back into public ownership. Prescott advocated a compromise formula, which became the model, to limit compensation to the value at the time of flotation, thereby refusing to pay for quick share profits on the privatisation. If the TUC and the Labour conferences reaffirmed the policy of confiscation, he said, it would only 'increase the division between the PLP [Labour MPs] and the party, undermine the authority of conference decisions and succour those SDP traitors who seek to exploit the differences within the Labour Party.'

One by one, over the years, the promises were discarded, gas, electricity, water ... He often spoke of the need for public ownership, but he was never wedded to one form of Clause Four nationalisation, as he showed when he became Labour's energy spokesman in 1987.

'As socialists, we have never been simply defenders of the status quo of institutions and organisations – although all too often we appear that way, simply reacting to the Tories' radical changes. Electricity is a good example. We wish to keep it in public ownership; but that does not mean that the public corporations are not in need of reorganisation and change …'

As early as 1987, he was arguing for workers to be given a stake in their own companies. 'The Labour movement has talked about the redistribution of wealth and about the redistribution of power – but not at the place of work. We should start at the bottom giving people real power over decisions about their working environment, training and investment programmes. Tragically, we have allowed Thatcher to capture the rhetoric of standing up for the individual, even though the Tories have massively reduced individual rights at work.'

The editors of the left-wing *Tribune* on 4 December 1987 described that as a 'radical revision of Labour's old belief in Morrisonian nationalisation'.

British Rail was Prescott's sticking point.

He wanted no clever phrases about that. He committed Labour to a publicly owned, publicly accountable railway, and he was convinced it would be a vote-winner with a public who felt standards – and safety – were being compromised for the sake of party dogma. Even Thatcher had drawn the line at the railways.

In a *Breakfast with Frost* interview in 1993, he had been unequivocal about the franchise companies. 'They only get a contract for six or seven years; they don't own the stock, they don't own the track. All I'll be doing is taking the contracts back. So make no mistake about it. It'll be coming back to a publicly owned network …'

FROST: That's an absolutely clear statement, you will revoke it?

PRESCOTT: Oh no doubt about it ...

FROST: Right, so you are going to renationalise it. How much will that cost?

PRESCOTT: That won't cost you a great deal because it depends how many contracts have been taken ...

FROST: So you can afford it?

PRESCOTT: It's not like taking gas or electricity where you're into billions of pounds ...

Tabs were also kept on the shadow Cabinet by the left. Lew Adams, the ASLEF rail union leader, kept a copy of a promise from a conference speech by Frank Dobson, then shadow Transport Secretary, covered with laminated plastic. It read: 'Let me give you this pledge. We will bring the railway system back into public ownership and control.'

The franchising of services was not a problem for an incoming Labour government, which would have to honour the contracts, and then take them back into public control, in a second term of office. The real problem was Railtrack, which owned the railway lines and the stations. If 'publicly owned' meant anything, it certainly meant owning the rails.

Brown and Blair were more cautious, and privately agreed that, if Railtrack was sold, Labour would not commit billions to buying it back. Prescott tended to agree, but wanted a hard policy to frighten off the investors to stop it being sold before the election.

Blair recognised that Prescott's passionate commitment to the publicly owned railways could be dangerous, if he threatened to resign over the issue. Blair therefore put Prescott in charge of a team to work out a policy with Michael Meacher, then transport spokesman, and Brown. By the time the government was preparing to sell Railtrack shares in May 1996, Meacher had been replaced by Clare Short, and the team were getting desperate.

Steve Hardwick, Prescott's adviser, did the number-crunching on a complicated formula with Lord Williams of Elvel, a Labour peer and former merchant banker with Barings, involving a British Rail share issue, and swap for Railtrack shares. They went to the City and obtained assurances that, given the Labour threat to buy back Railtrack, it would never be floated.

But Brown's office leaked to the *Financial Times* that Blair and Brown were determined to soften their commitment to buying back all or part of the UK's track and stations. The *FT* reported that the possibility of repurchase would not be totally abandoned, but held as a threat against the company if it failed to invest properly or the quality of rail service deteriorated.

However, in a strange flight of fancy for the *FT*, it compared Prescott to John Noakes, the swashbuckling erstwhile presenter of BBC's *Blue Peter*, and warned that his co-presenter, Val Singleton, had always ridden roughshod over Noaksey. 'Doing the same to the deputy leader is more dangerous.'

He fought hard in public and private to force Brown to accept a more explicit threat to renationalise Railtrack, if it was ever sold, which Prescott doubted would ever happen.

To force his case, Prescott went on LWT's *Dimbleby* programme on 3 March 1996, and promised the railways would be 'publicly owned and accountable', adding that a clause to this effect would be put into Railtrack's sale prospectus in May. The *Guardian* noted that his remarks suggested he had won the internal battle to ensure Labour would not simply seek tight regulation of the railways, as it proposed with other industries.

The politics, as ever, became mixed up with personalities. Short's deputy, Brian Wilson, was a talented Scottish journalist, who had run rings round her with leaks, press statements, initiatives and headlines on rail privatisation, earning him the nickname 'the deputy from hell'. Relations between Labour's number one and number two on transport were as strained as a garrotting wire.

The final act was played out while Gordon Brown was away in America on business. His place had been taken by Andrew Smith, subsequently given Short's job in the July 1996 reshuffle by Blair.

There was a flurry of faxes to and from America, as the battle over the policy went transatlantic, but Smith conceded the case to Prescott and Wilson. There was jubilation in the Prescott camp, but it was short-lived.

When Brown got back, he had a furious meeting with Blair. Blair called in the deal, and ordered it rewritten for the prospectus. Clare Short sided with Brown and Blair, leaving Prescott fuming in defeat. Prescott never forgave Short for what she had done.

Short supported a three-pronged attack on the privatisation: regulation would be used to enforce government control; the state subsidy – an annual £2 billion from the taxpayer – would be paid direct to Railtrack, instead of the operating companies, to influence its investment decisions; and British Rail would be charged with responsibility to oversee the system. Short said her own preference was not to buy back shares, but gradually to take a publicly owned stake in Railtrack.

It was all meant to put the City off the flotation. When Railtrack was sold, the shares went up in value.

CHAPTER NINETEEN

The Spin Doctors

Now we're going to have visions instead of roses.
John Prescott in *Tribune.*

The loyalty of John Prescott was strained to breaking point twice within twelve months of his becoming deputy leader.

The first big row with Blair occurred in spring 1995, after Prescott discovered he had been left out of a secret strategy meeting at the home of Chris Powell, an advertising executive, and brother of one of the Labour leader's aides.

Blair and his close allies gathered at Powell's house on 3 March 1995 at Fritham Lodge, Fritham, on the edge of the New Forest.

Chris Powell is the middle brother of three Powells – the other two being Charles, Baroness Thatcher's urbane former foreign affairs adviser at Number Ten (who pronounces his name with upper-class aplomb to rhyme with 'foal'); and Jonathan, the head of Blair's private office (who pronounces his name to rhyme with 'bowel'). Chris was a close ally of Peter Mandelson when he was head of the party's communications.

Blair's aides later said the meeting had been called primarily to introduce Blair to Powell, chief executive of the advertising agency Boase Masimi Pollit. The company was pitching to become Labour's sole advertising agency, replacing the 'Shadow Agency' made up of committed freelance experts, who had advised on the 1987 and 1992 campaigns.

But the key purpose of the meeting was to review the results of internal party polling, and its impact on how Labour was going to 'sell' the next phase of its economic and tax campaign to be led by Gordon Brown, the shadow Chancellor.

About a dozen were at the fireside seminar with Blair. The guest list included Mandelson, Brown, Jonathan Powell, Alastair Campbell, Tom Sawyer (the party General Secretary), David Miliband (head of policy and brother of Ed Miliband, who worked in Brown's office; both are now MPs) and Joy Johnson (appointed with Brown's support as the Labour Party's director of communications a few days before).

Although campaigning strategy was an essential part of Prescott's brief as deputy leader, almost incredibly he was not put on the list.

It was only later that Prescott's aide, Rosie Winterton, heard along the grapevine that there had been a meeting, and checked it out. A few telephone calls confirmed that it was true. Rosie, from a professional, Labour-supporting background in Doncaster, proved her weight in gold in Prescott's office, until becoming the Labour MP for Doncaster on 1 May 1997 in the general election.

Prescott was furious. Blair tried to calm Prescott down, assuring him it was an oversight, that he should have been there, that if it happened again, he would be on the guest list, that he was not being frozen out or excluded.

If he was going to resign, it was now. Those close to Prescott deny he did threaten to do so but the threat was in the air. He was a pragmatist, who wanted Labour to win power after years in the wilderness, and was not going to put that at risk. But the implication was clear: there was only so much he was prepared to take.

He later told friends that threatening to resign was something he could not do too often. It was like the ultimate deterrent. He was a fighter but being petulant had got him nowhere in the past, and it had destroyed one of his predecessors. Prescott had no intention of playing George Brown to Tony Blair's Harold Wilson.

'I give my advice privately. Nobody is free of constraints. I don't believe in the George Brown role where you threaten to resign every other day if you don't think something is right.'

Wilson and his deputy, driven by drink, had a stormy relationship and Brown ignominiously resigned in the midst of a sterling crisis, not over an issue of policy, but over an apparent snub by Wilson. When he went, he was hardly missed around the Cabinet table.

One of Prescott's allies warned Blair's camp that there were real dangers about appearing to go behind Prescott's back. 'I said he is one of the most honest people and loyal people you would ever meet. But he will not have dishonesty. He will have a difference of opinion, properly expressed, and he will respect you for it. What he won't have is dishonesty. He tells people sometimes in a rather bluntish way what he thinks – he is not like a politician; there is a gut conviction in Prescott.'

Prescott warned Blair that it would harm the whole modernisation project if he was kept out of the magic circle.

'He told Tony that he has got to keep his credibility with the left. If he loses that, it damages Blair as well as Prescott,' said the aide.

Prescott had already demonstrated his use to Blair. Within two days of winning the leadership, Blair told Prescott that he wanted to move Larry Whitty out of his job as General Secretary of the party. Whitty was held by Blair to be responsible for trying to slow down the move towards OMOV, ensuring the review group was biased against radical change, and he was seen as an obstacle to future modernisation. Prescott was shocked by Blair's vehemence that he wanted Whitty out. He could see there was no way he could prevent it happening, but he wanted to defuse the situation.

It could have proved explosive. Whitty was angry; he was appointed by the NEC, not the leader. Whitty was a union man with loyal friends; he could have taken his case to the annual party conference and appealed for the support of the unions. It was possible Blair could have been threatened with his first big defeat on the NEC by the union barons over Whitty, or at least a damaging party conference debacle. Prescott quietly worked behind the scenes and defused the row. He made sure that Whitty was not demoted into an academic role Blair had in mind, but moved sideways into a liaison role with unions and MEPs in Europe, a job in which he has won Blair's praise. Whitty was invited to a meeting in Prescott's office, high in one of the turrets overlooking Parliament Square, before a meeting of the NEC, which was to confirm the new post created specially for Whitty. It was cloak-and-dagger bordering on French farce. I had been called in by Prescott to write a piece about the new job. As Whitty slipped in unnoticed by one door at 1 Parliament Street, Prescott ushered me out of another. Whitty accepted the move with good grace and was eventually replaced by Tom Sawyer, a subtle, former deputy to Rodney Bickerstaffe in NUPE. Working to Tony Blair and Prescott in the European role, Whitty's work for Blair, including operating an early warning system with inside intelligence on Europe, forced Blair to revise his views. He became a highly valued member of the leadership team. Whitty is now a peer and a junior DEFRA minister.

Sawyer was a shrewd operator behind Kinnock's drive to modernise the party, and played a crucial role in keeping the unions on its side while shifting the party away from trade union influence in the block vote. As General Secretary of the party, he did the same for Blair, downgrading of the influence of the NEC by returning it more to its original role as a management committee for the party machine, rather than a supreme policy-making body.

Prescott's intervention over the movement of Larry Whitty – which has not been disclosed before – was a mark of Prescott's value to Blair, particularly of his understanding of the unions, which Blair – coming from a different background – has never matched.

Their relationship depends on mutual respect and trust. After the row over the Powell meeting, it was restored. Alastair Campbell, Blair's press secretary, played a crucial role in maintaining good working relations between Prescott and Blair. Campbell is a staunch Blair supporter and no wimp – he once took a swing at Michael White of the *Guardian* for playing the fool when Robert Maxwell died. He can be just as plain-speaking as the deputy leader, and Prescott respects Campbell for that. In the aftermath of the 1992 general election defeat, Campbell had written a stinging attack on Prescott in the *Daily Mirror*. The next week, the *Mirror* carried Prescott's counterblast.

> *Campbell also takes me to task for attacking the 'spin doctors', the image builders as he calls them. I was a member of the leader's committee, he says, which had access to all campaign plans. Indeed I was. But it met just three times and when it did it was to rubber stamp decisions reached by another committee, packed by smart people in smart suits who'd never won an election in their lives. They hijacked the campaign and there's no point saying they didn't ... We need less spin-doctory and more straight talking about where we stand.*

The piece was largely written by Campbell under Prescott's by-line. He has helped smooth the path between the two leaders whenever there have been tensions. Blair's own friends admit it was crass to leave Prescott out of the Powell meeting. Prescott accepted the assurances, and simmered down, blaming the Blair aides, not Blair, for the omission. But he did not forget.

The uneasy calm between the Blair aides and Prescott erupted again, in the middle of the TUC conference in September 1995, when a copy of a memorandum by Philip Gould – another advertising adviser to the party, who had helped set up the Shadow Agency with Mandelson ten years earlier – was leaked to the *Guardian*. It recommended a 'unitary command structure leading directly to the party leader', and an ambitious programme of further modernisation, including abolishing the block trade union vote.

It caused a furore among the trade unions and Prescott blew his top. 'My main concern was not so much about the meeting but about the [Gould] document which seemed to be giving the impression that everything should be run by advisers but it gave the wrong impression. Advisers advise. Politicians decide and I couldn't be in a party where it wasn't the politicians making that clear.'

He had not known about the Gould memorandum until it was leaked. It had been circulated around the time of the secret Powell meeting, but it was easy to see why the deputy leader of the Labour Party was not on the mailing list. It appeared to confirm all his suspicions about the hidden agenda of the leader's aides, the clever college boys who had gathered around Blair. Prescott had anticipated this would happen; he had warned against attempts to 'Clintonise' the party two years earlier. 'It's not about strengthening a party; all the ideas from Clinton are an elite few running a party on the basis of the information they get from the polls. That is not the way the Labour Party has been run, and while we've tried it in the last couple of elections, it does seem to be that we've lost, doesn't it?'

Rodney Bickerstaffe called on Blair to dissociate himself from the 'top-down leadership' run by a 'small coterie'. Blair devoted the core of his TUC speech to denying that charge.

Blair and Prescott held a private council at the TUC; Prescott's loyalty again won over his anger.

His readiness to accept the assurances about Gould's memorandum was partly due to the fact that Gould, a Robin Gibb lookalike, was a freelance adviser on PR, and his memorandum was so blunt that it resembled a taped message in the movie *Mission: Impossible* – within 24 hours it had started to self-destruct. Blair's aides tried to defuse its impact by pointing out that by the time it was leaked it was palpably out of date. It complained there was no political project to match Thatcher's in 1979; but by September 1995 the 'modernisers' with Prescott's backing had rewritten Clause Four of the party constitution.

The Gould memorandum also gave damaging hostages to fortune, which were fully exploited by Conservative Central Office. It was subtitled 'Labour is not yet ready for government; it needs to complete its revolution'. Michael Heseltine, the Deputy Prime Minister, said it proved that Labour was 'not fit to govern'. It was so counterproductive as to strengthen Prescott's hand against the 'aides'. He could now say to Blair, 'I told you so.'

But there were other items in the Gould agenda that have proved remarkably prescient: the 'unitary command structure' would require reducing the power of the national executive, which Tom Sawyer is studying; a 'new culture' was achieved – the party had been renamed 'New Labour', and it was more than an image-maker's invention; the unveiling of a 'revolutionary' policy agenda at the 1996 party conference – Blair planned to have the manifesto outline endorsed then; and a 'new building' – John Smith House, Walworth Road – became the headquarters.

The two snubs were hard for Prescott to suffer. Barely a month went by without John Major making a joke about Labour's deputy leader being kept in the dark. Blair put in a great deal of effort to win him round, but there remained the nagging doubts that the spin doctors were casting their spell over the leadership. Prescott had an almost clinical aversion to spin doctors from Kinnock's period of leadership, and it was happening again.

In June 1992, in the bitter aftermath of the fourth election defeat, Prescott said in *Tribune*: 'The Labour Party has run away from challenges in the last few years. We've become managers rather than the organisers of change and that I think has been very detrimental to us and the polls have told us to use the same warm language ...'

There were lots of warm words offered to Prescott about his exclusion from the Powell presentation meeting, but those around Prescott believed he was deliberately left out. That view is supported by Blair aides who privately admit that Prescott is 'not the most positive person' to have at the table when issues of presentation are under way. He was regarded as a disbeliever on public relations; some of the aides thought, naively, they could keep him out, Prescott suspected. It increased Prescott's anxiety about the influence of the PR men on the direction of party policy. 'The Labour Party was using polls through its Shadow Agency. It's often you know a political agenda can be pursued through the kind of answers you get in a poll which are reflecting the way the question's been put. There's a lot of evidence for that ... I think if a political party totally takes its messages solely from those polls, it must at least begin to question them ...'

The techniques were similar to the agenda-led journalism that Mandelson once practised brilliantly on *Weekend World*, the London Weekend TV current affairs programme presented by Brian Walden. Buzzwords and opinion polling were combined on *Weekend World* with tightly scripted, short interviews with MPs, commentators, journalists and academics to put Tory ministers or Labour shadow ministers on the spot. Being interviewed by Mandelson for the 30-second 'talking head' slots in the programme was an uncomfortable business, under the arc lights in a rented hotel suite, mixing soft furnishings with hard sell. Mandelson would sometimes cajole those taking part into using particular words, which fitted in with the script, which had been worked out in advance. Everything had to fit neatly into the package. It was part of the spin doctor's kit also used by the Tory Party practitioners.

Precise words and neatness were not Prescott's forte. During the 1992 general election, he was asked to use the word 'opportunity'.

'Opportunity is a word they tell us that the polls [say] is very nice – so the Tories use it and we use it.'

In addition to using polls to ease the party away from allegedly unpopular policies, Prescott feared the spin doctors were adopting another Clinton strategy of distancing Labour from the trade unions. Philip Gould was involved in the Arkansas governor's campaign team – there was a story at Westminster that he had been in Clinton's Little Rock headquarters when the Limey Prime Minister Major telephoned to congratulate the President on his election victory, in spite of having turned over his Home Office file for use by the Tory Party's friends in America. Brown and Blair were assiduous in keeping up contacts with the Democrats, and their advisers were active in sharing intelligence on campaigning with Clinton's team.

'I do not think it's been proven that Clinton won the election because he broke his contacts with the trade unions … We've gone chasing that extra 2 per cent from the Liberals on this basis if we got rid of the vested interest, if we could have proportional representation, this has dominated our thinking; that is Clintonism.'

He was against severing Labour's historic link with the trade unions. 'If you are questioning the relationship between trade unions and the Labour Party, then you question the very fundamental being of the Labour Party.'

There was also a practical reason for sustaining the link: he acknowledged that, without the unions, the Labour Party would not be able to afford to fight a general election.

He sought and was given an assurance by Blair that there would be no further changes to the trade union relations with Labour, particularly the block vote, until after the general election. He gave an interview to the *Independent* in which he hinted that there could be changes to the way trade unions sponsored MPs in their constituencies. It was a small change, possibly allowing the money to fund campaigns where it was needed in the marginals, for which he had special responsibility. But it caused Prescott grief, because he feared it would be seen as welshing on the deal. He is careful to keep his promises, and play straight, but he has learned that spin doctors do have their uses. He appointed his own press officer in July 1996.

Prescott has learned that leading with the chin can open Labour to unnecessary punishment by its opponents. In the run-up to the 1979 general election victory, Margaret Thatcher refused to give clear commitments about the Conservatives' tax plans, insisting that Sir Geoffrey Howe, the shadow Chancellor, had first to see the books before he could be expected to deliver his Budget. The *Daily Mail* famously ran its double-page spread denying the '12 Labour lies'. They included the assertion that VAT would be doubled. In fact it was raised from 8 per cent to 15 per cent. In spite of his natural distrust of the spin doctors, by 1996 Prescott said it was stupid to expect Labour to release its tax plans before the election.

It was not the end of the tensions, however. Prescott and Gordon Brown had never got on together. It was no secret that Prescott believed Robin Cook would have made a better shadow Chancellor, and there had been rows.

Brown's determination to hold Labour to strict financial rectitude caused increasing alarm among his shadow Cabinet colleagues in the run-up to the general election. It came to a head after Brown announced at a press conference that young people could lose welfare benefit if they did not take up one of a range of work schemes offered by a Labour government. It caused consternation in the Prescott camp. In fact, Brown had made the point in answer to a question; there had been no change of policy – it was already the case that young people would lose benefit for appearing not to be seeking work or work experience, but it sounded ominously like the American 'workfare' scheme.

The deputy leader had it out with Brown about the failure to be consulted. Brown also faced criticism from colleagues for appearing to announce in a speech that universal child benefit would be ended to pay for enhanced financial support to enable young people to stay on at school, go on to college or take a training course. The speech was unexceptional; the problem arose because the background briefing by some of Brown's aides was more explicit. The spin doctors again seemed to be developing policy, without the shadow Cabinet either being consulted or even knowing who was responsible for the headlines.

CHAPTER TWENTY

Right Hon.

I'm certainly not a monarchist ...
John Prescott.

The deputy leader of the Labour Party was sitting in his office under the clock tower at the Commons when he was asked whether he would take a call from the Prime Minister. Prescott assumed it was one of his friends playing the fool. 'I always take a call from the Prime Minister on Wednesday.'

Number Ten said they were quite serious. The Prime Minister wanted to speak to him.

In a moment, Mr Major's unmistakable monotone was telling Prescott the good news. 'I want to offer you the only honour worth having.'

Prescott was invited to become a member of the Privy Council.

'I won't have to bow to the Queen will I?'

Memories flooded back of the time when the Queen paid a visit to Hull in the 1970s to open the new dock complex of shops, offices, a Trust House Forte hotel and a marina. Prescott had not been prepared to bow to the Queen on that occasion.

The encounter between Prescott and the Queen in Hull was one for the aficionados.

As he was introduced to the Sovereign, the member for Hull East stood stiffly upright, unbending, refusing to bow. Then she spoke to him. Not quite being able to catch what she said, Prescott stooped to hear. To the spectators, it clearly looked as though Prescott had bowed.

Round one to the Queen.

The town had turned out for the occasion, the Queen's band had played, the Lord Lieutenant of the County appeared in uniform and sword, and local civic dignitaries escorted the Queen to the opening ceremony. Photographs of it are proudly displayed in the Marina hotel foyer, with the MP for Hull East clearly visible, tucked in at the rear of the royal procession around the docks, performing his civic duty.

That night, there was a reception on board the royal yacht *Britannia* moored in the dock, and the Prescotts had been cordially invited to be guests of the Queen on board. Prescott was reluctant, but Pauline had bought a new outfit, a stunning black dress; Prescott knew there was no way out. He would have to go.

As he walked up the gangplank with his wife, a voice could be heard over the cheerful playing of melodies by the royal band: 'You're a hypocrite, Prescott.' It was like his conscience screaming at him, but he went through the performance, ill at ease.

After being introduced, Pauline waited for the right moment to hand the Queen a letter. It was from their youngest son, David, then aged three. A few weeks later, the Prescott household received a letter from the Palace. It was to David, from the Queen. A few weeks later, they found David writing another letter. 'Dear Queen, It's David again ...'

They had a little monarchist in the family. Round two to the Queen.

Duty now called again. To be a member of the Privy Council is to be one of the Queen's Ministers, held to the ancient rules of secrecy, like a form of Masonic Lodge. This raised another question in Prescott's mind.

'I won't have to wear an apron, will I?'

He was assured that aprons were not de rigueur. It was imperative for him to join, however.

Prescott's hero is Oliver Cromwell. Cromwell, the Puritan defender of the faith, the defender of the Commons, and the commander of the army, who was reluctantly responsible for the execution of the King.

His enthusiasm for Cromwell overflowed when the Sealed Knot – the society dedicated to the authentic re-enactment of Roundhead–Royalist battles – staged an event in Hull. Prescott's adopted city is steeped in Roundhead tradition: John Hotham closed the city gates against the Duke of York in 1642, when the Civil War began, and the citadel was held by the Yorkshire Puritans under Sir Thomas Fairfax against Royalist siege. Prescott invited the 'Roundheads' back to 'Prescott's Castle' for tea and sandwiches after the conflict, where, being a stickler for detail, he could not help pointing out that the King was blond but the head pulled out of the basket by the axeman had brown hair.

Prescott is one of nature's Roundheads, but he would not go

so far as Cromwell. He has strong republican tendencies, although he accepts the role of the Queen, recognising that support for the Queen is strong among his own staunch Labour voters in East Hull. Like many people, he would prefer to see a slimmed-down monarchy, if the institution is to continue.

Asked whether he was a republican, before he became deputy leader, Prescott said, 'I'm certainly not a monarchist, so that makes me a republican in a democratic sense.'

Did he favour getting rid of the monarchy? 'I don't think it's an important issue … I find my way of dealing with it. You know when we have to swear our allegiance to the Queen to get our wages? To get wages without mentioning the word "Queen", I affirm, but … I don't say it. I mumble it. That's one of my little compromises …

'There's a constitutional monarch who's head of state. I'm quite happy to live with what the country has decided is to be the head of state.

'You have to do compromises in this game, where you don't want to offend people who strongly believe in the monarchy, right? I don't. But there's a constitutional head, which I recognise.'

As a member of the Privy Council, Prescott would become one of the Queen's closest political advisers.

Only members of the Privy Council are allowed the prefix 'Right Honourable' in front of their names, and it is a necessary step to becoming a fully fledged minister of the Crown. It is more than a mere courtesy title. Members of the opposition become members of the Privy Council in order to be given confidential briefings on state secrets, under oath.

Its origins reach back to William the Conqueror, and the Norman Magnum Concilium, composed of the great landowners, which had developed into a Parliament representing barons, clergy and commons. Gradually, it divided into two houses, the Lords and Commons, a separation given substance under Henry VIII, who was the first to use the term 'House of Lords'. The practice had grown up under medieval kings – as with all modern political leaders – to create a smaller inner circle of advisers, the Curia Regis, to agree on the important matters of state, including taxation, without summoning the Parliament. It included key ministers such as the Lord Chancellor, the Lord Treasurer, leading judges and the Lord Keeper of the Privy Seal. By the thirteenth century, it was known as the Privy Council, with paid members who took an oath to give the King good advice. Its composition was decided solely by the King. The Privy Council reached its zenith of power under the Tudors, and its Court of Star Chamber – named after the stars on the ceiling of the room in which it sat in the Palace of Westminster – became notorious for political trials, and the use of torture to extract confessions. It was abolished by Cromwell during the Commonwealth, but was restored with the monarchy in 1660 with reduced powers. There are about 300 members of the modern Privy Council, which meets as a body only when the Sovereign dies or announces an intention to marry, but it has a quorum of three. It meets regularly, standing up, in a room at Buckingham Palace with the Queen to give effect to Cabinet decisions by Orders in Council;

the judicial committee may also sit as a court of appeal for some Commonwealth countries; and it can appoint special committees to investigate highly sensitive issues, such as telephone-tapping. The leader of the opposition and his deputy are routinely sworn in to the inner circle. It is essential to be members if the Prime Minister wishes to brief members of the opposition in total secrecy on 'Privy Council terms'.

Having become Deputy Leader of Her Majesty's Opposition, it was a requirement of the job that Prescott be made a Privy Counsellor. On such occasions, the Queen is always present.

Palace aides briefed Prescott on the strange induction ceremony: he would not be required to bow to the Queen, but he would have to kneel on a stool, and hop to another stool, then kiss the Queen's hand, 'brushing the lips lightly' over her fingers. On receiving the honour, he would stand up, and tread carefully backwards, to join the other members of the Privy Council, but always making sure he did not turn his back on the Queen, in a sort of crab walk.

His mother Phyllis proudly kept a cutting of the Court Circular recording the event on 27 July.

> *The Queen held a Council at 3.00 p.m.*
>
> *There were present: the Lord Mackay of Clashfern (Lord Chancellor), the Rt Hon. Antony Newton MP (Lord President), the Baroness Trumpington (Baroness in Waiting) and the Rt Hon. William Waldegrave, MP.*
>
> *Mr Anthony Blair, MP, was sworn in as a Member of Her Majesty's Most Honourable Privy Council.*

> *Mr John Prescott, MP, made affirmation as a Member of Her Majesty's Most Honourable Privy Council.*
>
> *The Rt Hon. William Waldegrave took the Oath of Office as Minister of Agriculture, Fisheries and Food, and kissed hands upon his appointment.*

He recognises that whatever his own republican sympathies, the Queen remains more popular than the rest of the Royal Family, making the monarchy secure. 'It's certainly safe in my hands. Certainly in the sense that the public are very [great] admirers of the monarchy though they've gone through a change of opinion in the last few years, [and that is] a lot to do with the antics of some members of the Royal Family.'

In affirming the oath, Prescott also demonstrated another side of the Deputy Leader of Her Majesty's Opposition. In addition to being in his heart a Roundhead, he is also a card-carrying member of the agnostics.

His attitude to religion has hardened as he has got older. He was baptised as a member of the Church of England, and went to Sunday school as a boy in Brinsworth. He was married in a Church of England parish church in Upton, but he does not believe in God now. He refused to have his two sons baptised, leaving them to make up their own minds. Neither has gone through the adult baptism.

He does not make a big issue of his lack of faith in an all-powerful God, but does not have much time for the dressing up, the mumbo-jumbo and the other trappings of religion. Nor does he have much time for mixing religion with politics, and is sceptical of the brand of Christian socialism preached by his party leader. Mr Blair is a devout Christian, who was heavily influenced by the teachings of John Macmurray, Grote Professor of Philosophy at London University, and one of his later 'disciples', Peter Thomson, a minister of the Australian Anglican Church reading theology at St John's when Blair met him at Oxford University. 'Blair's idea of community, which is perhaps his most distinctive theme as a politician, derives directly from Macmurray,' says one of his biographers.

'It is precisely the combination in Macmurray of Christian socialism and a "conservative" critique of liberalism which underpins the apparent novelty of Blair's political philosophy.'

Prescott prefers to tackle the problems of the break-up of community, and 'the family', without the Christian morality with which the Christian socialist informs his analysis. Blair has laid heavy emphasis on the principles of Christian socialism in recent speeches, making some shadow Cabinet meetings uncomfortable for the non-believers.

'Shadow Cabinet meetings are getting like prayer meetings,' said one Prescott supporter. 'They're split between the Christians and the atheists.'

Labour is a sufficiently broad church to accommodate both views. Tony Benn found no difficulty in reconciling the teaching of the Bible – taken as the text of faith for the Levellers, who believed it prohibited the domination of man by man – and the tradition of humanists in the Labour Party, or non-believers, such as H.G. Wells. 'Christian, humanist and socialist moralities have in fact co-existed and co-operated throughout history and they co-exist and co-operate today most fruitfully and not only within the Christian Socialist movement itself,' Benn has written. 'The British trade union and Labour movement, like Anglicans, Presbyterians, Catholics, Methodists, Congregationalists, Baptists, Jews and campaigners for civil rights, have all gained inspiration from these twin traditions of Christianity and humanistic socialism.'

The Levellers, Benn pointed out, at first campaigned with Cromwell and then against him, ultimately to be defeated by Prescott's hero. Benn asserted that, while Marxism was 'one of the many sources of inspiration' for the Labour Party, it was less influential than Christian socialism, Fabianism, Owenism, trade unionism, and even radical liberalism.

The disestablishment of the Church is not part of the Labour programme, but it would find support in strange quarters in a multicultural Britain. Even Prince Charles has suggested that the monarch should become the defender of faiths.

The question of the monarchy is more difficult for the Labour leadership. As shadow Welsh Secretary, Ron Davies created a storm when he questioned the fitness of the Prince of Wales to become King. He was forced immediately into issuing an abject apology to the Prince, but he had succeeded in his objective of expanding the envelope of front-bench discussion on the subject. His aim had been to raise the issue of the monarchy; it was not, he made clear to friends later, an accidental slip of the lip in an interview he thought would be little noticed. There was a strong feeling within some parts of the shadow Cabinet that the issue of the reform of Britain's constitutional monarchy will have to be dealt with at some point. Some, like Davies, are republican. Others, like Jack Straw, believed the time has come for the monarchy to be reduced in scale. The royal marriages have proved to be the best recruiting sergeant for those who would like to see an elected head of state, on the lines of the successful Irish presidency. The scandals and controversies surrounding the Prince and Princess of Wales and the Duchess of York significantly altered public opinion, according to all the available opinion poll evidence. The Royal Family itself came to the conclusion that change was inevitable, and was reviewing how this could be done. The tensions in the shadow Cabinet on the subject also remained unresolved.

A Palace garden party was in full swing on the lawns outside the window, and the Queen and the members of the Privy Council exchanged pleasantries in the secure knowledge that it would all be kept on 'Privy Council' terms.

When the audience was over, Blair and Prescott shared a car back to the Commons. As they swept out of the gates of the Palace, the deputy leader of the Labour Party asked Her Majesty's leader of the opposition for a quick look at his Bible.

Those who swear the oath are given the Bible as a souvenir. Those who affirm leave empty-handed.

Prescott had been told that the Bible given to Privy Councillors is signed by the Queen. He was curious to see if it carried her inky signature. 'Let's have a look,' he said.

Inside the cover was a signature: Antony Newton, Lord President of the Council. A Tory.

CHAPTER TWENTY-ONE

DPM

I waited years to do this.
Prescott entering Downing Street to be confirmed as Deputy Prime Minister.

In May 1996, Blair called some of his senior shadow Cabinet colleagues and read them the Riot Act. 'He said if we didn't stop the infighting we'd blow it. We'd lose the election,' a shadow Cabinet source said.

Blair had been angered and alarmed by the open feuding on his front bench. The split in John Major's Cabinet over Europe was more fundamental, and the tensions between the Cabinet 'bastards' were driven by the manoeuvring for their long-term leadership ambitions. Blair had command of his shadow Cabinet – he taunted Major: 'I lead my party – you follow yours.' But Labour had gained its lead over the divided Tories by reuniting behind Blair. He did not want that put at risk by petty rivalries.

There was a feud between Prescott and Brown, Clare Short and her deputy Brian Wilson, and Brown and Mandelson. The tensions had been growing; for months, and as the deadline of the election neared, scores were being settled between the shadow ministerial teams and their advisers.

Prescott had become increasingly restive about his own role as Brown appeared determined to force the pace of change through speeches and briefings to the press. Brown had developed an economic strategy designed to avoid the Tory 'tax bombshell' being dropped again on Labour's election platform.

Labour had gone into the 1992 general election with two big public expenditure commitments on pensions and child benefit. This time, Labour's new spending commitments would be pared down to a jobs and training package, funded by a windfall profits tax on privatised utilities, water and electricity.

No new taxes meant that spending commitments on other programmes, including the NHS, would have to be met by savings elsewhere. That iron rule led to some hard decisions, and Brown's refusal to repeat the 1992 pensions pledge provoked a 'grey' protest campaign by veteran former Cabinet minister Barbara Castle.

But the pace of the changes to the welfare state, hinted at in background briefings to the press, caused a mini-revolt in the shadow Cabinet. On 18 April, Brown's press officer, Charlie Whelan, briefed selected journalists that the shadow Chancellor was proposing in a forthcoming speech to cut child benefit – which went to all families regardless of income – for children aged between sixteen and eighteen years of age to help fund an unspecified training and education programme. It was a precursor of Brown's determination to target help on the needy, rather than the middle classes, whom Blair was keen to win over.

Brown's speech never contained the specific threat, but the incident confirmed in the minds of Cook, Prescott and Chris Smith, the shadow Social Security Secretary, that either policy was being decided by the spin doctors or it was being driven by Brown and Blair without proper consultation.

Cook and Smith insisted the future of child benefit had not been decided. Cook said, 'What Gordon announced … was a review.' Smith resisted until he was moved in Blair's July 1996 reshuffle, when Blair handed responsibility for the social security review to Harriet Harman.

Prescott was restless. His commitment to making the deputy leadership a campaigning role – on which he had fought his three elections for the job – had served its purpose, and was now becoming a straitjacket. He privately told friends that he wanted to concentrate more on the direction of the party's policy, particularly on the economy.

The time was coming, he felt, when he would have to make his move, from jolly campaigner handing out sticks of Labour Party rock, to take responsibility for policy direction, matching the power of Michael Heseltine, the Deputy Prime Minister and First Secretary, whom he shadowed.

Brown got his strike in first. On 1 May, Brown said the Treasury under Labour would be 'both a ministry of finance and a ministry for long-term economic and social renewal. It will be innovative rather than obstructive, it will be open rather than secretive, and it will encourage new ideas not stifle them.'

It would be a Super-Treasury, thought Prescott, and he was not going to stand for that. But before Prescott could challenge

Brown's power play, *The Times* reported on 11 May that Blair was concerned about the existence of another long-standing feud, this time between Brown and Mandelson. Brown had never forgiven Mandelson for easing him out of the way so that Blair could have a free crack at the leadership in 1994. Brown and Mandelson had not been on speaking terms since then. Brown was bitter over his thwarted ambition to be leader one day; a bitterness which he still nursed. There was speculation that the report, suggesting Blair wanted to heal the wounds, was placed by Blair's camp in order to force a rapprochement between Brown and Mandelson. It sparked a brushfire of stories in the press about the feuds and the tensions around Blair's leadership. Prescott knew he was going to cause trouble if he pitched in now, but he could not help himself. He felt he had been silent long enough. Fourteen days after Brown's opening salvo in sleepy Bournemouth, to the unimaginably boring conference of the Public Service Tax and Commerce Union, Prescott fired his response.

'It would surely be detrimental to allow an overbearing role for the Treasury ... Too often in the past, the dead hand of the Treasury has stifled initiative and motivation, in the public and private sector with a rigid inflexibility in the interpretation of Treasury rules.'

Blair now felt the fire started by the Brown–Mandelson story was getting out of hand. He decided to intervene, telling his senior Cabinet colleagues they were risking throwing away the chance of power unless they were united. It pulled them up sharply, and led to a serious effort to avoid their personal ambitions sabotaging the party. At the end of May, Prescott was involved in another struggle with Brown over the detailed policy for the privatisation of Railtrack, the part of British Rail which owned the rails and stations. When the crunch came, Clare Short, Labour's shadow Transport Secretary, sided with Brown, and Prescott had to accept defeat, but the deputy leader never gave any hint of his dismay which could have damaged the party. He had come to the conclusion that he was not going to be able to undo the deal that Blair struck with Brown at Granita, and it would be better to work with the shadow Chancellor.

Brown, too, was told by close friends that he needed more friends around the shadow Cabinet table, and set about to correct that. There had long been rivalry between Brown and the other big player in the shadow Cabinet, the shadow Foreign Secretary, Robin Cook – a spiky, intelligent, bearded Scot, who Prescott believed would make a better, less conservative shadow Chancellor. The opportunity for a rapprochement with Prescott came when Brown's office obtained two courtesy tickets for the England–Scotland match at Wembley in the European Championships. He gave one ticket to Prescott. There was an eve-of-match party thrown in the luxury Park Lane penthouse owned by Geoffrey Robinson and half the shadow Cabinet were there. Robinson, the Labour MP for Coventry North West, later appointed Paymaster General by Blair in charge of sorting out the problems with the private finance initiative, had a reputation as a brilliant entrepreneur who was chief executive of Jaguar Cars at 33 and made his millions from an engineering business. He also owned a Lutyens manor in Hampshire, a villa in Tuscany, and the *New Statesman*. The next day, Prescott and Brown sat together at the match, and Prescott began to come to terms with the dynamics within the shadow Cabinet: he was never going to be able to prise Blair away from Brown; it would be better to work with him.

Short was demoted by Blair in the July reshuffle, from transport to overseas aid, before Blair flew off on his summer holidays to Robinson's Tuscan villa, leaving Prescott to mind the shop. Bitterly upset, Short gave an interview to the *New Statesman* in which she criticised the 'people in the dark' behind Blair, which the press assumed to be an attack on Mandelson; and she complained Labour was stripping down policy to appeal to readers of the *Daily Mail*. Media critics said Prescott would need his own 'minder' for the summer when Blair left him in charge, but his deputy showed that he could spin-doctor as expertly as any in the 'Millbank Tendency' as he defended Blair in his absence. In a late-night call from Blair to praise his deputy for dealing with the summer storm over Short's remarks, Prescott told Blair it would blow over, but made it clear in the bluntest terms that Blair needed to heed the warnings or there would be trouble ahead.

Prescott's good intentions were stretched to breaking point as the summer wore on, and one Blairite initiative after another appeared in the press as the conference season approached. At the TUC conference, over grilled sole in the Fish Restaurant, Blackpool, Stephen Byers ruminated on cutting the links with the unions. Kim Howells, another moderniser, suggested the term 'socialist' should be humanely slaughtered. Privately,

Prescott was incensed, but publicly he continued to reaffirm his principles, proclaiming his commitment to democratic socialism by waving his membership card at a manifesto rally in Luton. Prescott saw a joined-up campaign from the Blair camp behind these apparently disparate events, and he was probably right, although when it comes to a choice between the cock-up or conspiracy theory of politics, Prescott is on the side of Machiavelli every time. He even saw the dark hand of the Kinnock camp behind the demotion of his mini-portrait in the official painting of the House of Commons. It was based on a photograph of the Commons with Prescott sitting as he usually did on the front bench. When the painting was unveiled, Prescott's face was relegated to the second row. He has one of the limited edition prints on his wall at home in Hull as a reminder of what a snake pit the Commons can be.

As the election approached, Tory supporters in the media were gleefully asking how long it would be before, like a volcano, Prescott would blow. The relationship between the leader of New Labour and his older, traditionalist deputy was crucial to Labour's electoral chances. Prescott said that Blair reached parts of the party that he could not, and the leadership was stronger for it.

Throughout the summer of 1996 as the sound of hatches being battened down for the elections could be heard across Westminster, Prescott put down a series of well-placed markers about his anxieties, beginning with an on-the-record interview with me for the *Independent*, just before he left for the Democratic convention in America. He was relaxed, and seemed totally at ease with himself. Putting his feet up on his coffee table, he expounded on the support he had given to Blair in building New Labour. After this lengthy exposition, I switched the tape off, but he asked me to put it on again. He had more to say. He then spoke of the 'unease' in the party about the pace of change being driven by Blair, and how he felt Blair's camp had failed to recognise properly the self-discipline shown by the Parliamentary Labour Party in supporting the status quo slate in the shadow Cabinet elections, which averted a rebellion against Harriet Harman for allowing her son to go to a grammar school. Instead of being grateful for the party's support, Blair aides hinted that troublemakers could lose the whip. Prescott's mind went back to his own experience in the 1960 seamen's strike, and his warnings to Kinnock: 'You have to bring them with you – courage is not enough.'

The interview was clearly intended by Prescott as a warning shot, but it went largely unheeded. The leadership was determined to set out its modernising agenda, and used the TUC conference as a platform to inform the voters that Blair would not be in hock to the unions. Short was right; the leadership wanted to appeal to the *Daily Mail* readers, precisely because it could not win the election preaching to the converted. Blair, at the end of his Clause Four campaign, had told a meeting in Lewisham how one disgusted old Labour supporter had complained that even Tories supported the party now. That was the idea, he said with a grin. The press suggested that the TUC conference was a debacle for Labour, but for the Blair camp, it successfully got the message across. A hard-headed television journalist, Joy Johnson, had been appointed to the party press office with Brown's backing to balance Mandelson's influence, but she was frozen out by Blair's aides, and walked out on her £60,000 job in January 1996 after less than a year. She later complained: 'The party's language has become more elaborate and obscure. It's ironic that one frontbencher who does speak in plain words – Clare Short – has been demoted, for thinking the unthinkable without a licence.'

Blair used his 1996 Blackpool conference speech to deflate with a clever joke the criticism that was building up of his autocratic style of leadership – highlighted by the 'New Labour new danger' campaign by the Tory Party depicting Blair's grinning face with 'demon' red eyes. 'First it was Stalin. Then it was Kim Il Sung. Now it's the devil with demon eyes. Can't we just go back to Bambi? Or maybe Kim Il Sung's official title? "The Great Wise Leader, President for Life, Dearly Beloved and Sagacious Leader". Why not? That's what John Prescott calls me … sometimes.'

The Tory attacks continued but the expectant, high-spirited mood in the Labour Party at the Blackpool conference was sustained through to the general election, which no one in the party dared or cared to spoil. The publication in February 1997 of the first edition of *Fighting Talk*, however, brought to a head an issue which had been simmering for months: what role would Prescott be given if Labour won the election? I knew that Prescott had been promised the role of Deputy Prime Minister in broad terms by Blair, but I wrote that Blair would not countenance Prescott being given the freewheeling power around Whitehall of Michael Heseltine, operating from a vast office in the Cabinet Office, dubbed '10A Downing Street'. Michael Brunson, the political editor of ITN, on a flight back from Amsterdam was told by Blair that Prescott would be Deputy Prime Minister. When Brunson reported it, there was a flurry in Millbank Tower, the Labour election campaign headquarters, where Mandelson was based, but the rebuttal unit did not go into action, and it caused Prescott to talk to Blair to find out whether it was an authorised leak about his future. He later sent a 'thank you' note to Brunson for his assistance. Prescott was due to go on the BBC *Breakfast with Frost* show and needed to clarify how much he could say.

In fact, Blair and Prescott had reached an agreement on his title in the spring of 1995, when Prescott erupted after discovering through the diligence of his then political adviser, Rosie Winterton, that there had been a private planning meeting about economic strategy to which he had not been invited. Prescott, furious at what he had learned, telephoned Joy Johnson at home to challenge her about whether she had gone to the meeting. She had admitted to Prescott that there had been a meeting. For Prescott, her decision to go – she was under pressure having just joined the staff – without telling him amounted to choosing sides. Prescott said, 'Now we know whose side you're on.'

Bristling with anger, he boarded a train at Doncaster for London. He was due to meet Tony Blair, who was getting on at Newark, to discuss details of the changes to Clause Four of the party's constitution. Blair came down the first-class carriage, all smiles, his hand outstretched in greeting, and Prescott let him have it, with both Prescott barrels: 'Sit down … What's all that crap you sold me about Old and New Labour working together?' For the next hour or so, the leader and deputy leader thrashed out exactly what title Prescott would have in a Blair government as the train made its way to London. It is unclear what the other passengers must have thought as the leader and his deputy had their frankest exchange since winning the leadership elections. Prescott, as he had with Kinnock, made Blair set their agreement down in writing and Prescott still has the handwritten note saying he would be Deputy Prime Minister.

When they reached London, Blair said they should go to his home in Islington to sort out the Clause Four strategy. When Cherie came into the room, she said, 'Oh, I didn't think you'd be here.'

'Nor did I, love,' said Prescott.

Before he left, he made sure the note was safely in his pocket. It was a mark of Prescott's lack of confidence at that time that he needed the security of a piece of paper, but Prescott had enough political nous to know that even with a guarantee in Blair's handwriting, he could not take it for granted that he would be given the title Deputy Prime Minister in a Blair Cabinet.

A garbled version of this story was tested on Prescott by Sir David Frost when he went on *Breakfast with Frost*. Frost asked him about the row after he got on the train at Newark. Without a flicker of doubt, Prescott denied it point-blank. Later, worried I had got it wrong, I checked with Prescott why he had denied it. 'I got on at Doncaster,' he said.

The Frost interview and the publication of *Fighting Talk* precipitated more negotiations about his role. Prescott wanted the freedom, carved out by Heseltine as Deputy Prime Minister, to range across Whitehall to ensure that manifesto commitments were being carried out. Blair flatly refused.

They discussed other options, including Foreign Secretary – a post that was expected to go to the shadow minister Robin Cook. It was a post that carried portentous precedents for Prescott's relationship with Blair – there was the good example of Ernie Bevin, Clement Attlee's Foreign Secretary, whom Prescott saw as a loyal but powerful role model; but there was also the warning of Harold Wilson's troublesome deputy and Foreign Secretary, George Brown. The post had changed with the passing of empire, Britain's world role, and the changes to the Atlantic alliance with America. It was now likely to be dominated by European affairs, limiting its appeal to Prescott, who knew that the main negotiating tasks at Amsterdam and later summits would fall to Blair.

Prescott and Blair also discussed Prescott becoming Home Secretary, although it was not a serious option for long. But Blair made it clear he wanted Jack Straw to take the post; if Prescott could have been a liberal Home Secretary like Roy Jenkins, he might have taken it, but the current climate of law and order retrenchment meant the time was not right; Prescott saw it as a bed of nails with crime statistics and the intransigent problems of prison conditions. There was also the problem of the high level of personal protection that goes with the job. It would have turned his house into a fortress with Pauline virtually a prisoner in her own home; he did not want that.

He discussed it with his close friend Dick Caborn, the Sheffield Labour MP, whom he had known for years. As the 1997 general election neared, Caborn agreed to meet Prescott at the Woodall service station on the M1 in South Yorkshire. It was a convenient place, handy for Caborn's home in Sheffield and a useful stopping-off point for Prescott at the wheel of his Jaguar on his way back to Hull. Prescott pulled in for the meeting in the café with Caborn, where they discussed Prescott's Cabinet post over tea and motorway service station sandwiches. Prescott was still angry at being kept out of the secret negotiations by Blair and Brown, which laid the ground for the tax promises on the election pledge card, and saw the Home Secretary's rank as a way of protecting his status. Caborn told him bluntly he would be mad to go for the Home Secretary's post. Having sympathised with the miners and been identified by Wilson as a dangerous revolutionary during the seamen's dispute, Prescott as Home Secretary would be a target for the press from day one, said Caborn. Caborn urged him to go for a department with economic clout in the Cabinet. He strongly urged Prescott not to press for the creation of the Deputy Prime Minister's Office, which Caborn feared would have no clear responsibilities and no authority.

Blair, who had not yet learned to trust Prescott, had also made it clear to Prescott that he wanted his deputy fully occupied with a great department of state, and was against putting Prescott into the Cabinet Office.

Prescott did not need much convincing. His mind was already moving in this direction, and accepted Caborn's advice.

The possibility of an employment role, taking bits of training responsibility from the merged Department of Education and Employment to implement the 250,000 jobs pledge, was raised and discarded; given the lack of clarity in the separation of powers, it would have meant difficulties in the relations with the Department of Education, and it may have brought Prescott into conflict with the unions over trade union reforms.

Surrounded by truckers and travellers in the service station café, Prescott and Caborn mapped out the idea of a department that combined the environment, which included housing and local government, with transport – on which Prescott had made his mark in opposition – and regional affairs, a hobby horse he shared with Caborn. 'We thought putting it in the title would keep regional government on the agenda,' said Caborn.

Prescott was very attracted to the proposition because it would give him the chance to put into action the ideas he had championed for years in opposition. He hoped to persuade Gordon Brown to institute a new financing plan to build more council houses, by allowing councils, like housing associations, to take out loans on their rental flows. Blair accepted Prescott's request to take over local government, transport and the regions.

Reassured about his own position, Prescott took to the road for the general election with none of the old worries about being excluded from the manoeuvrings of those in the 'inner loop' at Millbank Tower. A growing maturity in their relationship had made Prescott and Blair more at ease with each other, enabling Prescott to jump on board the Prescott eXpress, his campaign bus, in April with a new confidence. Blair was due to unveil the party's campaign posters – simple messages listing election promises – to party supporters in the sunshine at a country house in Kent, but Blair asked for Prescott to come along too, to symbolise their unity. Prescott's bus came equipped to a high standard – it had been used by pop groups before – and the executive toys included stress-relieving vibrating cushions. I boarded the Prescott eXpress for the return to London and reported that Prescott would not need the vibrating cushions; I had not seen Prescott looking as relaxed as this before. As we raced through the Kentish countryside, he told me: 'We are basically seen as a team. Tony is doing that. It's kind of the head and the heart. I'm happy with the heart though I would like to say I've a head. The "bruiser" image doesn't come up any more and I think that's because over the years, they have got to see me laughing – they see somebody who has got a strong mind, but I don't get that even from the Tories these days. I think they have a great deal of difficulty dealing with me. John Major makes a great point of the "bar steward" but it blows up in his face; at the same time, he is saying, "I am from Brixton, I am the ordinary lad." I think their focus groups tell them that we look to be a team. Where they are suspicious is Brown – "Will there be a strong voice to tell him something else?" [the focus group answer is] "Yes." Where I am strong is [on the question] "Would Blair be bullied by me? No – because he is firm about it." What has come out of this is a kind of happy blend, in a way "traditional values in a modern setting". It looks as if it would work. It's true that we do talk quite frankly; but Blair doesn't personalise politics – I might do more than him.

'I am a lot easier in myself because we have come to an agreement that I no longer have to worry that I am at the centre of things. I am a guy much more at ease with myself as this has developed over the months. I no longer have that feeling that I have to prove to myself, while I'm out in Norwich, that I'm not being exiled.'

The Tories still poked fun at Prescott being exiled to the Outer Hebrides on his bus, but Prescott, ever the shrewd politician, knew there were now advantages to being away from the centre. 'I laugh at it sometimes but it never does me any harm to be outside the immediate pale of the inner core. My image is that "John will go in and tell them they are going too far".' He could preserve his position on his tour of the 90 target seats, if the election campaign, carefully directed by the strategists back at Millbank Tower, ran off the road. There was also the reassuring presence of the mobile telephone and the fax machine on board to iron out difficulties during the campaign. Prescott was in daily contact with Blair and the issues they discussed included the idea that the Labour candidate in Tatton should stand down to make way for Martin Bell, the respected BBC war correspondent, to stand against Neil Hamilton over sleaze allegations that dominated the first two weeks of John Major's strategy for a long, six-week campaign. Prescott had his reservations about the local party being asked to make way for an Independent but went along with the idea. Bell had a sensational victory on a spectacular night.

The start of Major's campaign was to be the theme for the rest of the six weeks – he went to Luton to be heckled by a mob in the market square, and was pleased with the result on the six o'clock news, only to have the whole stunt completely overshadowed that night when the *Sun* came out to back Tony Blair. Major spent the rest of the campaign in a frenetic tour of all four corners of Britain, helicoptering, travelling in his battlebus, shouting down hecklers in market squares from Carlisle to Brecon from his soapbox platform, and swinging from fleeting hope to black moods of despair as the opinion polls continued to point to a disastrous defeat. I was told during the campaign that he had asked one of his aides: 'How will history judge me?' She was diplomatic, and assured him it would judge him well; there was no blame attached to him for the debacle in the Tory Party, except that he was their leader. The Euro-sceptic splits deepened, his party refused to reunite in spite of his appeals, and the Tory Central Office election machine failed to land a direct hit on Labour, which had learned from 1992 to present a moving target. When Labour was attacked, as it was over confusion on the tax-raising powers of a Scottish Parliament, it retreated.

Regarded before the election as the Achilles' heel of Labour, Prescott covered 10,222 miles by coach, train, boat (a canal barge in Chester), plane and car with hardly a false step, although he wore out a pair of shoes he had bought for the campaign. The only stumble occurred when the *Sunday Times* writer A. A. Gill, under the headline LOOSE CANNON ON A ROLL BESIDE THE SEASIDE, reported on 13 April that, as the battlebus headed for Great Yarmouth, Prescott had said off the record that he could not tell the whole truth about the minimum wage causing unemployment. The Tories called a press conference at Central Office that

Sunday to denounce Prescott's 'lies'. Heseltine said he had 'blown Labour's bond of trust to smithereens'. Brian Mawhinney, the party chairman, said it was a 'defining moment' of the campaign. Prescott said it was 'an utter travesty of the truth'. He said he had made clear to Gill he had said in 1992 the minimum wage would cost jobs, but evidence published since then 'has proved those fears to be groundless'. That evening, I met Gill when we both boarded the sleeper for Penzance to cover the Prime Minister's tour of the West Country, and I said Prescott was demanding the transcript of their conversation. Gill, an engaging and intelligent television reviewer and not a member of 'the Lobby' – the journalistic pack attached to the Commons – told me he did not use a tape recorder for interviews 'because you don't listen' to the answers properly; he did not take notes because he was dyslexic; but he had a good memory. It was his memory against Prescott's press release, and the row became a 24-hour wonder. There were Tory attempts to open rifts between Blair and Prescott over privatisation, but they were ill informed. Prescott sketched a map, involving three connecting circles, of his plans for semi-privatisation for the Royal Mail, the London Underground and the railways, and he told Blair during the election he was not averse to seeing sell-offs where necessary to raise receipts for improving public services; he was prepared to contemplate the privatisation of the Royal Mail, to raise finance for investment in public transport. But he saw each privatisation as part of an interconnected strategy. Part of his plan was to raise finance from the sale of up to 49 per cent of the London Underground, although after the election, leaked papers showed he had asked Geoffrey

Robinson to include in the options allowing the majority of shares in London Underground to be sold. The deputy leader visited 89 out of 90 target seats; the odd one out, Brecon and Radnorshire, was the only one not to be captured by Labour.

The history of the general election on 1 May 1997 was being rewritten within minutes of the first result being announced – a massive swing to Labour in Chris Mullin's Labour seat in Sunderland South – so that only a visitor from Mars would have been in any doubt that a landslide was going to happen. Tory spin doctors were saying shortly after midnight, as the results were still coming in, that the Tories had lost it on Black Wednesday, when the pound was blown out of the ERM along with their reputation for economic competence. On the ground, it never seemed quite like that. Prescott thought Labour would win, but had never dared dream it would be by a landslide. Everyone assumed there would be a muted repeat of 1992, with Tories turning out to narrow the gap on polling day. There was a high turnout early on 1 May, but as Pauline said excitedly, it was the voters from the council estates that were turning out in droves. Prescott's arrival in London was delayed by the need to attend his own constituency count in Hull East.

When his plane touched down in Stansted, Prescott could not believe the news – Michael Portillo was one of six Cabinet ministers to lose his seat, and Labour gains across the country were taking Labour into areas that had never featured on their target seats, or even their lists of 'possibles'. Prescott and his aides were taken from the airport in the early hours of 2 May in a people-carrier to the Labour Party results party on the South

Bank, and they could not resist a short spin around Smith Square to witness the scenes outside Conservative Central Office. Alastair Campbell ordered Blair not to speak until the moment when the sun was rising so that Blair theatrically could say 'a new era is dawning over British politics ...' It delayed the procedures for half an hour. Prescott, sitting in the front row, let his face show how he felt about that. Mandelson remarked later that it was only John who could scowl on such a morning.

There had been jokes during the election about Mandelson changing Labour's colour to purple, but the political map of Britain was turning red. Nobody in the Prescott camp had any sleep that night and with the heady feeling of a party still celebrating in the warm May air, the Prescott eXpress made its final journey, to Downing Street, where Blair had earlier made his entry to cheering crowds of children – who turned out to be a walk-on cast of party workers and their kids waving Union Jacks. The deputy leader of the Labour Party jumped off his bus, and strolled down to Number Ten to be appointed as Deputy Prime Minister. As he approached the door, he waved to the cameras and said: 'I waited years for this.' It was the first ministerial rank he had held since entering the Commons as an MP 27 years earlier.

A month later, reflecting on the victory, Prescott told me: 'It just captured the moment. It said to lots of people in the party, who have waited a bloody long time for this, something about the sheer pleasure of the moment. My face has communicated most of my politics and it said it all. It was just the sheer joy and pleasure that it had been a long road, and it was over.'

CHAPTER TWENTY-TWO

First Term

> *John decided he would make an historic peace with Gordon.*
>
> Prescott ally.

Touring around Labour's key seats during the 1997 general election campaign, Prescott had plenty of time to contemplate his future as he bounced around the byways of England, Wales and Scotland in the back of his campaign bus, the Prescott eXpress. During his three weeks on the road, Prescott came to a strategic decision which had been forming in his mind for months, and it was to have an enormous impact on his own political fortunes, and those of the government.

Prescott decided to end his rivalry for influence over the economic strategy of the government and form an alliance with Gordon Brown.

It was a decision which was to form a pivotal relationship in the Blair government for the first term of office, and which most people outside the government failed to recognise. Prescott's strategic decision also had a profound effect on another potential contender for the leadership: the late Robin Cook.

Prescott could have formed an alliance with Cook, whose early friendship with Brown had collapsed long before Blair came to power and who, at one time, was seen by Prescott as a better prospect for Chancellor but in the weeks of the campaign, Prescott decided to leave Cook to his own devices, which had the long-term effect of making Cook more isolated in the Cabinet. Cook, who died in August, 2005 during a hiking expedition with his second wife Gaynor in the Highlands, had a formidable reputation for his forensic political skills, but he had failed to nurture a constituency of loyal support at Westminster or among the unions. When he came to resign from the Cabinet in the second term over the war on Iraq, his lack of any powerful allies in the Cabinet protected Blair from what could otherwise have been devastating consequences.

As the Blair government enjoyed an unprecedented honeymoon period with the press, stories still circulated of the power struggle between Brown and Prescott. They were based on the old public disputes they had had over the direction of economic policy, when Prescott had warned against 'the dead hand' of the Treasury, but these reports were out of date by the time Blair arrived at the steps of Downing Street on election day.

Having decided he could never beat Brown in the power battle behind Blair, Prescott decided it would be better to unite with Brown to achieve their ambitions together for the government. Casting himself as Ernie Bevin to Blair's Attlee, Prescott was committed to remaining totally loyal to Blair's leadership but Prescott would support Brown on his economic strategy. Over the coming years, their relationship was to form a solid foundation at the heart of the Blair government that few outside fully understood, and it paid dividends for Prescott as he did deals with the Chancellor over transport finance.

'John decided he would make an historic peace with Gordon,' said a Prescott ally. 'Gordon responded by telling John, "I want you to understand this is a proper economic department." He was telling John he would not interfere in his finances, unlike health or social security or the other departments.'

In the closing weeks of the Major government, Prescott held a secret meeting in the north of England with Andrew Turnbull, the Permanent Secretary at the DoE, to discuss the outline of the super-ministry comprising environment, transport and the regions: the DETR. Turnbull – later to be knighted by Blair and made Cabinet Secretary after a stint at the Treasury with Gordon Brown – was committed to helping Prescott make the disparate responsibilities work.

It would be based on the Department of the Environment under John Gummer, which three months earlier had moved out of the crumbling 1960s triple tower block in Marsham Street and into an ultra-modern, glass and steel office block called Eland House, at Bressenden Place, around the corner from Victoria station. Caborn was among Prescott's trusted friends who joined the 'super-ministry'. Caborn was appointed minister for the regions. Prescott made Alan Meale his Parliamentary Private Secretary. He replaced Rosie Winterton, who had won a seat in her own right as the MP for Doncaster, with Jo Irvin as his special adviser. Blair appointed Michael Meacher as Prescott's environment minister. David Taylor, who had helped

Prescott on 'Real Needs – Local Jobs' was appointed as an unpaid special adviser. When Prescott arrived after being appointed by Blair, the staff crowded around the balconies overlooking the atrium entrance and cheered, a gesture he found moving. He also enjoyed the eco-friendly design of the building, which automatically switched off the lights when he left his ministerial office, or rolled down the blinds when the sun shone on the windows. 'If you smoke, it blows you up,' he warned visitors.

It was essential to his grand vision for the environment that transport was brought firmly under his control when he took office. However, as Prescott was taking possession of his new department, a quietly spoken Scot, Gavin Strang, the shadow Minister for Agriculture for the past five years, received the call from Downing Street for which all members of the shadow Cabinet were waiting. Apart from a two-year stint as employment spokesman, Strang had been steeped in agriculture for over a decade, both as a junior minister in the last Labour government under Callaghan, and as an opposition spokesman from 1979 to polling day. He therefore arrived at Number Ten expecting to be appointed as the new Minister for Agriculture. He was astonished to be told by Blair that he was putting him in charge of transport with a seat in the Cabinet.

Strang remembers being told by Blair that he would have 'autonomy' over transport. Thus Blair allowed the transport brief to begin with two Cabinet ministers who both thought they had complete control of the portfolio. Strang went off to the Ministry of Transport at Great Minster House, astonished and flattered, to meet his own Permanent Secretary, thinking he was to be head of that department. Strang's Permanent Secretary, Patrick Brown, had to break the news to Strang that he could not be the Transport Secretary. 'The title has already gone,' he told Strang. Prescott had taken a string of titles including Secretary of State for the Department of Environment, Transport and the Regions. There could not be two transport secretaries, and Strang was informed he had to settle for the less grand title of Minister for Transport, in spite of having a seat in the Cabinet.

'Strang was quite upset. He said, "You are going to be my Permanent Secretary," but I said, "I don't think that is quite how it's going to happen,"' Patrick Brown said later. He blamed the lack of experience in the Blair administration in running a government for the misunderstanding, but a less charitable view would be that it was another example of a minister leaving a meeting with Blair and believing he had got what he wanted, only to find that the truth was somewhat different. The next day, a Saturday, Prescott and his team descended on Great Minster House and found Strang in conclave in another room with Brown. Watching their chat through a window, there were suspicions in Prescott's camp that Strang was being briefed to keep his department separate from Prescott, and they were reinforced when Strang told Prescott he would like to run his ministry from Great Minster House instead of moving to Prescott's main office. It was not something that Prescott would tolerate, and from that moment on, Strang felt that his card was marked.

Patrick Brown, as a senior civil servant, had helped to deliver the policies that Prescott had spent half his political career fighting against – the privatisations at the Department of Transport under the Thatcher government in the 1980s and the privatisation of the water industry in England and Wales, after he was moved to the Department of the Environment, where he was promoted to Permanent Secretary. He moved back to the Department of Transport in 1991, presiding over the botched privatisation of the rail system by the Conservatives. He was therefore well known to Prescott when the DPM came visiting. 'There was bad blood between them,' said one Prescott ally. Brown dismissed that suggestion, and said simply: 'I was a civil servant.' He knew that two permanent secretaries into one merged department would not go, and within weeks had decided to leave. Turnbull took over as Permanent Secretary for Prescott's DETR empire. Brown was later knighted and, though critical of the manner in which the rail industry had been privatised by the Tories, joined the board of the Go Ahead rail group in 1999 as its non-executive chairman on a salary of over £60,000.

Prescott, a keen political historian, had been careful in taking his titles. He was DPM, Secretary of State for the DETR and, although it was little noticed at the time, First Secretary of State – the position last held by Michael Heseltine. While his election as deputy leader rooted his authority in the party, this title secured his authority in the government, putting Prescott above Brown, Cook, Straw and all the clever, rising Blairite stars in the pecking order of the Cabinet. It is a mark of his early lack of confidence that he put such store by this, and it was not long before his confidence was tested to destruction in the chamber of the Commons. Prescott had never been comfortable in the 'public-school' atmosphere of the chamber, and while he could bluster through his own sessions of questions, his performances deputising for the Prime Minister were sometimes excruciatingly tense affairs. Having damaged an eardrum diving years before, he said he found it difficult to hear above the noise in the chamber while standing in for Blair at Prime Minister's Questions. He could not hear a question by Tory MP Sir Michael Spicer about the obscure 'withholding tax'. Looking around for help, he found Clare Short next to him, gazing at the ceiling. Caborn, his most trusted friend, who had been unable to get closer to him, was the other side of Short, too far away to help. Prescott hit back with a reply about council tax. Steve Richards of the *Independent* said it was the 'most damaging and confidence-shattering half-hour of his political career'. During the Balkans War, Prescott had to make a late-night emergency statement to the House and tripped up over the pronunciation of the Serbian leader, Miloševic. Prescott was due to do another session of Prime Minister's Questions, and over lunch with Dick Caborn we discussed how he could get round it. I suggested that Prescott should call him 'the Serbian dictator'. Caborn thought about it, but said, 'You can't – he was elected!' As it happened, it never came up again, but Prescott had good reason to hate taking Prime Minister's Questions in Blair's absence.

As a student of Labour history, Prescott also was well aware of the historical battles fought in previous Labour governments over the status the title of First Secretary carried.

'I realised there were the battles between Castle and George Brown over who was the First Secretary of State. I remember reading it in the diaries. I am senior by being the First Secretary, not by being the Deputy Prime Minister,' he said.

The ultra-cautious Labour election campaign appeared at times to be based on the strategy of saying nothing beyond the five commitments on the pledge card, but after the election, the pace of change under Blair was breathtaking, and no department was more energetic in the drive to make a difference than the newly created DETR. Within days of taking office, Prescott threatened Railtrack – after reporting £339 million in dividends for its shareholders – with action to force the company to invest more in rail infrastructure. Water companies were summoned to a 'water summit' to be presented with an investment plan of action within weeks. He waded into the chaotic financing of the Channel Tunnel rail link and, wearing his DPM's hat, got down to business chairing Cabinet committees to push ahead with Labour's manifesto commitments, including the minimum wage. Prescott and his close ministerial ally Ian McCartney, later appointed the chairman of the party, worked with the unions and pushed Blair for a higher figure, but settled on a compromise that could be pushed up later. The Tories later dropped their claims that the minimum wage could cost jobs.

Prescott marked World Environment Day by announcing that a Transport White Paper would be published in 1998 on cutting pollution, reducing emissions of greenhouse gases and improving the quality of life in towns and cities. He hinted that there would be green taxes to persuade more people to leave their cars at home. In a BBC *Today* interview, he was challenged about his 'green' credentials and his use of a fuel-guzzling Jaguar. How could they be compatible? Prescott said he sometimes used the Tube. This was noted with glee by at least one Fleet Street news editor who, assuming Prescott never travelled on the Tube, ordered a political correspondent to get to work on 'hypocrite' Prescott's love affair with the Jaguar motor car. The report was 'spiked' when the department announced that the DPM would be travelling to the conference in Kensington on the Underground.

Prescott may not have a reputation for being environmentally conscious but his brand of socialism, including a passionate belief in integrated public transport to persuade more people to commute without cars, fitted neatly into a green agenda. One environmentalist tried to trip up Prescott at the World Environment Day press conference by asking the DPM whether he knew what biodiversity was. Prescott readily admitted that after weeks in the job, he did not, but he was learning, a reply that won him many friends in the environmental lobby.

When MPs and ministers trooped to the Lords to hear the Queen's Speech, Prescott found himself next to his old adversary, Michael Heseltine, the former Tory DPM, in the procession. Heseltine, who was criticised for his own grandiose ambitions in Whitehall, made small talk by commenting to Prescott that he had a big department to look after. Prescott asked, 'How do you manage an office that size?' Heseltine said without hesitation: 'Delegate.'

Prescott's great regret, however, was that there was nothing in the Queen's Speech on transport. Blair was not interested in the issues of which he had put his truculent deputy in charge until transport became a liability.

The transport section of Labour's 1997 manifesto was buried on page 29 at the back of the document among pledges on sport and voluntary bodies. The New Labour design team for the manifesto chose a prescient picture to illustrate Labour's policy on transport for the future: a photograph of a mother and child enjoying a ride on a gilded horse on a merry-go-round.

Prescott, in his heart and soul, was in favour of renationalisation of the railways, but had conceded in the row with Brown and Short before the election that it was not financially possible. The manifesto said: 'Our task will be to improve the situation as we find it, not as we would wish it to be.'

To the dismay of many on the left, Prescott resisted calls for Labour to take the railways back into public ownership. The deciding factor, as ever, was the need to pay compensation. Prescott had refused to pay compensation for the return of the bus companies to public ownership, and he could not do it for the railways. Renationalisation 'wasn't on the table', he told me in July 2004 in an interview to mark the tenth anniversary of the Blair–Prescott leadership. 'I was in favour of it remaining in the public sector. The dilemma for me – and this is one of the disappointments [of the first and second terms in office] I was faced with – was whether you nationalise the industry and pay compensation – billions of pounds …'

Brown made it clear that he did not have billions of pounds to spare to compensate shareholders of the privatised train operating companies (TOCs) and the privatised track company, Railtrack. Prescott believed they would get fat enough without compensation.

As a sop to those demanding public ownership of the railways, the manifesto carried a promise to 'establish a new rail authority combining functions currently carried out by the rail franchiser and the Department of Transport, to provide a clear, coherent and strategic programme for the development of the railways, so that the passenger expectations are met'.

Prescott hoped the Strategic Rail Authority (SRA) and a new rail regulator, Tom Winsor, would impose a squeeze on Railtrack and force up standards by Railtrack and the train operating companies. Prescott's successor at transport, Stephen Byers, abolished Railtrack in 2002, to howls of protest from shareholders, who eventually were paid limited compensation but sued for more. He replaced it with a not-for-profit company, Network Rail, but it caused an acrimonious row with Winsor, who was blocked from intervening to rescue Railtrack. A series of rail disasters culminating in the Hatfield crash turned rising public anxiety about rail safety into a national scandal over the long-term lack of investment in Britain's rail infrastructure (see Crisis p 422). Public confidence in the Blair government's ability to deliver improvements in the public services plummeted. These were Prescott's most testing years in office, but he believed he was strengthened by them. Byers, his successor at transport, saw his glittering career cut short in as a panicky Downing Street fought to restore confidence in the Government's ability to get a grip on the rail crisis after the Hatfield disaster. Blair and his advisers had no intention of reviving old 'Clause 4' shibboleths by taking the rail network back into public ownership, in spite of growing public support for such a policy, but were eventually forced to act to restore public confidence. In July 2004, Alistair Darling, the Transport Secretary, announced he was abolishing the SRA, and taking over most of its powers himself.

Prescott's support on the left undoubtedly suffered over the rail fiasco, but his alliance with Brown began to bear fruit in the early months of the Blair government when Prescott was able to usher in the principle of 'hypothecated taxes' in the form of earmarked charges for transport. It was made public when he announced the introduction of powers for local authorities to impose congestion charges on motorists, though it was not without a final fight with Brown.

'Prescott was about to go into the chamber with his speech to announce it, and we had calls coming in from Gordon's office saying, "You cannot announce it – we haven't signed it off yet." Prescott refused to take the call, and went ahead,' said the Prescott source.

Brown was furious at being treated in this way, but Prescott used his muscle in the Cabinet to make the DETR a tax-raising department. Congestion charges for London were to be the test bed for the idea, and they were to be followed in other cities with both congestion charging and, in the longer term, road pricing, which is only now being seriously studied. Brown also promised Prescott that all rises in fuel duty above inflation would be ploughed back into transport, until the fuel protests of September 2000 brought an end to the annual real-terms increases in prices at the pumps.

In 1998, Prescott got Brown's backing for the introduction of a measure that was dear to his merchant seaman's heart. The tonnage tax sounded prosaic – it allowed shipowners to pay tax on the tonnage they owned rather than their profits – but it had a dramatic effect in reviving the red ensign. By January 2003, when the French-built Cunard liner *Queen Mary 2* was named by the Queen in Southampton, 61 company groups had joined the scheme with over 700 ships, half of which were sailing under the British flag. The tonnage flying the red ensign more than tripled from 2.8 million tonnes in 1997 to 12.1 million tonnes, including the *QM2*. Prescott listed the tonnage tax among his ten major achievements in the first two terms of office. In recognition of this, Prescott was given honorary membership of the Baltic Exchange for his efforts, an honour only bestowed on two other politicians, Attlee and Churchill.

Prescott had more pressing problems, however, over the London Underground, when Labour came to power. The Tube needed billions of pounds in investment, and Brown could not find the money from taxation to meet the bill. Prescott and Brown agreed it was an ideal vehicle for Prescott's beloved public–private partnership idea by selling off franchises to the private sector to raise the money for investment in the public service. He even toyed with somehow linking the Tube lines to overhead stations in London, but dropped it when it turned out to be impractical.

Brown asked his Treasury Minister, Geoffrey Robinson, to advise Prescott on the financing of the London Underground PPP. Robinson, the Paymaster General, acted as the Treasury interlocutor with Prescott before Robinson was brought down

the subsequent general election campaign, Brown, with Smith sitting beside him, refused to give a guarantee that National Air Traffic Services – the system guiding millions of planes each year in and out of UK air space – would not be sold off. In fact, Brown's Treasury team was working on a 'doomsday book' of assets that could be sold off to raise much-needed finance. Charlie Whelan, the Chancellor's spin doctor, briefed trusted journalists that Brown was looking to sell off NATS, the Tote, the Commonwealth Bank, and the London Underground.

It was a mark of how far out of the loop he was being kept that Transport Minister Gavin Strang only discovered that NATS would be sold when he opened his ministerial papers during a foreign trip on Prescott's behalf, and read an exchange of correspondence between Joe Irvin, Prescott's special adviser, and Ed Balls, the Chancellor's chief economic adviser. Irvin and Balls gradually established a close working relationship that was to have a profound effect on establishing trust between Prescott and Brown on a range of issues, starting with NATS.

NATS needed an estimated £100 million in investment for essential modernisation of its centres, and the Treasury was refusing to provide it. By selling off NATS to the airlines who were its customers, NATS could raise the finance for its own investment, said Balls.

Strang had been a strong supporter of John Smith, and was no devotee of New Labour. He believed passionately that if Smith had lived, Labour would have renationalised the railways. He could not believe his eyes when he read the proposals for the sale of NATS. They appeared to be finalising the details, and the

Transport Minister was astonished because this was the first he had heard of the plan. He immediately made his objections clear to Prescott, not knowing that the NATS sale was one small component of the wider strategic alliance that the DPM had with the Chancellor. Strang had clashed with Brown before the Chancellor's first Budget by suggesting there could be a 'windfall tax' on the bosses of the private rail companies, which Brown had immediately slapped down. Now he was taking on his own boss. There could only be one winner.

There had been a whispering campaign against Strang for being ineffective within weeks of his appointment. Some Whitehall whispers suggested he was suffering from a viral infection and nodding off at meetings, although Strang vehemently denied the rumours, and insisted he was in good health. After only fifteen months in the ill-fated transport seat, he was sacked by Blair in the reshuffle of July 1998. Also chopped were David Clark, from the Cabinet Office; and Harriet Harman, from the Department for Social Security. Blair brought in two of his key allies: Peter Mandelson, as Trade and Industry Secretary; and Stephen Byers to the Treasury under Brown. Nick Brown, a key Gordon Brown ally, who would have run the Chancellor's leadership campaign had it gone ahead, was given a Cabinet seat as Minister for Agriculture – a post that dramatically changed from a cushy number attending summer shows to crisis management when the foot-and-mouth outbreak happened.

On the backbenches, Strang joined the rebels and played a prominent role in trying to stop the NATS sale going through.

Prescott fought a bitter battle, rejecting warnings by the Labour-led Commons Select Committee on Transport, chaired by his old adversary Gwyneth Dunwoody, that air safety could be compromised. Having known him all his political life, she complained that Prescott 'confused activity with action'. Prescott rejected demands by Strang and the rebels to make NATS a non-profit-making body like the system adopted in Canada. Prescott was also having rows with the Treasury, which wanted to go further by selling off 50 per cent of the shares to the private sector. Prescott negotiated a compromise package for the flotation that was finally concluded in July 2001. Under a public–private partnership, 42 per cent of the shares would go to a consortium of airlines for nearly £800 million. They comprised British Airways, bmi British Midland, Virgin Atlantic, Britannia, Monarch, easyJet and Airtours. To quell the protests, he gave 5 per cent of the stock to NATS staff. The UK airport operator BAA plc took 4 per cent, and the government kept 49 per cent with a golden share. From Prescott's point of view, the sale of NATS was not an ideological issue. He believed in 'sweating' public assets to get the best return for the taxpayer.

Prescott had a more complicated deal in mind with Gordon Brown. In return for selling NATS, Brown allowed Prescott to prepare a ten-year plan for transport, which would provide stable funding over a decade; the Chancellor conceded the hypothecation of the money raised from congestion charging for investment in local transport schemes; and he sanctioned Prescott to enable four regional airports, including Manchester, which was owned by the local authority, to expand by raising private finance on the commercial markets. Brown's decision to sell NATS was seen by Prescott's aides as a dramatic symbolic gesture to the City in the early months of the new Blair government to show that they could trust Brown not to return to Old Labour 'tax and spend' policies. It also helped to produce the prospect of finance for the Exchequer at a time when Brown was building his reputation for prudence. At that stage, the Treasury mandarins, led by John Gieve, Director of Budget and Public Finances at the Treasury, had no idea that within a few years, they would be producing record financial surpluses at the Exchequer. When Brown arrived at the Treasury on his first day, he was shown the books by Gieve, who had been in charge of public spending under Kenneth Clarke, the outgoing Conservative Chancellor. Gieve told Brown that Clarke had pared down the departmental budgets so that Tory ministers could bid up from them in the spending round that would automatically follow the election.

Gieve said to Brown that they would have to be increased. 'I won't do that,' said Brown.

Ken Clarke told me the spending totals were far too tight, and if Major had been re-elected, Clarke would have immediately increased them. Gieve, later the Permanent Secretary at the Home Office, believed sticking to the Tory spending straitjacket was a master stroke by Brown. It enabled him to establish his own reputation as the 'Iron Chancellor', laying to rest the accusation that Labour could not run the economy and laying the foundations for the years of steady growth throughout the second term.

Left-wing MPs argued that the corset on spending for the first two years of Labour's first term was so tight that it contributed to the failure to deliver on promises until well into the second term. It led to the first major backbench rebellion against Blair in November 1997, over benefit cuts, which in turn led to Harman, the Secretary of State for Social Security, being sacked.

Even Blair tired of Brown's prudence. On 16 January 2000, Blair lost his patience and forced Brown to raise spending on health by declaring without Brown's approval on a *Breakfast with Frost* programme that Britain was to raise NHS spending to the European average, around 7–8 per cent of GDP. 'We will bring it up to the European Union average in time,' he promised. Brown was furious but raised National Insurance contributions (NICs) to do so. Blair also grabbed the headlines for that too. I was telephoned out of the blue one Friday morning while I was working on the *Independent on Sunday* by Alastair Campbell to be told that the interview with Tony I had asked for had been granted. It had been so long ago, I had forgotten I had written the letter. Something was clearly in the wind, and Campbell said the only snag was that I had to be in Dublin by 1 p.m. to catch the Prime Minister's plane back to London. With my colleague, Steve Richards, I managed to scramble there in time. It transpired that what Blair wanted to announce by this device was that the government would raise NICs to pay for higher spending on health. We had the scoop, and I also took a photograph of the PM on board the jet, but it was too grainy to use. A week later I got a letter from Campbell telling me not to try photography, saying: 'Keep the day job ...'

Nowhere was the early squeeze on spending felt more acutely than in Prescott's transport department. Cancelling roads was fine by Prescott, but he was desperate for money for the railways that had suffered years of underinvestment. Prescott could have changed the course of the Blair government – possibly for the worst – if he had chosen now to fight Brown over his parsimonious strategy. He was under intense pressure from his old supporters on the left of the party, and the trade unions, to do so.

However, Prescott used his speech to the IPPR in 1999 to give Brown his wholehearted backing: 'Let me say frankly that the first two years of this Parliament were tough. We were right as a government to put the public finances back into shape. The national debt had doubled. Public sector borrowing was £28 billion in the red. That required us to stick to the depressed spending limits we inherited.'

Prescott then offered the prospect of hope for the future. 'But in the long term, the Chancellor and I are in total agreement: poor transport is poor economics,' he said. Harking back to his days in the merchant navy, Prescott gave a self-effacing description of his relationship with Brown, saying, 'Whilst the Chancellor was up on the bridge plotting the course of the economy, I was in the boiler room ...'

Two Jags

When he became a minister, Prescott already owned an old second-hand Jaguar saloon that he continued to use for private engagements (under the ministerial rules, he was not allowed to use official cars on private business). On joining the Cabinet, like other senior ministers including the Foreign Secretary, the Northern Ireland Secretary, the Defence Secretary, and the Prime Minister, he was allocated a new ministerial car fitting his seniority in the Cabinet. It was a Jaguar.

It was therefore inevitable that as Prescott called for restraint in the use of the car for short trips, the defenders of Thatcher's 'great car economy' would accuse him of being a hypocrite for using not one but two thirsty Jaguars. The *Sun* began calling Prescott 'Two Jags'. He has a famously thin skin, in spite of appearances, but it was not the charge of hypocrisy that hurt him; it was a sense of injustice. Prescott was well aware that he would be pilloried for using a car with a big engine while asking motorists not to use theirs, at least for short journeys, and asked Jaguar to covert his ministerial limousine to run on LPG, liquified petroleum gas. In theory, this made Prescott more eco-friendly in his ministerial Jaguar than if he had squeezed with his chauffeur into a Mini. Short of putting a sign on the side of his car saying 'powered by gas', he felt there was not much more he could do about his public image, when it got worse.

At the Labour Party annual conference in 1999 in Bournemouth, a gale was blowing. Prescott was staying at the Highcliff Hotel, 250 yards up the hill from the conference centre, inside the security cordon. Instead of walking along the clifftop path, he and his wife Pauline got into a party Rover saloon and were chauffeur-driven down the hill to the hall. When he stepped out at the back of the conference centre, he was asked by a journalist why he had taken the car.

'Because of the security reasons for one thing and, second,

my wife doesn't like to have her hair blown about,' he replied. 'Have you got another silly question?'

He had intended the mention of Pauline's hair to be a joke. It backfired badly. John Redwood, Prescott's Tory shadow, said: 'Labour's hypocrisy knows no bounds.'

In fact, according to his aides, he was merely short of time. 'We had spent hours on the speech, and looked up and realised we had to be in the hall in five minutes. He just took the car because it was quicker,' said one of his assistants.

In the speech, an event always eagerly anticipated for its knockabout good humour, Prescott hit back at his critics, with a nod towards Blair, saying: 'The M4 bus lane trial now means buses and taxis are getting through quicker.

'Cars are also getting through quicker. Every week you get another alarmist news headline – seldom checked in case the truth gets in the way of a good story: "Reducing the speed limit from 70 to 50" – not true. "A policy to nick everybody, everywhere, driving over 30" – not true. "Anti-motorist" – not true.'

Pausing for effect, he added: 'How could I be anti-car, driving two Jags?'

Nobody now remembers a word of it. All they remember is the threat to Pauline's perfect hairdo. Clare Short, the International Development Secretary, did not help, commenting on BBC2's *Conference Live*: 'It's hard. Poor old John. But you know, if you say we must use our cars less, you should use them less …'

On occasions when the gas-powered car refused to start in the mornings, another ministerial Jaguar saloon with a petrol engine came to Prescott's rescue as back-up to the LPG model.

His love of Jags was noted by Chester Zoo, which invited him to open their new enclosure for jaguar cats. The manufacturers of a bicycle under the same name also presented him with a Jaguar bike. It was kept in the Prescott garage at Hull. Thus he should have been dubbed 'Three Jags'.

I once asked Prescott why he did not ditch one of the Jags for a smaller car to avoid the charge of hypocrisy. He dismissed the idea outright as giving in to media pressure. 'I won't be dictated to by the press,' he said. I never raised it again.

His sheer bloody-mindedness played a role, but Prescott is also a stickler for being 'paid the rate for the job' and he saw the ministerial Jaguar as part of his public office. When Blair decided to make an example of wage restraint to others in the public sector by declining an increase in his salary as PM, Prescott led a Cabinet revolt. Acting as Cabinet shop steward, he told Blair that the others would not stand for it. The pay awards went through for Prescott and the rest of the Cabinet, and Blair persisted with his personal pay demo on his own.

From time to time, he did show some response to the 'Two Jags' taunts, avoiding using his own Jag on party occasions to stop it becoming the story instead of the party event, but the press image still rankled with some members of the public.

In 2003, he sold his sixteen-year-old Arctic-blue Jaguar XJ6 to a West Sussex dealership. It was bought for £2,400 at an auction by an irate 55-year-old antiques dealer who threatened to burn it in protest at government policy on immigration. Prescott traded in the car for a second-hand Jaguar XJS. He had toyed with buying an even sportier XJS soft-top, but after being hit by an egg in the 2001 general election, was dissuaded from doing so by friends, who said he would be the target of more missiles if he put the top down.

Peter the Crab

One of the first Cabinet decisions in which Prescott played a decisive role had nothing to do with his ministerial brief, and would dog the Blair government through to the next election.

The Millennium Dome had been conceived as part of a regeneration scheme for the east London Thames corridor by Michael Heseltine when he was in the Major government. On coming into office, Blair was quickly faced with the difficult decision of whether to go ahead with the scheme to build the Dome, or to cancel it.

A Cabinet committee, including Mandelson, met in the Cabinet room to make a recommendation to the full Cabinet. Prescott had turned up for the Cabinet meeting and was carrying his ministerial papers and cooling his heels outside the Cabinet room, impatient to get on with the main meeting. The Cabinet Secretary said to Blair: 'The Deputy Prime Minister is outside, Prime Minister.'

'Bring him in,' said Blair.

Blair gave him a summary of the issue they were discussing. Blair said they had to decide whether to cancel the Millennium project or proceed and ask the taxpayer to foot the bill for hundreds of millions of pounds.

'What do you think, John?'

Prescott responded with hardly a second's thought: 'I remember the Festival of Britain. We were proud of it. If you cancel it now, they will say you lost your nerve.'

It may have been the answer Blair and Mandelson wanted. Mandelson's grandfather, Herbert Morrison, who had also been Deputy Prime Minister, had been responsible for the Festival of Britain.

Blair finished the meeting quickly, because he had an official engagement at a church service. He left Prescott to chair the Cabinet meeting which followed. As Blair left the room, his wisecracking deputy said: 'Say a prayer for the Dome.'

One ex-Cabinet minister recalled: 'As soon as Blair was out of the room, everyone started, shouting down one another. Prescott had clearly done a deal with Blair as had Gordon to get the Dome through.'

Brown said it should only be allowed through if the government was confident it would not cost more money. Mo Mowlam said Blair had said the Cabinet should give it their backing, and she thought they should support Tony. Harriet Harman said she was in favour. Chris Smith was reluctantly in favour. Ron Davies and Jack Cunningham said they should close it down and blame the cost on Heseltine. Clare Short was vitriolic in her opposition. Robin Cook was 'snooty' in his contempt. Donald Dewar said three times, 'I am not sure I can vote for this.' Nick Brown, the Chief Whip, said to himself: 'You are not going to get the chance to vote on it …'

Members of the Cabinet remember that Prescott, in his usual

style, went through the business briskly, saying that the recommendation from the Cabinet subcommittee on the Dome was to go ahead. 'Agreed?'

To the Chief Whip, this first major decision was a worrying portent of the way that Blair was to run the Cabinet. 'I knew that a majority were against it, and Blair was going ahead with it. It was a good example of the Cabinet government we were going to get,' said Nick Brown. 'I remember thinking that Prescott's skill was that he managed to close it without a vote.'

The Dome went massively over budget, and has yet to reopen as a concert venue for international stars. As a structure, the Dome proved something of a success, placing a new iconic shape on the London landscape, which chimed in with the 'Cool Britannia' image that followed New Labour into power. It even became a favourite landmark for BA pilots to announce to passengers on the flight path to Heathrow.

In July 2004, Prescott went to America to seal the deal on the takeover of the Dome by an American entrepreneur promising to turn it into an international concert venue surrounded by regeneration, including offices, shops and housing. It is also earmarked for use in the 2012 London Olympic Games.

'The site can be converted from a poisonous place at the heart of London with a Dome that is going to be one of the major sporting centres,' Prescott told me in 2004. 'We took a lot of stick for it, but for every £1 we brought in £7 – £7 billion is being paid in investment.'

The content of the exhibition it housed, called the Millennium Experience, proved more problematic. Tasked with inspiring a new generation with the discoveries that had made Britain one of the leading industrialised countries of the world at the close of two thousand years of history, Mandelson's committee appeared determined to shun 'old' industry for a vision of modern New Labour Britain. The Work Zone, which could have shown children what it was like to go down a pit, or stand on the footplate of a steam engine, featured a row of paper-shredders. Many critics said they should have been employed on Mandelson's ideas.

Brown made no secret of the fact that he regarded the Millennium Experience as a confounded waste of money, telling one meeting of European finance ministers (Ecofin) as all the European capitals prepared to celebrate the special New Year for 2000: 'You are spending a few thousand pounds on fireworks. We are spending £700 million on the Millennium Dome.' Ecofin ministers were left open-mouthed at the figure.

The media's love affair with New Labour may be judged to have come to an end at midnight on 31 December 1999. Security was so badly organised for the New Year Party to see in the new millennium at the Dome that VIP guests were forced to stand in line for hours, freezing in evening dress, while their bags were methodically checked. They included the editors of most of the national newspapers, who were delayed so long that some of them reached their seats after the show by 'New Labour' acts such as Simply Red had started. Many complained they could not even get a glass of champagne and the food had gone. The editors got mad, and they also got even: they savaged the Dome and New Labour in the weeks that followed. The spectacular show in the Dome, including a *Mad Max*-style high-wire act, ran for a year and attracted 6.5 million visitors – way below the original target of 12 million, but still the biggest attraction in the country. It was later to raise £550 million from its sale and draw in £4bn in private investment to turn it into an entertainments complex. That did not matter. In the public's mind the Dome became synonymous with financial disaster, and New Labour.

Prescott had one priority for the millennium night, and that was to make sure that the Jubilee line, connecting central London to the Docklands redevelopment area and the Greenwich peninsula where the Dome is sited, was open for New Year's Eve. Most of the Cabinet travelled in comfort in one of the new Underground trains from Westminster to the Dome in 20 minutes, while the VIPs shivered at a holding point which a bureaucrat had chosen to site miles away from the venue, at the Underground station at Stratford in the East End of London, a place most editors had never visited before and vowed never to do so again.

The Jubilee line was the first Underground line to be built in London for 25 years. Its airy station architecture became an instant hit with magazine picture-editors, but its signalling system was inadequate and it was plagued by operational delays in its early months. It was opened two years late, and about £3.5 billion over budget. Prescott, who had inherited the scheme, repeatedly made the point to doubting ministerial colleagues that it was a prime example of why Britain needed private finance initiatives to fund public sector schemes in future. He said in future, any cost overruns on PFI projects would be borne by the private sector consortiums that built them, rather than the taxpayer.

Prescott wanted a cheaper alternative for the public to celebrate the millennium. In addition to the Dome, he secretly urged ministerial colleagues to create a 'People's Park' on land next to the derelict Battersea Power Station. The centrepiece would be a huge funfair with spectacular rides. He remembered that the long-gone Battersea funfair had been one of the great popular successes of the Festival of Britain, although it was now largely forgotten by the intellectuals, who preferred to discuss the few remaining architectural traces of the Festival on the South Bank. Prescott had even persuaded Railtrack to provide a spur to a new station at his 'People's Park'. Mandelson stopped the idea, however, on the grounds that it would detract from the Dome.

Responsibility for the Dome was later taken over by Lord Falconer, a lawyer friend of Blair's, but the donation of £1 million towards one of the zones, the Faith Zone, by the Hinduja Foundation was to lead indirectly to Mandelson's second resignation from the Cabinet on 24 January 2001. He made enquiries about naturalisation for one of the billionaire Hindu brothers, Srichand Hinduja, behind the foundation. Mandelson was cleared in March 2001 by the Hammond inquiry of any impropriety, and in March 2004 was rewarded by Blair, who felt guilty over his resignation, by appointing his friend as Britain's sole European commissioner. Blair was tempted to fulfil Mandelson's dream of bringing him back into the Cabinet, but Prescott, Brown and Straw were among those who successfully urged him against it.

Prescott's view of Mandelson was complicated. Their relations were strained long before they reached government, partly for personal reasons – Prescott was kept out of the limelight by 'the beautiful people', the New Labour stars hand-picked by 'Mandy' when he was in charge of Labour communications. However, Prescott recognised in Mandelson a fellow member of the Labour 'tribe'. Mandelson also praised Prescott's readiness to accept new ideas, and support, however grudging, of Blair's modernisation of Clause Four of the party constitution.

Prescott's main objection to Mandelson was his passionate belief in a centre-left alliance, secured by a change of the voting system from first-past-the-post to a form of proportional representation (PR). Mandelson saw that this would not only keep the Tories out of office but would also stop a hard-left rump of 50 or so Campaign Group Labour MPs holding Blair to ransom if his majority over the Tories was narrow. It became known as 'The Project' around Westminster. Mandelson believed electoral reform could help to make Labour the dominant force in the twenty-first century that the Conservatives had been in the twentieth century. Blair put a commitment to review PR in the manifesto, and also established a joint consultative Cabinet committee on which, for the first time, Liberal Democrats sat down with members of the government to discuss constitutional reforms including removing the hereditary peers from the House of Lords. Roger Liddle, a former leading light in the SDP, and Mandelson had collaborated in writing the unofficial New Labour manifesto, *The Blair Revolution*, in 1996. After the election, Blair hired Liddle as an adviser in Number Ten until he became Mandelson's aide when Mandelson was appointed to the European Commission.

Prescott went along with allowing the Liberal Democrats a role in the reform of the Lords, but he remained an implacable obstacle to an alliance with the Lib Dems and the introduction of PR for both Westminster and local elections. Prescott made it clear in the early months of the Blair government that he would accept PR for Westminster only over his dead body. The same applied to Blair's tentative plans for a Lib–Lab coalition, and the offer that Paddy Ashdown claims Blair made to allocate two seats in the Cabinet to Ashdown and Menzies Campbell. It was also claimed privately by one senior Lib Dem figure that the deal broke down because Blair would not accept a third place for Alan Beith. However, Blair could not deliver on any such promise. Prescott threatened to resign rather than join a Lib–Lab government, bluntly telling Blair: 'When Ashdown walks through that door, I walk out.'

It was one of the rare moments when Prescott threatened to use his nuclear button and walk out of the Cabinet. It marked one of the indelible lines beyond which Prescott could never be persuaded to step. To discover the reason he made a coalition with the Lib Dems one of his main sticking points with Blair, you needed to go back to the lessons Prescott learned on his grandfather's knee about the betrayal of Labour by Ramsay MacDonald in 1931 when the Prime Minister surrendered Labour's control of power to a coalition government to overcome the world economic crash.

Blair privately treated Roy Jenkins, the SDP leader, as his mentor, but Prescott treated Jenkins and the SDP 'Gang of Four' as traitors. Prescott's opposition to a deal with the Lib Dems came to a head when Lord Jenkins – anathema to Prescott, who saw him as a claret-drinking, patrician 'toff' – was asked by the Prime Minister to produce a report on electoral reform for Westminster parliamentary elections. Prescott believed it was a device to get Ashdown a seat in the Labour Cabinet.

Blair had a majority of 179 and absolute control of his party, but he was forced to shelve PR, the Jenkins report, pacts with the Lib Dems and 'The Project' to avoid a damaging split with the Cabinet and his unmovable deputy. After winning a second overwhelming majority in 2001, Blair never needed a Lib Dem buffer against the hard left or the Tories.

There was one other lasting memorial to Prescott's role in the Millennium scheme, however: the Greenwich Millennium Village – a mix of luxury private apartments and social housing overlooking the Thames, all constructed on eco-friendly principles, as a sustainable development with the latest high-tech prefabricated techniques, including insulation to reduce wasteful heating.

The estate, within walking distance of the Jubilee line station for the Dome, was designed without garages to discourage car use, and had its own wildlife water park included at its heart. The Thames embankment was planted with reeds to encourage wading birds, but the habitat was threatened by a foreign invader, the Chinese mitten crab, which had become a pest in the Thames, undermining the banks of the river by burrowing holes into the mud. During his first summer in charge of the government in 1997, while Blair was away on holiday at Berlusconi's villa in Italy, Prescott took a trip with the media to Greenwich to see progress on his maturing estate. At an impromptu press conference, he held up a jar with a mitten crab in it for the cameras. Prescott playfully suggested the crab was called Peter and was looking for a seat on Labour's national executive.

Not for the last time, his sense of humour got him into hot water. He realised the moment the words had passed his lips that he had turned an easy media event into a political row. Having compared Mandelson to a particularly obnoxious form of pest, the press had a field day, and left Prescott deep in gloom at what he had done. Prescott's 'gaffe' was reported with photographs the next day in all the newspapers, which were grateful for a bit of light entertainment on a thin summer news schedule. Prescott telephoned Mandelson to apologise immediately the press event was over. He was doubly annoyed with himself for Mandelson had been a powerful ally in preventing the press from intruding into his personal life a few weeks earlier over the discovery that his wife had a 'love child'. Mandelson was typically gracious, and told him not to worry. He assured Prescott that he would not take personal offence; that he fully understood that it was a remark intended as a joke.

However, Prescott lived to regret poking harmless fun at 'Mandy'. While Blair has been away, Prescott has handled the difficult government arrangements surrounding the death and funeral of the weapons expert David Kelly, and the disaster relief after the Asian tsunami, but every time he does the summer shift in charge of the government, while Blair is away on holiday, the newspapers resurrect the photograph of 'gaffe-prone Prescott' holding up the jar with the crab called Peter.

Walking and Talking

The 1997 election manifesto committed Labour to creating a 'green' office in every Whitehall department. The 'Two Jags' tag clouded the fact that Prescott took more seriously than anyone else in government his responsibilities for tackling climate change, on which he devoted a great deal of his time and energy throughout Labour's first two terms of office. His priority was the Kyoto conference in December 1997 on reducing carbon dioxide 'greenhouse gas' emissions responsible for global warming.

Prescott had excellent contacts with US Democrats, which came as a surprise to Blair's advisers. In opposition, Philip Gould, Blair's polling expert, had introduced Chris Dodd, the Democrat senator from Connecticut, to the shadow Cabinet. The Blairites were surprised when Prescott walked in and Dodd jumped up, and said, 'John, I haven't seen you for a long time. My wife sends her regards.'

Prescott recalled: 'They all sat there agog because they didn't think I knew anyone in American politics ...'

He met Dodd when the senator organised a dinner for visiting Labour politicians, including Prescott, and Walter Mondale, Jimmy Carter's vice-president. Prescott had been left at Dodd's home, without Dodd's knowledge. 'He came into his house and said, "Hello – who are you?"' said Prescott.

En route for Kyoto, Prescott secretly stopped off in Washington for talks with Vice-President Al Gore. They immediately struck up a rapport. Clinton, in spite of his personal support for Blair, said America would cut US emissions by zero per cent, but Prescott reached an understanding with Gore that the US position was negotiable.

In Kyoto, Prescott threw himself into negotiating with environment ministers from around the world, on the hoof, which he called 'walking and talking'. He drew on his experience as a union negotiator, focusing on the detail, bridging gaps in countries' needs by a system of tradable permits, to bring reluctant nations, such as Russia, to sign a deal. The EU – represented by lowly Luxembourg, which had the presidency – wanted a cut of 15 per cent but said they would not cut more than the US in any event. Prescott, on behalf of the UK, outbid the world with the offer of a cut of 20 per cent. After days of bargaining, Prescott had lined up a deal in which the US would take a cut of 7 per cent over 1990 levels by 2012, and the EU a cut of 8 per cent. It depended on the Japanese, who were hosting the event, taking a cut of 6 per cent. The Japanese Environment Minister offered 5 per cent, which was the minimum figure to emerge from Kyoto.

'The Japanese Environment Minister was nearly in tears. He said he would have to resign if he went further. Prescott got Blair to phone the Japanese Prime Minister,' said a member of the Prescott team. 'He knew the Japanese would move because they did not want to lose face with no deal at the conference, because it was in Kyoto.'

In fact, US levels rose by more than 10 per cent between 1990 and 2000. Prescott continued pressing for deeper cuts at the global warming summit in Buenos Aires in 1998, saying: 'I am walking and talking – we got it last time [in Kyoto] and hopefully we will get it this time.'

When Clinton's two terms at the White House ended, to be replaced by a Bush administration dominated by oil interests, the prospects for Kyoto looked grim. Bush announced shortly after taking office that he intended to repudiate the Kyoto protocol because it would harm America's economy. Prescott continued to drive for the US and Russia to sign up to the Kyoto agreement, negotiating in November 2000 in The Hague between the EU and the Bush administration. He negotiated for 30 hours without sleep and felt that a deal was within his grasp, but at the last minute, EU ministers rejected the package. French Environment Minister Dominique Voynet said: 'Britain had conceded too much to America.'

Prescott stormed out, declaring: 'I'm gutted, the talks are off. They are all gone.'

The day of drama had started with high hopes when Prescott brokered a deal aimed at breaking the deadlock between the head of the US delegation, Frank Loy, and a group of EU ministers. The key stumbling block – EU splits over the amount of carbon dioxide America wanted to be absorbed in carbon 'sinks', forests and areas of plants, without making any changes in energy use – proved insurmountable.

A furious Prescott accused Voynet of backing away from the deal because she had got 'cold feet'. Prescott said Voynet 'said she was exhausted and tired and could not understand the detail and then refused to accept it'.

'That is how the deal fell,' he added. 'There comes a time

when politicians have to use their own guts, their own judgement.'

As the recriminations flew, Voynet accused Prescott of adopting a 'standard macho attitude'. Prescott parried the accusation of male chauvinism, saying: 'Moi?'

However, Voynet repeated the charge. Writing in the *Guardian*, she said: 'According to Prescott, a woman is necessarily incompetent and can't physically last the course in such negotiations.

'Such an argument is laughable compared with the stakes we face.'

Prescott angrily told colleagues the environment ministers 'fucked it up' with the backing of the Greens at The Hague. He sent a memorandum to Blair saying it was vital for the world leaders themselves to take over the search for a way through the impasse. Responsibility for Kyoto was taken out of the hands of the environment ministers and taken on by the world leaders at the next summit in 2001. In Labour's second term, Blair left Prescott in charge of international negotiations for the UK, although in a messy compromise, Margaret Beckett was given Cabinet responsibility for environment policy in the UK and she took part in Kyoto negotiations in Bonn in 2001.

It was Prescott's natural talent for wheeler-dealing, Gore later told Blair, that helped make progress on Kyoto. Prescott regards the Kyoto protocol as one of his top ten achievements in office. It may seem contradictory, but when Prescott drives out of the gates of Downing Street for the last time, the Kyoto deal on reducing CO_2 emissions will remain a lasting legacy to Two Jags.

Crisis

With perfect timing, to demonstrate the need for a deal on global warming, the heavens opened up in the autumn of 2000 and flooded large parts of England, including the historic city of York. Prescott's aides warned him not to go for a photocall in the flooded areas. 'We told him you are responsible for a lot of things, but you can't be responsible for holding back the rain,' said one aide. He went and was vindicated in his judgement.

Prescott donned an emergency jacket and waded in big wellingtons through storm water, some of it not smelling too sweetly. 'People really appreciated the fact he had gone out to share the misery,' said the aide. Prescott pronounced at a UN conference in The Hague that the freak weather was a 'wake-up' call about global warming, and privately went cap in hand to Brown for money for flood defences. Brown already had to contend with the cost of the foot-and-mouth epidemic, which spread throughout England and Wales, leading to the slaughter by 19 October of 3,915,000 animals, with compensation for the farmers which would run into billions, but he found the extra money needed for Prescott's schemes.

The Chancellor also agreed with Prescott to impose annual increases in duty on petrol and diesel as part of his contribution to Prescott's plans to curb car use. However, Brown's fuel 'escalator' provoked an unprecedented public protest by lorry-drivers and farmers.

On 11 September 2000, Blair was beginning a regional tour during the recess of Parliament, from his constituency in

Sedgefield, when a spontaneous fuel protest by farmers in Wales at an oil refinery began to snowball elsewhere.

Prescott was celebrating his 30th anniversary in Parliament with a party at his favourite Chinese restaurant by the marina in Hull, and Blair was due to be guest of honour. Downing Street had denied there was a crisis over the fuel protests, but in Hull, Prescott saw motorists queuing for petrol. Pro-fox-hunting protesters had also found out Blair was due in town. Prescott feared there would be mayhem and called Blair to tell him not to come. Blair cancelled the regional tour and headed back to London to handle the crisis, leaving Prescott to apologise to his party for Blair's absence.

Prescott was indignant at the actions of the fuel protesters, and suspected there was a more sinister side to the blockade that threatened to bring Britain's economy to a standstill. 'They said we will give you 60 days' notice and if you don't do it, we are going to come back, Mr Blair, and we are going to get rid of you. I cannot think of any more blatant political motive. Even we, as the "politically motivated men" in the seamen's strike, never said we would get rid of a Labour government …'

He was also furious with environmental groups for not backing the government more vocally. 'Hell, we had snow in Hull in August. I said to the Cabinet do not forget the environment equation. You hear Friends of the Earth going around saying get tough … where are they? They are great yackers but when they can get on the *Today* programme, when there are real problems, and they can get on [radio], they say bye-bye baby.'

The fuel protests petered out when Brown announced a

review of the fuel regulator, but it had been nip and tuck. Gus MacDonald, the Transport Minister, had secret, effective talks with the leaders of the tanker drivers in the Transport and General Workers' Union. 'If the tanker-drivers in the T&G had obeyed the picket lines, Britain would have ground to a halt,' said a senior official in the DPM's office. This time it was a wake-up call to Blair and the government about the need to plan for civil contingencies, which, after 11 September next year would become brutally obvious.

To add to the sense of disaster surrounding Blair and Prescott, in October, a GNER passenger train, heading from London to Leeds, was travelling at around 115 miles an hour when it crashed 17 miles into its journey at Hatfield. There had already been two major rail crashes since Labour came to power: Southall, in September 1997, in which seven people died; and Ladbroke Grove, Paddington, in October 1999, in which 31 passengers died.

The Southall and Ladbroke Grove crashes caused an outcry about safety procedures over the lack of warning systems in cabs, and, in the Paddington disaster, a badly sited red light, but the Hatfield crash had more far-reaching consequences. It was quickly established that the Hatfield crash was caused when a rail disintegrated, and turned the endemic problems of Britain's railways – decades of underinvestment, coupled with corporate confusion over track maintenance – into a national scandal.

The calls for the railways to be renationalised became louder, and Prescott was sympathetic, but resisted the pressure on the grounds that it would mean breaking contracts awarded under the previous Tory administration to the train operating companies (TOCs), and that would not help to provide the resources that were desperately needed to modernise the rail system.

Looking back in 2004 at that troubled period, Prescott said he regretted not being able to force Railtrack to spend more on railway maintenance. There was another regret too: Prescott was thwarted in repeated attempts to introduce a new offence of corporate killing to punish the bosses of companies held responsible for the deaths of people in rail or marine disasters in future.

However, Prescott gained strength from being forced to contend with a series of blows to the government that tested his pragmatic approach to politics to the limit. As Blair appeared to be struggling to cope with catastrophic 'events', his deputy privately grew in confidence about his own ability to govern through adversity. 'I am increasingly recognising that Tony is not Superman,' he told friends. 'He makes some mistakes. I have every respect for Tony. He is a very good Prime Minister. But he is human.' Anthony Seldon in *Blair* noted that Prescott was 'wracked with doubt which he would share quite openly with Blair, who was touched and engaged by his honesty and trust'. By the second term, Prescott's inner confidence had grown, as he reflected that Blair had come to rely more and more on his loyal deputy to provide a steadying influence in the Cabinet at times of crisis.

CHAPTER TWENTY-THREE

Second Term

If it had been anyone else, they could have been finished, but John has a lot of public support.
Prescott ally.

Two Jabs

Wednesday, 16 May 2001 was the day that the general election caught fire, and John Prescott's Cabinet career nearly came to an end.

His punch – an instinctive boxer's jab with the left fist – divided the nation, and became a talking point from Rhyl, north Wales, to Sydney, New South Wales.

The Deputy Prime Minister had gone up to Birmingham on a train chartered for the Cabinet and the media for the launch of the 2001 general election manifesto – bland even by the standards of manifestos – by Tony Blair.

Gordon Brown, who had taken total control of the election campaign and the manifesto, smiled and joked. Blair chatted amiably. Prescott kept up some running gags. Labour were a massive 15 points ahead of 'Hapless Hague' and the Tories in the polls – the *Guardian*/ICM poll that morning put Labour on 46 per cent, the Tories on 31 per cent and the Liberal Democrats on 16 per cent. They appeared as though they had not a care in the world.

The launch in the heart of Middle England to emphasise that New Labour was not a metropolitan party was successful, although, in a pointer to future battles with Brown over 'choice', Alastair Campbell briefed journalists that there would be no ideological limit on the use of private clinics to get NHS patients treated free of charge for things such as hip replacements. Afterwards, Cabinet ministers were sent from Birmingham to the corners of England to do regional manifesto launches.

Blair visited a local hospital to promote the health policies in the manifesto and ran into a media disaster. At the entrance to the Queen Elizabeth Hospital, Birmingham, Blair was ambushed by Sharon Storer. Her partner had cancer and she was furious he could not get a bed on the bone marrow unit. With the television cameras rolling, she demanded to know what Blair was going to do about it. Blair looked uncomfortable as he listened to her one-woman demolition of his 1997 election promises 'to rescue' the NHS.

Gisela Stuart, the local MP and a junior Health Minister, stood next to the Prime Minister as Ms Storer harangued him. In Labour's campaign war room on the first floor of the Millbank office tower, London, where TV coverage of the campaign was minutely studied, Labour apparatchiks messaged Cabinet ministers on their pagers that the PM had been challenged about cancer beds, just in case they were 'doorstepped' by local news crews about the row. Gordon Brown's election campaign team also noted that German-born Stuart, who was not as experienced as most ministers at electioneering, appeared to be nodding but doing little to help the PM get out of the situation. She was sacked in the reshuffle four days after polling day.

Meanwhile, Jack Straw, the Home Secretary, ran into the second media disaster of the day at the annual conference of the Police Federation in Blackpool. Straw was there to draw attention to the law and order promises in the manifesto, but was jeered and heckled by a thousand of Britain's bobbies. They burst out laughing when he said that being a policeman was a popular job.

Prescott was in good spirits, unaware of the PR disasters to befall Blair and Straw, when at 6.35 p.m., the Prescott Express eased to a halt near the Little Theatre, Rhyl.

Brown had gone back to London and was holding one of the many conferences he chaired in the boardroom of the Millbank headquarters. Having been forced to share control of the campaign team four years ago, Brown had insisted on Peter Mandelson being kept out of the team for 2001 election. Brown was now in control, although Mandelson kept in regular contact with Tony Blair. Brown had brought in as his lieutenant Douglas Alexander, a fellow Scots Labour MP and a rising star among the modernisers, who claimed to have coined the phrase 'the People's Party'.

Grouped around the table with Brown and Alexander were Ian Austin, Gordon Brown's special adviser; Lord Falconer; Lance Price, the party's chief press officer; and focus group guru Philip Gould. They were discussing regaining the initiative at the next day's press conference when a Labour official, a woman, dashed into the room and whispered to Margaret McDonagh, the widely feared General Secretary of the party.

They watched as the woman started gesticulating. 'She was waving her fists about, as though there was a punch-up. We all thought, this looks interesting,' one party source told me.

The official left the room and the meeting continued, but she returned to speak to McDonagh again. McDonagh then told the meeting: 'There has been an incident in Rhyl. We don't know the details but we think that John Prescott may have punched someone.'

There were desperate attempts to contact Prescott's team by mobile phone but it was proving frustratingly difficult. The Labour Party had issued Orange mobile phones to all staff and Cabinet ministers, who were stripped of their ministerial phones for the duration of the campaign. Orange had poor cell coverage in Rhyl.

Joe Irvin, acting as Prescott's 'eyes and ears' at party headquarters, as he had for the 1997 election campaign, was inside Labour's war room when he saw the first newsflash on Sky News.

Shirley Lewis, Sky's correspondent in the north-west, who had the 'scoop', breathlessly reported there had been a fracas involving the Deputy Prime Minister. There were no live pictures being screened, but she said Prescott appeared to have thrown the first punch. Sky were rushing pictures back to the studio as she spoke.

On the journey back to London from Blackpool, Straw, unaware of what was happening elsewhere, gloomily shared a bottle of wine with an aide in the belief that the police assault on the Home Secretary would be leading the news. As their train rattled south through the Midlands, his aide checked out the running order of the news and found out they were not the first item, or even the second. They were third, after Prescott's punch and the Prime Minister's row with the partner of a cancer victim. Gordon Brown's carefully laid plans for the manifesto launch were in ruins.

There was mayhem in the open-plan war room, as staff ran from one television to another, and tuned into the BBC, Sky and the 24-hour programmes to try to catch the first pictures of the incident. Austin told an official to start videoing the news. Every member of Brown's team including Alexander and Falconer gathered around the television sets in the war room.

Adam Boulton, political editor of Sky News, who was broadcasting live about the incident from their Millbank studio, received a telephone call from an official in Labour's Millbank HQ half a mile away. 'A press officer at Millbank said I would be sued for libel,' he told me. 'They would have denied it, if we didn't have the evidence.'

That threat died as Sky News began broadcasting film of the incident. Boulton, who was acting as the anchorman in London for the election, told viewers it was so serious that Prescott could be forced to resign.

Stephen Byers, the Trade and Industry Secretary, and a close Blair ally, had also returned from campaigning to Labour's Millbank headquarters.

'I wasn't listening to the news. It was a bad day. Earlier in the day I got paged and told the PM has had a problem. Someone has had a go at him. Then we were told that Jack Straw, who was then Home Secretary, had got jeered by the Police Federation annual conference. I got back to Millbank at about 7 p.m. I was discussing with some colleagues – I think it was Alan Milburn – how we could regain momentum tomorrow when someone rushed in, and said, "Prescott has just thumped somebody."' Byers joined Brown and his campaign aides watching the television.

Brown's camp stood by Prescott, and were determined to get ahead of the news by issuing a statement claiming it was self-defence.

Lance Price, a former BBC political correspondent in charge of the party's media strategy, refused to put out any statement before they had seen the pictures for their own eyes. The party's pollster Philip Gould was also convinced that the public would never stand for a DPM who went round hitting people and said that Labour's poll rating would be floored by Prescott's punch.

Meanwhile, a shaken and downcast Prescott telephoned Alastair Campbell on his mobile. Campbell took the call as Blair was about to record an ITV election programme, *Ask Tony Blair*.

'It's John,' said the gruff familiar voice on the end of the line.

Campbell put the story in his one-man show when he left Downing Street. He recalled there was an ominous silence, and with the DPM that always meant there was a problem.

'I've hit someone,' said Prescott.

'What?' asked Campbell, who could not believe his ears.

Campbell was incredulous as Prescott told him what had happened. Campbell decided not to tell the Prime Minister until his show was over. Prescott's friends say Campbell told Prescott he thought he would have to apologise.

Prescott snapped back: 'You didn't apologise when you hit that lad on the *Guardian*.' He was referring to the incident when Campbell, then political editor of the *Daily Mirror*, had punched Michael White, the political editor of the *Guardian*, in the *Daily Mirror* office at the Commons when the *Mirror*'s ogreish owner, Robert Maxwell, had been found dead at sea. White had popped his head round the Mirror's door and playfully suggested the *Mirror* headline should be BOB BOB BOBBING ALONG. Campbell, harassed, did not see the funny side.

As Blair, Campbell and Blair's gatekeeper, Anji Hunter, now Boulton's partner, drove back from the recording studio, the grim view on board was that Prescott was in serious trouble. Blair asked Hunter what she thought. She had no hesitation in telling the Prime Minister it was terrible. 'Middle-class England will not understand it,' she said.

Campbell had a lot of time for Prescott, and had helped defend him when the press had been intruding into his private life over Pauline's love child, Paul, but landing a punch in a general election campaign was, Campbell thought, beyond the limit.

The consensus in the Blair camp was that at least Prescott should apologise and some thought he should resign to try to limit the damage on Blair's campaign for a second term, which was partly based on a promise to deal with yobbish behaviour. Brown was more cautious, and delayed an opinion until they could get a clearer view of what exactly had happened. While the debate went on at Millbank over what they should do, Prescott's career hung in the balance.

That night, according to his allies, Prescott came to realise who his friends were.

There were some obvious questions to be answered: if Prescott was charged with a criminal offence, how could Labour pretend to be serious about law and order? And how could Prescott remain in the Cabinet?

When Joe Irvin got through to Prescott, Prescott felt crushed by the whole affair. Prescott told friends: 'I just felt terrible at letting the party down.'

In the split second when he was hit – by what he thought was a fist – Prescott's mind may have gone went back to the night on Monday, 9 February 1998, when he and his wife were drenched by a publicity-seeking singer in the band Chumbawamba at the Brit Awards. The singer, Danbert Nobacon, real name Nigel Hunter, jumped on Prescott's table and threw an ice bucket full of water over Prescott, splashing Pauline. That night he had been sorely tempted to give the man a thumping, but Prescott had kept his cool. After that, he had told friends he would never suffer that again.

Joe Irvin spoke to Blair, saying: 'If we apologise, we will be admitting responsibility.'

Brown, running the campaign, asked Lord (Charlie) Falconer, Blair's close friend and a fellow lawyer, to give his expert view of the footage, which they had videoed. Douglas Alexander, in spite of his youth, was also a highly respected lawyer in Scotland. Austin asked for the video footage to be screened in freeze-frame and they gathered round a television set. It was difficult to form an opinion from the Sky film, shot by a camera over Prescott's shoulder. Their view hardened when the BBC began broadcasting their own footage of the incident from a different angle, facing Prescott as he walked towards the Little Theatre and the protesters shouting on the right. It clearly showed the egg being thrown at Prescott from point-blank range. Prescott instinctively ducked after being struck on the left ear. Then he turned and let fly with a short left jab to the jaw of the protester. The protester lunged at Prescott, grabbed him and they fell to the ground, a meaty fist pushed into Prescott's distorted face, which was the image used on many front pages the next day.

In his lawyerly way, Lord Falconer turned to Alexander and said: 'What do you think, Douglas? I think we could make a case of self-defence …' Alexander and Falconer, who both had experience of cases of fights on a Saturday night in Glasgow, were of the opinion that there were good legal grounds for arguing that it was self-defence, and on no account should they offer an apology. Lance Price bowed to their judgement and they rushed out a press statement saying it was self-defence. The Brown team informed Blair and Prescott how they intended to handle it.

The first objective of the Millbank team was to stop Sky News running the highly damaging incident as the lead item on their news bulletins. Falconer telephoned Boulton to tell him he was wrong about Prescott. Falconer told him it was clearly self-defence and he should stop reporting that Prescott would have to resign. Boulton refused to do so. Had it gone to court,

Prescott had a video recording of the whole incident taken from his bus as a souvenir of his campaign tour, which would have shed more light on the incident. It shows Prescott looking out of the windows to find a line of about 25 protesters, mostly farm workers, who were shouting and waving placards protesting about their plight in the wake of the foot-and-mouth epidemic. It showed Prescott remonstrating with a police officer, saying it was a mistake to walk in front of what he could see was a baying mob.

Prescott believed it was organised by the Countryside Alliance, the campaign against Labour's threat to ban fox-hunting, as a payback for his speech to Labour's annual conference in September 2000. Prescott had said: 'Every time I see the Countryside Alliance and their contorted faces, I vow to redouble my efforts to abolish fox-hunting.' Prescott was convinced the Rhyl attack was a set-up. That is denied by the Countryside Alliance, although Sky News reporters have confirmed that they were tipped off by the farmers to be there with their film crews.

Prescott was also furious with the police. Instead of holding the protesters behind a metal safety railing that ran along the footpath, they were on the footpath, inside the barrier, where Prescott had to run the gauntlet to get to the venue. Two police officers preceded Prescott's small team, but his nearest protection as he stepped as nonchalantly as possible along the footpath within reach of the protesters was Joan Hammell, the special adviser to the Deputy Prime Minister; and Beverley Priest, another female assistant. They had gone only a few yards when a man in a blue shirt hit Prescott in the head with the egg.

Prescott felt it draining down his neck and thought it was blood.

Craig Evans, the farm worker who threw the egg and wrestled with Prescott, was arrested but no charges were brought against either of them.

Prescott issued a statement saying: 'I responded to defend myself in the mêlée. I tried to get away as soon as possible from the incident. It was a frightening and regrettable incident, which involved two female assistants being knocked to the ground.'

In the morning, the tabloid newspapers were hostile, but – largely because it was 'two-Jags', at whom they enjoyed poking fun – the headlines were tinged with humour. The *Sun* front page banner headline said: TWO JABS.

Those around Prescott said it was the most difficult moment of his career which had hung in the balance. 'If it had been anyone else, they could have been finished, but John has a lot of public support,' said one Prescott ally.

By the morning Blair was confident his deputy would ride out the storm without damage to Labour's campaign. Blair bounced into the morning strategy meeting and said: 'I cannot talk about it without finding it funny.'

Alastair Campbell also backed his old friend, saying: 'It will probably go down well with the D/Es [working-class voters].'

Blair succeeded in cauterising the issue at the morning press conference at the Millbank centre, paying a fulsome personal tribute to Prescott: 'You could not wish for a deputy more loyal, more true and more decent. He cares about his country and he cares passionately about his politics ...'

He was asked whether he personally would have punched a

protester, Blair said: no, but 'John is John and I'm lucky to have him as my deputy'. The phrase 'John is John' made the headlines, but it was carefully ambiguous. A Blair aide said: 'By saying John is John, Blair was making the point he would not have done that.'

Gradually, the cloud lifted over Prescott. There had been a gender split in Millbank, with some of the younger women around Blair appalled at his behaviour while the men around Brown supported Prescott. The Brown camp also noted that they backed Prescott when he needed their support but the Blair camp at best was equivocal and some believed he should go. Millbank received a flood of messages of support from all over the world. Prescott even received a request by Helen Clark, the Labour Prime Minister of New Zealand, 'to give some punch' to her election campaign. Older women too supported Prescott. Prescott's late mother, Phyllis, then 83, stood by her son, saying: 'He would have been less of a man if he had not reacted the way he did.' And she hinted at the remorse he was feeling for letting down his party in an election. 'John is a very thoughtful man,' she said.

Internet websites sprang up dedicated to Prescott and the egging incident. One, with a video of the incident, invited visitors to click on a button to see 'two jags go mental'. It too came down on Prescott's side, saying: 'It has been announced this morning that Prescott may be investigated for assault but we say fair play to him. Our respect for Prescott has gone up enormously.'

A few days later, he was back on the Prescott battlebus, campaigning among the marginals in the Midlands, and made a detour to the safe Labour seat of Mansfield to lend his support to his former parliamentary Private Secretary, Alan Meale. As the Prescott coach slowly passed a building site in the town centre, there were cheers from the building workers. Many of the men stopped laying bricks and waved their left fists playfully at the Deputy Prime Minister's coach. Prescott, in the front seat, on the mike, said simply: 'Thanks, lads.'

The Prescott wave, the clenched left fist, caught on across the country. As his motor coach sped on its way through the neighbouring seat of Geoff Hoon, the Defence Secretary, it was overtaken by a Golf GT, honking its horn. As it sped by, the passenger's left arm shot out of the passenger window, punching a clenched-fist salute to Prescott.

'It's happened quite a bit,' said Prescott, who was surprised by the support he was getting. The incident produced the most famous 30 seconds of news footage of the 2001 election campaign.

Calls for Prescott to resign continued in the media, though the official opposition avoided doing so. One BBC reporter predicted if Blair won the election, Prescott would be dumped, but it was no longer a serious question.

It did not appear Prescott suffered any lasting damage from the 'Rumble in Rhyl'. Indeed, his personal popularity appeared to rise afterwards as voters warmed to him for the first time. An NOP poll for the *Sunday Times* four days after the punch showed that 58 per cent to 35 per cent still thought he was fit to be Deputy Prime Minister.

There was one caveat in the good news for Prescott, though. His close friends thought the incident revealed Prescott was showing his age. His lifelong friend Rodney Bickerstaffe said: 'I told him it was a good left, but it had no weight. In the past, the lad would not have got up! He must be losing his touch.'

The Enforcer

At about 8 a.m. on 8 June 2001, the Prescott eXpress took another lap of honour around Smith Square, where the Tories had their headquarters, after Labour had won a second landslide victory over the Conservatives. Prescott gave the Tories a blast of Labour's campaign theme, 'Lifted' by the Lighthouse Family, for the final time, right outside the Conservative Party headquarters. William Hague, the Conservative leader, would shortly announce his resignation outside the same doors.

'We were doing the Lifted and he [Hague] got lifted shortly afterwards. Somebody said to me he resigned as soon as he heard our bus going round the Square,' Prescott said later.

Prescott had attended a dawn VIP party at the Millbank headquarters, where he was irritated at being assailed by media well-wishers, including a female newspaper editor who tried to kiss him on the cheek. He was not in the mood for burying years of mutual animosity with the media. 'I nearly said what are you coming over to me for, all the bloody stuff you have written about me. All she wanted was the picture,' he said.

When Blair went to Downing Street later in the day, the choreography of his arrival was deliberately different from the first victory in 1997. After foot-and-mouth, floods, rail crashes and the failure to deliver improvements across a range of public services – something Blair had admitted in a speech in the closing days of the campaign – it was not a moment for triumphalism. Blair publicly recognised that, and wanted to demonstrate he was getting on with the business of running the country. His first task was to reshuffle the government.

On the day before polling day he met Prescott secretly at his home in his Sedgefield constituency and confided to his deputy that he intended to move Robin Cook from the Foreign Office. Blair explored with his deputy the ramifications of moving Cook, which they both knew would lead to ructions, but Prescott did not ask Blair why he had decided to move Cook. Prescott felt it was important for Blair to make up his own mind about Cook.

Blair would have liked to move Brown, but so long as he was at the Treasury, it was better to move Cook – who had nothing like Brown's support. Cook was ardently pro-euro, and demoting him signalled that Blair was opting for an easier life with Brown over the vexed question of Britain's entry to the single currency.

Blair held a second secret meeting on polling day in Sedgefield with his close advisers, including Jonathan Powell and Sally Morgan, to discuss the reshuffle. Stephen Byers, the Trade and Industry Secretary, an ally of Blair's, was also there. Byers was told by Blair that he would be staying at the DTI, but Blair intended to give him an enhanced economic role by taking communications – broadcasting policy – out of the Department of Culture and putting it into the DTI.

When Cook arrived at Downing Street the next day for the

reshuffle, Blair was not looking forward to their interview. Cook was a prickly character and Blair knew that in spite of the media speculation that he would be moved, Cook would hit the roof. Prescott sympathised with Blair's predicament: 'Tony always has got bigger problems at the top. If you look at the thing, everybody comes with baggage – I come with baggage, Robin's got baggage, Gordon's got baggage, Jack [Straw] has got baggage. There comes a time when it's wise to move people around and they can take their baggage with them.'

Blair tried a gentle approach, telling Cook he had been Foreign Secretary longer than almost anybody, and there came a time when he had to make some changes in his Cabinet. It made little difference. Cook was furious and at first refused any other post in the Cabinet. Blair persuaded him not to resign from the Cabinet, but he argued about the terms of his departure from the Foreign Office for so long that it delayed the announcement of the other new appointments.

Jack Straw had been tipped off that he would be taking over transport and local government from Prescott in a revamped department and went over to Prescott's DETR office to prepare for the move. He was still being briefed about Prescott's department at 4 p.m. when he was eventually called in to see the Prime Minister. He was stunned to be told by Blair he was going to be the next Foreign Secretary.

In a last-minute change of mind, Blair opted to put Byers into a newly reconstituted Department of Transport with responsibility also for local government and the regions. Blair decided to put environment into a new department for food and rural affairs, which was to take over from the old Ministry of Agriculture, Fisheries and Food, discredited by the foot-and-mouth debacle. He chose a 'safe pair of hands' in Margaret Beckett to take charge of it.

Prescott had done a deal with Blair that after one Parliament at DETR, he would have his own department at the Cabinet Office. Now Blair honoured that bargain. The Cabinet Office had been the graveyard for a string of ministerial careers – David Clark, Jack Cunningham, and Mo Mowlam – but Prescott passionately wanted a role at the heart of government as Blair's delivery-chaser. Blair deliberately omitted to tell Prescott when they met in Sedgefield that he was going to dismantle the Department of the Environment, Transport and the Regions that had been created for him. Blair had been thinking long and hard about how he could get a grip on the transport issue, which was continuing to cause problems for the government.

The idea of bringing environment and agriculture together came from Michael Meacher, Prescott's Environment Minister, in a confidential memorandum to the Prime Minister's Office. Meacher complained to Jonathan Powell, the Prime Minister's chief of staff, about the failures of the old Ministry of Agriculture. Powell asked Meacher to put it in a paper, telling him: 'We are thinking along similar lines.' Beckett liked the idea of taking over environment, which enhanced her department. It also gelled with Blair's thoughts, and he rewarded Meacher by keeping him as the Environment Minister under Beckett. However, Meacher insisted later that he never intended that transport should be broken away from environment. 'I think that was a retrograde step,' he told me. 'It was not at all what I was recommending.'

Prescott was furious with Meacher for going behind his back and he was also irritated at losing control to Byers of the agenda for regional government that he had wanted to take with him to the Cabinet Office. He had been so confident of keeping his old department intact, in spite of the rumours to the contrary, that on the day of the reshuffle, he sent a note to his civil servants thanking them for their dedication and saying, 'We have kept it all together.' It was only at 8 p.m. on the night of the reshuffle that Prescott was told that Blair was moving environment to a new ministry.

However, Prescott was more concerned about his own ministerial future. He knew his position was stronger than his predecessors' in the Cabinet Office in two key respects: as the deputy leader of the Labour Party – elected by the party, not appointed by Blair – he could not easily be sacked; he also had more 'clout' in the Cabinet, with allies such as Brown, to develop it into the post he had always coveted – the Office of the Deputy Prime Minister, which Blair was still not yet ready to concede.

Prescott had written a confidential paper to Blair setting out what he saw as the remit for the Office of the Deputy Prime Minister which he believed Blair had promised him in 1997. Lord MacDonald, who had gained Prescott's confidence as Transport Minister, was moved by Blair into the Cabinet Office under Prescott as the progress-chaser on public service delivery, and MacDonald was dubbed 'the enforcer' by the media. But the idea that MacDonald could act as the Cabinet 'enforcer' as it was presented by Downing Street was not sustainable. MacDonald, though widely respected, lacked the weight and experience that Prescott carried within the Cabinet, and was eventually to leave both the Cabinet Office and the government after only two years.

Blair gave Sally Morgan, his political secretary, a seat in the Lords with a peerage, and put her into Prescott's office as a Minister of State, but that was to last only until November. She was then moved back into Downing Street to plug a gap left by Anji Hunter, Blair's gatekeeper, who resigned after a great deal of soul-searching from her newly enhanced role as Blair's £120,000 head of government relations in Number Ten to take up a private sector post with BP.

However it was packaged, both Blair and Prescott knew that Prescott's move to the Cabinet Office would be seen as a demotion by the press. To avoid any misunderstandings about his role in the future, and to give Prescott greater assurance, Blair issued a detailed description of Prescott's new 'enhanced role as deputy prime minister'. The statement said:

> *He will deputise for the Prime Minister in all matters. He will head a new deputy prime minister's office. He will act with the full authority of the Prime Minister in delivering key manifesto pledges and in matters of current importance dealing with cross-department issues, including social exclusion, devolution, regional governance; the regional coordination unit along with the social exclusion unit will be located in this Cabinet Office.*

Prescott would also represent the UK on the Council of the Isles – part of the Northern Ireland peace settlement – and retain the leading role in international climate change negotiations. 'On occasions he will also act as the Prime Minister's personal emissary on Kyoto issues,' said the statement.

He also would be responsible for the White Paper on regional government. But Prescott – tired of the sniping by the press – threw himself into the backroom job, the 'boiler room' of the government, chairing a number of key Cabinet committees, including the economic committee. On the face of it, this had dangerous echoes of Prescott's pre-1997 bid to share power with the Treasury. However, this was a very different Prescott, and it showed how close Prescott and Brown were that the Chancellor was relaxed about his ally chairing the meetings. 'I don't think there's any problem about Gordon and I working closely together anyway,' said Prescott.

Blair also wanted Prescott to step in and coordinate government for him when a crisis broke, such as the foot-and-mouth epidemic. 'He now wants me, where he designates, to play a part on his behalf,' said Prescott.

Added together, it did not sound like the portfolio of a man who was on his way out. On the contrary, those around him noticed a more relaxed, mature Prescott who was preparing for a second term. He was grateful to Blair for giving him the experience of running a department, saying: 'After four years in government, I have learned an awful lot about how departments work. I have developed my own relationships – I have a very good relationship with Gordon Brown which has come from that, and

Tony, and in that sense I am a lot wiser going into the next period of office. I can give support knowing how departments work and develop my own authority. I am a pretty good Cabinet committee operator as the chair. I can get agreement from people.

'I can use those skills to good effect inside government and make sure they have the machinery working to deliver, so we don't lose time right at the beginning, wondering, "If ..."

'We know at the next election there is one hell of an opportunity for Labour. What it is holding out now is the possibility of a third term ...'

The past four years in charge of the unwieldy department, particularly of the transport brief, had taken their toll on Prescott's apparently boundless energy. His friends believed he was too tired to carry on in that capacity, and he appeared to feel that too.

Before the election, he had been diagnosed by his local GP in Hull with diabetes, which had been confirmed on the election campaign trail by an optician when Prescott dropped in for a photocall. It caused pins and needles in his legs – something you could see when he got out of the bus on the fateful Rhyl trip – and the side effects of the medication caused dryness in the mouth. The illness was also associated with his weight problem, which he was trying to get down. His restless lifestyle made dieting impossible; he was not a big eater, but he still had a habit of snacking on sandwiches. Notoriously uninterested in most sports, apart from boxing, Prescott made one concession to the new 'get fit' anti-obesity culture being pushed by John Reid at the Department of Health and Tessa Jowell at the Culture Department: he had an exercise bicycle installed in a cupboard-sized room in Admiralty House, his Whitehall office complex.

Chairing Cabinet committees appealed to Prescott's style and, he told friends, played to his strength as a negotiator. He saw all the important Cabinet papers, and in spite of the press reports to the contrary, became more of a central player in Whitehall. His role as a troubleshooter also brought him in closer proximity to Blair and Brown at a moment when their relations were about to take a fresh nosedive.

Four Homes

I once telephoned Prescott's private flat on the top floor of Admiralty House and was greeted by a thick Liverpudlian accent: 'Hello – Golden Shot!'

Asked who that was, the Liverpudlian said: 'We are John's old shipmates.'

The Deputy Prime Minister had invited his former shipmates from the merchant navy to join him for a small party in 'the flat' at Whitehall, and Prescott the former waiter was doing the cooking himself.

When the DPM returned, he explained: 'I've been cooking sausages and my cooker broke down, so I had to use Margaret Beckett's.' Mrs Beckett had the flat below.

There had been many distinguished tenants in the top floor grace and favour flat at Admiralty House and the previous incumbent of Prescott's flat occupant before the Prescotts arrived was Michael Portillo, the former Defence Secretary. When the Prescotts arrived, they discovered the bedroom had been decorated in cerise, with an elaborate canopy over the bed, which was not quite to Prescott's northern tastes. It was later changed as part of a general refurbishment of the building. Other occupants of the flat have included Malcolm Rifkind, Peter Brooke and George Younger. The other flats in Admiralty House have had such tenants as John Major, Tom King, Patrick Mayhew and Norman Tebbitt.

Prescott was attacked by the Tories for allowing £1.1 million to be spent on his flat over five years; in fact, that was the cost of the complete refurbishment of the historic Admiralty House. They Prescotts undoubtedly enjoyed the privilege of a grace and favour central London flat with a spectacular view, but Prescott was meticulous about not abusing the trappings of power. In addition to the DPM doing his own cooking and waiting on his guests, Prescott and Pauline did the shopping at Marks and Spencer's Oxford Street branch. He also paid a notional commercial rent for the privilege of living 'above the shop' in Admiralty House.

One advantage of the flat is that it has an unrivalled view across Horse Guards Parade, offering a grandstand seat for the Trooping the Colour ceremony in June. If the VIP guests ever wondered where the sound of jazz was coming from, they might have spotted that the windows of the Prescotts' flat were open. Prescott likes to play jazz music loudly whenever he is relaxing. He and Pauline sometimes entertained a few friends to drinks and a buffet but did the catering themselves.

When Prescott moved to the Cabinet Office, he never used

the offices in Whitehall which had been allocated to his ill-fated predecessors. Instead, he took some garden rooms in the basement of Dover House, a romantic neoclassical building halfway down Whitehall used by the Scottish Office. Prescott sat in an office with French windows and a small rose garden separating him from Horse Guards Parade. However, he soon discovered that the military bands, parading up and down in preparation for Beating the Retreat and Trooping the Colour, interrupted his work. He chaired Cabinet committee meetings next door at a long table, shouting above the clash of cymbals and blare of trumpets. The then Scottish Secretary, Helen Liddell, joked to her tenant about putting up his rent and he joked about having it reviewed.

The building, restored to some of its former glory, had once been the home of the notorious Lady Caroline Lamb, where she seduced her lover, the poet Byron, and ministers found they were invited to meetings chaired by Prescott in a room decorated more like a ladies' boudoir.

Prescott was awaiting the completion of the new multimillion-pound Cabinet Office development, refurbishing the Admiralty House complex and opening up office space near the Whitehall Theatre. The historic buildings, the home of the Admiralty Board for 200 years, including the Napoleonic wars, are now used for ministerial meetings chaired by Prescott. Lord Nelson's body lay in state in the ground-floor Captain's Waiting Room before being interred at St Paul's Cathedral on a day of national mourning. Countless naval officers anxiously waited there before climbing up a wide staircase to receive their orders in the Admiralty boardroom, a hidden gem in Whitehall, which boasts spectacular panelling on one wall, carved by Grinling Gibbons in an outpouring of embellishments with a naval theme, including drums and guns and scientific instruments. Its centrepiece is a weather cock, which is still attached to a weather vane on the roof. It was intended to tell members of the board which way the wind was blowing as they ordered the fleet to embark on a new mission, and it is still in working order. Ministers are sometimes distracted from their papers by the noise of the arrow swinging with the wind in a sudden gust. The boardroom table is over 200 years old. Traditionally, the First Sea Lord sat at one end, in a chair given to the board by the Duke of Clarence (later William IV). George Ward Hunt, who was First Lord of the Admiralty in the 1870s, was so fat that he had a semicircle cut out of the table to accommodate his immense stomach. Prescott conducted ministerial meetings sitting at the same spot, and, pointing to the stomach-hugging gap in the table, would tell visiting ministers: 'Don't tell the press!'

Prescott also has the use of Dorneywood as his country residence. Gordon Brown was first offered the use of the Queen Anne house, near Burnham Beeches in leafy Buckinghamshire, which is owned by the National Trust and made available to ministers of the Crown under the terms of a charitable trust. As he already had a private mansion block flat in Victoria, and an official flat over Number Ten, he gifted his grace and favour country retreat to Prescott.

Previous Labour tenants included Tony Crosland, when he

was Foreign Secretary. Lord Hattersley recalled joining him at Dorneywood the week before Crosland died: 'It was his first visit to his official country residence. I was there to confirm his view that the trappings of office were absurd as well as offensive and to share his amused amazement every time that the resident butler rushed forward to prevent one of us from pouring his own drink.'

Prescott showed no such inhibitions, although it was no Jeeves and Wooster relationship – Prescott is on first-name terms with the butler. His reasons for accepting the privileges that come with the role of DPM are complex and not a subject he will easily discuss, even with friends. Prescott famously has no time for 'champagne' socialists, and rejects the idea that 'there's nowt too good for the working class' as a 'cop-out'. He was pilloried by the Tories for having 'two Jags and four homes' – he also had the house in Hull and a former union flat in Clapham.

For all that, Prescott shrugged off the charges of hypocrisy and enjoyed the peace of Dorneywood. The estate, with links to Kenneth Grahame, author of the *Wind in the Willows,* had been given to the nation during the war in 1943 by Lord Courtauld-Thompson and run by a trust, which limited the cost to the taxpayer. Prescott was delighted to find that its visitors' book reads like a *Who's Who* of twentieth-century politics, including the signatures of Attlee, Churchill and foreign leaders. Perhaps it was Prescott's belief in being paid 'the rate for the job' that enabled him to sleep easy at night in one of Dorneywood's eight bedrooms.

However, in November 2002 he was unable to get much peace

or sleep. He had gone for the weekend to Dorneywood in the middle of knife-edge negotiations between the Fire Brigades Union (FBU) and the employers, the Local Government Association (LGA), to avert a damaging national strike by the firemen. He held crisis talks on his mobile in the early hours with Gordon Brown in Number 11 and Nick Raynsford, his local government minister. At dawn, the talks collapsed in farce, amid recriminations and allegations that Prescott had vetoed a deal under orders from Brown. In the end, Prescott succeeded in forcing through a deal that required modernisation in return for higher pay, but it was one of the deepest low points of his term in office. He privately said he had offered an exit strategy to Andy Gilchrist, the FBU leader, only to have it rejected, and the experience left him bruised.

He was also bruised by a row over his union flat in Clapham with the RMT, led by Bob Crow, a Militant opponent of the Labour Party. Prescott felt it was becoming almost a personal vendetta, and stuck to his guns as a regulated tenancy-holder, but in 2003 was forced to give up his flat. He was also lightly reprimanded by a Commons watchdog for failing to declare in the register of members' interests that he got the flat – which he had once shared with Dennis Skinner – at a reduced rent of £220 a month compared to commercial estimates of £1,600 a month. When Prescott and five other Labour MPs were challenged by the RMT to support RMT policy in return for political donations to the party, Prescott, at great personal pain, resigned from the union rather than be dictated to by Bob Crow. He told me: 'What always motivated me is my belief in right or wrong.

It's the best guide for anybody in public life – you have to do what you think is right. Sometimes it's painful but your only guide must be doing what you think is honest and right.

'I have taken this for quite a time now. I can live with disagreements on policy but the policies I carry out are the Labour Party policies I argued out at conference.'

He said he had always been a 'union man' and would 'die a union man'. In July 2004, he quietly joined Amicus, the manufacturing, technical and skilled workers' union, led by Derek Simpson.

In the midst of Prescott's personal battles with the unions, his transport successor, Stephen Byers, endured a twelve-month battering, ending in his sudden resignation. Byers had also incurred the wrath of Tom Winsor, the rail regulator, over his get-tough attitude towards Railtrack, the failing rail network operator. Winsor had offered to try to save Railtrack, and Byers, who planned to replace Railtrack with Network Rail, had threatened Winsor with action to stop him if he tried. But the 'tipping point' came as a result of a poisonous row between his special adviser, Jo Moore, a former party apparatchik, and Martin Sixsmith, a widely respected former BBC reporter, who had become head of the transport press office. Moore had suggested in an email to staff that coverage of the 11 September terrorist attacks in 2001 made it a 'good day to bury bad news', and inevitably it was leaked. Symptomatic of the climate of spin in Whitehall, their dispute dramatised the tensions between the cadre of highly politicised New Labour ministerial special advisers and the traditionally neutral departmental civil service press officers.

Byers's failure was in not sacking Moore before it got out of control. At the height of Byers's difficulties, he received a telephone call, out of the blue on a Sunday morning. It was the Downing Street switchboard saying, 'I have the Deputy Prime Minister on the line.'

They had never been close – Prescott used to call him 'the fish man' for telling journalists in a seafood restaurant in Blackpool that Labour should break the link with the unions. Byers vividly remembers the call.

'John said, "I hope you are all right … All this talk about you in the press. Don't you take any notice. You are a bit New Labour for me but you are one of our lot."

'I could hear this splashing noise in the background, so I said, "John, what are you doing?"

'He said, "I am in the bath."'

Prescott disputes that detail, but Byers was genuinely moved by Prescott's support. 'John's pretty loyal and tribal,' Byers told me. 'It was a great credit to him that he should call.'

In spite of Prescott's supportive message, Byers bowed to the pressure and resigned as Transport Secretary on 28 May 2002, barely a year after taking office. Blair acted quickly, replacing Byers with Alistair Darling, an ally of Brown's, who was unspectacular but sure-footed. In the ensuing reshuffle, Prescott, a day before his 64th birthday, finally got the Whitehall department he craved: his own personal fiefdom – the Office of the Deputy Prime Minister.

Comparing himself to Heseltine, he told friends: 'Now I am definitely centre stage with the deputy prime minister's office with all I wanted to do. If you have a good prime minister, he can't do everything. I can take some of the strain of some of those things he has to do, whether it is getting the railways together or foot and mouth, or some emergency, or if he has to go abroad and cannot get there. He uses me abroad.'

In his biography of Blair, Anthony Seldon said that in the early years of the first term, Blair feared Prescott was becoming 'an unguided missile' in his huge DETR empire. Prescott acknowledged that Blair was hesitant about giving his deputy his own department effectively shadowing parts of Downing Street, but by the middle of the second term, a mutual trust had been established that enabled Blair to give Prescott what he had wanted all along.

'I think there were sensitivities I might be the chief executive running around everywhere,' said Prescott. 'But after four years in government I have learned an awful lot about how departments work. I have developed my own relationships – I have a very good relationship with Gordon Brown which has come from that, and Tony – and in that sense I am a lot wiser.'

9/11

Prescott was in his hotel bedroom at Brighton for the TUC conference, the television on Sky News, when he saw live pictures of the burning tower after the first jet ploughed into the building on 11 September 2001.

Blair was in a room across the corridor, preparing his speech for the conference.

'When I saw the first one I couldn't believe it,' said Prescott. 'I walked into his room and we saw the second one. We couldn't believe it.

'I said to him, "This is going to change the world."

'He said, "Yes, in a quite fundamental way."

'My response to that was that these problems will not be solved until we do something about Palestine and the Palestinian people.

'It was quite clear that he was visibly shocked by the whole thing. And when he gave evidence to the Hutton inquiry. I do think that was quite a seminal moment in his thinking about how we deal with terrorism …'

Blair made a short speech to the TUC and hurried back to London. The Prime Minister's Special Branch bodyguards had urged him to go to a safe house in the Brighton area where he could be better protected from any assassination attempt by Al-Qaeda, but he raced back to London in his car with his team of close advisers, leaving Prescott at the TUC conference. Prescott's aides recall that the workaholic continued to hold a round of union discussions, and held an evening ministerial meeting with Gus MacDonald.

In the ensuing months, Prescott was to play a crucially important role in helping Blair survive the traumas of joining a right-wing Republican President in a pre-emptive strike against Iraq. On the morning after the first crunch vote in the Commons on 26 February 2003, when 121 Labour MPs voted against the government and Blair survived on Tory votes,

Prescott was left in charge by Blair to sum up at a Cabinet meeting. The DPM turned it into a vote of confidence in Blair's premiership.

'My assessment of the mood of the Cabinet is that we're backing the PM,' he said, eyeing the Cabinet for anyone who dared dissent. 'Anyone want to say anything to the contrary?' Nobody did. Prescott said in that case he took it that they were all signed up to the policy.

However, Prescott was contemptuous of the neo-conservatives around Bush that Blair had embraced. In the immediate aftermath of the attacks on the World Trade Center, Prescott spoke to Vice-President Dick Cheney on a video link from Downing Street via the White House to a secure location where Cheney was being held.

Prescott said: 'Cheney was in some hideaway. I said, "You must share some feeling with Bin Laden who is also hiding away. But you have more luxurious surroundings than Bin Laden's."' Cheney replied with a expression that Prescott called 'an enigmatic smile'.

After the Iraq war, Prescott also tackled Cheney about Bush's refusal to honour Clinton's commitment to sign the Kyoto agreement. 'I told Cheney they were totally wrong not to endorse this policy and eventually they would have to do so,' he said. There was some movement over the reluctance by the Bush administration to sign up to the Kyoto targets in 2005, when the US entered negotiations with China and India on limiting carbon emissions.

In spite of Prescott's bravura performance in the Cabinet, he was becoming concerned about the way Blair appeared to be giving all-out support for Bush. On 11 March 2003, as Blair faced another crucial Commons vote, Prescott hosted a dinner for Brown and Blair at his flat in Admiralty House. It was one of a series of regular meetings Prescott had arranged to ease the tensions between Blair and Brown. It was intended as a general stock-taking supper, but it was dominated by a frank discussion about the forthcoming vote in the Commons on Iraq, which would be a vote of confidence in Blair. Brown and Prescott had left foreign policy to Blair, and over the next seven days, Brown, who was privately accused by Blairites of not fully supporting the Prime Minister, more than ever before lobbied Labour MPs, including Clare Short, to secure their support for the vote. Brown was instrumental in keeping Short in the Cabinet for the vote, although she resigned on 12 May, claiming Blair had broken his promise to her that she would help to lead the postwar reconstruction.

Peter Stothard recorded in *30 Days*, his insider's account of Downing Street during the war, that it was Prescott, not Blair, who stood at the podium outside the black door of Number Ten after a crucial Cabinet meeting to announce that the diplomatic process had broken down and that the next day, the Prime Minister would be asking Parliament to support 'the ultimate action of last resort'. If he was used – as the anti-war campaigners including Short believe – to push the Bush–Blair war agenda, Prescott is not resiling from his support now.

When I asked Prescott on the tenth anniversary of the leadership whether he regretted supporting Blair on the war with the benefit of hindsight, he had the opportunity to disown the policy, but he did not. He said he gave his support 'willingly'. He told me: 'I have been consulted on all the things that have been involved. I have been supportive and I don't depart from that.'

Some of his friends believe he has been too loyal, and has been used by Blair to bind the party into unpopular policies such as the war on Iraq. To have walked out on such a crucial issue as the war would have broken the back of Blair's government and brought it down. At no stage, however, did Prescott contemplate bringing Blair down.

Euro-Wars

In spite of their growing mutual respect and trust, Prescott still had rows with Brown, including one over Brown's refusal in June 2000 to allow the Cabinet a say over policy on the euro. Prescott supported Brown's extreme caution about entry, but did not agree with Brown's insistence that the Treasury had authority over the five tests for entry.

The DPM returned from a trip on Blair's behalf to Sierra Leone to visit British troops at the end of their dangerous mission to restore authority in that country to discover the increasingly strained relations between Blair and Brown at home. The running sore over the euro had become poisonous. Prescott was alarmed that the poison was spreading through the Cabinet, as ministers began to take sides in the run-up to a summit in Portugal.

Robin Cook, the pro-euro Foreign Secretary, had been told by

Blair's private office the week before to strip out offending sentences from a speech to the Commons shortly before he was due to enter the chamber, to avoid upsetting the Chancellor. However, Blair had authorised Stephen Byers, the Trade and Industry Secretary, publicly to push the case for entry to protect British jobs.

Brown's camp hit back with a whispering campaign, saying Byers was 'shallow' and 'uninspiring'. A Brown supporter told me Brown 'just doesn't rate Byers – he thinks he's no good at detail'. Blair called for an end to the infighting over the euro at a regular Cabinet meeting. Prescott believed it was necessary to bind the Cabinet into the decision, and told Brown: 'You can't clamp down the debate.'

The running Cabinet battle over Brown's determination to keep control over the policy on the euro continued throughout the early part of 2003 as Britain went to war over Iraq. It led to bizarre claims by Brown's camp that Peter Mandelson, the *bête noire* of the Brownites, had been overheard saying to Ken Clarke, the pro-euro former Tory Chancellor, in the Commons chamber that the assessment had been carried out by Brown, and it was no.

There were counter-claims by euro enthusiasts that the Treasury was trying to bounce Blair and the Cabinet into rejection of entry to the single currency. Mandelson fuelled the story by giving the impression that Blair was confident the tests would be met, which caused consternation over one weekend at the Treasury while Brown was in Washington chairing a World Bank meeting. Brown fell asleep in the chamber when he got back, having been 'knocked flat by jet lag'.

The Iraq war brought the three men closer together at the very moment the row over the euro and the 'noises off' by the opposing camps threatened to tear their relationship apart. 'It has always been difficult for those outside the inner circle, who have wanted to try to divide the relationship,' a Brown ally told me. 'They can have a corrosive influence on it. But during the war, Gordon and Tony have met much more often. They have met a lot of the time with Prescott. They were meeting every hour or so. There was no room for the corrosive words in people's ears to have an effect because they were so close.'

In May 2003, the divisions over the euro resurfaced. Blair's Cabinet allies were 'told to make a noise' to reassert the Cabinet's authority over the final decision. One Cabinet minister told me that Brown should not be allowed to deliver his euro report 'like the Budget to the Cabinet' (without an opportunity for amendment). On 15 May, the euro strategy was discussed by the Cabinet. Prescott had always been a Euro-sceptic, but his scepticism did not amount to ideological opposition to the single currency. He was prepared to take a pragmatic view, supporting Brown's tests for entry, which were unlikely to be met.

But Prescott had something else on his mind, however: his care and maintenance of Brown and Blair's relationship. It was now under renewed strain because of the euro and an amendment tabled by MPs associated with the Brown camp to weaken Blair's flagship modernising legislation on free-standing foundation hospitals. Brown was also engaged in a row with Blair about the financing of the UK's bid for the Olympics, and rang Prescott at

7.30 a.m. to discuss his objections, which he wanted Prescott to take up because he himself was having to deal with the euro.

Blair, Brown and Prescott met before the Cabinet to discuss the euro. Blair had been arguing late on Wednesday night for the Treasury assessment on the five tests to be taken as a 'yes' because there was enough to go forward for entry. Prescott, who was seeking a compromise on the euro, said it should be seen as a 'yes, but ...'. Overnight, Blair seemed to come round to Prescott's formulation.

In the Cabinet, Prescott won the case for the Cabinet to be consulted on the euro, and be bound by the conclusions. Brown's allies supported this tactic to stop the 'freelancing' by pro-euro Cabinet ministers such as that carried out by Byers and Cook in 2000. In the privacy of their pre-Cabinet meeting, Prescott privately warned Blair and Brown that the faction-fighting between their two camps was in danger of pulling down New Labour.

There was no let-up in Blair's ambitions for euro entry, however. Six days later I was told by a Blairite in the Cabinet: 'Tony could delay the election until the autumn of 2005 or spring 2006 if necessary to hold a referendum on the euro.'

On 6 June, the Cabinet had its discussion about entry to the euro. As he entered Number Ten, Prescott playfully waved a V-sign at the cameramen behind his back. The gesture sparked off another round of speculation about Prescott's fitness for office. On Sunday, Brown announced on *Breakfast with Frost* that the Cabinet had decided to make European membership the key issue in the coming months leading up to the election. This was wrongly reported on *Channel 4 News* as 'pro-euro', but Brown was making a very different point: Labour would accuse the Tories of wanting to pull Britain out of Europe.

On 12 June 2003, a Cabinet reshuffle would brush all news of the euro rows off the front pages. Blair had planned to create a new Department of Constitutional Affairs, handling the justice system, and abolishing the 800-year-old role of the Lord Chancellor. Lord Irvine, who had once employed young Blair and Cherie Booth in his chambers, was content to go, until it was discovered late in the day that, owing to a legislative hitch, the title could not be abolished without a new Bill, which would take another session. Derry would not be remembered as 'the last Lord Chancellor'. He therefore refused to budge, and after a desperately painful day, Blair had to sack his old mentor. In the midst of this farce, Blair telephoned Prescott for advice.

Prescott was sitting down to tea in the members' tearoom, where mobile phones are banned from use, when his mobile phone trilled in his pocket and the Downing Street switchboard put the Prime Minister on the line. He was talking to Blair about the Derry problem when a tall thin Tory MP in a blue suit – Andrew Robathan, the member for Nigel Lawson's old seat of Blaby – reminded Prescott that mobiles were barred. Robathan picked up a small metal notice of a phone with a red stripe from one of the tables and waved it in Prescott's face.

Prescott exploded at the Tory MP. Robathan three years earlier in 2000 had taken a complaint about Prescott and his failure to declare his union flat in the register of members' interests to the Commissioner for Standards and Privileges. Prescott received a mild reprimand and was advised 'in the current climate' he should have openly declared he was paying £220 a month for the flat in the RMT headquarters at Clapham. Now Prescott saw red, and told Robathan, a former SAS soldier: 'You're not in the sergeants' mess now – fuck off.' He then continued his conversation with Blair. Robathan complained about Prescott's boorish behaviour and breaking the rules. It all blew over, until a few days later when Prescott spotted a familiar tall thin Tory MP wearing a blue suit.

Prescott stormed up to the MP and gave him a verbal salvo. The MP was, in fact, Richard Spring, the mild-mannered Conservative spokesman on foreign affairs, who said he did not understand what he had done to upset the DPM so much, but whatever it was, he was sorry, and backed off. 'To the DPM, all Tory MPs clearly look the same,' Spring told friends later.

Some time after the altercation, Prescott was hosting a banquet for visiting Chinese dignitaries at Lancaster House, when he spotted Spring, who had been invited as a courtesy to the Tory foreign affairs team, sitting a few seats away from him. Spring took immediate action, shouting: 'I am not Andrew Robathan!'

Spring and Prescott have established friendly relations, and Spring enjoyed Prescott's self-effacing speech in which he told the Chinese visitors: 'In Britain, if you become a waiter, you can become Deputy Prime Minister.'

Speaking on his tenth anniversary as deputy leader, Prescott said he would have accepted the result of a euro referendum if the Cabinet had decided to go ahead with it.

'I was prepared to take a referendum on the euro,' he told me.

'I was one who campaigned to come out of the Common Market and the people said no. I am always conscious that the people made the decision to stay in, and they will take a decision on the euro in a referendum, and politicians should take account of that. I am pleased I belong to a government that is the only one that will give a referendum.'

He added: 'I was against going into the Common Market because I thought historically we would end up as a United States of Europe.

'I am not unconvinced about that but we certainly won't be in my time. I think it's forgotten now.

'It's a very important issue when you look at the two exponents of that, France and Germany: no longer are they saying they want the discipline of the euro; they are saying they want to change the rules so they can try to do what Labour has done which is to create full employment and keep public expenditure in the public services.'

While Blair had been eager for a referendum on the euro, he had been opposed to promising a referendum on the new European constitution. However, a number of pro-European Blair allies in the Cabinet were convinced such a promise would neutralise any Tory attempt to turn the next election into a referendum on Europe.

It was a mark of Prescott's central role that when a number of Cabinet ministers began pushing for a change of policy in favour of a pledge to hold a referendum on the EU constitution in late April 2004, they came to see Prescott. Jack Straw, the Foreign Secretary, and John Reid were among the senior ministers who privately lobbied Prescott to persuade Blair to hold a referendum, even though it would mean an embarrassing volte face. Straw also saw Blair privately in March and strongly urged him to reconsider the referendum as Blair went off on his Whitsun holiday. When Blair returned, he came back convinced that Straw was right. To Brown and Prescott, Blair returned with a determined look in his eye, which they privately described as his 'messianic mood'.

Brown, who was determined to hold to Britain's red lines against creeping European integration, including the threat to veto tax harmonisation, shared Prescott's view that if Blair was now committed to making the U-turn, a referendum could play in their favour. Blair seemed to Brown and Prescott to have a messianic look in his eyes about the referendum that they were not going to try to dispel. Instead, they decided to go along with Blair's new passion for a plebiscite, tempered by a heavy dose of pragmatism, which included delaying any real campaign until the French had voted.

'When Gordon sees Tony Blair in a messianic mood, he works with it, to keep Blair's feet on the ground,' said one Brown ally when the referendum was still in prospect. 'He could see that Tony had made his mind up. Gordon is going to campaign hard on the positives – that a referendum will be a big bargaining card to make sure none of our red lines are crossed, particularly on taxation.'

Prescott then faced the prospect of campaigning in another great European referendum after the election, but this time he would be urging the British electorate to vote yes. Any contortions that might have caused Prescott were avoided by the French and Dutch voting *non* and *nee* in their referendums in June 2005. On 6 June, Jack Straw announced that Britain was not proceeding with the referendum. That night, Prescott relaxed at the back of the Locarno Room at the Foreign Office as he attended a leaving party for Ed Owen, Straw's political adviser for twelve years. Blair was on his way to Washington for discussions with President George W. Bush in the White House on climate change and aid to Africa before the G8 meeting in Gleneagles in July. However, hovering in the background was the thought that if Blair no longer had to fight for a yes vote in the referendum, when would he step down?

The Tee-Bee Gee-Bees

On the Sunday before the 2003 Labour conference, Channel Four screened *The Deal* for delegates at the ultra-modern Imax cinema on the beach front at Bournemouth. I could not get a seat because it was packed out.

The Deal was a 'docu-drama' which attempted to recreate the Blair–Brown deal at Granita, then a fashionable Islington restaurant, on 31 May 1994, when Brown agreed to step aside for Blair to run for the leadership after John Smith's death. The only problem for the programme-makers was that there were no eyewitnesses to the talks. Only Brown and Blair know what was actually agreed and whether a deal was struck. The programme-makers overcame that problem by imagining their conversation.

One who was at the restaurant that night, writer Allison Pearson, described the scene to me: 'It was extremely clattery, open-plan, small tables, with absolutely no sense of privacy.

'I was sitting about halfway back in the restaurant. Susan Tully of *EastEnders* was sitting at the front near the window. Everyone was staring at her, and saying: "It's Michelle [the character Tully played in the soap opera]."

'Then I saw Tony. He was sitting by himself. Nobody was interested in him. My husband said: "You are a columnist, go and say hello." I was going to the loo and Blair said hello. He didn't seem to know exactly who I was, but he was very charming, extremely flattering.'

Blair asked Pearson: 'What do you think we should do?' Pearson, caught by surprise, said that New Labour needed to tap into the power of enlightened self-interest, to raise taxes to strengthen society as a whole.

Only later did it become clear to her that Blair might have been referring to the more pressing question of what he and Brown should do about the Labour leadership. 'I heard these footsteps behind me. I assumed it was Cherie. Then I turned round and saw Gordon with an aide.'

Ed Balls, Brown's chief economic adviser, had accompanied Brown by taxi to the venue. 'Gordon said: "How are you?" But it was very obvious that I had found myself in the ring between Muhammad Ali and Joe Frazier,' she said.

Balls stayed for the first course. Gordon kept prompting him to order, but he did not wish to intrude on their private talks. Balls left and retreated to Rodin's, a Westminster restaurant since renamed The Atrium, where he met up with more members of the Brown camp, including Paul Routledge and Nick Brown.

Blair still disputes what happened next. Brown had come under pressure from Blair's friends to make the sacrifice for the party. They included Mandelson, who had tried to act as a friend to both men, but who was later thanked as 'Bobby' by Blair in his victory speech. By the time they sat down together at Granita there was already intense speculation in the press, including my report for the *Independent*, that Brown would concede.

In fact, Brown's decision had been growing on him over a fortnight before the Granita meal. The night before the Granita dinner, Brown held a council with his allies Nick Brown, Murray Elder and Charlie Whelan at Joe Allen, a Covent Garden American diner and bar. Brown spoke about the need to avoid splitting the vote and made it clear to them that he would not stand against Blair. Nick Brown told him to stand and fight, as did Whelan, but Gordon's mind appeared to be made up.

Brown went to Granita with a list of demands on policy, but, according to one Brown ally, he was stunned when Blair volunteered a deal. A Brown ally told me: 'Brown arrived with a list of demands for guarantees on policy; he wanted the right to appoint people. He did not have a timetable for the handover. That was not part of his strategy. But Blair came and raised it himself. He was obviously thinking that is all we would talk about.'

Another Brown ally told me: 'I don't know what they said. But I get the impression Blair said, "Look Gordon, I can only do this for so long." The trouble is, Gordon would expect it to be honoured and would hold him to it.'

From the viewpoint of two rising stars in an opposition that had been written off as unelectable, a transfer of power after a second election victory must have seemed a far-off prospect, but the offer was etched in Brown's memory as if it had been cut in granite.

Brown, eager to get away, sipped wine with a nouvelle cuisine main course, and was still hungry when he left the restaurant. When he arrived at Rodin's, he ordered steak pie. 'It's nonsense that he didn't eat and only had water,' said one of his team.

It hardly mattered what Blair claims took place. What mattered was that Brown was convinced that Blair had offered him a deal. It became an obsessive point of principle for Brown, and as the years in the second term ticked by, he nursed a growing resentment that he was being denied his rightful inheritance, as promised by Blair.

As Brown's frustration grew, Whitehall was rife with stories about the destabilising squabbles between TB and GB, which were known as the 'Tee-Bee Gee-Bees'. Soon after Blair's second general election triumph, Brown went to Blair to demand to know when he was stepping down. 'He was very blunt about it,' said one of Brown's closest friends. 'He said, when are you off then. Or words to that effect.'

The *Mail on Sunday* claimed Brown tackled Blair at least six times soon after the 2001 general election to demand a date when Blair would 'fuck off'. One Downing Street insider told me: 'Only six times? It was every day!'

To Blair and his supporters, it was breathtaking arrogance to even broach the subject when Labour had been returned with a second huge majority, which they regarded with some justification as a tribute to Blair's ability to reach out to voters across the political divide. Downing Street reacted by actively promoting alternative candidates to Brown to show the Chancellor that whatever he thought Blair had signed up to in Granita, he would never be given a free run at the leadership.

Blunkett was the first to be put up by Blair's camp. That became obvious when an otherwise dull book launch for Blunkett produced a show of strength from the Blairites – Cherie Blair; her aide, Fiona Millar, Alastair Campbell's partner; Peter Mandelson; Alan Milburn; and Stephen Byers all turned up for the warm white wine at a meeting hall next to the old Westminster library, now an upmarket curry house called the Cinnamon Club. Each time a contender came forward, it would appear that Brown would knock them down in combat over their budgets. Brown's budget row with Blunkett, particularly over prisons, was so bad that it had to be resolved in private with Blunkett being invited up to Scotland to a dinner with Brown. Blunkett specifically asked for his dog not to be fed any of the steak they were eating, as it upset the dog's stomach. It was too late. Another friend of Brown's, Defence Minister Lewis Moonie, who was acting as the chef for night, had already fed the dog the meat.

Milburn then emerged as a potential contender, and a row broke out between Milburn and Brown over the direction of health policy. When Milburn resigned from the Cabinet to spend more time with his family, Charles Clarke became the favoured candidate, again walking into a Cabinet showdown with Brown over student top-up fees in 2003.

As Brown's allies briefed against Clarke, provoking a furious row across Whitehall, one Cabinet minister told me: 'What is going on now is enormous resentment. There is an enormous row behind the scenes as to why Gordon briefed. They are ever so jumpy in Downing Street about whether their friends are going to let them down.

'Gordon has thrown a hand grenade and everyone has dived into the bunker. Politically, he has played a blinder. He has created havoc. He has got to have a game plan. You don't do this unless you have a game plan.'

It seemed perfectly obvious to Brown's Cabinet colleagues that his game plan was the destabilisation of Blair and his modernising agenda. Prescott kept silent, even to his friends, but another Cabinet minister said: 'It's destabilisation and with the help of Dacre [editor of the *Daily Mail*] and Piers Morgan [then editor of the *Daily Mirror*] a coup – that is what it is all about either by pissing Tony off to the point where he jacks it in or by destabilisation where things go badly wrong and people say it's time for a change.

'He is using history because there is many a good Prime Minister who has had enough and stepped down. We have the fine example of Thatcher – someone who was "invincible" but who in the end went because the party decided it liked staying in power better. That can be his only game – why do it otherwise?'

The next serious challenge by Brown to the Blair agenda came at the crucial meeting of the Cabinet committee on top-up fees, chaired by Prescott at Admiralty House, but Brown played a weak hand. The Chancellor called for the plans to be shelved until after the next election, but he failed to carry his Cabinet colleagues with him because he failed to put forward a convincing alternative. One minister who was there said: 'It was all very sane and rational. It wasn't, as they have briefed, in any way a terrible row. It was thoughtful and sensible and people were trying to walk through a terrible problem. All Gordon's contribution amounted to was, could we defer all this until after the election? We couldn't because it's got too much steam behind it. I would have been sympathetic to a graduate tax. He hinted he would come back to it after the election, but he didn't put it forward. We know you have to say it now. You can't say to Charles, float the problems but we haven't got a clue how you deal with them. Charles had tried to do the best job he can with the commitments that have been made.'

Brown had no allies at the meeting because, I was told, 'nobody thought delay was credible.' However, Brown's allies said the Chancellor simply could not understand what all the rush was about. 'Suddenly we were being told that our manifesto commitment not to introduce top-up fees had to be overturned. Gordon said this was a ridiculous way to run the policy. He said you had to have a public debate about the strengths and weakness of the current system. He thought we ought to be going through a Wanless-type exercise taking a long time about it.'

However, Prescott felt caught in the middle of the argument between Blair and Brown. Another of Prescott's Cabinet colleagues told me: 'Prescott is furious with Brown that he has been dragged into it by Gordon. He is incandescent that reports today said Prescott is backing Brown. He isn't. Prescott failed to find a consensus and reported back to Tony that he [Blair] will have to resolve it.'

Prescott was put in an impossible position by Brown. Having been asked by Blair to act as an honest broker, Prescott's friendship with Brown was being used to play him off against Blair, which he would not do. Prescott insisted he would not have split loyalties, and had to remain neutral.

A key Blair ally told me: 'Brown has constantly set himself up as being more left-wing. I don't think JP is happy with what happened. When Tony asked him to chair the meeting to try to resolve it, he was doing just that – simply chairing the meeting. He rejects the headlines "Prescott backs Brown".'

Brown had more success with Prescott's backing in watering down the Blairite policy on foundation hospitals, which was being driven by Alan Milburn, then Health Secretary. It would have given hospitals financial independence from the NHS, but Brown insisted on limiting their ability to raise their own finance.

Prescott also had his own battles during this period. In the last week of June 2003, when Charles Clarke proposed direct funding of secondary schools to cut out the inefficient Local Education Authorities, Prescott blew his top, telling Blair in blunt terms he would not stand for it. There was an acrimonious exchange of notes around the Cabinet table, like sixth-formers at the back of the class, as Clarke scribbled a message to Brown and Prescott saying he had told Labour leaders of the Local Government

Association that he was going to do it in a speech at an LGA conference. Prescott wrote back saying that was great – it would be just before he and Brown were to deliver their speeches to the LGA. Prescott later included a putdown for Clarke's idea in his speech. Blair avoided the showdown with his deputy by avoiding any clear commitment to strip the LEAs of their power to allocate school funds. But in July 2004, Clarke announced in a five-year plan the government's intention to ring-fence the money for schools, achieving almost the same result by a different route.

Prescott's main concern, however, was that Brown's obsession with the leadership was endangering the hopes of securing a third successive election victory. He began the task once more of trying to persuade Blair and Brown to put their squabble to one side, and, for the good of the government, come to some new arrangement, by hosting a series of meetings between the two. Prescott was acting like a marriage guidance counsellor, urging them to hold their relationship together for the good of the party. Prescott had his own code name for the secret meetings between Blair and Brown, referring to them in private as 'Bed and Breakfast'.

All his efforts to keep a lid on the simmering row were blown apart at the Labour Party conference in Bournemouth in September 2003.

The Brown camp was already agitated by hints from the Blair camp that Blair had no intention of stepping down. This was made clear to me in an interview Lord Falconer gave me in his private office at the Commons. Without prompting by me, he volunteered that Blair had a zest for the job with no intention of resigning. It was published in the *Sunday Telegraph* with a headline – deliberately echoing Thatcher's remarks – saying Blair would go ON AND ON.

This message was reinforced after Blair had given an interview to the *Observer* for the Sunday of the Labour conference. The first edition, which was circulated at around 8 p.m. on Saturday, was picked up and given a new slant by the *Sunday Telegraph*, under the headline: BLAIR: I WON'T RESIGN. I'M GOING ON AND ON.

On the morning of the conference in Bournemouth Brown was irritated, but this turned to fury when he watched Blair on the BBC *Breakfast with Frost* programme. Blair was asked whether he had done a deal with Gordon at Granita.

Blair said there had been no deal.

A Brown ally said: 'We were taken aback when Blair said that.'

As Brown wrote his speech in his hotel bedroom, Balls, a keen footballer and a Norwich fan, sat nearby watching Manchester City versus Spurs on Sky Sports. It was a 0–0 draw but Balls was barely taking in what the Chancellor was telling him. Brown read out to Balls his peroration in which he took Tony Blair's words and threw them back in his face: 'We are at our best when we are at our boldest', but Brown added 'best when we are united – best when we are Labour'.

Brown's refusal to use 'New Labour' was a blatant challenge to Blair. The next day, Brown won a genuine standing ovation from a willing audience at the Bournemouth International Conference Centre.

It was immediately seen by Blair's allies as a crude attempt to destabilise Blair at the moment of his greatest weakness – having lost the trust of the public over the war on Iraq, Blair was also unpopular with his own party for pushing through reforms to health and education. Later, Brown nervously enquired of one of his aides: 'Did we go too far?'

The next day, the *Daily Telegraph* front page headline confirmed his fears: BOLD BROWN STAKES CLAIM TO BE LEADER.

Brown's allies confirmed to me that they believed Blair could still step down before the general election, even though it was less than two years away. That night, I wrote in my diary: 'X said, "We think Blair could go before the election. They [the Blair camp] will wait and see how it goes and then he could go."'

It was a jaw-dropping comment, and it seemed to me they were playing with fire. I was left in no doubt that two and half years into a second term – beyond the midway point of a four-year Parliament – Brown believed that it was time to call in Blair's tacit deal offered at Granita in 1994 to step down. If he failed to act now, Brown would have no time to obtain the smooth transition to power he needed to stand a chance of winning the next election, and he would have to wait for at least another four years for Blair to go. This was his last heave to remove Blair before the general election.

In the Blair camp, they angrily accused Brown and his acolytes of attempting 'a coup' from the platform at the party conference. Blair could not leave Brown's move unanswered. On Tuesday, in his keynote leadership speech, he hit back, reminding the party that he had led them for six and a half years continuously in government, something no predecessor had achieved, but the core of his speech was an aggressive attack on the critics of New Labour. He did not name him, but no one was in any doubt who he meant.

'After six years, more battered without but stronger within. It's the only leadership I can offer. And it's the only type of leadership worth having,' said Blair. It was a bravura performance that showed all his skills as the actor-manager of the Labour tribe who had held them together through two election victories. 'I can only go one way,' he declared. 'I've no reverse gear.'

That comment was to cause merriment in the Cabinet, with Jack Straw later joking with Blair at a Cabinet meeting that he would show him how to do a three-point turn.

Blair's supporters were thrilled by his performance. Clarke told allies: 'Tony is stronger now because Gordon has overreached himself.'

This was also Prescott's view. Prescott had long been a restraining influence on Brown, and privately warned him he might not succeed in lifting the crown, if he was seen to wound Blair. However, he also wanted to be scrupulously honest with both men, who had come to respect his advice, knowing that he was one of the few around the Cabinet table with no interest in the premiership for himself. He told them both bluntly that their behaviour was 'stupid'.

One Cabinet minister told me Brown would never become the leader because he was too disliked by his colleagues. 'We don't like him. He will never be leader,' he said.

Prescott had done everything he could to avoid their rivalry breaking out into the open, but now he felt he had no alternative. He used his own speech on Thursday, the last day of the conference, to knock their heads together:

'Two powerful speeches from Tony and Gordon,' he recalled. 'And this conference knows, this party knows, the whole country knows, that these two achieve more by their common endeavour than they do alone.'

He then lectured the Blair and Brown camps on the need for party discipline. 'Conference, this is where we sort out our differences, within the party.' Prescott added this warning: 'If we fail now, if we tear ourselves apart as we have done in the past, that would truly be a betrayal.'

It was an astonishing public warning to the two men at the centre of the government that they were imperilling their hold on power by their feud. A couple of weeks later, Prescott did what he normally does on Saturday afternoons to relax. He settled down to watch a film. This time, it was the video of the Channel 4 reconstruction, *The Deal.*

However, there was to be no let-up in the real-life war between Blair and Brown. There was another flashpoint in November 2003 when Blair kept Brown off the NEC before the vote to readmit Ken Livingstone to the party and fight for re-election as mayor of London as a Labour candidate. One of Brown's allies said: 'Gordon would never have accepted Livingstone back into the Labour Party. That is why they did it.' Prescott thought Blair was being petty, and sided with Brown over the row.

Prescott invited both Blair and Brown to dinner in his flat at Admiralty House to talk over their differences. Prescott, like the rest of those on the outside, did not know – and largely did not care – whether a deal had been struck at Granita in 1994.

However, he actively encouraged them to agree a 'Granita 2' for the good of the government.

Close colleagues said Prescott bluntly told them both: 'You have to sort out an agreement between the pair of you. I don't want to know about it. I just want to know that you are working together.'

In fact, Prescott had begun his role as marriage guidance counsellor to Blair and Brown much earlier. Prescott's allies said he had been pressing them 'for ages', from Labour's first term of office, to reach a fresh accord on a handover of power that would limit the damage their corrosive dispute was threatening to do to the government. He hosted a secret dinner for Blair and Brown at Dorneywood in early 2002 and again at his flat in March 2003.

He regarded Blair and Brown as the outstanding politicians of their generation, and found it deeply frustrating that their friendship had been spoiled by their rivalry. He told Brown privately he was 'head and shoulders' above the rest of the Cabinet, and did not need to waste energy fretting about the inheritance which Prescott was convinced would be his.

Some of Brown's camp were worried that by the time Brown did succeed Blair, he would inherit a hollowed-out husk of the mass membership party they had launched in the heady days of 1994. 'One is worried about his inheritance and the other is worried about his legacy,' Prescott gloomily told friends. However, there were real differences over political direction, and Brown led Cabinet opposition to the more radical aspects of the 'choice' agenda for the public services being pushed by the Blairites for inclusion in the 2005 general election manifesto.

Again, Prescott believed Brown was making a mistake by allowing himself to be portrayed as Old Labour. Gordon still appeared to be bitter, said Prescott. 'He makes the modernisers seem like some evil force, but they are not. We are all modernisers. Gordon is a moderniser. I am a moderniser.'

One day a blue plaque may be put on the wall of the formal dining room in the top flat at Admiralty House as the place where Blair and Brown discussed the handover of power with Prescott acting as the waiter, serving out the shepherd's pie from the flat's galley kitchen. With its long polished banqueting table that could comfortably seat twelve with elbow room, and huge landscape paintings on the walls, it was not an informal setting to ease tensions, but it had one advantage – secrecy. Brown cut the ice by demanding a change of chair because his own was too low, and uncomfortable. Prescott got a more upright chair for the Chancellor and asked Blair whether he wanted one the same. Blair broke the ice by joking: 'No – it's all right, Gordon has always looked down on me.'

Behind the tense bonhomie, there was serious business. The main course for the evening was Blair's future. Prescott has refused flatly to discuss their private conversations even to friends, so what took place has to be pieced together from scraps from friends, allies and colleagues, and subsequent events. Blair admitted that his personal poll ratings were plunging after the war on Iraq, the death of David Kelly and the failure to find Saddam's weapons of mass destruction. The Hutton report into Kelly's death was hanging over Blair like a sword of Damocles, and Blair knew if it came down against him, he was finished. He was at his lowest ebb. One of Blair's close aides told me, 'Tony said to Gordon – please work with me to help me through the next year.' Brown allies have confirmed to me the account in Robert Peston's *Brown's Britain* that Blair told Brown: 'I think I'm going to be vindicated but I'm not going to turn this around for a very long time. Therefore I am going to stand down before the election.' I was told, 'Blair made it clear he would stand down at the party conference in 2004.' Brown agreed to support him to get through the next twelve months so that he could stand down around the time of the party conference in October 2004, giving Brown six months to prepare for a probable election in 2005.

News of the dinner leaked out and my colleague Andrew Grice wrote on 10 November that a Blairite had told him Blair had warned Brown that he would continue to influence the government, but ultimately Blair was in charge. 'You can't have two Prime Ministers,' Blair is said to have told Brown. This report infuriated the Brown camp for the implication that Blair was still firmly in the driving seat, in spite of the deal which Brown now felt he had. In the weeks that followed, relations became more strained. One Blair aide said: 'Gordon was obsessive about the cuttings. He would come in with bunches of them, and say, "Look – you're briefing against me."'

Blair's political crisis came in late January, when by a coincidence of timing, the crucial vote on student fees took place on the eve of the publication of the Hutton report. Alastair Campbell used to joke that journalists were forever writing that 'this is the worst week faced by Tony Blair … since the last one.' However, it was now true. The ringleaders of the rebellion on the Higher

Education Bill were two of Brown's allies, Nick Brown, the former Chief Whip; and his ex-deputy in the whips' office, George Mudie. It was seen by Blairites as confirmation that Brown was still up to mischief. The lines between the Blair and Brown camps were hot. Anji Hunter telephoned Sue Nye, Hunter's opposite number in the Brown team, to tell her to 'call off' Gordon's people, including Nick Brown. But Nye told her that they were not under Gordon's control. That was frankly met with disbelief in the Blair camp. 'Tony had asked Gordon to help him through the year, but it was pretty clear that Gordon wasn't working with Tony,' said a Blair aide. However, in the week before the vote, Brown met his part of the bargain to help Blair by lobbying his allies to call off their rebellion. Every Cabinet minister, including Jack Straw and Tessa Jowell, had a list of Labour MPs to lobby, and Prescott complained, 'I've got the hard one!' He had to put the squeeze on the ring leaders of the revolt in the Brown camp.

However, in spite of Brown's appeals to his supporters, they appeared determined to press ahead with a rebellion. Blair saw George Mudie but was unclear what the rebels wanted, and called in Prescott to negotiate. Prescott met Mudie on a Saturday in a roadside café on the A1 in secret to discuss their concerns. Officials had suggested meeting at a police station, but Prescott thought that would only confuse matters if it leaked. As he sat down with Mudie, Mudie received a call from Nick Brown, which he had to take outside. Brown was ready to cave in, but Mudie held out for more concessions. Prescott reported back to Blair that Mudie had some constructive points to make, and was given a second meeting with Blair at Chequers lasting two and a half hours. Prescott then held a meeting with Gordon Brown in his Whitehall flat with Mudie to discuss financing. By the day of the vote on 27 January, Nick Brown announced he was backing down. Blair, sensing victory, applied the screw by turning the vote into a confidence motion in his own leadership. That was enough to reduce the rebels to a rump but it was a close-run thing. 'It was a team effort,' said Prescott, underlining the help Brown had given Blair.

The next day, Lord Hutton delivered his 328-page report and it exonerated Blair over the death of Dr Kelly, the weapons expert. It criticised the reporting of BBC journalist Andrew Gilligan, saying that allegations he made against Downing Street of 'sexing up' the intelligence on Saddam's weapons of mass destruction were 'unfounded'. Alastair Campbell, who was also exonerated, told friends: 'If the vote had gone the other way and Hutton had gone the other way, Tony would be dead. So everyone is very relieved.'

Blair had feared he would have to resign immediately over the Hutton report, but its total exoneration of him changed the picture completely. Blair told Brown at a second private dinner hosted by Prescott that he felt that if he resigned now, he would be admitting culpability after Hutton had brought in a 'not guilty' verdict.

However, as the terms of the November dinner leaked out, Blair's allies in the Cabinet became alarmed that he was contemplating resigning. By late spring 2004, as Blair was having second thoughts about going before the election, rumours were sweeping Westminster that Blair was about to announce his resignation. Andrew Marr, political editor of the BBC, reported that Mr Blair had been persuaded out of resignation by visits from Cabinet ministers, which provoked immediate ministerial denials. In fact, the stories were broadly true – ministers had gone to plead with Blair not to step down before the election, but by that stage, he was having second thoughts anyway. I was astonished during one division in the Commons to be approached by three Cabinet ministers in succession, who all volunteered to me the importance of making sure that Tony was going to stay on. One of them told me that they had been to see Tony to impress on him their views. Alastair Campbell had drilled into ministers the need to avoid lobby journalists in the Members' Lobby by leaving the chamber by the back entrance at the 'back of the Speaker's chair'. As a result, catching a Cabinet minister during a division was a rare event. Being approached by three Cabinet ministers amounted to a coordinated campaign.

Blair survived the spring 'wobble', but there was a bizarre postscript to Prescott's role in the B and B soap opera – an unguarded interview in *The Times* on 15 May 2004, and the Loch Fyne 'accord'.

In his *Times* interview, Prescott said: 'I think it's true that, when plates appear to be moving, everyone positions themselves for it.'

By referring to the seismic shift caused by the moving of (tectonic) 'plates', Prescott triggered a feverish bout of renewed speculation that Blair was being forced out. I noted at the time that Prescott seemed 'very down' about the whole affair. He was mortified by the coverage, and insisted his remarks were intended as a warning to some members of the Cabinet to stop publicly positioning themselves. 'The plates are moving – it was bloody well what everyone has been doing, everyone has been giving statements – Clarke, Reid, Straw – all interpreted by the press as manoeuvring for a possible changeover at some time. I am just saying to people, stop positioning yourselves.'

Prescott was firmly behind allowing Blair to fight the next election, if he wanted to do so, telling friends: 'Tony says he is going to stay and fight. Tony is a party man. He will do what he judges is good for the party. He will go on and fight the next election and win it. He might not win it with as big a majority, but he will win it.'

Clarke, Reid, Tessa Jowell and Hilary Armstrong, the Chief Whip, were among the senior figures who urged Blair to stay on when he contemplated quitting in the summer of 2004. Some of the Blairites, bolstering Blair's position, insisted he would go 'on and on' for another five years, a promise that was calculated to further enrage Brown.

As the row over the 'plates' was dying down, the Scottish *Sunday Herald* reported that on the previous Sunday, 17 May, Prescott and Brown had had 'a lengthy private discussion at the Loch Fyne Oyster Bar to discuss the Labour party succession and how to minimise a damaging leadership contest when Tony Blair leaves Downing Street'.

Prescott and Brown (though significantly not Blair) had been to John Smith's windswept graveside on Iona for a memorial service to mark the tenth anniversary of his death with his family and other Labour figures. On the way back, they shared a car and after two hours on the road, pulled in at the Loch Fyne Oyster Bar where they spent 90 minutes in deep conclave in the car, broken only when Brown stepped out to use his mobile telephone. The next day, the media had a field day reporting how Brown and Prescott had privately discussed a smooth handover of power to Brown. Film crews descended on the Loch Fyne Oyster Bar to interview bemused customers about the historic event. The car park and the Loch Fyne Oyster Bar for two days became as famous as Granita.

I made a note in my diary: 'I actually phoned JP at the time. He said: "I've got Gordon in the car!" Hardly the action of a man who wants to keep it a secret.'

Reid, one of Blair's toughest lieutenants, was in the car behind them, with Douglas Alexander, and had also pulled in at the Oyster Bar car park. The idea that Brown and Prescott used the Loch Fyne car park to hatch a conspiracy was risible, and the row descended into low farce.

However, Prescott was determined to puncture another media myth when he opened the Hoxton Apprentice restaurant at a training scheme in east London: he said he had (working-class) kippers at Loch Fyne, not (upper-class) oysters.

On Wednesday at Prime Minister's Questions, Michael Howard, the Conservative leader, tried to raise *l'affaire kippers* with Blair, but two protesters from Fathers4Justice threw two purple flour bombs at Blair and that wrecked the whole session. The Speaker suspended the sitting. Prescott covered up the dust with an order paper – fatal if it had been anthrax or ricin, a lethal chemical. Prescott said he was reminded by the attack in

1970 in which CS gas canisters were thrown on to the floor of the chamber by Irish republicans shouting, 'See how you like it.' Tom Swain, a Labour mining MP, threw his body over the CS gas canister at that time. Prescott settled for his Commons order papers, and left the chamber with everyone else.

Later I discovered what Blair, who was prepared for a kippers jibe, would have said if his final soundbite had not been so rudely interrupted:

'As the Right Hon. gentleman is in the business of promoting Scottish food, let me tell him that kippers are not the only good thing from Scotland – Scotland voted every single Tory out at the last election.' There was also a sideswipe at Scotland being used to try out Howard's beloved poll tax. The words were never uttered.

Why did Prescott want kippers? Prescott had bought the kippers to serve to Fiona Millar, Alastair Campbell's partner, who is a vegetarian, at a dinner for a few friends at his Admiralty House flat, including Caborn, and Rosie Winterton. When Prescott came to serve up the famous kippers, Campbell quietly had to explain to the Deputy Prime Minister that it was not just meat Fiona would not eat – it was also fish. Prescott went straight out and bought her a serving of macaroni cheese from one of the shops over the road.

Prescott hosted dinner on 18 July for B and B at the Admiralty House flat, when Blair's change of mind became clear. Blair, bolstered by his allies and his escape from blame over the death of Kelly, told Brown: 'I need more time – I can't be bounced'. Brown had already lost trust in Blair's private assurances that he would give up the crown for his Chancellor, and they agreed that Blair would go after one more general election campaign, but that Blair would announce his decision at the party conference, as earlier planned. From Brown's point of view, that at least was something concrete at last.

Blair kept the dramatic announcement secret during the conference week, but immediately the October 2004 conference was over, he announced that he would be going into hospital for a small operation to correct an irregular heartbeat and that he would stand down *after* the next general election. There was one caveat, however, that was to cause further pain to Brown: Blair said he would go after serving a 'full term'.

Prescott took over the helm temporarily when Blair went into hospital for the successful operation, but Blair's announcement meant that Prescott's role as the critical friend to both Brown and Blair would now subtly change. Instead of being the neutral referee, he would be required to act as the manager of the handover, telling friends: 'I have an agreement to bring those two together. We are working on that. Gordon's view is that he needs me when he becomes leader and I will support him.' Prescott's friends say that Gordon Brown has a role for him when Brown becomes leader. Quite what that role will be is so far a secret between the two of them but Brown's most senior allies say he has not ruled out Prescott going on as his deputy after Blair stands down. That would put the final seal on their alliance, and their growing friendship.

Conclusion

So did Blair and Brown agree a Granita 2? If Prescott knows, he has never confided to anyone that it exists, or what its contents may be. But it appears clear that no firm date has been set. A handover in mid-2007, when Blair will have been in power for ten years, would seem an appropriate point for him to step down, but the abandonment of the referendum on the EU constitution has removed a natural climax to his term of office, and, buoyed by the G8 and EU presidency, there were signs that Blair may wish to go on longer. One key ally of Blair told me: 'Blair never set a date for departure at Granita. We would have known, but he didn't. Tony would never say that he is going to go by a certain date. That's just not his way. He won't stand at the next election, but Tony himself doesn't know when he will go.' The Brown camp are confident that they do have an agreement that he will step down for that smooth transition of power in 2007 and are content to bide their time. Before the 'showdown' at the Parliamentary Labour Party which I described in the introduction, Prescott bluntly told Blair that neither Brown nor the party would stand for another four years of uncertainty about the timing of the handover. That seems to have worked, but there is always the threat that the Brown camp will make their move, if Blair appears to 'ratting' on Brown again. 'They [the Blair camp] want to be reasonable, and that is the case at the moment. If that changes, then our attitude will change,' said a Brown supporter.

Meanwhile, Prescott's contribution to the Blair government is being reassessed in a more positive light. Anthony Seldon, who interviewed Prescott for his Blair biography, wrote that Prescott's importance to the Blair government 'cannot be over-estimated'. Nicholas Soames, who had mocked him as 'Giovanni', genuinely shares the admiration for what Prescott has achieved, telling me – with a slight barb in the tail – in spring 2004: 'Prescott is a big figure. In many ways he is a remarkable chap. I love the way he bestrides the Commons. He tries to hold the line between old and new Labour. He is irre-placeable. God knows what they would have done without him. Anyway, he has provided a great deal of pleasure in Parliament.'

Prescott is seen by fellow ministers as the glue which has held Brown and Blair together during the moments of crisis in their leadership. Nick Brown had no hesitation in identifying the most important feature of the Blair government as 'Prescott's relationship with Blair'. Prescott's role in the B and B saga, however, should not be allowed to obscure the importance of Prescott in influencing the direction of the Blair government.

When I interviewed Prescott in July 2004, he described his relationship with Blair as being like the brakeman on the back of a toboggan going down the Cresta Run. When necessary, he has persuaded Blair to slow down, and to bring the party with him. He helped to inform Blair's leadership how to make its reforms more palatable, and practical, and bluntly told Blair when he had overstepped the mark, for example after Blair's 'wreckers' and 'scars on my back' speeches attacking the unions.

Prescott, who resented being cast as Old Labour, having developed the concept of the public–private partnership, continued to play a decisive role in modernising reforms – he secretly worked with David Blunkett on the production of ID cards a year before they were announced, although he later questioned the timing of the scheme to stop it becoming an unnecessary distraction for the 2005 election. He also went along with the war on Iraq. Old allies on the left of the party may say that Prescott failed to apply the brake on Blair at the most important moment in recent history, but Prescott had never been a pacifist and, like Blair, believed in the intelligence on Saddam's weapons of mass destruction. He was a member of the Ministerial Committee on Intelligence Services (CIS) chaired by Blair. The Butler report found there were too few formal ministerial meetings and too many decisions taken on the hoof like *The West Wing*, but the CIS met formally on 18 December 2002, with Prescott, Brown, Straw, Blunkett and Hoon, long before the fighting took place, when it would have been possible to raise serious objections to the already apparent commitment to join the Bush administration in 'regime change'. When I asked Prescott in mid-2004 whether he still went along with his unqualified support for the war, he said yes.

His biggest disappointment was undoubtedly the defeat in the referendum for regional government in the north-east, which set back his cause for a generation or more. When Prescott came into Parliament, most northern MPs wanted a regional power base in the north-east to counter the power of Scotland in winning financial support for regeneration. By the time of the referendum, a sceptical electorate, growing tired of the Blair government, wanted nothing to do with an extra costly tier of government in the regions. The Prescott camp felt Blair delayed a full-blooded campaign for a 'yes' vote until it was too late, but Prescott knew he was launching his boat after the tide had gone out, and suffered a humiliating defeat for his efforts. Given it was one of his passions, he took its rejection with reasonably good grace and has not given up hope of elected regional assemblies. Caborn, who was equally passionate on the subject, told him: 'We might have lost the battle, but we will still win the war.'

Critics of Prescott accuse him of being a failure at transport, and David Hare wrote a scathing critique of his role in a play about the aftermath of the rail crashes at Potters Bar and Paddington. Prescott is prepared to take the brickbats, but believes his main achievement at transport – a ten-year funding plan – is a legacy that will be running long after he steps down from front-line politics. When I asked for his assessment of his achievements for his tenth anniversary as leader, the fax machine spilled out a lengthy document from his private office. It contained this list (the comments in brackets are mine):

1. *Full employment with 2 million more in work than in 1997.*
2. *Climate change and the UK commitment to the Kyoto negotiations.*
3. *Communities plan, including £38 bn for good quality and affordable housing.*
4. *Devolution of power to the regions, including the creation of the directly elected London regional assembly.*
5. *Countryside – the 'right to roam' legislation, the creation of three national parks with the South Downs in the*

pipeline, and [in spite of critics' claims to the contrary] *enlarging the green belt.*

6. *Tonnage Tax, which brought more ships, including the* Queen Mary 2, *under the red ensign.*
7. *The Channel Tunnel Rail Link, rescuing the scheme when the financing was in doubt.*
8. *Congestion charge – traffic cut by 15 per cent within the zone.*
9. *Water quality – returning life to dead rivers such as the Thames, and enforcing investment in water supply to stop wastage.*
10. *Local government – funding up by 30 per cent.*

Prescott had it within his power to bring down the Blair government, if he had been minded to do so by resigning from both the Cabinet and the party role to which he was elected with Blair in 1994. Had he triggered an election for the deputy leadership, it is unlikely that Blair could have survived the upheaval. One of Prescott's aides told me: 'He has the nuclear button, but he's never pressed it.' His Labour critics such as Clare Short accuse Prescott of making it easier for Blair to implement his policies, but the Deputy Prime Minister has also stopped Blair from a number of things too: the introduction of PR for Westminster, a coalition with the Liberal Democrats, a fully elected chamber for the House of Lords, and probably more we do not know about. Liberals and democrats may be critical of these interventions by Prescott but they show, warts and all, that he remains a tribal figure, and his family is the Labour Party.

INDEX